NEW NETHERLAND
and the DUTCH ORIGINS
of AMERICAN RELIGIOUS LIBERTY

EARLY AMERICAN STUDIES

Series editors:
Daniel K. Richter, Kathleen M. Brown,
Max Cavitch, and David Waldstreicher

Exploring neglected aspects of our colonial, revolutionary,
and early national history and culture, Early American
Studies reinterprets familiar themes and events in fresh ways.
Interdisciplinary in character, and with a special emphasis
on the period from about 1600 to 1850, the series is published in
partnership with the McNeil Center for Early American Studies.

A complete list of books in the series
is available from the publisher.

NEW NETHERLAND

and the DUTCH ORIGINS

of AMERICAN RELIGIOUS LIBERTY

EVAN HAEFELI

PENN

UNIVERSITY OF PENNSYLVANIA PRESS

PHILADELPHIA

Published by
University of Pennsylvania Press
Philadelphia, Pennsylvania 19104-4112
www.upenn.edu/pennpress

Printed in the United States of America on acid-free paper
10 9 8 7 6 5 4 3 2 1

Library of Congress Cataloging-in-Publication Data

Haefeli, Evan, 1969–
    New Netherland and the Dutch origins of American
religious liberty / Evan Haefeli. — 1st ed.
       p.   cm. — (Early American studies)
    Includes bibliographical references and index.
    ISBN 978-0-8122-4408-3 (hardcover : alk. paper)
    1. New Netherland—Religion.   2. Religious
tolerance—United States—History—17th century.
3. United States—Religion—17th century.   4. United
States—Church history—To 1775.   5. Dutch—United
States—History—17th century.   6. Netherlands—
Religion—17th century.   I. Title.   II. Series: Early
American studies.
    F122.1.H34   2012
    323.44′2097309032—dc23   2011046060

To Ieneke,
who opened the door
and let me into Amsterdam

and Andries Suidman,
who then brought me tea.

CONTENTS

Religious tolerance has become a matter of great debate in recent years. When I first wrestled with the topic in the 1990s, it had seemed a fairly straightforward matter. However, since then, incidents and controversies on both sides of the Atlantic coupled with a new burst of more sophisticated scholarship have convinced me that tolerance is a much more complicated matter than we think. Though it is a central theme of American history, there is still much that we do not understand about what tolerance is or how it came to America. Dutch tolerance in particular became a topic of political controversy during the uproar over New York's so-called "9-11 Mosque" in the summer of 2010. Mayor Michael Bloomberg invoked the legacy of Dutch tolerance in defense of the construction of an Islamic religious center in lower Manhattan, while Dutch politician Geert Wilders drew on it to oppose the very same institution. How could the religious tolerance of New Netherland lead to two such diametrically opposed interpretations? Barriers of language, culture, and history make the case of the Dutch and their way of managing toleration particularly difficult for Americans to understand. Nonetheless, as Bloomberg and Wilders made clear, it remains a vital part of American culture and politics.

What follows is a new telling of an old story. This is not the first account of religious toleration in New Netherland, nor have I uncovered a trove of hitherto unused sources, though I have cast my research net wider than earlier scholars. Many of the Dutch sources I rely on are published and have been available in English translation for a hundred years or more (though it is always best to go back to the Dutch originals). Yet my version is significantly different from earlier accounts, in both scope and approach. Recent work in several languages by scholars on both sides of the Atlantic has helped me to set the story of Dutch America firmly within its broader Dutch context. Though I am an American historian, and my training and interests in that field led me to this topic, I have gone to some lengths to write a book as relevant to the Dutch as to Americans, in the hopes of provoking both to think more deeply about tolerance (a quality both nations claim to possess) as well as the history of New Netherland that connects us.

So far, the history of religious tolerance has tended to remain aloof from other methods of historical inquiry. Only recently scholars have embraced a social historical approach to the topic. My work drew inspiration from the relatively new fields of Atlantic world history and borderlands history. Atlantic world history builds on the recognition that the American colonies were part of a trans-Atlantic world that included Europe, Africa, and the Caribbean in very important ways. Much of the work in the field is about motion, circulation, networks, and connections, tracing people, trade, and objects as they move about from place to place, only some of which wound up in the future United States. Religious issues, and a problem like religious toleration, have remained a secondary concern in the field, but there are clear parallels. In many ways, this study can be seen as an example of Atlantic world history as I feel it should be done, one aware of the connections, comparisons, and differences between various parts of a trans-oceanic community, in this case the Dutch world of the seventeenth century. Borderlands history, though it tends to focus on the American Southwest, has brought an awareness of the permeability of borders in early American history, and the importance of connections and conflicts between different groups of people across and around border zones, that is also relevant to my approach. Borderlands existed across the Americas, and between groups of Europeans as well between Europeans and indigenous Americans, the field's usual focus.

Above all, I hope my work will be of interest to students of religious tolerance. As religious tolerance comes under increasing scrutiny from a growing range of thinkers, it is becoming clear that it means different things to different people. We often presume there is—and was—a shared understanding about tolerance, yet on closer inspection it becomes clear that advocates for tolerance vary in their visions for coexistence. The seventeenth century was no different. Only then there were far more people who argued that tolerance was a bad idea than do so today. I have chosen to write an account of a particular time and place—New Netherland—because I believe the specifics of where, when, and how tolerance exists are not trivial. They are, in fact, essential. Examining the specifics makes clear that what we too often group together as "tolerance" contained a great diversity of possibilities and relationships. Connecting one instance with another, as with New Netherland and American religious liberty, turns out to be more of a challenge than had long been thought. It certainly cannot be taken for granted. My approach has been both chronological and thematic, uniting what have hitherto been treated as separate accounts into a single narrative, one that stresses the broader, Dutch context of what has long been considered an American story. My narrative, I hope, will encourage readers to think anew about a familiar story, a story of relevance to the histories of America, the Dutch and their empire, and religious tolerance.

Translation is a crucial issue in the history of New Netherland, where many of the sources are in Dutch but have been translated into English, but not always perfectly. Where there is no English translation easily available, or with certain important phrases, I have made my own translation or checked to confirm the strength of the existing translation. However, since my primary goal is to pull Anglophone readers into research and thinking on the Dutch world, I have generally used the existing English translations of Dutch documents, preferring the recent translations of Charles Gehring to earlier ones whenever possible.

Dutch spelling of town names and certain words has been retained. The most important issue to keep in mind is the Dutch "ij," pronounced "aye" (like a cinematic pirate). Common terms, like south (zuid) and new (nieuw) have been rendered in English even as I have tried to preserve as much of the Dutch flavor as seems reasonable for an English-reading audience. With personal names I have followed the Dutch usage, where Pieter van Rooden or Jan de Meier is referred to as Van Rooden or De Meier but listed in the bibliography under Rooden and Meier rather than van or de.

Several Dutch cities, like Vlissingen, had English versions of their names, in this case Flushing. When discussing Dutch places in a primarily Dutch context, I have endeavored to use the Dutch name, but have used the English name when discussing the same place in a prevailingly English situation. Other towns had several names that changed over time, usually from a Lenape-related term to a Dutch and then an English one, as with Mespath-Middelburgh-Newtown. In these cases I have preferred the name that reflects the sovereign power claiming authority over it at the time, with the exception of The Hague (Den Haag).

When transcribing seventeenth-century English, I have preserved the existing spelling as much as possible. However, in cases of unusual spelling, where an "i" functions as a "j" or a "u" as a "v," for example, I have generally corrected it to modern usage to avoid confusing modern readers unfamiliar with the older conventions.

The Dutch switched to the modern calendar some two centuries before the English did. Consequently, dates are in New Style, with the occasional exception from after the conquest, when the English imposed their Old Style system of dating, which was ten days ahead of the New Style system.

NEW NETHERLAND

and the DUTCH ORIGINS
of AMERICAN RELIGIOUS LIBERTY

INTRODUCTION

What is religious tolerance and how does it happen? For Americans these are more challenging questions than one might think. From the beginning of its existence, the United States of America has done without a national religious establishment of the sort that was long a trademark of European history. Consequently, Americans have been able to take tolerance for granted in a way Europeans (and others) have not, for religious liberty was assimilated into America's national experience from the beginning. As a result, scholars of the American past are more preoccupied with the question of when, where, or with whom tolerance started, not how it came to be in the first place. Was it Revolutionary statesmen like Thomas Jefferson and James Madison? An earlier colonial figure such as William Penn or Roger Williams?[1] A particular denomination, such as the Baptists?[2] Or a particular colony like Rhode Island, New York, Pennsylvania, Maryland, or South Carolina?[3] One persistent candidate in the debate over the origins of American religious liberty is the Dutch, the subject of this book.[4]

For some forty years in the seventeenth century the Dutch possessed a colony in North America called New Netherland. The colony stretched from the Delaware River Valley to the Hudson River Valley and Long Island, claiming all the land between Maryland and Connecticut: the Mid-Atlantic region of the future United States. For a few years, a sub-colony run by the city of Amsterdam called New Amstel existed on the Delaware River. After the English gained control of the region, they divided it up into separate colonies: New York, New Jersey, Pennsylvania, and Delaware, together known as "the middle colonies." By the eighteenth century, the Dutch inhabitants had been joined by a range of migrants from England, Ireland, Scotland, Germany, and France, ensuring that the Mid-Atlantic contained a greater mix of European ethnicities and religions than any other part of colonial North America. The diversity, and the religious toleration and pluralism that accompanied it, have distinguished the middle colonies' place in early American society ever since. They are widely recognized as the birthplace of American ethnic and religious diversity, pluralism, and religious freedom. In one way or another the Dutch must be credited with laying the foundation on which the middle colonies were built. But how? It is generally agreed that they brought tolerance and religious diversity to America—certainly more than their neighbors in New England and Virginia did. It is also acknowledged that then, after being conquered and incorporated into the English empire, they became part of the diversity. But is that the whole story?

My goal is not to judge whether New Netherland was more or less tolerant than other American colonies. It was different, but that is only part of the point. In many ways, this book carves out a place for the Dutch in America's history of tolerance by taking them out of the framework of American history and situating them within the wider Dutch seventeenth-century context. It is also an effort to prompt a new, more site specific and contextualized approach to the history of religious tolerance whether in America, Europe, or elsewhere. A close analysis of the workings of religious liberty in Dutch North America, it addresses in particular the question of the degree to which those who did not belong to the official Dutch Reformed Church could express their religious difference. The story emerges from the available sources—official correspondence, court records, church correspondence, and some Quaker literature—sources that chronicle the struggle of Jews, Lutherans, Quakers, and, to a lesser extent, Baptists and other radical Protestants to exist as such within New Netherland. In these sources some evidence on individual attitudes about religious tolerance emerges, but that is an issue of secondary concern here. My focus is on group activities, and particularly confrontations over gatherings for worship and the laws, ideas, and actions that affected those struggles. The conflicts reflect something of the range of possibilities and attitudes at work within Dutch tolerance while at the same time being only one particular manifestation of it. In the end, I hope this work will add to the study of tolerance in the Dutch world despite its focus on the Dutch contribution to early American religious pluralism.

Dutch historians have not made my task of reconciling Dutch and Anglo-American priorities easy. Jaap Jacobs, a leading historian of New Netherland, maintains that the colony has little place in America's history of religious liberty. The Dutch authorities never dreamed of bringing religious freedom to America. Instead, they simply extended to the colony

Figure 1. One popular version of the history of tolerance in New Netherland is conveyed in this American cartoon, which emphasizes the role of local events affecting English Protestants. Courtesy DC Comics.

the traditional Dutch policy of freedom of conscience and never altered it. Freedom of conscience meant that colonists had "the liberty to believe whatever one might like, not the liberty to act upon that belief." Any effort to challenge and expand the range of tolerance in Dutch America thus demanded much more of Dutch tolerance than it had ever promised. Though freedom of conscience was "never," Jacobs argues, "violated in New Netherland," this cannot "be taken as proof of tolerance." He reminds us that the Dutch drew distinctions that Anglo-Americans have a hard time grasping. In the eyes of Dutch authorities and Dutch law, there was a crucial and self-evident difference between an individual's liberty to believe and a group's freedom to worship.[5]

Restoring New Netherland to its proper Dutch context brings up a series of obstacles that any analysis of Dutch tolerance must recognize. Jacobs's distinction between "tolerance" as something relating to a public gathering and liberty of conscience as something restricted to private belief has deep roots in Dutch law and history but not the Anglo-American experience. Swallowed up in the Anglo-American world that produced the United States, New Netherland has existed in a very un-Dutch realm of analysis for centuries. It is too often evaluated more for what it was not, the future middle colonies, than for what it was: an unusually Protestant manifestation of Dutch tolerance. Ironically, precisely because New Netherland later became New York, more has been written about the history of toleration there than for any other Dutch colony and even many parts of the Netherlands, giving New Netherland a disproportionate interpretive influence on Anglo-American ideas about Dutch tolerance. Consequently, though New Netherland was a minor colony in the Dutch overseas empire, to study religious tolerance there is an excellent place to challenge the greatest obstacle to studies of Dutch tolerance everywhere, namely, the persistent habit of evaluating the Dutch by non-Dutch standards (something the Dutch themselves are not immune from). At the same time, the great effort needed to restore New Netherland to its Dutch context should be a warning to Dutch scholars that the Dutch-ness of their subject matter is not self-evident or uncontested.

To address the specifics of the history at hand alongside the bigger challenge of reconceptualizing the history of religious tolerance, my method is simultaneously narrative and analytical, stressing change over time and the dynamics of that change. Previous historians have taken a more synchronic approach organized by denominations, telling a serialized story of individuated struggles for religious liberty by Jews, Lutherans, and Quakers. The approach has its merits. In fact, each of these groups did wage its own struggle apart from the others. However the denominational focus is premised on the idea that there was a single ideal of tolerance for which each was striving and that the various groups shared a common desire for it. While it has its virtues, such an approach obscures the way Dutch tolerance actually worked. Moreover, by placing an unexamined ideal of toleration at the center, it holds the Dutch authorities and those who challenged them up to standards that were not their own. The result tends to be more a pronouncement about the Dutch capacity for some presumably universal quality of tolerance than an assessment of what was actually at stake at the time.

"Dutch tolerance" is not a formal category of analysis. It is a concept I am invoking here in an effort to locate my topic within the broader history of tolerance. Describing Dutch tolerance is not as easy as it might seem, for both "Dutch" and "tolerance" are amorphous categories with contested histories. Historians bold enough to employ them must navigate a thicket of conflicting interpretations if they want their analysis to be understood on its own terms. Before proceeding, then, it is necessary to clarify what I mean by Dutch tolerance. Briefly put, it is the form of religious tolerance practiced within the Dutch world, that is, in those areas where the United Provinces of the Netherlands, often referred to as the Dutch Republic, held power and authority. Crucial to any understanding of Dutch tolerance is an appreciation that it developed alongside the nation and its colonies. Before 1566, to be Dutch meant nothing other than to be associated with the northwest corner of the Holy Roman Empire. The actual parameters of the Dutch world would remain in tremendous flux until the late seventeenth century. The relevant parts of Dutch history will be treated more fully in Chapter 1. At this point I will just say a few words about current approaches to the history of religious toleration, how it has been studied in Dutch America, and how my approach differs.

Tolerance and toleration are strange terms to rely on for historical analysis. Though many people believe their meaning is obvious, scholars are not so sure. Varying definitions of the terms exist, often linked to different approaches to studying the topic. Until recently, most histories of tolerance focused on the ideas of notable thinkers such as John Locke or Roger Williams. Now historians are exploring what could be called the social history of tolerance, and this has prompted them to redefine the terms. For example, Benjamin Kaplan, drawing on his studies of early modern Dutch religious life, uses "toleration" to refer to "a form of behavior: peaceful coexistence with others who adhere to a different religion." It is a "social practice, a pattern of interaction" among neighbors "living together in the same village, town, or city." His interest is in the social and cultural experience of those who were "not just intellectuals and ruling elites," like John Locke. Drawing a distinction between "toleration" and "tolerance" underscores the methodological difference between his social and cultural approach and earlier accounts concerned more with the history of ideas, while acknowledging that they are still related topics. "Tolerance," for Kaplan, is "the ideal" or set of principles articulated by philosophers and theorists who proved so crucial in giving it positive connotations. He reminds us that "most Europeans continued to the very end of the early modern era to use the word tolerate in its traditional meaning: to suffer, endure, or put up with something objectionable." His interest in the "nitty-gritty" experience of regular people, sometimes referred to as "confessional coexistence" or "religious pluralism," has made him suspicious of accounts that treat tolerance as an ideal. He criticizes studies that ask "only *how much* tolerance prevailed in a particular time and place" because they fail "to acknowledge that qualitatively different *kinds* of tolerance may exist." Kaplan is right. Assessing different kinds of tolerance along a single spectrum running from more to less tolerant is misleading. It misses important dimensions of what was at stake then as well, I would argue, as of its interpretation now.[6]

Another recent approach builds on the negative connotations tolerance used to have to stress the intellectual and moral ambivalence of toleration. If one truly cared for one's fellow humans, one would lovingly yet firmly bring them to the True Religion. Alexandra Walsham, a historian of early modern English religion, goes so far as to claim that "toleration is a form of intolerance," not "religious freedom. Nor did it proceed from indifference or neutrality." Rather it was "a paradoxical policy, a casuistical stance involving a deliberate suspension of righteous hostility and, consequently, a considerable degree of moral discomfort." As she points out, the strongest defenders of "true religion" had nothing but negative words for toleration. They called it "a diabolical device, the hallmark of the Beast, 'the last and most desperate design of Antichrist,' 'the whore of Babylon's backdoor.'" Not until the era of the French Revolution would it "lose its negative and critical overtones," if only for some people. As "late as 1832 Pope Gregory

XVI declared 'liberty of conscience' an 'absurd and erroneous opinion, or rather delirium,' which sprang from 'the most foul well of indifferentism.'" Accordingly, "persecution" was in the eyes of the beholder. For those who practiced it, it was often defined as a necessary "correction" encouraging its victims along the path of truth and salvation and saving them from their obstinate errors and heresies. To tolerate them would be to let them damn themselves. One man's persecution was another man's loving care.[7]

As histories have moved away from the long-standing focus on ideas and philosophy and toward a concern for social and cultural experience, historians have drawn ever more distinctions between tolerance and toleration. Ned Landsman, one of the most important historians of the middle colonies, sees "toleration" as the official policies permitting the coexistence of more than one faith within a single colony, policies drawn in part from the history of ideas as well as political circumstances. "Tolerance," on the other hand, is for him the "willing acceptance of diversity" by individuals— something expressed more in day-to-day interactions. Since neither necessarily implies the other, they can with justification be treated separately. I am not so sure that such a strict separation of terms is very helpful, if only because scholars do not yet agree on how to deploy the terms. To stick just to the few cases discussed here, while toleration is understood by Kaplan to be "a form of behavior," Landsman and Walsham place it more in the realm of ideas. Where Walsham and Landsman see tolerance as about "actions rather than words," social expressions of "charity, harmony, and peaceful coexistence," Kaplan places it in the intellectual realm. Landsman's point is a good one. Just because multiple faiths coexisted does not mean people approved of it. Moreover, the opposite is true as well. As Stuart Schwartz has recently demonstrated for the Iberian world, even when coexistence was forbidden, people could favor it. How much does it help to label the one toleration and the other tolerance?[8]

The increasing number of definitions of "toleration" and "tolerance" is less a sign of growing intellectual rigor than evidence of the expanding awareness of the complicated issues surrounding the phenomenon. Rather than come up with a new or more precise distinction of my own, I am deliberately blurring the terms. I find the two aspects so deeply intertwined that to hold them strictly apart can be misleading. Can one really separate the ideas from the attitudes, and both from the policies, and each from the enforcement, and all these from public representations and private experience? From the beginning, the history of toleration has been plagued by

efforts to draw distinctions and take sides, to judge and categorize everything from other faiths to particular nations, policies, ideas, and philoso-
phies. Efforts at drawing distinctions of any sort within and around
toleration risks accentuating one dimension over others and possibly one
party over another. This dynamic is very much what tolerance is all about.
Both tolerance and toleration imply a relationship between two or more
different religious groups, in which one group has more power, authority,
or influence than others. It is that relationship—whether accommodating,
hostile, cautious, liberating or otherwise—rather than any putatively
abstract category of "tolerance" or "toleration" that is the heart of my
story.

At the same time, the insistence by a wide range of scholars that there
is a universal category of tolerance suggests that there is a common topic,
even if we cannot fully agree on its contours. I suspect there will never be
complete agreement on what tolerance and toleration are or should be. In
fact, given the nature of the issue, I believe it is impossible. Rather than
propose an ideal standard of toleration, it is time to come to grips with the
multiplicity of its manifestations and sharpen our conceptual use of tolerance. My focus on Dutch tolerance deliberately emphasizes that it was distinct from, say, English tolerance. Yet even within Dutch tolerance there

was a range of experiences and possibilities. New Netherland's tolerance was just one version of what was possible in the Dutch seventeenth-century world. Too many accounts of tolerance either treat it along a judgmental and presumably universal spectrum running from more to less, arguing there was either too little or too much, or portray it as operating in a binary framework of tolerance versus intolerance. Such approaches not only tend to take sides, they also miss out on the politically contingent and locally specific nature of tolerance by assuming that there is a single ideal to which all should adhere. It will no longer do to simply invoke tolerance as a transparent tool of analysis. It is time to start specifying the elements involved and the implications of the relationship between them. To judge the degree to which the Dutch were tolerant is a political statement that obscures how toleration worked in the Dutch world by holding it up to some other standard. There was never any doubt that the seventeenth-century Dutch lived in an environment of religious diversity and coexistence of some sort, even if it did not satisfy the standards of all who witnessed it. Dutch tolerance was a dynamic, complex, constantly negotiated process that could be (and has been) called tolerant and could be (and has been) called intolerant. By calling it Dutch tolerance, I am not claiming an inherent affinity between the Dutch and the phenomenon of toleration, but emphasizing that there is no universal standard of tolerance. How toleration happened when the Dutch were in charge was simply one of many variants, none of them universally applicable or desirable.[9]

The subjective quality of tolerance is more apparent in the case of the Dutch than, say, the English, for Dutch tolerance was never entirely in the hands of Dutch people. Since the Dutch state was expanding in Europe and abroad at the very time it was also becoming independent, even the issue of who was Dutch kept shifting with battle lines, immigration trends, and colonial acquisitions. Jews, immigrating initially from Iberia and later from central Europe, together with Lutherans, often from German or Scandinavian lands, and a range of English Protestants could be found in New Netherland as well as the Dutch Republic. Foreigners, visitors, immigrants, refugees, diplomats, traveling merchants, seasonal workers, slaves, and philosophers from around the world all experienced Dutch tolerance at some point; challenging it, misunderstanding it, loving it, loathing it. During the Dutch "Golden Age" (c.1600–1680), Dutch tolerance was not just something the "Dutch" did. It was what happened or perceived to happen under Dutch authority, a phenomenon that evolved through interactions between

Dutch and non-Dutch people in the expanding republic, across Europe, and throughout the nascent Dutch empire.

The intercultural and interwoven character of Dutch tolerance poses a special interpretive challenge, for discussions of Dutch tolerance come laced with a heritage of conflict and antagonism dating back to the sixteenth century. The Dutch themselves were remarkably laconic about their tolerance, which they generally described as simply liberty of conscience. In no small part because of Dutch unwillingness or inability to go into much detail about what liberty of conscience was and why they permitted it, the most influential accounts of Dutch tolerance have come from foreign observers or those outside the official Dutch Reformed Church. Unfortunately, political motivations lay behind these descriptions, whether those were to justify a war against the Dutch or wage a campaign for or against toleration within or without the Dutch world. Forgetting that these observations were never neutral, scholars have adopted much of the contemporary polemic as putatively objective analysis. As a result, prevailing understandings of Dutch tolerance have not moved much beyond those of the seventeenth century.

English accounts of Dutch toleration have been the most influential to interpretations of Dutch tolerance—too much so. In the seventeenth century, the English relationship to all things Dutch was fraught and dangerous, sometimes filled with awe and admiration, other times mocking and disrespectful. For example, when the English began the first of a series of wars against the Dutch in 1652, their propaganda gave Dutch tolerance a negative gloss, as in the pamphlet *Amsterdam and her other Hollander Sisters put out to Sea*. This tract accused the Dutch of having, "in plain English a Gally-mophrey of all Religions; except only what's true and pure: Their main Nest is Amsterdam, which hath as many Sects as Chambers, for they let out Lodgings to all people, and if they pay, they regard not how they pray; so they can prey upon them: That this is so, take a view of some, as Calvinists, Hugenots [sic], Lutherans, Brownists, Anabaptists, Arminians, Socinians, Pelagians, Papists, Jews, Swinglians, Remonstranten, Contra-Remonstranten, with divers others not fitting to be named, much lesse to be allowed." In short, the Dutch "account the best Religion which brings most gains to them for toleration, were it the Turks Alchoran." The emphasis on the presence of non-Christians ("Turk-Christian-Pagan-Jew") deliberately diminished the Christian character of the Dutch Republic while also exaggerating and misrepresenting the extent to which non-Christians existed within it. The accusation is that the Dutch desire to make money overrode any concern for Christian piety. Their "best God" is the one "that brings the most Gold; if the Cantore [store] be full, let their Churches be empty." One should keep such criticisms in mind whenever reading interpretations that claim Dutch tolerance grew out of a pragmatic preference for trade over a desire for religious truth. That such an idea was used in the seventeenth century to justify attacks on the Dutch should give us pause before adopting it as a scholarly interpretation.[10]

The English were not the only ones to draw such invidious portraits of Dutch tolerance. During the Dutch Golden Age, "Holland's trade and religious freedom were celebrated and feared," as historian of France Jacob Soll writes. "Dutch wealth became legendary in art and poetry." Their European neighbors "marveled at, and also expressed mistrust about, Dutch wealth, tolerance, and difference. Many of these works claimed that the Dutch were essentially pirates and parasites, growing rich at the expense of the French and English." A piece of French anti-Dutch propaganda from the 1670s extends criticism of the Dutch for putting trade above religion into an attack on the legitimacy of their colonial endeavors: "All other sorts of Christians" promoted Christianity in their colonies "by the great number of Missionaries, whom they send into the East and West-Indies" even the English, "the Dutch only excepted." The Dutch "would rather see all those People Perish eternally in their Ignorance, than . . . that they should share with them in the advantages of their Commerce." Such statements should be kept in mind when religiosity in New Netherland is depicted as weak or subservient to issues of trade, as many scholars do, both Dutch and American. For example, Cornelis Goslinga, Dutch-born and educated author of an important study of the Dutch Caribbean colonies, claims that, when it came to religion, the "Dutch all-consuming desire for profit left no room for any other concern." The interests of commerce created a "permissive atmosphere" that allowed "more tolerance of Catholics than Protestants experienced in Spanish and French colonies," he continues, citing a remark by the English governor of Jamaica that, on the Dutch island of Curaçao, "'Jesus Christ was good, but trade was better.'"[11]

Familiar with the concept of separation of church and state, many American scholars often describe religious life in New Netherland in terms of opposing binaries, whether Church versus State or piety versus trade. They seem to find the idea that European merchants more intent on profit than piety laid the foundations for pluralism in New York and later the

United States appealing. Such scholarship emphasizes the importance of the broader trans-Atlantic social and political context, particularly the role of the West India Company (WIC), whose directors in Holland ultimately set the policy for New Netherland. The WIC, these scholars claim, deliberately encouraged religious diversity in the fledgling colony, in the hopes of turning it into a thriving commercial society like Amsterdam. Dutch historian Willem Frijhoff, with some awareness of the propagandistic origins of these views, has criticized the "general stereotype of the Dutch in seventeenth-century Europe as a commercially skilled people but in foreign affairs destitute of moral inhibitions and religious principles." One "should not oppose commercial interest to religious concern" he cautions. Indeed, his work demonstrates the power of religion in the colony, a place where a Dutch minister could bring down a colonial governor not once but twice, as Frijhoff's own biographical subject Everardus Bogardus did. The ability or willingness to distinguish between religion, politics, and economics was not as common in the seventeenth century as many modern scholars presume. It was, as it remains, a political choice that could be made in more than one way.[12]

Freedom of conscience was never straightforward in the Dutch world. The interactive quality of Dutch tolerance helps explain why it is not enough simply to affirm that liberty of conscience was the law of the land in New Netherland, as Jacobs does. Where the conscience begins and ends is and always has been a matter in great dispute. For example, Jeremy Bangs, an authority on the Leiden-based Separatist Pilgrims who established the colony of Plymouth, ignores Jacobs's distinction between liberty of conscience as an individual right and toleration as a group freedom of worship when he criticizes the ostensibly "tolerant New Netherland" for engaging in "sophistry bordering on hypocrisy" with its promise of liberty of conscience. The freedom "to believe whatever they wanted, as long as their belief did not extend to religious exercises outside the family circle" implied a series of restrictions on vital aspects of religious life: "no preaching, no prayer meetings, no group discussions of theology, no public marriage ceremonies (except civil marriages before magistrates in remote regions where no Reformed clergy could be found), no non-Reformed baptisms or burial ceremonies, no communion outside the Reformed Church." Inhabitants could "disagree with the Dutch Reformed, but only if they kept silence about it outside their own homes, and only if their beliefs led to no visible actions in society." Though non-Dutch Reformed people could live there, "the reality in New Netherland was scarcely freedom of religion." Bangs's criticism reflects the potent plasticity of Dutch tolerance, which lay precisely in the disagreement over what it was. The willingness of individuals to push at its borders, including Dutch Mennonites, Remonstrants, and others, I argue, was as much a part of Dutch tolerance as any official interpretation of liberty of conscience.[13]

The enforcement of liberty of conscience varied across the Dutch world, both raising and crushing hopes of tolerance depending on the local circumstances. The Dutch historian Maarten Prak affirms that tolerance "varied from place to place" within the republic and "had little chance of prevailing in regions with a low degree of urbanization, in areas where the cities experienced little growth, and in cities where representatives of the citizenry directly influenced the authorities." Some areas, such as "the insular and largely rural province of Drenthe," were heavily Reformed. Toleration "could never be taken for granted, even in Holland." Prak feels the Dutch regulation of religious diversity is best described as the "politics of intolerance." Most scholars of New Netherland would agree that "intolerance" is the better term to describe the colony's relationship to religious diversity. This consensus goes back to the first proper study of the topic, by a scholar educated at Belgium's ancient Catholic University of Leuven, Frederick J. Zwierlein, who forcefully argued in 1910 that New Netherland actually had an active religious policy of conformity and repression.[14]

Recent Dutch scholars may stress the lack of tolerance, but there is a strand of work that argues that the Dutch in New Netherland were in fact tolerant. Its first and perhaps best representative was Dutch Reformed scholar Albert Eekhof, whose thoroughly researched histories focused on the individuals who ran the colonial church. Eekhof maintained that these were pious men who rejected persecution of the sort Dutch Protestants had suffered at the hands of the Catholic Inquisition. Eekhof did not address Zwierlein's criticisms so much as shift the terms of debate from formal policies of toleration to individual capacities for piety, understanding, and kind dealings. The divergence illustrates how interpretations of Dutch tolerance can vary depending on what one looks for and one's own vantage point: whether one's nationality and scholarly training is Dutch, Belgian, or American and one's religious background is Dutch Reformed, Roman Catholic, or otherwise. The conclusions of Zwierlein and Eekhof are incommensurate because their priorities lead them to emphasize different aspects of tolerance. For the Catholic scholar Zwierlein, tolerance was the ability to exercise a dissident religion in some sort of public capacity, something Catholics lacked in the Dutch world. For the Dutch Reformed Eekhof, the absence of punishments for lack of conformity to the Dutch Reformed Church, as well as the ministers' heartfelt efforts to bring in as many people as possible, made the Dutch tolerant, unlike the Catholics with their Inquisition. The unmistakable partisan inflection to these interpretations demonstrates that, while tolerance may be a universal tool for analysis, it is not a neutral standard.[15]

The tensions between how Dutch tolerance is depicted, how it was practiced, and how it was experienced is of direct relevance to this study at several levels. First, since many of the ostensibly scholarly interpretations of Dutch tolerance can be traced to anti-Dutch propaganda, one has to be careful with any sort of pat analysis of what Dutch tolerance was and why. Resurrecting ideas once deployed in hostile propaganda does not summon up the Dutch reality so much as it does the polemical image created by its jealous neighbors. Second, depictions of Dutch tolerance that focus on Amsterdam to the exclusion of the rest of the republic produce a very skewed image of who the Dutch were and why they did what they did. Heavily Reformed, comparatively homogeneous Dutch provinces like Zeeland or Drenthe, much better comparisons for New Netherland, are lost to view. Finally, such scholarly depictions of Dutch tolerance often grow out of, or reflect, ongoing struggles between different groups and positions, whether Belgian Catholic (Zwierlein), Dutch Reformed (Eekhof), Protestant dissenters (Bangs), or letter of the law (Jacobs). For me, Dutch tolerance is a combination of these various views.[16]

Pure objectivity on an issue like Dutch tolerance is impossible. Indeed, one of my findings has been that the only people who really thought about toleration in anything like the way modern scholars do were those who most opposed it—in this case, Dutch Reformed clergymen. To say that "toleration" was or was not extant, or to judge whether it was growing or diminishing, is a rather dubious form of analysis. It risks reproducing more the perspectives of those who fought it (albeit with a positive estimation of tolerance) than the aspirations of those caught up in it. My preference has been to be as comprehensive as possible, analyzing the specifics of the situation and the actors on their own terms, rather than by an anachronistic standard of toleration. Having come to the conclusion that to write a truly nonpartisan account of tolerance is infeasible, my goal has been to produce a history that makes the clashing partisan perspectives and actions a central part of the story. When emphasizing the particulars of the people, places, and times involved, what becomes clear is that no single group fully determined the shape of tolerance in New Netherland. Rather, it contained the sum of the aspirations of a variety of groups and their conflicts with one another. Dutch tolerance, in other words, was a multiparty system.

If one adopts a somewhat longer vision of Dutch religious history, looking beyond the commotion of the Dutch Golden Age, the striking result of Dutch tolerance is a society with much less religious pluralism than one would expect. Dutch Reformed Protestants were never the demographic majority in the Dutch world, but their proportion of the population was much bigger at the end of the seventeenth century than at the beginning. In no small part this came from their social and political dominance, embodied in the persistent restriction of others to second-class citizenship. Catholics made up the single largest group of the non-Reformed. Then came Lutherans, Mennonites, and, on a much smaller scale, a few other Protestant Dissenters and Jews. All these groups had been present in the mid-seventeenth century, and simply persisted into the eighteenth. There was no perpetual efflorescence of new faiths and denominations in the Dutch world. However, to call this situation intolerance merely conveys a sense of what the Dutch were *not* rather than what they were (which as everyone will agree permitted more religious diversity than its archenemy Spain). Scholarship has yet to offer a clear sense of what it was, exactly, that the Dutch were doing, and why it happened. As Frijhoff notes, opinions "diverge as to which term is the most apt to qualify the religious pluralism that existed in Holland in the seventeenth century." Whatever it was, it was very Dutch, even if scholars have trouble embracing it as very tolerant.[17]

Dutch tolerance in New Netherland was not what the colonial government did or failed to do; it was the whole process of negotiating religious coexistence, a political process involving people and ideas on both sides of the Atlantic. That it turned out differently in America and Europe is emblematic of the phenomenon, which varied across the Dutch world. Instead of questioning the Dutch commitment to a universal cause of toleration, or doubting their capacity to think and act in terms of principles above and beyond those of economic logic and social stability, I want to return the discussion to its particular social and political context. Like all other humans, the Dutch were not entirely practical or market-driven people. They could and did act according to ideas and principles, even if their interpretation and implementation of them was conditioned by their specific context. This was perhaps nowhere more evident than in New Netherland, which existed within a trans-Atlantic geopolitical framework with Amsterdam playing the central, though not the determinative, role. Most of the religious and political authorities supervising the Dutch North American colonies were based in Amsterdam, the colony's primary economic link to Europe. New Amsterdam, capital of New Netherland, deliberately modeled its government, if not its society, after Amsterdam. New Amstel was named after the river that gave Amsterdam its name (Amstel-Dam). The largest, richest, and most powerful city in the most powerful province of the Dutch Republic, Amsterdam was not the capital of the Dutch Republic, but had far more influence than any other Dutch city, including the actual capital in The Hague.

There were both connections and divergences between Amsterdam and the Dutch colonies in North America. New Amsterdam, a small town of 1,400 people at the southern tip of Manhattan Island, had much in common with the rapidly expanding metropolis of the Dutch Republic and its roughly 200,000 inhabitants, but there were significant differences. Being in America rather than Holland, on a small not large scale, scattered widely rather than compact—all these factors made life in the colony different. However, simply to say it was more "American" is equally misleading. Dutch America is better compared to frontiers of the Dutch world like Twente and Taiwan than to its cosmopolitan heart. Thus the history here is set in the context of the entire Dutch world, from Europe to Brazil and Asia, wherein existed many more apt comparisons to the religious situation in New Netherland than Amsterdam. Historians of the Anglo-American colonies, coming to similar conclusions on a range of topics from trade to religion, politics, and culture, have adopted a new framework of analysis called Atlantic history. In many ways my thinking has benefited from developments in Atlantic history, even if my focus on the Dutch has taken me beyond the usual confines of the field. Hence my recurring invocations of "the Dutch world," which in the mid-seventeenth century included all the Americas, parts of Africa, and significant portions of Asia as well as an expanding frontier within Europe itself.

The chapters of this book are designed to illuminate the texture of Dutch tolerance as well as to analyze the particular case of New Netherland. They are organized into aspects of Dutch tolerance that are relevant to the story but may not be well known to readers from the Anglo-American tradition. Each is coordinated with the chronology of actual events in the colony in the 1650s and 1660s. First, I provide an overview of the relevant religious and political history of the Dutch Republic from the early sixteenth century, when Protestantism first appeared in the Low Countries, through the 1660s, when New Netherland was lost to the English, explaining the Dutch relationship to liberty of conscience that justified their struggle for independence. Readers unfamiliar with Dutch history will find useful orientation here to the key events and religious groups relevant to the Dutch American story. The European context sketches out the realm of possibilities and the terms of debate that shaped Dutch tolerance in the colonies. Chapter 2 focuses on Amsterdam and Holland, where the practice of connivance allowed aspects of Dutch tolerance to take on the appearance of religious freedom, at least to outsiders. An informal and subtle process, connivance was in many ways the preferred method of Amsterdam's rulers for coping with religious diversity; one that would occasionally find parallels overseas.

After outlining the basic dynamics of Dutch tolerance, the book explores incidents where the Dutch went beyond connivance to grant formal recognitions of other religions' rights to worship. Chapter 3 thus looks at publicly acknowledged forms of toleration in the Dutch world. Such grants were actually quite rare, arising only in some places and certain circumstances. Only one, the case of New Sweden, occurred in Dutch North America, but others elsewhere provide crucial context for the colonial struggles. Chapter 4 expands on the previous two chapters to demonstrate how the Dutch integrated non-Christian peoples, including Jews, Chinese, Africans, Muslims, and Native Americans, into their religious world. Dutch tolerance proved remarkably adept at accommodating a wide range of religious difference while simultaneously placing distinct constraints on it. The end result was neither formal toleration nor religious freedom, but something closer to connivance, though not even always that. Again, the particular—specific adjustments to accommodate certain groups at precise times and places—turns out to be central to understanding Dutch tolerance.

Dutch tolerance was designed from the beginning to cope with religious diversity, not to foster it. Chapter 5 examines how the Dutch on both sides of the Atlantic responded to the growing religious diversity and demands for toleration in New Netherland. This chapter underscores the role of petitions, lobbying, and negotiations in shaping Dutch tolerance, arguing that it was a much more nuanced and variable phenomenon than it is often credited for. The habits and possibilities of both connivance and toleration come into play in New Netherland at this stage. Chapter 6 analyzes the radical challenge posed by the sudden appearance of Quakers in New Netherland. Confronting their aggressive proselytizing pushed Dutch tolerance to the extreme in New Netherland, as both very narrow and very liberal interpretations of it began to be applied by different individuals in different places. Most notable was the Flushing Remonstrance, the one great articulation of ideas on religious tolerance made by colonists. This document provides a rare chance to explore in some depth something of the ideological range at work among English colonists living under Dutch rule. As ever, Dutch tolerance was not something entirely within the control of Dutch authorities. Liberty of conscience could, and did, take on multiple connotations.

Remarkably, the Amsterdam authorities in charge of New Netherland meddled less in the management of the colony's church than their counterparts did in Amsterdam. However, by 1658 they felt compelled to take a stand and implement what on the surface seems a small alteration in church policy—the phrasing of the baptismal formula. Chapter 7 argues this change reveals that much more was at stake than baptism. The West India Company directors sought to resolve the struggles over toleration by returning the church to its public function and downplaying its ideological content. The result was that the ideological tenor of the colony's church was somewhat different in its final years than it had been earlier. Nonetheless, it remained an officially Dutch Reformed colony. Chapter 8 examines how some groups, Catholics and Quakers in particular, took advantage of New Netherland's neighbors to sustain faiths that officially had no place in the colony. The close proximity of borders with foreign powers put limits on the extent of Dutch authorities' control over religious life, reminding us that a study of tolerance in the colony must take into account more than just the trans-Atlantic Dutch world.

Much of the story of Dutch tolerance in New Netherland seems, in hindsight, to be little more than a good deal of tumult over a fairly limited range of possibilities. However, by the 1660s the Dutch Republic was at its most radical and libertarian, as the famous philosopher Spinoza perfected his thinking and shared his ideas with friends and colleagues. Chapter 9 examines how some of those in the radical intellectual and religious circles of Amsterdam began thinking of implementing a radical new form of toleration in New Amstel. The one proposal actually put into practice was arguably the most extraordinary expression of tolerance the Dutch colonies would ever see. It did not last very long. Conquest, and the wars that made it possible, was the most fundamental aspect of Dutch history from the day the revolt began until the end of the Golden Age, when the dimensions of the Dutch republic and its empire had stabilized. Chapter 10 presents the impact of the English conquest on Dutch North America. Continuing through the brief Dutch reconquest of 1673–1674, it demonstrates that in this case, the real force for change in policies and practices of toleration was not philosophers or liberal overseers in Amsterdam, but war and foreign domination. The Dutch themselves, for all their vaunted connection to toleration, had a difficult time when they were no longer in charge of setting the parameters of the toleration with which they had to live. As the Dutch reconquest demonstrates, the Dutch preferred to manage religious diversity in a very different way from the English. For better or worse, the English way ultimately proved the more decisive for American history, as the Dutch finally turned over their North American territory to the English in the 1674 Treaty of Westminster.

In the end, one could say that, thanks to the Dutch, the United States of America wound up with a religious freedom it would not have had without them. However, this influence, albeit important, was mostly indirect. It was the English who took over from the Dutch who implemented the religious liberty that made the middle colonies, and thereafter the United States, so famous as a haven and harbor for religious pluralism. Those English—the English of the Restoration period of the 1660s to the 1680s— were a very particular group of individuals living in a peculiar moment of their nation's history, which goes a long way toward explaining how and why they were so open to pluralism (other English at other times were much less so). Perhaps, in the end, the greatest Dutch contribution to American religious diversity was to hold the Mid-Atlantic out of the English orbit until this singular period of English history. Had the Mid-Atlantic become English earlier—or later—American religious history would be radically different.

CHAPTER 1

DUTCH TOLERANCE

. . . each Individual enjoys freedom of religion and no one is persecuted
or questioned about his religion.

With the words, "each individual enjoys freedom of religion," the Union
of Utrecht inscribed tolerance into the heart of the Dutch Republic.[1] Individual freedom of religion was soon qualified as liberty of conscience, and
liberty of conscience became the fundamental law of the land in all the
Dutch provinces and colonies. The cornerstone of Dutch tolerance, it
evolved along with the Dutch state and empire from the signing of the
Union of Utrecht in 1579 until the fall of the republic in 1795. Exactly what
it meant varied over time and from place to place. The union was a political
alliance binding together the northern provinces of the Low Countries in
their eighty-year war for Independence from Spain. It served as the closest
thing to a constitution for the Republic of the United Provinces. Ultimately
seven provinces had full recognition within the States General, the republic's national assembly: Holland, Zeeland, Utrecht, Gelderland, Overijssel,
Groningen and Friesland. Another province, Drenthe, governed itself but
had no representation at the national level. Parts of other provinces liberated from Spanish rule, like north Brabant, Zeelandic Flanders, and the
Overmaas, were designated as Generality Lands and governed directly by
the States General. The Generality lands lacked the sovereignty over internal
affairs, including religion, guaranteed the other provinces, which governed
themselves through their own provincial assemblies, or estates. The combination of the long-running war for independence and the political union
of otherwise quite autonomous provinces proved fundamental to the shaping and evolution of Dutch tolerance. The Dutch carried the political and

religious arrangements of the Union of Utrecht to their colonies when they started expanding overseas in the 1590s. The Dutch tolerance, colonies, and nation were created together.

Whether at home or abroad, the Dutch never could, or would, force or even expect religious conformity and unity. Herein lies the root of Dutch tolerance. Initially it was not articulated as a positive principle but rather "a refusal of Catholic monopoly," one Dutch historian explains. Article 2 of the Union of Utrecht specifically opposed reestablishment of Catholicism as the only religion. From this beginning, the emergent Dutch state gradually embraced "the refusal of any religious monopoly." Instead it "placed itself under the banner of freedom of conscience." Under it, Reformed Protestants gained hegemony within the Dutch world without ever being an absolute majority of its population. Calvinists could attack and restrict the worship of Catholics and others but "did not dare attack the fundamental law of freedom of individual *conscience*," Dutch religious historian Willem Frijhoff emphasizes.[2] To this constitutional refusal to question or coerce an individual's faith one can add the demographic fact that the Dutch Reformed *never* formed a majority in the Dutch world, though they achieved majority status in various areas. Considering how few the Dutch Reformed were when the revolt began, the growth of the Dutch Reformed Church that accompanied tolerance is quite impressive. Developments in Dutch religion and politics through the 1660s provided crucial context for the events in Dutch America. It is the story of the emergence of a nation called Dutch out of the collection of provinces known as the Low Countries and of Protestants out of Catholics.[3]

What I am calling "Dutch tolerance" the Dutch themselves called liberty of conscience or freedom of belief (*gewetensvrijheid* or *geloofsvrijheid*), ignorant of there being anything particularly "Dutch" about it.[4] Yet most non-Dutch scholars agree there was something distinctive about the Dutch manner of handling religious diversity. Jonathan Israel, for example, has accorded the Dutch a central role in the broader history of toleration. Unlike myself, Israel believes toleration is an autonomous quality distinct from the contexts in which it takes place and advocates a certain form of toleration as the true sort. Nonetheless his overview is a useful starting point. The Dutch Revolt (1568–1648) was in part a fight for tolerance as well as independence, and "shaped the toleration debate down to the early eighteenth century" across Europe, he claims. Israel is clearly ambivalent about the revolt's place in the broader history of tolerance, saying that it was both a victory and a defeat "for toleration." Though not everyone who fought for Dutch independence was a Reformed Protestant, loyalty to the Reformed Church and loyalty to the cause of the revolt were often seen as the same thing. The political loyalties of those who were not Dutch Reformed could always be called into question. "Public criticism of the Reformed Church was simply not tolerated," Israel points out, "nor indeed was any kind of open, formal religious or intellectual dissent."[5] Though the Dutch Reformed lived and worked with a range of religious diversity that most other Europeans found almost inconceivable, they did not make such diversity a virtue.

The connection between religious and political rights and loyalties in the Dutch world remained confused precisely because it was never fully resolved. The peculiar history of the Dutch Revolt deprived the Dutch of an established church that could force people to join it and adopt its creed, as in England or France. Instead, it created what the Dutch called a public church, a church that enjoyed the monopoly of state sponsorship and prestige, but that could not force people to conform to it. Nor, because this church was an arm of the state as a public entity, did it have full control of religious matters. Government authorities always had the final say. As a result, even though inhabitants of the Dutch world were not forced to adhere to the Dutch Reformed Church, those who were not Reformed Protestants lacked freedom of religious practice—they could not build separate churches or hold publicly visible religious services, such as processions in the case of Catholics. Consequently, it was not always clear if the Dutch were fighting for liberty of conscience, as some of its leaders insisted, or for the Reformed Church, as others claimed. For some they were essentially the same cause. In different times and places, there could be more or less religious pluralism in evidence. In Amsterdam, there was an extraordinary religious diversity with a variety of religious groups—Lutherans, Jews, Quakers, Catholics, and Mennonites—peacefully coexisting in the shadow of the public church. In other cities, such as Middelburg or Franeker, the range and visibility of religious diversity was much less. The Dutch did not coerce religious uniformity, but that does not mean they encouraged religious diversity.

The religious diversity of the Dutch world was a direct result of the complex process by which the "Dutch" were created. A major challenge when speaking about Dutch tolerance in the seventeenth century is that during these years, both politically and religiously, what was and was not Dutch was constantly changing. The "Dutch" did not exist as a distinct group until the revolt made them so. The revolt brought together roughly a dozen provinces in the northwest corner of the Holy Roman Empire that had for a time (in some cases only briefly) shared a single sovereign in the form of Hapsburg ruler Charles V (who became king of Spain in 1516) but little else. Since the days of the Roman Empire the Low Countries had been a frontier zone, politically, culturally, and geographically divided around the rivers Maas and Scheldt. The southern and western regions were more Celtic and Roman, while Germanic peoples—Franks, Frisians, and Saxons—dominated the north and east. Centuries of social change eventually created a remarkably stable linguistic frontier with French speakers dominating the southern, and Germanic speakers the northern, Low Countries. Yet even there linguistic identity was mixed. The Frisians to this day retain a separate language, while inhabitants of the northeastern provinces shared the Saxon dialect of their German neighbors. Modern Dutch only began to take on its current shape and sound in the sixteenth century. Much of the political elite, including national hero William the Silent, Prince of Orange, who first spearheaded the revolt, spoke French, while the language of religion and learning was, of course, Latin. After 1585, refugees, especially French-speaking Walloon Calvinists from the southern provinces, and immigrants, including German Lutherans, Jews, and English Protestants, added to the linguistic and cultural diversity of the Dutch Republic.

Unlike England and France, the Netherlands had no traditional center. The revolt actually began in the southern provinces. However, since they were soon recaptured by the Spanish Crown, the "Dutch" ended up being those living in the northern provinces, with Holland the wealthiest and most powerful. Amsterdam became the economic powerhouse of the Dutch Republic after the loss of Antwerp in 1585, yet it was never the political capital of the republic, which was in The Hague. Meanwhile the intellectual and (arguably) religious capital was in Leiden, with its Protestant university founded in 1575. The long war, which involved overseas expansion and conquests after 1590, gave birth to the Dutch Republic but also at times threatened to extinguish it. From the moment the struggle for independence began in 1568 until 1674, the frontiers of the Dutch world were extremely unstable. Cities, provinces, and colonies (including Brazil and New Netherland) were won and lost. The borders of the Dutch Republic were not set until the 1648 Treaty of Munster. Even then, the republic was radically reduced in size by the French and allied invasion of 1672. Only a hard-fought war restored the republic's 1648 frontiers. Battles and diplomatic negotiations would continue to shift Dutch borders well into the nineteenth century.

Politically, linguistically, and religiously, then, the seventeenth-century Dutch were a mixed and evolving lot. When talking about "the Dutch," historians and commentators are usually referring to an inhabitant of Holland. Yet there was much more to the United Provinces than Holland, a crucial factor for understanding Dutch religious politics in the colonies. Zeeland, for example, remains famous as a strongly Calvinist province and played a large role in Dutch overseas expansion. Religiously and culturally it had much in common with its neighbors and long-time trading partners, the southern provinces of Flanders and Brabant, also famous for producing strict Calvinists. Refugees from those provinces would settle in Zeeland as well as Holland in the 1580s. The war eventually allowed Zeeland to annex part of Flanders, creating Zeelandic Flanders. Its main fortress town, Sluis (captured in 1604), lay on the military frontier with the Spanish Netherlands and gained a reputation as one of the most staunchly Calvinist communities in the republic. Calvinism had entered the Netherlands through the French-speaking southern provinces first and gained a stronger hold along the southern Dutch military frontier than in Holland.

Over the course of the revolt Calvinism became closely—but never completely—identified with the Dutch Republic and its empire, yet originally all the Netherlands had been Catholic. How the Dutch became Protestant has long been a subject of debate. The degree to which people willingly became Protestant and what sort of Protestant they became (Calvinist or not) are central questions to Dutch national identity, not least because many stayed Catholic. A leading Dutch Catholic scholar has argued that the Dutch people did not become Reformed Protestants of their own volition. Instead, most had been forced to abandon the Roman Catholic Church. Other Dutch historians reject this, pointing to the popular support for the revolt and the comparative lack of persecution by the Dutch Reformed in their rise to dominance to suggest that Protantism was widely embraced by the Dutch. Among Dutch Protestants there has been a debate since the seventeenth century over whether Calvinism, coming as it did from the southern French-speaking parts of Europe, was a maladapted foreign import or a natural fit for the Dutch character. More liberal sorts of Protestants have pointed to pre-Reformation figures like the famous intellectual

[Brackets] indicate territories not represented in States General.

50 Miles

North Sea

Emden

GRONINGEN
• Groningen

• Franeker

FRIESLAND

• Assen

TEXEL

[DRENTHE]

Enkhuizen•

• Kampen
• Zwolle

Amsterdam
Ouderkerk
aan de
Amstel

Haarlem

Naarden

OVERIJSSEL
TWENTE

HOLLAND

Rijnsburg

• Leiden

GELDERLAND

The Hague

Woerden

• Utrecht

• Delft

Gouda

UTRECHT

• Arnhem

Brielle

Rotterdam

• Nijmegen

Dordrecht

Waal

ZEELAND

• Cleves

WALCHEREN
ISLAND

Zierikzee•

RAVENSTEIN

• Wesel

Heusden•

Middelburg

• Breda

• Tilburg

Vlissingen

[NORTH BRABANT]

• Sluis

Maas

Rhine

[ZEELANDIC
FLANDERS]

• Antwerp

Ghent •

Scheldt

• Mechelen

Cologne•

DENMARK

Area shown on
larger map

1•
2•
3•

• Maastricht
[OVERMAAS]

•4

POLAND

A

•5

• Liège

SILESIA

Neuwied•

Elbe

B

BLACKMER MAPS

HOLY
ROMAN
EMPIRE

•7

KEY

A Dutch Republic
B Spanish Netherlands

•6

HUNGARY

FRANCE

Rhine

1 Friedrichstadt   5 Munster
2 Gluckstadt   6 Paris
3 Hamburg   7 Heidelberg
4 Berlin   8 Geneva

OTTOMAN
EMPIRE

•8

Figure 2. Dutch Republic and neighboring territories, c. 1648.

Erasmus and mystics like Thomas à Kempis as emblematic of a long-standing Dutch religious tradition that placed an emphasis on individual belief and private practice outside the structure of the Church as fundamental to Dutch spirituality. Strict Calvinists, on the other hand, argued the Reformed Church gave Dutchness its distinctive edge. Without it, the Dutch Republic would have been impossible.[6]

In a suggestive resolution to how Dutch religious affiliation was crafted that holds important relevance for the Dutch colonies, Peter van Rooden has tied the fate of religion in the country to the progress of Dutch state-building. He notes that the "truth of the thesis that the Dutch were forcefully Protestantized by political means lies in the undeniable outcome of the years up to 1625, which proved that the Reformed were right in their assumption that once the correct structures were in place and political support was assured, the hearts and minds of the population would follow. In all areas where political authority had effectively suppressed dissenting Christian organization before 1625, the population became homogeneously Reformed. Interestingly, those areas form a continuous belt, running . . . along the military front as it had been more or less stabilized at the turn of the sixteenth century." This is the contemporary Dutch Bible Belt, a stretch of territory running across the interior of the country, from Zeeland through southern Holland and Gelderland to Drenthe, known for its conservative Calvinism. The Dutch military frontier with Spain at the time of the Twelve Year Truce (1609–1621) thus became a religious frontier with lasting consequences for Dutch society. To the north and west lie Holland, Friesland, and Groningen, which never experienced the same degree of forcible Calvinization, and thus had more mixed religious environments. South and east are the heavily Catholic regions of North Brabant and Limburg, incorporated only after 1621.[7] Consequently, at precisely the moment when the Dutch Reformed Church was gaining new lands and people overseas (New Amsterdam's church was founded in 1628), it was reaching the limits of its expansion within Europe. The Dutch Reformed Church presided over the Dutch Republic, but it never encompassed all its inhabitants, especially on the periphery, from Batavia to Brabant and Brazil.

Within the core provinces of the Dutch Republic, especially Holland, a series of religious and political transformations ensured that religious diversity was a fixture of Dutch society, though exactly how varied over time. A heavily urbanized center of trade and industry, the Low Countries quickly gained access to the new religious thinking in the wake of Martin Luther's protest against the Roman Catholic Church in the 1520s. Lutheranism denied the power of the Catholic Church, its saints, monasteries, convents, and most of its sacraments to enable salvation, claiming only faith in Jesus Christ as taught by ministers (the term rejected the spiritual powers associated with Catholic priests) properly educated in Biblical interpretation could do so. Lutherans restored the church to the secular world, encouraging ministers to marry and abandoning the Catholic Church's claims to autonomy under the pope, placing their churches under the authority of their secular rulers instead. Though Lutheranism gained a number of supporters in cosmopolitan Antwerp, which had extensive trading contacts with the north German and Scandinavian territories that adopted Lutheranism, it did not take much hold elsewhere in the Low Countries.

More important in the northern provinces was Anabaptism. Arriving via the many trade connections to southwest and central Germany, where its radical rejection of traditional religious authority had mixed with the social revolution known as the Peasants' War (1524–1525), Anabaptism was a far more dramatic rejection of the authority and hierarchy associated with the Roman Catholic Church. Meaning literally baptized again, Anabaptists abandoned the Catholic and Lutheran custom of baptizing infants, claiming that only an adult could demonstrate the repentance and acceptance of faith necessary in a baptized Christian. With the Bible as their primary spiritual authority, they also rejected the claim that ministers and priests must be of a specially educated class. Instead of having formal priests or ministers, they granted commoners the power to preach and lead their fellows in all things religious—which at times was difficult to separate from other dimensions of life. For a time it seemed that Anabaptists might effect a revolutionary transformation of European society. Though the Peasants' Revolt was brutally suppressed, ten years later another radical movement gained control of the city of Munster, drawing thousands from the northern Low Countries including a Dutch tailor, John of Leiden, who became one of its leaders. Anabaptists launched a parallel coup in Amsterdam, but failed to capture the city. Savagely repressed in Munster after a long siege, Anabaptists thereafter abandoned efforts at social transformation and moved toward pacifism and withdrawal from worldly politics, especially under their leader Menno Simmons, a Frisian, from whom Dutch Baptists derived the name Mennonites.

Reformed Protestantism, the last strand to be incorporated into the range of Protestant religious diversity of the early Dutch Republic, arrived in the 1540s. Developed in the Rhineland and Switzerland by figures such as Ulrich Zwingli and Jean Calvin, it rejected both the radicalism of the Anabaptists and the conservatism of the Lutherans. Reformed ministers had to be specially educated (hence the creation of Leiden University) in languages and theology, and they baptized the infants of their congregations. However, they went farther than the Lutherans, rejecting the authority of bishops and denying that God was really present, in body and blood, in the Eucharist—perhaps the most important difference between Lutherans and Reformed. The French theologian Calvin, who made Geneva his base, is particularly associated with predestination, the idea that God had foreordained whether an individual would be saved or damned regardless of that individual's qualities or actions in life. Entering through the southern, French-speaking provinces, Reformed Protestantism caught on slowly in the Dutch-speaking north.

Philip II, who became king of Spain and lord of the Low Countries in 1556, fiercely resisted the growth of religious diversity. Philip promoted the Catholic Counter-Reformation in Spain and introduced it to the Low Countries, but did not trust Netherlanders to enforce the new demand for religious conformity to his satisfaction. Instead, he continued the policies of his father, Charles V, taking decision-making power away from the provinces, their nobilities and assemblies, and concentrating it in his court. These policies undermined local control over religious matters as well. Philip created new bishoprics so that there were more bishops able to work closely with the Inquisition and supervise the new orthodoxy. A Spanish institution designed to ensure conformity of belief and punish individuals for heretical thoughts as well as deeds, the Inquisition offended the local pride and moral sensibilities of many in the Low Countries, both Protestant and Catholic, who had an aversion to coercing individual beliefs even if they did not favor religious pluralism. The Inquisitors' methods, developed in the Spanish Catholic struggle to root all traces of Jewishness out of their society after having forcibly converted (or killed or expelled) all Spanish Jews, relied on an intense investigation of people's personal beliefs and represented yet another institution disrupting Netherlander control over local affairs. The Inquisition's arrests, trials, and public executions formed the most severe persecution in Europe. From its appearance in the Low Countries in 1521 to the end of the sixteenth century about 2,000 Netherlanders were executed for heresy. Some 800 of the executions took place in the northern provinces, about 400 in Holland alone. Witchcraft

was persecuted along with Protestant heresy, with some 200 people executed for witchcraft in what later became the Dutch Republic. Several legal
decisions in the 1590s officially put an end to government trials for witchcraft in the United Provinces—the first European state to do so—a hundred years before the Salem witch trials. In later memory, the idea of
witchcraft trials would be grouped with the Inquisition as evidence for
many Dutch Protestants of the backwardness and oppression of Spanish,
Hapsburg, and Roman Catholic rule.[8]

The religious and political issues provoked by King Philip's government
came to a head in 1566, in what have gone down in history as the iconoclastic riots. After a group of Low Country nobles persuaded the Spanish
regent to stop the operation of the Inquisition, thousands gathered publicly
in crowds to hear Reformed ministers preach. Prohibited from preaching
in the churches, they usually gathered in fields outside town. One of the
key themes of this so-called "hedge preaching" was the importance of rid-
ding the community of the "idolatrous" and false elements of religious
worship decorating all the Catholic churches and institutions around the
country. In a sudden burst of activity that summer, inhabitants of the Netherlands took down or destroyed statues, paintings, altar elements, and a
range of other paraphernalia associated with Roman Catholic worship. This
"rioting" was often well organized and sometimes quite peaceful. The most
militant provinces were Flanders and Brabant.[9] The resulting repression by
the Spanish crown turned a fight for control of the Low Countries' religious
landscape into a war for political sovereignty.

Idolatry was a concern first raised in opposition to Roman Catholic
worship, but it carried over to the non-Christian world as well. To Protestant minds idolatry was a fundamental error in religious worship in which
not God himself but images and "idols" representing him or some other
false God were worshiped. For the Reformed, the dramatic scale and success
of the iconoclasm, as it came to be called, was a divine confirmation of
their faith and actions. As one leader later wrote, it was not human "strata-
gems" that brought it about "but the manifest providence of God who
wanted to show how much He detests and abhors the abominable idolatry
committed around these images to the disgrace of the name of Christ and
the whole of Christendom. He wanted to stigmatize and ridicule the foolish
imagination of people who always wish to contrive new ways to worship
Him." To adore and serve images was "contrary to God's commandment."
Those who defended it, saying they knew "the images were only wood and

stone, and that they did not adore them but only what was represented by them," were resurrecting the false arguments of "the ancient pagans." Unfortunately, "the poor people committed and are still committing every day such horrible and abominable idolatries in connection with these statues, that every God-fearing man cannot fail to shudder with horror." The work of Reformation had just begun.[10]

Geneva-educated Huguenot Francis Junius (François du Jon, 1545–1602), who as chaplain to William of Orange and later as professor of theology at Leiden played an important role in shaping Dutch Calvinism, proposed a solution for King Philip II "to obviate the troubles and commotion about religion and to extirpate the sects and heresies that abound in the Low Countries." The answer was simple: publicly recognize the Reformed churches alongside those of the Roman Catholics. It was a revealing statement of why the Reformed thought that they, and they alone, should be tolerated, and not just in private, but permitted "the public worship and ceremonies" without which religion could not exist. Heresy was understandable as a misdirected response to the "grave abuses in the Church," the Roman Catholic Church, that is. The best way "to exterminate such heresies" would be to "permit, nay expressly to command that all who profess the religion called reformed or evangelical, assemble openly and keep a strict discipline in accordance with the obedience due to God and the authorities, and correct all vices and licentiousness." With the Reformed, together with the established Catholic Church "there will be only two ways of public worship in public sight, each of them keeping to the obedience due to God and king. Even if there were no other benefit, this would be valuable enough in the maintenance of public order. And as soon as a new opinion arises, it will be very easy to show by the word of God that it is false."[11] It was an argument from below, made by a Reformed Protestant in a world ruled by Catholics, but barely concealing the Calvinist sense that their faith was the only true one. It was not what King Philip chose to do.

Philip blamed the people of the Low Countries, not his policies, for the troubles. According to him, "the condition of religious affairs in the Netherlands" required stricter enforcement of the law, not leniency. The "cause of the past evil and its subsequent growth and advance has been the negligence, leniency and duplicity of the judges," not the laws they were expected to enforce. There was no question of getting rid of the Inquisition. "It is the only means the Church has at her disposal of making every one live and behave according to her commandments. It is an instrument which has been applied since ancient times and is fully legitimate according to canon and civil law, to Holy Scripture and natural reason. Its purpose is to see that those who don't behave as they should and fail to do as the Church commands, should be admonished and brought back to the right path and reprimanded, if necessary. If the inquisition were abolished, this would no longer be possible, and it would seem that then every one would be permitted to live almost as he likes."[12] No one on either side of the revolt wanted that. The question was who would be in charge, and how would they enforce a moral society?

In reaction to the iconoclastic riots, Philip sent the duke of Alva with an army of thousands of Spanish soldiers to bring the Low Countries firmly under his command. Even though local authorities had largely suppressed the rioters long before Alva and his army arrived, the Spanish authorities came down hard on the Netherlanders. Alva brought back the Inquisition, which tried thousands for their role in the riots. Others, including several leading nobles, were tried in the so-called "Council of Troubles," and executed. William the Silent, Prince of Orange, fled the region rather than face Alva's justice. Beginning in 1568 he started launching raids from neighboring German provinces, but it was not until 1572 that his fellow rebels finally gained a foothold in Holland with the capture of Brielle. Towns across Holland and Zeeland, unhappy with the Spanish military occupation and the new taxes it brought, started to join the rebels. Amsterdam stayed loyal longer than most, holding out for the Spanish king until 1578. In January 1579 the seven northern provinces of the Low Countries united in the Union of Utrecht. Over the next few years other provinces including Flanders and Brabant joined the Union, only to be recaptured by the Spanish.

Because of the war, Dutch history was a near-run thing. In 1584 a Catholic agent assassinated William of Orange. In 1585 the rebels were driven out of Flanders and Brabant, including Antwerp, the heart of the Low Countries' international trade. As late as 1588, the year of the great Spanish Armada, it seemed that the armies of the Spanish king might recapture all his rebellious provinces and return them to obedience to him and the Catholic Church. Fortunately for the Dutch cause, William of Orange's son and successor Maurice (Maurits in Dutch) proved to be a military genius, and the Spanish overextended themselves by getting involved in the French wars of religion. Maurice reorganized the Dutch armies and renovated tactics to the point where the Dutch superseded the Spanish as the most sophisticated military in Europe. Expensive siege warfare became increasingly important as the holding and capture of cities and forts became the basis of painstaking territorial gains. By 1609, when the exhausted parties settled on a Twelve Year Truce, Maurice had gained control of much of what would ultimately become the territory of the Dutch Republic. After the Truce expired in 1621, fighting between Dutch and Spanish resumed until the 1648 Treaty of Munster finally secured Dutch Independence, guaranteeing at the same time that the southern provinces, essentially what is now Belgium and Luxembourg, remained Spanish and Catholic.

The desperate years of the 1580s were the crucible of Dutch tolerance. Jonathan Israel traces the beginnings of a distinctively Dutch debate on toleration to this period.[13] Before 1579, the Dutch struggle and debate over toleration fit into the broader European pattern. William of Orange initially fought for a bi-confessional country, governed by a so-called "religious peace" where Catholics and Protestants could both worship freely and openly in the same cities, towns, and provinces. In this he was in tune with elsewhere in Europe. In France, the 1598 Edict of Nantes granted Reformed Protestants rights of public worship alongside the Roman Catholic Church in designated places. In Switzerland, certain provinces had stayed Catholic while others became Protestant, and a complicated system of government was arranged to share power between the two religions. In several German provinces and cities of the Holy Roman Empire, Catholics and Lutherans were both granted rights of worship in an arrangement called "simultaneum." Sometimes they even shared the same church, each getting half, with all sorts of elaborate arrangements to monitor and restrict conflict between the two. However, no "religious peace" lasted in the Low Countries. Only in Maastricht and parts of the Overmaas, conquered by the republic in 1632, would a simultaneum be granted. Everywhere else, only one faith could worship openly.[14]

The Union of Utrecht guaranteed liberty of conscience, not a religious peace. Stating that no one will be "persecuted or questioned about his religion" and "each individual enjoys freedom of religion," it prevented any single church from being fully established, but it could deny other churches the privilege of worshipping in public if worshipping and believing were held as two distinct categories, as they often were.[15] As the war continued, Reformed Protestants, who had everything to lose in a Catholic Spanish victory, argued that Catholics could not be trusted to defend Dutch liberties as well as they could. The rebellious provinces passed laws prohibiting

Catholics from worshipping in public and excluding them from political offices, but also proscribed the activities of non-Reformed Protestants, Lutherans, and Anabaptists, claiming they also could not be trusted to run the country or defend it from its enemies. None of these groups was absolutely forbidden, forced to convert, or expelled from the republic. However, they could no longer hold important positions of secular authority nor could their religion be publicly acknowledged. By 1581, the Reformed Church was the public's only officially available church in all rebel-held territory. It had the monopoly on church buildings, higher offices, and state support. Rather than becoming a bi-confessional state or even one with religious freedom for all, the Dutch had more or less reaffirmed the pre-Reformation world—where there was officially only one church in town, only one place to get baptized, hear a sermon, participate in public rituals, and pray with one's neighbors—only now it was the local authorities rather than the pope who were in charge and the religion was Reformed Protestant, not Roman Catholic. The Dutch called this the public church (*de publieke kerk*), and it was inseparable from Dutch tolerance.

Some Dutch rebels had a more expansive view of religious liberty. The great advocates of freedom of conscience in the United Provinces tended to be born in Holland. Perhaps the best known and most outspoken was Dirck Volckertszoon Coornheert. Though he was marginalized after his death in 1590, many of his ideas would resurface later among seventeenth-century radicals. The son of an Amsterdam cloth merchant, his great skills in Latin made him a favored secretary of William of Orange. A loyal citizen of the republic while also a Catholic, Coornheert placed a stress on internal spirituality and outward peace, claiming that the structure and order of church life were secondary. For this reason he defended the Roman Catholic Church by arguing that the external aspects of the church so often criticized by Protestants as idolatry had no bearing on salvation (they were what some called *adiaphora* or "things indifferent"). Consequently there was no reason to reject it, for it still conveyed the essentials of Christian faith.[16] In his last work, *Proces van 't ketterdooden ende Dwangh der Conscienten* (Trial of the Killing of Heretics and the Constraint of Conscience, 1590), he argued against forcing individuals to believe a certain way, claiming that coercion and execution of heretics only produced false converts and undermined true religion. Though he engaged in polemics with virtually all available Christian religions, he was an unflinching advocate of liberty of conscience. For him, liberty of conscience and freedom of expression were essential for the discovery of truth, and he denied that any single faith had a monopoly on the truth.[17]

Notwithstanding the advocacy of Coornhert and a few others, only one church was officially permitted within the republic. Initially, only a small minority of the population was Reformed. The bulk of the population had to be converted, but without the coercion associated with the Roman Catholic Church under Spanish rule. Church services were open for all to attend, and any Christian could be baptized in the Church. However, those who wanted to play a role in running the Church or hold high political office were required to become full members, conforming to the Church's beliefs and discipline (enforcement of those beliefs and the corresponding behavior expected of a church member). Over time, with no other public religious options available, more and more people joined the Dutch Reformed Church. However, full members never formed more than a small majority of the Dutch population. A significant number of Roman Catholics, together with Mennonites and Lutherans, could be found across the Dutch Republic and its colonies.

Exactly what it meant to be Dutch Reformed was not settled until 1618, when the national Synod of Dort proclaimed the public church to be Calvinist. Before then, theological matters were more fluid. The importance of the years from 1580 to about 1620 in shaping Dutch religion has drawn the bulk of scholarship on religion and politics in the Dutch republic over the last three decades. Reflecting in part the decentralized structure of Dutch politics and society, there remains no authoritative overview of the political and religious struggles in the United Provinces. Instead, those wishing to come to grasp with the history must pull together a range of smaller-scale studies in a way that can only be gestured at here. Important studies have been done of the provinces of Holland and Friesland.[18] Cities have been served by excellent studies of Haarlem, Leiden, Utrecht, and elsewhere.[19] Amsterdam—an enormous topic—has proved more difficult to grasp, but a number of important partial studies exist.[20] Finally, a few studies of small communities illuminate the social and religious transformations on the local scale.[21] One of the most important points to emerge out of this work is the variety from place to place, notwithstanding the overall national hegemony of the Reformed. The religious complexion of no two cities or provinces was quite the same. Given the long-standing insistence on autonomy by local authorities in the cities and provinces, this should not come as a great surprise. This complexity would have great consequences when the Dutch went overseas, where the religious make-up of the different colonies would echo the variety found in the republic.

The ambiguity of religious identity in these years gave birth to several terms specific to the Dutch context. Calvinists, claiming the center of Reformed identity even before 1618, called those who were Reformed but did not support a fully Calvinist church "libertines," suggesting they were too permissive in doctrine and discipline. Those who regularly attended and supported the Reformed church without becoming full-blown members were referred to as "liefhebbers"—sympathizers with the Reformed Church. In the early seventeenth century the "liefhebbers" generally outnumbered the full members in any particular church. People could attend the Reformed Church and benefit from its services, but did not have to believe everything the Church said. Or did they?[22]

In the 1580s the debate over religion in the Dutch Republic shifted from the previous Protestant-Catholic question to an internal, Protestant matter. There was no longer a question of allowing Catholics to exist on equal terms with Protestants. Now the question was about the nature of the public Reformed Church and its relationship to the beliefs of the republic's citizens, Reformed or not. The University of Leiden, founded by William of Orange in 1575 to train Reformed ministers, became the focal point of the struggle because, though the Dutch Reformed Church was the public church everywhere in the republic, it had no central national authority. As early as the Synod of Emden in 1571, the principle was established that no one church should have authority over any other. Local churches were largely self-governed by a consistory, or council, consisting of the minister and several lay elders and deacons. Only classes (councils of several churches) or provincial and national synods (councils of several classes) could draft and enforce new policies on individual churches. In other words, the church of Amsterdam had no more power in the Dutch Reformed Church than the church of Arnhem or Middelburg. They each interpreted and enforced the rules and regulations of the Dutch Reformed Church on their own. Of course they did so in consultation with other churches, but in the end each church had a certain amount of autonomy, being as influenced by the local government as by national church policy. This helps explain why a theology dispute between two professors at Leiden exploded into a political and ecclesiastical coup in 1618.

The nature of Dutch tolerance and the orthodoxy of the public church were inextricable from the politics of the republic. As Frijhoff notes, the

Union of Utrecht provided for both government intervention in the church and particularism—the sovereignty of each province in regulating its own social, political, and religious order. This curtailed the extent to which the Dutch Reformed Church could apply the national Presbyterian synodal model of church government in ways the Scots, for example, did. Instead, provincial synods "continued to support their specific rulings and followed their own political lines." Even the ways a minister was appointed varied from province to province. The 1618 Synod of Dort respected this arrangement. Apart from affirming the Calvinist doctrine of the public church, it could not enforce a uniform Church policy across the Dutch world. By the time New Netherland's church was founded, the public church was undeniably Calvinist, but it swam in notably different seas depending on the local circumstances.[23]

The Synod of Dort was made possible by a political coup. The Union of Utrecht had created a new State: the United Provinces, a republic in a world of monarchies. In this, the Dutch had achieved something revolutionary. However, their radicalism more or less stopped there. The Dutch Republic was not a new government so much as the old form that had shed its meddling monarchs and their aggravating supporters. Regents still governed the towns. Estates (or States, the legislative assemblies) still governed the provinces. The States of Holland, the States of Zeeland, etc., were the representative assemblies of particular provinces. There was a States General that represented the union, but its powers were as vague as the nation itself. It could not easily impose its will on the provincial States. Hugo Grotius, the great Dutch political thinker and scholar, articulated a theory of sovereignty to justify this arrangement. According to him, the States General were a voluntary federation of sovereign provinces. As allies, they could cooperate but not impose their will on one another. The States General was not a powerful Parliament like that in England but rather a mediator, more a meeting place than a source of authority.

Only some Dutchmen accepted Grotius's theory about their constitution and almost all of them lived in Holland, of which Grotius was a true son, born in Delft and educated at Leiden. Equal in theory, in practice Holland was the most powerful of the provinces. In fact, Grotius's theory of provincial sovereignty justified Holland's relative independence from the national assembly of the States General. From an early stage in the revolt Holland had made a habit of using its considerable influence to coerce the other provinces into following its lead, regardless of the will of the States

General, which sometimes outvoted Holland. When that happened, Holland appealed to its sovereign right not to obey the vote, and there was little the States General could do to compel compliance. The emphasis on the supremacy of provincial power, as embodied in its representative Estates, gave supporters of this constitutional theory their name in Dutch: *staatsgezind* (inclined to favor the Estates), often rendered Republicans in English (not to be confused with Anglo-American Republicans, though both shared an aversion to anything resembling absolutist monarchical rule). Because of Holland's power within the republic, the most influential man in the States of Holland became the most powerful politician in the United Provinces. At the time Grotius wrote that man was Johan van Oldenbarnevelt, pensionary (legal advisor) of the States of Holland. Even though he held no national position, Oldenbarnevelt was de facto leader of the United Provinces from 1586, when he acquired the office, to 1618. Deposed in 1618, Republicans would return to power in 1651, opening new possibilities for Dutch tolerance in America.[24]

The greatest challenge to Republican rule came from the stadholders. Stadholders had been minor viceroys of the Spanish crown, with control over executive and especially military functions in the provinces. With the revolt, most stadholders chose the side of the crown, with William of Orange a crucial exception. Representatives of an executive power that no longer existed, the Dutch stadholders now depended on the right of each province to choose its own stadholder. Holland and Zeeland traditionally chose a descendant of William of Orange. Since those were the most important provinces, their stadholder became the most powerful in the republic, though he was not the only one. Another branch of the family generally held the stadholdership of Friesland and Groningen in the north. In a nation without a political center, the stadholder of Holland served as a powerful token of national unity. The princes of Orange led the nation's army and held special status as not just a nobleman but a sovereign prince—albeit of the tiny principality of Orange in the south of France. Those who stressed the primacy of the Prince of Orange in the Dutch constitution were known as Orangists (Oranjegezind) or supporters of the Prince (Prinzengezind).

The stadholders' political role in the republic was ambiguous. In theory, their powers and the prestige of their office gave them the potential to rule almost as monarchs, with authority over the military and foreign policy as well as some executive rights in provincial government. Stadholders needed a strong, centralized government capable of coercing obedience from recalcitrant provincial States (especially Holland). Consequently they supported a stronger States General than Grotius did. This made them a natural ally of anyone who resented the dominance of Holland. Oldenbarnevelt's foes included a mix of poorer inland provinces, Dutch nobles, strict Calvinists, and some urban crowds. The Orangists argued, contrary to Grotius, that every province had sacrificed some of its sovereignty to the greater entity of the United Provinces. For them, the States General was a national representative body with genuine powers over all the provincial States. The Republicans' vision was of a "small Netherland" that would preserve the power of Amsterdam and prestige of Holland by not becoming too large. The Orangists' vision was of a "big Netherlands," expansive and inclusive. Through 1650 the stadholders and their supporters did not give up the dream of annexing the southern provinces.[25]

Since the 1580s, the public church had become an increasingly important political force, with a constitution and governmental structure of its own. Key to its strength was the way its institutions grew up from local constituencies. The fundamental unit was the congregation, made up of all the members of the local church. Membership had to be earned, either through a convincing confession of faith before the congregation or, if one's parents were members, through baptism. Membership could also be proven if one moved from one town and church to another (or to the colonies) by a letter attesting to membership from the person's original congregation and authorizing him or her to transfer it to the new congregation. The governing body of the congregation was the consistory, which enforced what the Calvinists called "discipline," the morality and standards of membership. Though the minister of the congregation was part of the consistory, secular members, appointed as elders and deacons, ran the business of the church, maintaining the church building and its social welfare programs. Above each consistory was a classis (what the British called a presbytery) made up of delegates from the various consistories under its authority. Classes were grouped into the regional unit of a synod, whose members were appointed from the classes. In Holland there were two synods, North Holland, dominated by Amsterdam (and, through Amsterdam's classis, including many of the colonial churches), and South Holland. Theoretically a national synod would preside over the regional synods, but there was none after Dort. The church was arguably the most national, democratic, inclusive, and egalitarian institution in the Dutch Republic: as long as you were Dutch Reformed.

When the Dutch spoke of the public church, they meant it. Churches and church property became public property, belonging to the community, not the churchmen. Former monks and nuns who could find no other employment received pensions from the state. Secular authorities oversaw the finances and had at least some say in governing. Classes and consistories ordained and called ministers but always in cooperation with the secular authorities. This allowed communities to install ministers of slightly different theological dispositions within the overall structure of the Reformed Church. Depending on whether the local government was Republican or Orangist, they could have different political inclinations as well. The nature of the public church meant that it is impossible to describe Dutch affairs as falling on a line of "Church versus State." The overlap between political and religious power and affiliation also helps explain why the biggest political crisis of the Dutch revolt began as a religious dispute: the Arminian controversy.

The Arminian controversy was theological in origin, pitting so-called "libertines" against Calvinists over the question of predestination. Had God determined ahead of time the fate of all souls, condemning them to perdition or granting them salvation regardless of the individual will or actions of the person? Calvinists argued yes, the libertines—who could point to teachings of Calvin that did not insist on the matter—argued not quite. There was, possibly, some role for human free will to accept or reject the salvation granted by God. These theological positions corresponded to contrasting visions of the public church and its relationship to both the wider society and the secular authorities.

Libertines, or Arminians as they were also called, preferred a more flexible theology because they wanted as inclusive a church as possible, hoping the church could retain the communal role it had played before the Reformation of uniting all neighbors in a single congregation. Only through exposing the maximum number of people to true religion could the cause of salvation best be served. This led them to be tolerant theologically—as long as people stayed within their church. Apart from certain uncontroversial fundamentals, they avoided being specific about the rest of their religious doctrine, enabling as many people as possible to fit comfortably within the public church. However, precisely because the church was so inclusive, they saw no reason to tolerate dissenters from it. Libertines discriminated against Calvinists wherever they held power, refusing to let Calvinists worship separately, as some began to do in the 1610s. As Jonathan

Israel has pointed out, they did not have a theory for tolerating the open worship of anyone who did not belong to the public church.[26]

The Arminian controversy drew its name from Amsterdam minister and Leiden professor Jacobus Arminius.[27] Arminius had studied in Geneva and was seen by his congregation in Amsterdam as a good Reformed Protestant and valued minister. However, starting in the 1590s, one of his fellow ministers, Flemish immigrant Petrus Plancius, began denouncing Arminius's teachings about the role of free will in salvation. Plancius was from what had been one of the most radically Calvinist corners of the Netherlands—West Flanders. The iconoclastic riots of 1566 had begun there and were more ferocious than in Holland, Arminius's native province. Having fled Brussels in disguise after its capture by Spanish troops in 1585, Plancius became a minister in Amsterdam, where he soon gained a reputation as a "fiery Calvinist." A foe to all who were not strictly Calvinist, Plancius was a man who could affirm over dinner "that the Catholics were as dangerous enemies as Jews and Turks."[28] Strict Calvinists like Plancius wanted the church to be as independent of magisterial authority as possible. Ironically, given their pretensions to national hegemony, the Calvinist emphasis on restrictive membership, intense discipline, and high but narrow standards of belief and behavior made it difficult to include the bulk of inhabitants within their purview. From the beginning they considered themselves an embattled minority surrounded by reprobates. This attitude tended to make them combative rather than indulgent of diverse opinions, though it also led them to acknowledge religious differences more easily than Arminians.

Arriving at Leiden in 1602, Arminius and his teachings drew the opposition of his Calvinist colleague, and Plancius's fellow Fleming, Franciscus Gomarus. By the time the truce with Spain began in 1609, Arminius himself had died but the Arminian-Gomarist debate had just begun. Strict Calvinism, which stressed the importance of the individual's submission to church order and the inscrutable omnipotence of God's will, was relatively new to Holland, hence its close association with Flemish refugees in the Arminian controversy. Arminius's supporters preferred the tradition of Dutch piety that emphasized the importance of the individual's relationship with God for achieving salvation. Their differences soon congealed into two separate religious camps, called Remonstrant and Counter-Remonstrant.

Petitions, or remonstrances, provided the names for the major religious and political split that divided the public church in the 1610s. In 1610,

Arminians submitted a petition for government protection from harassment by Gomarists, who responded with a counter-remonstrance asking the government to support their cause. Oldenbarnevelt came down on the side of the Remonstrants and suppressed the Counter-Remonstrant campaign of harassment. The people who complained most loudly of persecution now were the Counter-Remonstrants. In places like Woerden, Holland, where they formed a minority, they seceded from the national church and formed their own shadow congregations.[29]

Oldenbarnevelt could take pride in presiding over a peaceful and thriving society. Yet his regime's success created many enemies. Some merchants earned a tidy profit in the peacetime economy. Others did not. Prices for many goods dropped while rents began to rise. The merchants and magistrates who had thrived on the aggressive wartime economy simmered with resentment. The States of Holland—representing many other cities, such as Leiden, that were not benefiting as much from the truce as Amsterdam was—also came to resent the overweening power of Amsterdam in the province, embodied in Oldenbarnevelt and his policies. Even within Amsterdam's elite a growing number of Calvinists, like Reynier Pauw, resented Oldenbarnevelt's policies and refused to suppress the Counter-Remonstrants. Popular protests began, combining religious indignation with anger over economic difficulties. Stadholder Maurice, frustrated in his dreams of reconquest, fostered the growing resentment. By summer 1618, Oldenbarnevelt's allies could no longer maintain public order in Holland. Prince Maurice was able to take over the government in what was effectively a bloodless coup. He purged Oldenbarnevelt's sympathizers from town councils and the provincial States, justifying his actions with Orangist constitutional arguments. He had Oldenbarnevelt and Grotius tried for treason by the States General, with Reynier Pauw on the bench. Oldenbarnevelt was condemned and executed, Grotius imprisoned.[30]

Prince Maurice reinforced his political coup with a religious one, convening a national synod at Dordrecht (known as Dort to the English) to settle the Arminian controversy. Since Arminian-like ideas existed in other countries as well, England, Scotland, and several German states took an interest and sent delegates or observers, making the synod the first major international synod of Reformed Protestantism. It found nearly 200 Dutch ministers, mostly from Holland, guilty of Arminianism. They had to sign a formula of submission to the Church as defined by the Synod of Dort or be barred from preaching and threatened with banishment. About forty signed and were rehabilitated. Another seventy were stripped of their posts, but allowed to remain in the republic as private citizens. Approximately eighty were banished.[31] It was the greatest break in Dutch religious life since the Reformation. For Dutch Calvinists it seemed their time had finally come. Condemning Arminians as heretics was only one of the synod's items of business. Its many resolutions on church matters formed a cornerstone for Reformed churches everywhere and would be of particular importance to the Dutch colonies, whose churches were to be organized along the lines specified at Dort.

With the support of Prince Maurice, Counter-Remonstrants began what they termed the Further Reformation, a puritanical program to promote a uniform code of beliefs and behavior across the country. Much like Puritans in England, they zealously attacked all forms of what they considered ungodly life. The list of prohibited activities ran from drunkenness and ribaldry to music, the theater, lack of respect for the Sabbath, and so-called "superstitious festivals," such as St. Nicholas Day (i.e., Christmas). The Further Reformation was never completed. However, it remained a persistent concern long after the death of Maurice in 1625 ended the Counter-Remonstrants' period of political dominance.[32]

By formalizing the Calvinist orthodoxy of the Dutch Reformed Church, the Synod of Dort also prompted the creation of a new Dutch Protestant church—the Remonstrant church, formed by proscribed Arminians in exile together with surreptitious congregations in the republic. Remonstrants initially denied they were creating something new, but simply preserving the true Dutch Reformed Church from before 1618. As long as Remonstrants retained the claim to be the true legal, public Reformed Church of the Netherlands, they were treated as a serious political and religious threat by the Counter-Remonstrants. Only after Maurice's death in 1625 would they be able to worship without harassment in the republic as a minority religion. Nonetheless, since it appealed to a number of the wealthiest and brightest individuals in Holland, it retained a strong cultural role in the republic out of proportion to its actual membership. Indeed, several of the most famous Dutch writers on toleration in the seventeenth century were Remonstrants.[33]

The Remonstrants are relevant to the story of tolerance in New Netherland because at least one, and possibly more, of the Amsterdam directors of the West India Company who oversaw the colony had close connections to, if not a downright affinity for, Remonstrants and their ideas. Around 1621 Remonstrant exiles started a publishing campaign, picking up some of the issues advocated by Coornhert in the 1580s. Leading Remonstrant ministers like Paschier de Fijne and Johannes Uyttenbogaert began denouncing persecution as destructive of human freedom and economic prosperity. Another minister, Simon Episcopius, set out what Jonathan Israel calls a theory of "a general toleration, a toleration which would not only guarantee freedom of practice, and expression, to all churches but also free the individual from compulsion, on the part of the secular or ecclesiastical authorities, or any body of elders, within each church." His *Vrije Godes-dienst* (literally Free Divine Worship or Religious Freedom) argued that "No human conscience is above another," nor could anyone "judge another, all having equal access to Holy Scripture and an equal right to interpret it according to his, or her judgment." Episcopius, like Coornhert, opposed persecution and dogmatism because they generated resentment and political conflict. Worse, they stifled "genuine debate about God's truth, reducing individuals to unthinking ciphers or hypocrites who in their hearts reject what outwardly they profess to believe." This was a rejection of a number of sixteenth-century arguments for conformity. Episcopius went so far as to argue that a "plurality of churches . . . produces a calmer, more stable society." Of course, since it was only after they had been excluded from the public church that Remonstrants advocated religious pluralism, their Counter-Remonstrant foes held it against them as evidence of their hypocrisy.[34]

The Synod of Dort ensured that the Dutch Reformed Church would be Calvinist on the eve of Dutch colonization in North America. In fact, New Netherland's church and government would have a distinctly Counter-Remonstrant character for its entire existence. The changes of 1618 also announced the close alliance between Calvinists and militant Orangists against Spain. Together they leaped back into the war, hoping to reconquer what they regarded as "Dutch" territory that was still under Spanish control. Another twenty-seven years of fighting brought some territorial gains in Europe. The United Provinces of 1648 was bigger than it had been in 1609. Overseas the territorial gains were tremendous. Dutch imperial claims were at their peak in 1648, spanning the globe from Japan through Indonesia to Brazil and North America. Wherever they could (Japan was a notorious exception), the Dutch set up their Reformed Church and made efforts to proselytize and convert whoever they could.

The Counter-Remonstrants had a clear but limited vision of Dutch tolerance, articulated in their resistance to the growing toleration of Remonstrants and others after 1625, when Maurice's religiously moderate younger brother Frederick Henry became stadholder of Holland and Zeeland. One writer maintained the Counter-Remonstrants were actually upholding the "principles of freedom enshrined in the articles of the Union of Utrecht and legacy of the Revolt against Spain" by harassing those who tried to worship outside the public church. They claimed Dutch freedom of conscience did not imply "freedom of practice." As Israel sums it up, they saw "absolutely no contradiction between upholding" freedom of conscience "and categorically denying, on principle, freedom to practice, dispute, criticize or publish views of which the public Church disapproved." After all, the States General "had never officially conceded the 'free exercise of their pretended religion to the Lutherans or Mennonites, much less to the godless Jews, in these lands, but that their gathering and holding services in some places happens only because the authorities turn a blind eye.'" In reply to the Remonstrant argument that Poland (at that point the most religiously diverse country in Europe) demonstrated how different religions could live side by side in peace, Counter-Remonstrants pointed out that Poland was "a land of ceaseless turmoil and strife." As if to reinforce the point, the South Holland Synod submitted a protest to the States of Holland denouncing Arminians as theologically and politically insidious in 1628—the year New Netherland's church was founded.[35]

Petrus Stuyvesant and his allies in New Netherland clearly came down on the Counter-Remonstrant side of the debate over liberty of conscience. Stuyvesant put it simply and dramatically in a confrontation with several English colonists in 1658. Liberty of conscience, he told one Englishman, "was in his breast, and withall struck his hand on it." The English claimed he was "speaking against Liberty of Conscience" but Stuyvesant rested on years of theorizing and polemicizing by Counter-Remonstrants over how to reconcile Calvinist aspirations with the Union of Utrecht.[36] Another incident the same year, involving Quaker missionary Humphrey Norton, illustrates that Dutch colonists had an acute sense of a distinction between persecution for belief and defense of the public church, one most English never fully grasped. On his way from Plymouth "to visit his seed under the Dutch government," Norton stopped in Southold, Long Island, then part of the New Haven colony. English agents seized Norton and carried him to New Haven, where minister John Davenport denounced him and the court sentenced him to be "severely whipt, and burnt in the hand with the letter H. for heresy" and banished, but not before being fined ten pounds for the court costs. The sentence was carried out that very afternoon. A "Drum beat, and the people gathered a great many." Norton was "stretched forth and offered upon their Altar-Stocks in the view of all the people," whipped and branded with a hot iron that burned "more deep then ever I saw any impression upon any quick creature," noted his fellow Quaker John Rous. In true Quaker fashion Norton refused to pay the fine or have anyone pay it for him even if it were "two pence." Then "a Dutchman whose face he never saw before, ingaged unto them for twenty Nobles altogether." He did it without Norton's "consent" but insisted on it to free Norton from the clutches of New Haven's magistrates. None of the English had stepped forward to assist Norton. When the Dutchman was asked why he paid the fine, he "said his own spirit within him made him do it."[37]

Together these two incidents—recorded with some bewilderment by their Quaker foes—reveal much about Reformed Dutch attitudes toward tolerance. Even a strict Calvinist like Stuyvesant accepted liberty of conscience. However, for him it had clear spatial limits, namely, the interior (spiritual, intellectual, and physical) of the individual. What happened to Norton in New Haven was precisely the sort of thing Dutchmen had been objecting to since the days of the Inquisition. Norton was traveling quietly as an individual when he was denounced and seized—not for something he had done in that territory (preaching or gathering an illicit congregation)—but for what he was known to believe. He was punished for his belief, as the "H" branded into his hand made clear. And he was punished publicly. Any Dutchman watching it would have seen echoes of the Inquisition's treatment of Protestants in the days before the Dutch Revolt. Such punishments not only went against the sensibilities of many Dutch people, they were unconstitutional and unpatriotic. No wonder the Dutch man in the crowd could not help himself. For all the talk of persecution in New Netherland, nothing like Norton's fate befell anyone in the colony.

The religious and political struggles in the republic of the 1610s and 1620s are especially important for New Netherland because in many ways they would be recapitulated in the colony during the 1650s and 1660s. However, the trans-Atlantic context would be significantly different. By the 1630s the governments of some of the most important towns in Holland (Amsterdam, Rotterdam, Delft, and even Dordrecht) permitted greater pluralism than the Netherlands had ever seen before. In Amsterdam the Lutherans and Remonstrants built churches while the Jews built a synagogue. Of course Amsterdam was, as ever, exceptional. Though Counter-Remonstrants could no longer dominate the States of Holland, they still held power in important cities like Leiden and Haarlem. In Utrecht they not only had power but an intellectual center as well. Outspoken Calvinist Gisbertus Voetius became professor of theology at the new Utrecht University in 1636. For the next forty years he would carry the mantle of Gomarus, claiming an ever more public and influential role in the debates over orthodoxy and toleration in the republic. Historian Jonathan Israel notes, "the defeat of the Counter-Remonstrants, and shift to a freer society in Holland, during the 1630s, by no means introduced a full toleration, religious and intellectual, or in any way ended the furious debate about toleration." However, there was evolution in the argument. As he puts its, "the emphasis slowly shifted from the 1640s onwards from a struggle for freedom of religion to a struggle for freedom of thoughts including thought about basic religious concepts." Given the close connections between Dutch politics and Dutch religious life, another political revolution in 1651 inaugurated the most radical phase of Dutch tolerance yet.[38]

The 1651 revolution in Dutch religion and politics was prompted by the failed coup attempt of William II, who became stadholder in 1649. Unhappy with the Treaty of Munster, which deprived him of the glory of conquering more lands from the Spanish, he plotted with men who tended to favor a strong Calvinist church (some wanted to turn the public church into an established church like that of England or Scotland) and a more centralized political structure to launch a coup in 1650. It almost repeated the successful 1618 coup of his uncle, Prince Maurice, but William II's sudden death from smallpox ended it and prompted a dramatic new shift in Dutch politics. As Republicans came to power, they successfully prevented a stadholder from emerging in either Holland or Zeeland for the next twenty years, until 1672. Sometimes referred to as the "stadholderless period," Republican leaders at the time called it the "True Freedom."

The new era of possibility create by the True Freedom provided the immediate context for the struggles over tolerance in New Netherland. It was given constitutional shape at the Great Assembly of 1651, a convention of representatives from the various provincial Estates. Holland's Estates took advantage of the occasion to reclaim the province's prevailing position among the United Provinces. The Great Assembly also set the terms for Dutch church–state relations for the rest of the century. The hegemony of the Reformed Church was not questioned, but it was not strengthened either. The Great Assembly ended official support for Further Reformation but did not reflect a new devotion to religious pluralism. "A promise was made to stop 'sects and denominations' from spreading further," Frijhoff notes, "as long as they only enjoyed mere 'connivance' rather than 'public protection'." Legislation against Catholics was actually revived for a few years. Catholics found themselves more harassed than they had been in the final years of the war. Nonetheless, there was no lasting transformation in Dutch religious policy. By the mid-1650s, magisterial laxity soon reasserted itself, "and everything stayed as it was." The General Assembly had agreed to oppose the establishment of tolerated churches (Lutheran, Anabaptist, and Remonstrant), but only in places where they did not exist already.[39] This last resolution would cause trouble for New Netherland's Reformed Church. If congregations of the tolerated churches existed in Amsterdam, could they be established in territories under Amsterdam's control?

Religiously, the 1650s were a significant turning point in Dutch religious history. Until then, most Dutch people had either been confused, ambivalent, or noncommittal about their church membership. Around 1650 most of the population sorted itself out into one church or another, usually Dutch Reformed or Catholic. As Frijhoff notes, it "was only after 1650, when Dutch society left its expansive phase and started a long period of consolidation, that the Churches managed bit by bit to incorporate these undecided or stubborn people and to give themselves a solid structure embracing the whole confessional group." The "religious landscape" of the republic had actually been "at its richest and most colourful" *before* 1650. Thereafter, the trend began toward what by the nineteenth century would become the "pillarization" of Dutch society into distinct, parallel confessional worlds of Protestants (subdivided into Mennonites, Lutherans, and Reformed) and Catholics.[40] In New Netherland, however, quite the opposite was the case. There, the challenge of diversity first appeared in the 1650s.

The Dutch Republic evolved in more liberal ways than its North American colony did. In the 1650s and 1660s, as New Netherland's authorities continued to battle local assertions of religious pluralism, a wide range of thinkers from outside the Dutch Reformed Church began publishing works advocating some form of toleration, marking a peak in what Israel identifies as the Dutch debate over toleration.[41] Most influential on an international level would be the young Philipp van Limborch, grand-nephew of the great

Remonstrant leader Simon Episcopius. Philipp van Limborch spent much
of his long life publishing Episcopius's papers and other early Remonstrant
documents to keep alive the Remonstrant faith. He befriended John Locke
when he was in Holland, which secured Van Limborch's fame in English
histories as one of the great Dutch advocates of religious toleration. In the
1660s, he was just beginning an impressive, life-long publishing career. By
1661, in addition to several collections of Remonstrant texts and letters and
a critical account of the Synod of Dort, he had published a tract explicitly
on toleration: *A brief response to a pamphlet recently published by Jacobus
Sceperus, called Chrysopolerotus, wherein among other things is discussed
mutual toleration.* It was the beginning of a lifelong involvement with the
cause.[42] Other thinkers had more impact on Dutch America.

New Amstel, the city of Amsterdam's colony on the Delaware River,
was more influenced by the new intellectual and religious developments
than New Netherland. The ideas of the philosopher Baruch Spinoza and a
new Protestant group, the Collegiants, had a bearing on religious arrangements there that would have been inconceivable for any other Dutch colony. The Frenchman René Descartes had been active in the republic in the
first half of the seventeenth century, but his philosophy did not have the
radical potential of Spinoza's. Jonathan Israel has recently bestowed a great
deal of attention on Spinoza as a key theorist of religious freedom and
leading philosopher of what he calls the "radical Enlightenment." Spinoza
was born in Amsterdam to a Portuguese Jewish merchant family who suffered heavy losses to English predations during the first Anglo-Dutch War
of 1652–1654, and the ruin of the family business seems to have encouraged
him to pursue his talent for philosophy. By 1656, his unconventional thinking had become well enough known to his fellow Jews that he was excommunicated from the Amsterdam congregation. By then, Spinoza had made
a number of friends and contacts among various liberal Protestants and
free thinkers in Amsterdam: Mennonites, Collegiants, and others. These
groups, open to the use of reason in religion, provided a congenial connection for Spinoza, whose ideas rubbed off on several key thinkers in both
groups. Unable to stay in Amsterdam, Spinoza moved down to Rijnsburg,
outside Leiden and the hearth of the ecumenically minded Collegiant
movement. There he began developing his ideas about religion, philosophy,
and toleration. After 1664, he moved down to The Hague, where he died in
the winter of 1677. Most of his work was published posthumously, but some
appeared in print before he died, as did the works of several men who

shared his philosophical circle. One of them, Franciscus van den Enden, drew up fascinating plans for new forms of tolerance in America, though they never were implemented.[43]

More influential for New Amstel than Spinoza were the Collegiants with whom Pieter Cornelisz Plockhoy, who did establish a radical community there, associated. Collegiants represented the most ecumenical and philosophical tendencies in the Dutch Republic at the time. They drew their name from the fact that they met in "colleges" rather than congregations to discuss Scripture and pray together. A small group located mostly in Holland, they included a number of wealthy and well-educated individuals and thus had an influence greater than their numbers, especially in Amsterdam and Rotterdam, where some important merchants and magistrates sat in on their discussions. Originating with Remonstrants who continued to meet on their own without a minister after the Synod of Dort deprived them of their ministers, Collegiants arose in one congregation in particular, at Rijnsburg, which discovered that it preferred meeting without a minister present. Rejecting the clandestine minister sent by the Remonstrant Church in the 1620s, they preferred debating religion among themselves to listening to a sermon. The Rijnsburgers' approach drew a few interested individuals from nearby Leiden University. By the 1640s, they were setting up colleges in other towns, most notably Amsterdam and Rotterdam. These colleges provided a spiritual and intellectual home for a variety of individuals who could not conform to or accept the teachings of one of the existing churches. Though they remained a religious group, Collegiants were not averse to some philosophy, and by the 1650s some were advocating reason informed by some of the latest philosophical thinking as an important part of their religious life. In the 1660s, this would include Spinoza's philosophy.

Collegiants shifted in favor of reason in part in reaction to the arrival of Quakers in Holland in the 1650s. Superficially, Quakers resembled Collegiants in many ways, and Collegiants formed some of the primary converts gained by Quaker missionaries. Both rejected a professional ministry. Both relied on the "prophesying" or interpretation of Scripture from their membership in their worship services. Both had strong connections to the spiritualist traditions of Christianity and used discussion to arrive at agreement on religious truth. However, the Quaker emphasis on the preeminence of the Inner Light, the spiritual force within each individual, as an authoritative source for interpreting Scripture and religious truth struck most Collegiants as excessive and disturbingly irrational. Over the previous decade they had developed a veneration of reason as an important instrument in arriving at religious truth. Collegiants had not become secular rationalists or philosophers, but they denied that spiritual inspiration alone was sufficient for religious truth. After all, it could be chaotic and unpredictable. Efforts to apply rationality opened a number of Collegiants to influences from Spinoza and Descartes.

Added to the mixture of Collegiant and philosophical influences that made an impact in New Amstel was the ecumenical Protestantism of some Mennonites, particularly the congregation around Galenus Abrahamsz de Haan in Amsterdam. The Mennonite community of Amsterdam generated its own tracts on tolerance as the result of a bitter division within the community that opened between 1655 and 1664. Known as the Lamb's War, it ultimately brought about a schism in the Mennonite church. However, it also brought to fore a sort of millennial ecumenicism that found particular appeal in Amsterdam. The leader of the Flemish Mennonites, the largest Baptist community in Amsterdam, Galenus Abrahamsz, as he is usually known, was from the town of Zierikzee, Zeeland, the town where Pieter Cornelisz Plockhoy (about seven years his senior) had grown up.[44] Perhaps there was something about this once great city reduced to a farming town that produced liberal Mennonites. Plockhoy would take his ecumenical ideas to England and then America. Abrahamsz took his to Leiden and Amsterdam.

Abrahamsz's ecumenical predilections lay at the root of the Lamb's War. A number of his fellow Mennonites worried that he was dissolving the confessional boundary between Mennonites and others that was so fundamental to their group identity and faith. "The Lamb" was the name of the building where the Mennonites met. Though many Amsterdam Mennonites found Abrahamsz's rather free-thinking approach to religion congenial, those who did not began to suspect him of Socinianism, the denial of Jesus Christ's divinity, which was the doctrine of a group of Protestants from Poland who arrived as refugees in Amsterdam in these years. Starting in 1655, his critics published a series of pamphlets attacking him as a hypocrite and enthusiast who presided over a "church of winking" ("kerk der oogluiking")—a reference to a common Dutch term for connivance. Abrahamsz replied with *Thoughts on the condition of the Visible Church of Christ on Earth, briefly presented in 19 Articles*, written together with his colleague David Spruit in 1659. In it, they appealed for the toleration of all Christians on the grounds that no one could know for sure what the true visible church was. All confessions and professions of faith needed to be rejected in favor of a pure reliance on Scripture as the guide to faith. Abrahamsz's subsequent efforts to convert Polish Jews underscore the Protestant millennialism that underlay his vision. Yet its ecumenical bent was bound to displease those who wanted to defend the integrity of the Mennonite faith. After a series of struggles and attempted reconciliations, in the course of which Abrahamsz was put on trial for Socinianism (a crime in Amsterdam at the time) and found innocent, about seven hundred Mennonites left to form a separate congregation in 1664.[45]

Galenus Abrahamsz was not alone in wishing for ecumenical Protestant harmony. Petrus Serrarius, a Collegiant, Protestant millenarian, and associate of Spinoza, strongly supported him. Like a number of other radical Protestants of the time, English and Dutch, both men dreamed of the conversion of the Jews and the coming of the millennium. They rejected the growing insistence on membership in a particular church and adherence to a strict creed. Instead, they saw the future in a return to the essentials of the faith, rooted in the Bible. Serrarius leaped to Abrahamsz's defense with *The Representation of the Holy City* (*De Vertredinge des heylingen Stadts*, 1659), arguing that no existing church was the true church, and thus pled for a general toleration to end all quarrels about faith. Topping off the trend toward Protestant ecumenicism was the 1656 arrival in Amsterdam of Jan Amos Comenius (1592–1670), the famous scholar, educational pioneer, and Moravian bishop. Comenius was fleeing the devastating Swedish-Polish War that had turned into a campaign against Protestants in Poland, including Socinians. He pled for, and received, the support of the city's council in his campaign to assist the Protestants in Poland. For the rest of his life, until his death in 1670, Comenius made Amsterdam his home. He published a constant series of works, including his 1659 *De Irenico Irenicorm*, laying out his irenical approach to religion, with hopes of encouraging cooperation between Protestants of all sorts.[46]

The Collegiants provided a common forum for many of these individuals to share and debate their ideas. The rise of their Amsterdam College fit with the general pattern of Dutch tolerance in the city. One of the first signs of its existence, from 1647, comes from the Reformed Church consistory's discovery that they were meeting in someone's home. The man they sent to report on the meetings said that they begin by "putting forward one or another question to dispute, everyone listening but no one condemning, their gatherings are some hundred people strong, and that good, respectable people attend and that they try and defend very scandalous pieces." As

with the Rijnsburger group, the Amsterdam Collegiants held religious services wherein the laity, not a clergyman, set the tone. Everyone had a right
to speak, and no one was expected to adhere to a particular dogma. The
Bible formed the basis of their services and discussions. Once a year the
Amsterdamers headed down to Rijnsburg to celebrate a common religious
service and baptize their new members through immersion in water, earning them the nickname of "immersers" ("dompelaars").[47]

The Collegiants inspired Van den Enden and Plockhoy to create a new
form of worship in America, but they were very much a metropolitan phenomenon. They gained acceptance from Amsterdam's authorities because
they knew the meaning of being "quiet" in a way none of the colonists in
America ever seemed to grasp. An officer who investigated their meetings
on behalf of the burgomasters reported that their meetings were very quiet.
They simply read a chapter out of the Bible and discussed it. If anyone
caused any trouble through confrontational tactics, it was the Reformed
spies. Thus, as long as they remained peaceful and did not disturb the
public peace or publish Socinian books, the Collegiants lived in security in
Amsterdam, however much the Reformed consistory tried to thwart them.
Their gatherings continued, and they remained open to visitors and sympathizers: Mennonites like Abrahamsz, spiritual seekers like Plockhoy, mystics
like Daniel Zwicker, Socinians, and philosophers and free-thinkers like Spinoza and Van den Enden. Nothing quite like it ever happened in Dutch
America.[48]

The story of Dutch tolerance in North America brings together elements
from several different stages of Dutch religious history. The Synod of Dort
and subsequent Calvinization of the Dutch Reformed Church had a decisive effect on the religious and political establishment of Dutch America,
which remained overwhelmingly Counter-Remonstrant in sentiment until
the conquest. However, as everywhere else in the Dutch world, Calvinists
did not have complete control over religious matters. The Remonstrants
had been suppressed after the Synod of Dort in 1618, but they persisted
in the republic, and their connections to certain members of the elite in
Amsterdam in particular insured their views had at least some impact on
religious policy in New Netherland. Meanwhile, the radical philosophical
developments of the 1660s reflected a very different Amsterdam from the
one the original colonists had set out from in the 1620s and 1630s. It would
have little impact on New Netherland, which remained a part of the West

India Company, albeit with oversight from Amsterdam. However, when Amsterdam acquired a colony of its own on the Delaware River in the late 1650s, the city's magistrates displayed a remarkable openness to permitting some of the radical experiments in religious liberty contemplated in the city to be transplanted to America. It was a unique and special time in Dutch history, and in the history of America. Altogether, Counter-Remonstrants, Remonstrants, religious radicals, and others contributed to the ideas and actions that shaped Dutch tolerance in North America, where the offshoots of the previous fifty years of Dutch religious history confronted one another on a very different basis from that of Holland.

CHAPTER 2

CONNIVANCE

. . . we daily and more and more find it to be the maxim of our high as well as lower authorities that on the subject of religion, other than their own, they are willing to connive to some extent and to overlook, but never, or very rarely, directly, by apostil, to give their consent to the public exercise thereof.

Dutch tolerance grew out of two seemingly contradictory facts. First was the persistent desire to bring as many people as possible into the Reformed Church. Second was the recognition that many inhabitants of the Dutch world were not and would not be members of the public church. As the Lutherans and English in Holland and America learned, connivance sometimes helped bridge the gap between aspiration and accomplishment. Connivance is a word with decidedly negative connotations in English, one that suggests abetting a crime or indecency. In Dutch the connotation is not quite so negative, partly because the concept is usually expressed through visual metaphors suggesting a willful limiting of perception: to wink at something, or to look at it through one's fingers. In perhaps the most famous line in New Netherland's story of religious tolerance, the West India Company directors would ask Stuyvesant to "shut your eyes, at least not force people's consciences, but allow every one to have his own belief, as long as he behaves quietly and legally, gives no offense to his neighbors and does not oppose the government."[1] These expressions imply a less than perfect acknowledgment of something that is happening, but theoretically should not be. Indeed, the lack of visibility, of public presence, was a key aspect of connivance, an informal tolerance of religious dissent that took

on many manifestations but no uniform character. The upshot of connivance in Amsterdam was frequently mistaken as religious freedom by foreigners fascinated by the religious diversity flourishing in its side streets,
attics, and warehouses.

How much the authorities could or chose to see was the key to connivance, which thus varied according to who was in charge and how strictly
they supervised local religious life. New Netherland was no exception to
this rule. In the republic, groups of those other than the Dutch Reformed—
Catholics, Mennonites, and (after 1618) Remonstrants—could worship in
certain times and places, but only so long as their presence did not become
so obvious that even a magistrate looking through his fingers could not
deny its existence. Often, particularly in the case of Catholics, a magistrate's
vision could be impaired with a regular bribe. In many places in the republic a system of regular payments to magistrates was worked out to guarantee
that they would leave the "hidden" congregations in peace. They generally
gathered in "hidden churches" (*schuilkerken*), sometimes called "house
churches" because they were often built in private homes. Clandestine services were also held in barns, warehouses, fields, and forests, but only in
properties owned by a member of the congregation could the requisite
paraphernalia for a worship service be installed. If the payments were not
enough, or a new magistrate came into office who did not share the ability
to overlook the idolatry and false worship going on within his jurisdiction
no matter how well hidden, there could be a sudden wave of raids and
arrests of congregants and their leaders until a new arrangement was
worked out or the religion was driven underground or out of town.[2]

The existence of contrasting habits of connivance played a crucial role
in shaping the struggles over Dutch tolerance in North America in the
1650s and 1660s. Because it was not a formal practice, only a rather flexible
set of expectations that the magistrates in various localities could interpret as they saw fit, connivance varied greatly from one place to the next,
such as Holland and New Netherland or New Netherland and Brazil.
Reviewing how connivance operated in Amsterdam before 1650 elucidates
what was the major point of reference for all participants in the subsequent struggle over connivance in New Netherland. Amsterdam housed
the religious and political heads of New Amsterdam, the Amsterdam
Chamber of the West India Company, whose directors, often prominent
city magistrates and merchants, supervised the colonial government, as
well as the Amsterdam classis of the Dutch Reformed Church, whose

deputies for Indian affairs supervised the colonial church. Amsterdam was also the major trading partner, point of departure, and experience of all things Dutch for many of the colonists. Even those who had never been to Holland would have had at least some thoughts on the religious situation in Amsterdam. It was the primary reference point for all European discussions of religious diversity (pro and con) from the late sixteenth through the early eighteenth century. Much of our story turns on the complex, multivalent relationship between the religious atmospheres in Amsterdam and New Amsterdam.

Liberty of conscience (the term the Dutch generally used instead of tolerance) was the tool of an embattled but ambitious Dutch Reformed minority fighting for hegemony in a vast and hostile world. Though it ensured that the Dutch Reformed Church could never aspire to a monopoly of the devotion of all those within the Dutch state, unlike the Church of England or the Catholic Churches of France, Spain, and Portugal, comparisons with such well-established national churches within countries that had existed for centuries are inapt. A better comparison for the Dutch case would be the Church of Ireland, comprehending a small island of Protestants in a vast sea of Catholics but having the full backing of the state. The apparatus of Dutch tolerance, as well as a vigorous Reformed Church, was built from such materials. Connivance developed to smooth over some of the rough edges created by clash between the pretensions to hegemony of the Dutch Reformed Church and the reality of its incomplete hold on the hearts and minds of the inhabitants of the Dutch world.

Dutch connivance was not a theory or philosophy that was ever propagated or written down. It was what Dutch authorities did in certain situations, for reasons they rarely fully articulated. As Amsterdam's Lutheran Church consistory tried to explain it to the Lutherans in New Netherland, most of whom were not Dutch and had little grasp of how connivance worked, Dutch "high as well as lower authorities" were "willing to connive to some extent and to overlook" the practice of a religion "other than their own . . . but never, or very rarely, directly . . . to give their consent to the public exercise thereof." Connivance was not a formal recognition of a different religious group or its right to worship. Nonetheless, it could produce results that were sometimes far more spectacular than any formal grant of toleration and must be considered a form of tolerance, however ambiguous and ambivalent it was.[3]

Explaining connivance is a real challenge. Dutch historians have not been able to improve much on the analysis offered by Amsterdam's Lutheran consistory. In the words of Willem Frijhoff, the "distinctive feature of the Dutch solution" to religious diversity "was precisely a generalised practice of toleration that had nothing to do with legislation, and which [sic.] limits were inevitably vague and changeable. It was based on a new and largely implicit relationship between the ecclesiastical and civil authorities, itself based on a new idea of the civic body." Joke Spaans is a bit more specific, arguing that Dutch tolerance did not emerge from a "passive attitude, refraining from persecution or too much harassment, or ignoring the claims of the Reformed Church to cultural hegemony." Instead a combination of "several, overlapping religious policies" produced "a chaotic jumble of arrangements made at the local level." The product of the political structure of the Dutch Republic (highly decentralized) and the character of the Dutch Reformed Church (exclusive), it was a perennial situation "without a clear periodization," meaning it did not simply wax or wane over time. Instead, conflicts recurred again and again without a definite resolution as long as the republic existed.[4]

Since the Synod of Dort and Calvinist coup of 1618, the Dutch Reformed Church had abandoned aspirations to be a comprehensive national church even for the nation's Protestants. Thus, though it was "public" and had the support of the state, it was never synonymous with either the public or the state. For this reason Dutch Reformed churchmen and Dutch magistrates could often be at odds, even though both adhered to the same faith. The magistrates always had to take into account the many who were not members of the Dutch Reformed Church. The ministers did not. They sought to protect those who were members and aspired to convert some of those who were not. The overall result was a society in which religious stratification mirrored economic and political stratification. Certain groups, like Lutherans, and Jews, were associated with immigrant foreigners. Others, like Mennonites and Remonstrants, represented what were often quite elite and entrepreneurial slices of indigenous Dutch society, while Catholics filled the countryside and infiltrated the cities at all ranks from laborers to wealthy merchants. "All this made for a society which was very stable and by contemporary European standards harmonious, but at the same time highly authoritarian," Spaans points out. The "public recognition and relative freedom for dissident groups" was the result of "a rather strict disciplinarian regime and a considerable amount of social engineering."[5] Connivance was the term by which Dutch magistrates permitted this stratification to happen.

Foreigners easily mistook connivance for a sort of religious freedom. For example, the famous Pilgrim leader William Bradford and his fellow English Separatists decided to seek refuge in the Dutch Republic because "they heard" it offered "freedom of religion for all men."[6] By the 1640s a visitor to the city could see a Jewish synagogue, a Lutheran church, and an English Presbyterian church while Catholics, Mennonites, Remonstrants, and English Separatists could be seen heading in and out of their "hidden churches." What to outsiders was a staggering degree of religious diversity was, in the eyes of Amsterdam's magistrates, a carefully calibrated system of social and political stability. Connivance provided a cover under which religious diversity could thrive so long as the various groups could both find a niche in the local economic and social structure and not become a public burden or a nuisance to the public church. How it worked in Amsterdam reveals much about why it did not work so well elsewhere.

For New Netherland's history, the most important manifestations of Amsterdam's connivance involved the Jewish, Lutheran, and English communities. The Jews, as both non-Christians and foreigners, existed in a separate category that will be treated later. The Lutherans and English, as both Christians and Protestants, had a much more intimate connection to Dutch tolerance as they both were precisely the sorts of people the Dutch Reformed hoped to absorb. The Lutheran experience demonstrates how drawn out and uncertain a process connivance could be.[7] Because Lutherans were not entirely foreign in language and religion they were under regular pressure to assimilate into the public church. Most early Netherlandish converts to Lutheranism had been in Antwerp, the region's great cosmopolitan trading port with extensive links to the German and Scandinavian territories that had become Lutheran by the mid-sixteenth century. The only place in the north where a local, native Lutheran community existed before the fall of Antwerp in 1585 was in the town of Woerden, which had a Lutheran tradition dating to the earliest years of the Reformation that was never extinguished. The flight of Antwerp's Protestants added a sizable number of Lutherans to Holland, including important merchants. In 1588 the refugees petitioned the city of Amsterdam and the States of Holland for the same right to public worship that they had had in Antwerp before 1585. Both entities rejected the petition, saying the religion preached in the public church of Amsterdam did not contravene the tenets of Lutheranism, thus the Lutherans should attend the public church. Though the States of Holland recommended to Amsterdam that it let Lutherans worship undisturbed in private, the hope was clearly to absorb the Lutherans quietly into the public church.

Instead of quiet, however, the city found itself caught up in a religious dispute. During the 1590s, the consistory of Amsterdam's Reformed Church, led by Petrus Plancius, embarked on a preaching campaign against Lutheran teachings. The Lutheran minister in Woerden and another in Hamburg responded, criticizing Calvinist teachings. Lutheran and Reformed inhabitants of Amsterdam extended the dispute down to the street level, attending each other's services and criticizing their respective teachings. A theological split within their own community pitted Lutherans against Lutherans, and both against the Reformed. The response of Amsterdam's burgomasters was this: Lutheran meetings for worship were forbidden; Lutheran books were seized; religious leaders who organized religious services were banned from the city.

Had Lutherans remained a small group of Low Country natives, they could well have been suppressed. However, they quickly developed an international veneer and thus became something more than just a domestic Dutch issue. After the initial influx of refugees from the south, Lutheran immigrants from Scandinavia and the German territories poured into the city. Lutherans became a growing community of laborers, soldiers, sailors, and merchants—all roles crucial to Amsterdam's international trade, the source of its wealth and power. Economically, Amsterdam benefited tremendously from Antwerp's fall, picking up its vital trade connections to German cities like Hamburg, and the Scandinavian countries, especially Denmark, crucial to the all-important Baltic trade. Consequently, it inherited Antwerp's relationship with the Lutheran territories of northern Europe. Whether as labor or international trading partners, Lutherans were vital to Amsterdam's prosperity. The foreign states and princes acted as patrons for the Amsterdam Lutheran community. Their wishes could not entirely be ignored.

The foreign connections enabled Lutherans to form the most visible Christian congregation in Amsterdam outside the public church. As early as the 1590s, Hamburg merchants stepped in to protect the fledgling congregation in its time of trouble. The Hamburgers had long possessed a chapel within the city's Old Church. It had supported the first Lutheran services in Amsterdam, and funds from the chapel helped pay for two laymen from Amsterdam's Lutheran community to lead religious services in private homes until 1600, when they began meeting in a rented warehouse at the southern end of the city. The pressure from the Dutch Reformed church was finally removed in 1604, when a combination of the prince of Brunswick and Brandenburg and the king of Denmark persuaded Amsterdam's burgomasters to prevent any further harassment of the Lutherans. In 1606, the Lutherans were able to buy the warehouse they had been worshiping in and a neighboring house. They eventually joined the two into a single "hidden church" by knocking down the adjoining wall. By 1631, the Lutherans owned several houses and warehouses all next to one another. On the outside the buildings retained their nominal function, but on the inside they housed religious services led by what were now four different ministers. Upon petitioning the city council that year, they were granted the right to build a proper church on the spot, which was completed in 1633. The division within the Lutheran community had been smoothed over since the 1610s, primarily because German Lutherans had become the majority within the church and would remain so until the 1670s. Nonetheless, church records and preaching were supposed to be in Dutch. The immigrant nature of the community meant that the publicly visible Lutheran church could be understood more as a concession to important foreign partners in commerce rather than a right extended to Dutch citizens, even though there were some native Dutch Lutherans involved.

The Dutch Lutheran community grew rapidly. From barely noticeable beginnings in the sixteenth century, Lutheranism became one of the largest faiths in the Dutch Republic by the mid-seventeenth century. Since few native Dutch converted, the amazing growth of the Lutheran community reflected the tremendous Dutch dependence on immigrants. Over 160,000 Lutheran immigrants married in the Lutheran Church of Amsterdam during the seventeenth century. Another 34,000 acquired citizenship, giving them access to the city's guilds and their restricted markets. As the workers, sailors, and soldiers who did the grunt work of building the Dutch empire, Lutherans formed an omnipresent and ambivalent part of the Dutch religious mix.

As with all other aspects of Dutch tolerance, the connivance of the Lutherans was site-specific. Amsterdam, as usual, was a great exception in the Dutch world. As its Lutheran church represented the largest and most influential Dutch Lutheran community, the governing consistory of the

Lutheran Church became the central organizing and directing force for Lutherans everywhere in the Dutch world, from Groningen to America. Its church book bears witness to the many Lutheran struggles for recognition across the Dutch world, most of which did not turn out anywhere near as well as the situation in Amsterdam. The consistory appointed comforters of the sick (lay religious leaders) and ministers for covert congregations across the provinces. It requested ministers not to use "harsh words" from the pulpit. It noted the conversion of an Augustinian monk and a Jew. It had Lutheran Bibles printed, but outside of Dutch jurisdiction in the imperial enclave of Ravenstein. It received a request for advice from the congregation in Maastricht on how to deal with the prohibition against religious freedom (as they term it). It considered the persecution of Lutherans in Enkhuysen and more. Being tolerated in Amsterdam did not mean one was tolerated everywhere else in the Dutch world.[8]

The colonies are largely noticeable by their absence in the Lutheran consistory's accounts. The bulk of the consistory's seventeenth-century business concerns Lutheran communities in other Dutch cities: Leiden, Arnhem, Medemblik, Groningen, Breda, Harlingen, Edam, Kampen, Zwolle, Enkhuizen, Den Haag (The Hague), Middelburg, Leeuwarden, Hoorn, Nijmegen, Bensdorp, Sardam, Weesp, Woerden, Rotterdam, Deventer, Haarlem, Delft, Cuylemburg, Naarden. Virtually no mention is made of the East Indies except for the reception of a delegate from Batavia in 1651. International contacts within Europe are also important, especially with the German world: Hildesheim, Hamburg, Aachen, Altena, Giessen, Rostock, and Hanau. There was even an effort in April 1661 to obtain freedom of worship in London. There is no mention of Brazil or any other Dutch American colony except New Netherland, which came to play an exceptionally important role in the story of Dutch Lutheranism overseas. New Netherland fit a European pattern of many individual struggles for recognition. Amsterdam's church book describes it as a "gemeente," a congregation, the only Lutheran one overseas in the seventeenth century. Not until the mid-eighteenth century would Lutheran congregations overseas attain anything like what they had in the republic.[9]

The publicly visible Lutheran Church in Amsterdam demonstrated the possibilities as well as the limitations of connivance. Amsterdam's rulers were willing to tolerate the exceptional visibility of religious difference, but only under certain conditions, primarily the foreignness of Lutherans as well as their importance to the city's international economy. Catholics, for example, still a significant portion of the city's native population including some of its wealthiest merchants, never gained such tolerance. Outside of Amsterdam things looked rather different. Lutherans had to fight to gain any sort of recognition and often failed, whereas at times and places, as in Haarlem and Maastricht, Catholics could retain a noticeable institutional presence. The one other Dutch city where something resembling Amsterdam's religious diversity occurred was in The Hague, the capital of the republic. There, diplomatic delegations from France, Spain, Venice, and the German principalities could open their chapels to local Catholics and Lutherans (indigenous Mennonites and Remonstrants had no such outlets). Everywhere in the Dutch world, the Dutch Reformed Church sought to minimize the damage religious diversity inflicted on its hegemony. Its ministers and institutions policed boundaries, encouraged conversions, and kept as many Dutch natives as possible away from the opportunities offered by these foreign establishments. In The Hague, for example, where the Dutch could not infringe on the diplomatic rights of the ambassadors, they could insist that services not be performed in Dutch.[10]

When Lutherans in New Netherland made a move to emulate the situation in Amsterdam in 1649, it was the first time Lutherans attempted such a thing in any Dutch colony.[11] Ultimately it would not be until the mid-eighteenth century that the East India Company (Vereenidge Oost-Indische Compagnie, VOC in Dutch) and West India Company (WIC) would permit separate Lutheran congregations to be formed. As soldiers, sailors, workers, farmers, and merchants, Lutherans were crucial to the success of Dutch colonialism. Yet in none of the seventeenth century Dutch colonies east or west were they permitted to worship on their own. Lutherans who wanted a church service had to worship within the Reformed Church. However, a German Lutheran who served at Fort Nassau in the 1640s complained, they were not allowed to partake in the Lord's Supper along with the Reformed. For him, it was " 'the greatest loss, and dissatisfaction, that he and others devoted to the Lutheran religion, experienced.' "[12] Compelled to a second-class status, Lutherans in the wider Dutch world were faced with a series of disappointments. Among other dilemmas before Amsterdam's Lutheran consistory in 1649 was the question of whether Lutherans could participate in the Reformed communion with a clean conscience in places where there was no Lutheran preacher.[13]

As elsewhere in the Dutch world, there was a notable degree of coexistence between the Lutherans and the Reformed from the beginning of New

Netherland's existence. This was most vividly expressed through intermarriage. Dominie Everardus Bogardus, who grew up in Woerden, the one
Dutch town with a native Lutheran population, had married a Lutheran
woman and had children by her. Jonas Bronck, the Danish Lutheran after
whom the Bronx would later be named, married a Dutch Reformed
woman. He kept his Lutheran books and Lutheran religion while she stayed
Reformed. Willem Frijhoff cites these as examples of what he calls "everyday ecumenicity," a defining characteristic of everyday life in the religiously
diverse Dutch Republic where interfaith arrangements were common, even
if never officially acknowledged. He suggests that in New Netherland "participation of Lutherans *as Lutherans* in the life of the Reformed congregation was" acceptable to both sides until around 1650, "on condition that
the community ritual was recognized *as a full community ritual*, not as a
denominational confession of faith," emphasizing both their acceptance as
Lutherans and the fact that the colonial community served by the church
was more than the Dutch Reformed. The ministers were, after all, the ministers "for all the colonists, not only the Calvinists." The result was a sort
of "confessional pluralism and cultural unity" within the public church.[14]

At the same time as everyday ecumenicity may have permitted the existence of confessional difference within an otherwise unified community,
one can see in it also the means by which the public church could gradually
incorporate those who were not Reformed. New Amsterdam's ministers
called this enjoying "the full benefit of our religion in this province." Since
the emergence of the Lutheran community in Amsterdam in the 1590s,
Reformed authorities had insisted that Lutherans were Protestants whose
differences in belief did not warrant a separate church. It was the hope of
the Reformed that Lutherans could gradually be persuaded to drop their
errors and join the public church as full members. At times this succeeded.
New Amsterdam's ministers explained, "as long as no other religion than
the Reformed has been publicly allowed, all who wish to engage in public
worship come to our service. By this means it has happened that several,
among whom are some of the principal Lutherans, have made a profession
of religion, and united with us in the Lord's Supper," something only full
members of the public church could do. Deprived of a church of their
own, some Lutherans were converting to the Reformed faith. And not just
Lutherans: a Mennonite asked to join New Amsterdam's Reformed Church
in 1660. Intermarriage could also produce converts. The Lutheran wife of
Dominie Bogardus eventually joined the Dutch Reformed Church and their

children were raised Reformed. The Reformed considered this validation of their policy of liberty of conscience a benefit. Lutherans, however, described it as "lamentable and a great sorrow to the steadfast that owing to the lack of free exercise of our religion so many of us have struck out on other paths, which they never knew before, whether they were fit to walk on or not." Everyday ecumenicity was threatening to erase the colonial Lutheran community.[15]

Everyday ecumenicity was not as affable or satisfying a situation as the term might suggest. New Amsterdam's Lutherans did not willingly participate in the public church as the Lutheran part of the community. Instead, when several of them were in Amsterdam for business in 1649, they approached the Lutheran consistory asking for help in organizing a congregation. For that, they needed "a pastor and the public exercise of religion according to the Augsburg Confession."[16] They wanted a publicly accepted church of their own, as in Amsterdam or Augsburg, an imperial city where both Catholics and Lutherans could worship publicly and had strictly regulated political and religious rights, known as parity.

Why New Netherland's Lutherans decided to agitate for freedom of worship must be deduced from circumstances. Most important was the longstanding connection between Lutherans and New Netherland. Lutherans had actually been operating in the region years before the colony existed. Inspired by Henry Hudson's discovery of a bountiful new source of furs along the river that now bears his name, Amsterdam's fur merchants, including Lutheran exiles from the southern Netherlands, had monopolized the North American fur trade in the guise of the New Netherland Company, formed in 1614.[17] The fur merchants employed some Lutherans, and the WIC even more after it too began colonizing the area in 1624. By 1653, Lutherans amounted to "about 150 heads of family strong," living "on the Manhatans, at Fort Orange, as well as on Long Island" (especially in Middelburgh, it seems). It was a growing community. By 1659 they claimed to be "considerably stronger than before; at Fort Orange there are from 70 to 80 families, here at the Manhatans and on Long Island also fully that many, including many permanent residents and mechanics, but mostly farmers." Most important, there were men, women, and children, and thus the seed of a self-perpetuating community.[18]

The fact that the Lutherans in New Netherland were able to form families with fellow Lutherans was probably the most important factor in making them so much more assertive than in other Dutch colonies. In most

Dutch colonies, Lutherans tended to be just men—soldiers, sailors, company employees—who planned to return to Europe after several years of overseas service. For example, there were Lutherans on Curaçao as well, even though they were not attempting to form a congregation. A 1650 letter from a representative of the Reformed Church indicates they were mostly soldiers (along with Englishmen, who also served in Dutch armies in significant numbers). After a recent epidemic "almost the entire garrison was exterminated; also most of the brethren-in-religion; so that not more than six or seven remained, besides some Englishmen; as for the rest, the most of them were Lutherans."[19] New Netherland's Lutherans were more than soldiers trying to survive their enlistment. They had families, farms, and a future.

Other reasons for the colonial Lutheran activism must remain speculative. Perhaps the very Protestant-friendly environment, with virtually no Catholics and (initially) no Jews to offer competition for the right to toleration, was encouraging. Maybe they had witnessed the grants of charters guaranteeing liberty of conscience to immigrants from New England and thought they could achieve something similar. The relative proximity and connection to Amsterdam no doubt helped. It was quicker and easier to get back and forth from New Amsterdam than from Batavia or Recife. Maybe the United Provinces' newfound peace and independence, guaranteed by the 1648 Treaty of Munster, along with the concomitant Treaty of Westphalia, which settled the religious disputes of the Holy Roman Empire, was inspiring. The idea of a church of their own also had a community-building appeal to those committing themselves to live out their lives in the colony. A common Lutheran religion provided comfort and a sense of fellowship to the "small group of people from divers lands in Europe" who found themselves "in these parts of America." Whatever the motive or inspiration, they felt it was time to have a church of their own and had hopes of success.[20]

The response of Amsterdam's Lutheran consistory reveals the Lutherans' dependence on, and sensitivity to, the political forces in the republic. After receiving the colonists in the fall of 1649, it did nothing. Rather, the consistory decided "not to hasten with the final resolution and answer concerning" the request, "as it is a matter of far-reaching consequence and the most serious considerations to engage therein, in view of the state of the country and the situation of our churches at this juncture in time." In the republic, Lutheran efforts to expand their rights of worship were meeting with increasing resistance. In Alkmaar they had begun building a church in 1641 but the local authorities stepped in and dismantled it. In Leiden and Haarlem, magistrates, prompted by local Reformed ministers, removed inscriptions above the doors of the local Lutheran house churches that proclaimed them as entryways to houses of God. In Zwolle, the Lutheran congregation had been able to build a house church in 1649, but the magistrates rejected their requests for the right to worship publicly in 1650 and 1651. Worse, until about 1660, Zwolle's magistrates repeatedly fined Lutherans for gathering to worship in their house church.[21]

Events in 1651 opened new possibilities for the colonists. The death of William II led to a dramatic shift in Dutch politics. The Great Assembly of 1651 agreed to oppose the establishment of tolerated churches (Lutheran, Anabaptist, and Remonstrant), but only in places where they did not exist already.[22] If congregations of the tolerated churches existed in Amsterdam, could they be established in territories under Amsterdam's control? On a smaller scale, the arrival of Paulus Schrick, a Lutheran merchant from Amsterdam, provided the Lutheran colonists with a man whose wealth, profession, and contacts enabled him to serve as a crucial trans-Atlantic intermediary with the Amsterdam Lutheran consistory. The majority of the colonists, mostly former soldiers, artisans, and farmers, lacked Schrick's wealth, education, and networks, so their contacts with Amsterdam were largely fortuitous, as in 1649. Shrick's regular trans-Atlantic voyages meant he could deliver messages, petitions, and information back and forth, and so wage a steady campaign for Lutheran rights of worship.[23]

The Lutherans waited until fall 1653 before resorting to petitioning. They had hoped their mother church in Amsterdam would have worked something out with the Amsterdam directors of the WIC since the 1649 plea from "some members of our community." Having heard nothing, they were trying again, but "this time in writing." They drew up two petitions, for the States General and for the Amsterdam Chamber. The petitions asked for "permission to plant here in this country the exercise of the Augsburg Confession, and at our own expense to procure a good and faithful pastor, which will serve for the glory of God, the salvation of our souls." They added an argument designed to appeal to the spirit of Amsterdam's more liberal burgomasters, claiming freedom of religion for the Lutherans would be "for the advantage and benefit of these places in helping to populate them more and more." They made no bones about the fact that they wanted "the Unaltered Augsburg Confession" to "flourish in these parts."

They even argued that this was one of the distinguishing aspects of the Dutch Republic where "the kind toleration of" the States General allowed Lutheranism to flourish "in the Netherlands"—mistaking connivance for formal grants of toleration as many foreigners did.[24]

The Lutherans petitioned Dutch authorities on both sides of the Atlantic simultaneously, turning a petition in to Stuyvesant on October 4, 1653, and forwarding two more to the Lutheran consistory of Amsterdam. They asked both to forward their petitions to the States of Holland and the WIC directors. Stuyvesant told them "he had taken an oath in Holland before the supreme authorities not to allow any other religion to be established in this country." Nonetheless, "he would not obstruct" the Lutherans "if we ourselves could obtain permission to do so from the supreme authorities." The Lutherans felt this was a good start. "God is granting us his blessing," they wrote, urging the Lutheran consistory "to promote these matters with all diligence." They would soon learn how dilatory the Dutch petitioning process could be.[25]

In Amsterdam, the Lutheran consistory proceeded cautiously. Paulus Schrick presented the colonists' letter and petitions in January 1654, requesting the consistory "to exert means and efforts" on the colonists' behalf. It responded with the advice "not to address himself to the High and Mighty Lords of the States General, nor to the Directors of the West India Company," foreseeing "dangerous consequences" from such acts and recommended that instead he "quietly seek to contract with someone to go thither" to serve as a Lutheran pastor until Lutherans "be admitted to public worship." The consistory promised to "lend him the helping hand," but "no available person who might be suitable and inclined thereto" was found. It took no other action until Schrick let them know in April 1655 that he was "about to depart to return" to New Netherland. Then the secretary of the consistory wrote a letter, dated May 4, 1655, explaining matters to the colonists. What they described was connivance from the point of view of those who had obtained it.[26]

The consistory had to explain to the colonial Lutherans how tolerance worked in the Dutch world because, after all, most of the colonists had spent relatively little time there. Coming from various parts of Europe they were, like most Lutherans in the Dutch Republic at the time, recent immigrants. When Lutherans wound up in the colonies, it was often after only a brief stay in the republic, usually in Amsterdam, which would have given them a skewed impression of what Dutch tolerance actually looked like.[27]

The aspirations of the colonial Lutherans drew on experience with the Holy Roman Empire more than the Dutch Republic. In the empire there was open, official tolerance, not connivance, and established churches, not a public church. Lutheranism had long been recognized and protected by princes of the empire, an arrangement recently formalized by the 1648 Peace of Westphalia, which granted official toleration to Lutherans, Catholics, and Calvinists (and no one else). Often more than one faith coexisted in the same city or province, each with access to a church (sometimes sharing a church with another group in simultaneum), and its own ministers or priests. New Netherland Lutherans expected something similar to be possible in America.

The consistory's letter was the product of its over fifty years of experience with Dutch ways. It explained that the petitions "will hurt rather than promote your cause and intention and that they would only be thrown into the fire." As the consistory "daily and more and more" learned, it was "the maxim of our high as well as lower authorities that on the subject of religion, other than their own, they are willing to connive to some extent and to overlook, but never, or very rarely, directly, by apostil [that is, in writing], to give their consent to the public exercise thereof." Forthright petitioning and edicts of toleration were not the Dutch way. Rather, "by the grace of God," the Lutherans in the Netherlands had gained such toleration as they had "in no other way than in length of time, by connivance." The consistory held onto the petitions, refusing to forward them, and advised the colonists to follow the path Amsterdam's Lutherans had pioneered. They should, "as far as possible," work to "keep the community and members of Christ [i.e., the Lutherans] together and seek to increase their number" by "meeting among yourselves" until "such a person as you desire for your spiritual leader" could be found—much as Amsterdam's Lutherans had done over fifty years earlier. The letter would not reach the colonial Lutherans until around July 1655 at the earliest. In the meantime, much had changed on both sides of the Atlantic.[28]

As the consistory feared, the Lutherans' forthrightness undermined their cause. Their petitions provoked a response that reveals how New Amsterdam could exist under the influence of Amsterdam while avoiding its approach to religious diversity. Unlike the Lutherans' trans-Atlantic connections, the Dutch Reformed networks were official, legitimate, and effective. It took about two months for a letter to cross the Atlantic Ocean. The mobilization of the Reformed establishment on both sides of the Atlantic after the Lutherans presented their petition to Stuyvesant illustrates how fast matters could progress through the Dutch bureaucracy when backed with political clout. The Lutherans had turned their petitions in to Stuyvesant on October 4, 1653. Two days later, New Amsterdam's two ministers penned an urgent letter to the Reformed classis of Amsterdam, its power-broker for colonial religious policy, for aide in opposing the Lutheran campaign.

The Reformed ministers, Johannes Megapolensis and Samuel Drisius, presented the public church's case against open toleration for Lutherans. In it, one sees that they recognized how the everyday ecumenicity outlined by Frijhoff benefited their church. Freedom of worship for Lutherans "would tend to the injury of our church, the diminution of hearers of the word of God, and the increase of dissensions, of which we have had a sufficiency for years past." Worse, it "would also pave the way for other sects, so that in time our place would become a receptacle for all sorts of heretics and fanatics." In America, the ministers were fortunate enough to have a magistrate, Petrus Stuyvesant, who supported them to the utmost: "Our governor here is zealous for the Reformed Religion," they proudly noted. He "would rather relinquish his office than grant permission in this matter, since it is contrary to the first article of his commission, which was confirmed by him with an oath, not to permit any other than the Reformed religion" (in fact the matter of the oath would turn out to be Stuyvesant's primary and most effective line of defense against the Lutherans). They asked that the classis "use your influence with the Honorable Directors of the Company, that they may so provide and determine, that the project of our Lutheran friends may be rejected, and thus the welfare, prosperity and edification of the church in this place may be promoted." The Reformed ministers had nothing against the presence of Lutherans in the colony. What they opposed was Lutherans organizing as such. Tolerating separate Lutheran worship would restrict the power and influence of the Reformed Church.[29]

The Lutherans' petition had the opposite effect from what they had intended. Instead of getting them their right to worship, it mobilized the Dutch bureaucracy to put explicit limits on Dutch tolerance in America. By the end of 1653, the classis of Amsterdam obliged the colonial ministers, submitting a petition to the Lords Nineteen, who had ultimate authority over the directors of the Amsterdam Chamber, "to prevent Lutheran Preaching and Public Assemblies in New Netherland." Naturally, it supported the ministers' argument that to allow the Lutherans to "call a pastor from Holland and organize public assemblies . . . would be a circumstance very injurious to the Reformed doctrine there." On January 1, 1654, just three months after the colonial Lutherans had drawn up their petitions and before Schrick had even presented their petition to the Lutheran consistory, the classis recorded its success. At the classis's prompting, the WIC directors had concurred. They "were inclined to oppose the plan of the Lutherans" and shared the belief "that such permission would be very injurious" to the colony. The WIC's existing policy of tolerance was not in conflict with the demands of the dominies, as the Dutch Reformed referred to their ministers. Quite the contrary, the directors shared "their fear that other evil consequences might result; that the Mennonites, as well as the English Independents, who are numerous there, might seek to introduce like public assemblies." Like the dominies, the company directors supported the presence of non-Reformed colonists in Dutch America but opposed the idea of them organizing into separate congregations.

The classis had gained an important concession. However, learning the Lutherans had "made known their request" to the States of Holland as well as the WIC, it continued to worry. Dutch bureaucracy was notoriously diffuse and extensive. No single authority had absolute power in decisions like these. Though not always a bastion of tolerationist sentiment, lately the States of Holland had displayed an inclination to favor tolerance of dissenters over the hegemony of the public church. The classis "feared that" it "might grant their petition" and persuaded the WIC directors to promise "that they would take care in this matter, that in case the Honorable States should incline thereto, they would give opposing reasons; that they would bind themselves to resist the request of the Lutherans." Thus from "the church in New Netherland, in the city of New Amsterdam" to the classis, to the nineteen managing directors of the WIC, and then on to the States of Holland (at this point the most powerful political body in the republic), there ran a chain of opposition to freedom of worship for Lutherans in Dutch America that no other available power could easily oppose. In classic Dutch Republican style, power came from a series of overlapping authorities, not a single, central source.

In most of the Lutheran states of Europe, a major policy question such as toleration of public worship for dissidents was a matter for a single, prince-like individual such as a duke of Brandenburg or king of Denmark to determine. For example, in 1617, Danish king Christian IV had established a new city, Gluckstadt (Fortune City), in Danish territory along the north bank of the Elbe just downriver from Hamburg, hoping it would draw off some of the international trade that was making Hamburg so rich. Inspired by the example of Amsterdam, he judged that Jews and Dutch Protestants would be the keys to success. Consequently he made Gluckstadt the only haven for Sephardic Jews in Western Europe outside Amsterdam, allowing them to build the first synagogue on Danish soil. He granted freedom of worship to Dutch Reformed Protestants and Mennonites. After 1618 this was extended to Remonstrants. Though Catholics also moved to the city, only Protestants could worship openly. Then Duke Friedrich III of Gottorf in Schleswig-Holstein, also taking advantage of the fall-out of the Synod of Dort, granted Dutch Remonstrants "free exercise of their religion" in his newly established city of Friedrichstadt, which he too hoped would become a cosmopolitan center for trade on the model of Amsterdam. As in Gluckstadt, the toleration was explicitly limited. It did not extend to all other religions, and the Remonstrants' freedom to practice their religion in Friedrichstadt did not imply that they could "preach in other cities and towns in our territories." Nonetheless, it was an extraordinary act of executive power, done against the will and advice of his Lutheran ministers. Friedrichstadt thus became the first place in the world with a publicly recognized Remonstrant Church. Competition for trade persuaded the town of Altona, on the western outskirts of Hamburg, to open itself up to settlement by Jews, Catholics, Calvinists, and Mennonites around 1600. Originally an autonomous fiefdom and then, after 1640, a possession of the Danish crown, Altona's actions prompted a debate in Hamburg over the economic benefits of religious toleration. However the conservatively Lutheran city, which considered itself a new Zion, did not formally tolerate any other religious worship until 1785. This did not prevent Hamburgers from congratulating themselves on their tolerance.[30]

The republic had much more in common with Hamburg than the duke of Gottorf or king of Denmark. The one princely hope of the Lutherans would have been the stadholder. Unfortunately for the Lutherans, these were the years without a stadholder for Holland. There was no executive power to override the various assemblies and councils that supported the appeal of the colonial ministers. The Lutherans, lacking savvy about current Dutch politics, actually had addressed their appeal to the less influential parts of the Dutch power structure: the States General, the national assembly of the republic, and the Amsterdam Chamber of the WIC. The States of Holland dominated the States General in the 1650s while the Amsterdam

Chamber was still subservient to the WIC's supreme council of directors, known as the Lords Nineteen. Perhaps the Lutheran consistory realized this when it judged the petition campaign to be doomed to failure.[31]

Within four months, the Reformed establishment on both sides of the Atlantic had been successfully mobilized against any attempts to secure a right to public worship, whether by Lutherans or another group. On February 26, 1654, the classis reported back to the colonial dominies with praise: "you have acted very well and prudently in that you have not only attempted to hinder" the Lutherans' "purpose through your Honorable Governor, but have also transmitted to the Honorable directors your complaint" and "requested our Classis to lend you their helping hand. This we have willingly undertaken." The directors confirmed to the classis that "they have refused the request of the Lutherans in every particular, and have resolved to tolerate no other exercise of divine worship in New Netherland except that of the true Reformed Religion" and would "transmit their action to their Governor, by the first vessels, and have the same promulgated there." Indeed, the directors passed the news on to Stuyvesant in early March. "We have decided absolutely to deny the request made by some of our inhabitants, adherents of the Augsburg confession, for a preacher and free exercise of their religion, pursuant to the custom hitherto observed by us and the East India Company, on account of the consequences arising therefrom." The directors reiterated their religious policy, and told Stuyvesant "not to receive any similar petitions." The Lutheran strategy had backfired.[32]

Toleration of alternative forms of worship in New Netherland would not be able to work its way up from the people through the process of petitioning. True, Stuyvesant was ordered "to turn them off in the most civil and least offensive way," but the directors shared the assimilative goals of the ministers. Instead of heeding any more petitions, Stuyvesant was "to employ all possible but moderate means in order to induce them to listen, and finally join the Reformed Church, and thus live in greater love and harmony among themselves." The classis breathed an audible sigh of relief. Now it did "not doubt but that the Reformed Doctrines will remain unembarrassed, and be maintained without being hindered by the Lutherans, and other erring spirits." It was not just a triumph over the Lutheran campaign, but a precedent for policy against any other Protestant dissenters who might try something similar.[33]

Exactly when the news of the directors' decision reached New Netherland is unknown, probably sometime around May 1654. Thus, within
roughly eight months of the Lutherans' presentation of their petition to
Stuyvesant, news had been communicated and decisions made that effectively shut down their campaign before it even got off the ground. It would
be another year before Amsterdam's Lutheran consistory sent over its letter
of advice with Schrick. In the meantime, the colonial Lutherans waited and
hoped.

The English had a much more complicated set of relationships to the Dutch
and their tolerance than the Lutherans. The public church had an assimilative power to which they were particularly vulnerable. In the case of the
Lutherans, living in the Dutch world tended to enhance their attachment
to Lutheranism, but for the English, it had a tendency to break down whatever group cohesion they had. Some joined Dutch congregations. Others
split off into smaller groups. Few were unaffected by their exposure to the
possibilities of living in a society with a Reformed Church (the dream of
most English Puritans) that did not coerce conformity to its doctrine.

The English were both closer to and farther away from the Dutch
Reformed than the Lutherans. Their relationship with Dutch Christianity
goes back to its beginnings, when the Anglo-Saxon monk Willibrord converted the Frisians and made Utrecht the seat of the bishopric of the northern Netherlands. Trade across the North Sea added mercantile and political
connections over the course of the Middle Ages, with the Netherlands textile industry becoming the prime consumer of English wool. The close trade
relations ensured that religious interaction was intense during the Reformation. Dutch and English religious thinkers read and influenced one another
on everything from mysticism to Calvinism. In the 1560s, Queen Elizabeth
offered refuge to Dutch Protestants fleeing the persecution of King Phillip
II. Their church in London served as a model Reformed congregation for
English Puritans and a home to London's Dutch community into the eighteenth century. Beginning in the 1590s, Holland returned the favor by providing a refuge for dissidents from Elizabeth's Church of England.

The Anglo-Dutch connection tightened after 1585, when Queen Elizabeth signed the Treaty of Nonsuch, adding a military alliance to the long-
standing ties of trade and religion. Several thousand English soldiers were
sent to the Dutch Republic. Stationed in garrisons in Flushing (the English

rendering of Vlissingen), Brielle, and smaller fortress towns near the battle-front like Heusden, they came into close contact with the Dutch, to the point of occasionally marrying Dutch women. Some of these soldiers would join the religious refugees and make their way to New England and New Netherland after 1630. Trade disputes and an intricate set of diplomatic issues created by the English revolution of the 1640s pushed Anglo-Dutch relations to their extreme. By 1650, the revolutionary English Republic actually urged a union with the Dutch Republic, then, in 1652, declared war on it when the Dutch refused. In between the many twists and turns of Anglo-Dutch relations, a sizable English community developed in the Dutch Republic that had a powerful impact on the English relationship to Dutch tolerance in both the republic and the Americas.[34]

English Separatists probably did more to test Holland's reputation for tolerance than any other group of immigrants. Called Brownists by the Dutch after Robert Browne (c. 1550–1633), one of the first and most distinguished men to become a Separatist, Separatists represented the extreme expression of Puritan qualms about the Church of England. Beginning in the 1580s, rather than try to reform the church from within—the essence of the Puritan impulse—they renounced their membership in the English religious community entirely and formed a separate congregation of their own. Separatists refused to be associated with the religiously and morally impure and so had very high standards for church fellowship. Outside of that, however, they could be extraordinarily tolerant. Unlike all the other Christian churches that wanted to include as many people as possible and aspired to the status of official legitimacy and governmental support, Separatists neither wanted nor expected any of this. They simply desired autonomy over their religious life—something the Dutch system granted them. Even then, the Separatists repeatedly tested its bounds.

The Brownists actually found it more challenging to be tolerated than persecuted. Persecution had reinforced their convictions. Toleration produced behavior in some that tested the patience of their Dutch Reformed hosts, while leading others to defect to the public church. The first Separatists arrived in Middelburg, Zeeland (long an important trading city for the English) in 1582 with Robert Browne, "'fullie perswaded that the Lord did call them out of England.'" The lack of persecution in Middelburg quickly proved detrimental to group unity. According to English accounts, the Dutch ministers were "'not ill affected unto Browne and his followers.'" In fact some Middelburgers who understood English attended the Separatist services Browne held in his house. He and his second-hand man Robert Harrison were even able to publish several books. Soon the Separatists turned their zeal inward, against themselves. In a series of fallings out, Browne was deposed and reinstated as the congregation's pastor at least three times. When some of the members wished to return to England, Harrison approved, saying they "'might Lawfully Returne . . . Because thei Were Wearied of the hardnes of that countrie,'" meaning Zeeland. Browne warned that "'England was as AEgipt'" and those who wanted to return there "'did sinn.'" In the end it was Browne who returned to England (via Scotland) with a handful of followers, while Harrison died in Middelburg around 1585. Thereafter the congregation disappeared. The Separatists had worn out their welcome. Dutch ministers resented the Brownists for "'the stirring up of our church members, even to the slander of our own religion and church government and to the reinforcement of their own errors.'" Any other Englishmen who wanted to serve as a minister in Zeeland thereafter would have to "'deliver a testimony of their faith and life from the place where they have come to the classis under which they will serve.'" In other words, they would have to prove they belonged to the Church of England and were not Separatists. Thereafter, Separatists went to Holland instead.[35]

Shortly after the Brownist community in Middelburg disintegrated, another group of like-minded men formed a Separatist congregation in London in 1592. By summer 1593, three of them had been executed, fifty thrown in prison and those still at liberty had fled to Amsterdam. Though they rejected the label of Brownist as a "nickname" ("'We are no Brownists, we hold not our faith in respect of any mortal men'") the name stuck. The Amsterdam Dutch were not well disposed toward the Brownists, no doubt in part because they had heard of their behavior in Middelburg. When the city's church consistory learned of their "'disreputable preaching'" they sent the famous minister Arminius and a colleague to warn the English against any further such activity. In fact Arminius, often noted for his advocacy of liberty of conscience, was at the forefront of the Amsterdam church's struggle against the Separatists. This does not mean he was a hypocrite. His liberal vision of Protestantism, like that of his fellow Remonstrants, was predicated on an inclusive church, which of course precluded Separatism. The Separatists responded by moving away, first to Kampen in

Overijssel, which was advertising for immigrants "'of whatever nation'" and offering easy terms for citizenship, then to Naarden, in eastern Holland. By 1596, they were back in Amsterdam. The years on the road had been rough. They had lived in poverty, fought with one another, and sometimes gone over to Anabaptism. By the time they were back in Amsterdam, only about fifty remained.[36]

The second time around, the magistrates of Amsterdam did nothing to support the Separatists, but they did not harass them either. The Dutch Reformed Church (and, after 1607, the English Reformed Church) regularly denounced them and did what they could to limit their influence. Nonetheless, the Separatists were able to build a house within which they held services and set up a printing press that brought Separatist works into print for consumption in England and Holland. Those in England had nothing like the freedom of expression of their fellows in Amsterdam and began migrating to Holland, like the congregation from Scrooby that included William Bradford and many other of the future "Pilgrims" who would found Plymouth colony. The Separatists reached a pinnacle of development in Amsterdam unimaginable anywhere else. By 1610, there were at least five English congregations in the city, four of them Separatist. The Separatists numbered some three hundred members, including prominent merchants and many artisans. Their theology unfolded. The role of the covenant grew as the defining core of their church (something that would influence the Puritans who moved to New England as they set up their Congregational churches). Then they began to turn on each other.[37]

As in Middelburg, Dutch tolerance proved to be a mixed blessing for the English Separatists. The intensity of their demands on and expectations of each other, the clash of personalities among their leaders, their habit of taking their fights to the public through print and open confrontations, and the lack of any sort of infrastructure to resolve conflicts soon made the Separatists into something of a laughingstock in the city. Congregations split off and denounced one another. Others dissolved as members moved into the English or Dutch Reformed Churches or even became Anabaptists. By the 1630s, only two English congegations remained in Amsterdam, the Reformed Church and a single Separatist gathering, whose numbers and status gradually declined until it finally disbanded in 1701.[38]

Given this fate, one can understand why John Smyth, another important English Separatist preacher, was initially intimidated by the freedoms of Amsterdam. We "being Now Come into a place of libertie are in Great danger if wee look not well to our wayes, for wee are like men sett upon the Iyce and therefore may ezely slyde and fall," he was quoted as telling his congregation shortly after they arrived in 1607. Slide he did. Within about a year, he had become convinced that "all existing churches had become apostate" and rebaptized himself and then his followers. This act of "se-baptism" soon began to trouble Smyth. It implied contempt for all surrounding churches. He had developed a respect for the Waterlander Mennonites in Amsterdam and sought a union with them. Several of his congregation objected and seceded. Led by Thomas Helwys, they returned to England in 1612, founding the English General Baptist movement. Those who stayed behind affiliated with the Waterlander Mennonites in 1615, after Smyth died. They met for services in a bakery until the early 1640s, when what remained of the English congregation merged into the Waterlanders.[39]

Living with Dutch tolerance was not conducive to group cohesion for the English. William Bradford's congregation had gone first to Amsterdam, but the troubles of the Separatist community quickly drove them to Leiden. Leiden was a different environment from Amsterdam. A manufacturing town of over 44,000, many immigrants to its booming textile industry, Leiden fostered a very distinct religious climate. Its university was the intellectual center of the Dutch Reformed Church and a leading center of study for Reformed Protestants internationally. Lacking Amsterdam's dependence on international trade, Leiden was much less hospitable to both Jews and Lutherans and generally a stronger supporter of the power of the Dutch Reformed Church and Calvinism in Dutch society. The Separatists were so small in number—roughly one hundred people—that they were hardly even noticed by the authorities.[40]

After ten years in Leiden, the absence of official harassment and the bustling economy was pushing the Separatists in two directions. Some were assimilating into Dutch society. Others had become so alienated that America seemed preferable. One of the main reasons Bradford gave for the fifty or so Leiden Separatists' decision to leave for America was that their children seemed to be growing up Dutch: "'how like we were to lose our language and our name, of English.'" Another was their inability to compel the Dutch to uphold strict observance of the Sabbath. Yet another was the poverty they (like many of the other immigrants to the city) lived in. As the leading historian of religious life in Leiden in this period has pointed out, "Perhaps the Reformation in this city was enough to turn Separatists into Pilgrims." Those who did not leave eventually merged into Dutch

Reformed society, beginning with their minister, John Robinson, a well-respected Calvinist theologian who enrolled at the University of Leiden and took a turn at denouncing Arminius and Arminianism. Over time, he became increasingly amenable to the Dutch Reformed Church and rejected strict Separatism. After his death in 1625, his widow, children, and several others from the congregation would join the Dutch Reformed Church. Those who did not leave for America in 1620 or join the Dutch Reformed church after 1625 continued to meet without a minister until about 1645. Thereafter they disappear from the record. The Leiden Separatists had been engulfed.[41]

It is perhaps not a surprise that Dutch society had the capacity to absorb small groups of English sectarians into the public church. Dutch tolerance could assimilate even more robust English dissident groups into the Dutch Reformed order as well. From the time of the 1585 alliance, a Calvinist consensus had provided a powerful bond between puritanically inclined English and strict Dutch Calvinists, who represented a majority, but not all, of the Dutch Reformed before 1618. The pro-Calvinist earl of Leicester, who initially presided over the English forces in the Netherlands, set the tone. He favored puritanically minded ministers for the English troops. So did his successors, the Veres. Well into the seventeenth century the military chaplains of the English regiments would serve as an outlet for English ministers who could not fully conform to their national church, including the important Calvinist theologian William Ames (1576–1633) who later became a professor of theology at the University of Franeker in Friesland. Ames almost moved to New England, but went to Rotterdam instead, where he died.[42]

With the support of Dutch authorities, Reformed English churches spread across the Netherlands together with the growing numbers of English soldiers and Puritan religious refugees. Relations between these English churches and the Dutch authorities varied from place to place depending on religious and political differences. For example, in Rotterdam, noted for its support of the Arminian cause, the English did not get any government support until 1619, after the Calvinists drove Arminians out of the church and government. The Arminians had given them permission to do no more than hold occasional meetings in a nonecclesiastical space. In 1619, however, the new pro-Calvinist government gave them permission for a church and minister of their own, put the minister on a government salary, and turned over one of the local churches for their use.

Leiden permitted an English Reformed Church that proved a little too strictly Calvinist for local taste. Its Puritanical minister Hugh Goodyear was much harsher toward his own congregation than Dutch Reformed ministers were toward theirs, leading Dutch authorities to step in a few times to moderate his strict enforcement of church discipline. Smaller English churches existed at The Hague (presided over by the chaplain to the commander of English forces), in Flushing (where the "'people of Zealand openly grumble and grudge us the money that they provide for our maintenance'"), Brielle, and the garrisons at Heusden and Gorinchem. As more Puritan refugees arrived in the 1630s (the years of the great migration to New England), additional churches were built in Utrecht and Arnhem.[43]

The Puritan connection was strongest in Amsterdam. Until 1607, Separatists had offered the only English language worship services in the city. Then an ex-Separatist, Matthew Slade, complained to the Dutch authorities about the errors of the Separatists (they concurred) and petitioned for a church for those English Protestants who did not know Dutch and could not join the Dutch Reformed Church as he had. The Dutch authorities granted the English a chapel that had belonged to a Catholic women's organization (the Beguines) and put the congregation's minister on the city payroll, just like the other Dutch Reformed ministers. John Paget, an ardent Presbyterian, became the first minister, serving the church until 1637. Separatists received no such support from the government. Paget cooperated closely with the Dutch Reformed classis of Amsterdam to keep more radical forces out of his church and agitated against the Separatists as much as possible. When the consistory of his church wanted to hire the noted refugee Puritan ministers Thomas Hooker and John Davenport (both of whom later went to New England) in the 1630s, Paget, realizing they were already moving toward Congregationalism, successfully prevented the Dutch authorities from accepting them.[44]

By 1621, the number of English churches and chaplains was such that the English ministers (with a few exceptions, including Paget in Amsterdam) gathered together to form an English synod. The synod met a few times, but never had much power. Not all the churches cooperated, and by the 1630s, England's Archbishop William Laud was actively trying to suppress it along with the other Puritan tendencies of the English churches in the Dutch Republic. Nonetheless, its very existence is telling about the possibilities opened up to Englishmen in Dutch territory, including New Netherland. Many of those who came to New Netherland via New England had

had a stint in Holland first, or knew someone who had. Consequently, as we will see, English ideas about Dutch tolerance played a major role in New Netherland, more so than anywhere else in the Dutch world.[45]

Connivance was an almost unavoidable outgrowth of the Dutch constitutional respect for liberty of conscience. Everywhere in the Dutch world, including comparatively modest New Amsterdam, there were individuals who adhered to a variety of faiths, lending plausibility to descriptions of Dutch lassitude in matters of religion. This combination of circumstances has provided fodder for countless descriptions of Dutch tolerance and pluralism, all of which have their roots in the religious and international politics of the seventeenth century, and none of which adequately capture what the Dutch were doing. For most Dutchmen, liberty of conscience referred to a personal, individual right, the domain of which rarely extended beyond the privacy of one's home. Its opposite was the public visibility and authority of the public church. Between domestic privacy and public hegemony was a wide range of possibilities for connivance, with the emergence of the Lutheran Church in Amsterdam one of the most outstanding examples.

On closer examination, it becomes clear that connivance contained pluralism even as it refused to suppress it. Lutherans, Catholics, Separatists, and Mennonites could challenge their circumscribed religious life, but even in Amsterdam they did not always succeed. There was no obvious economic logic that led necessarily to religious liberty. There were a series of struggles—assertions on the part of the non-Reformed, suppression or avoidance thereof on the part of Dutch authorities—with a range of outcomes. Exactly how matters turned out depended largely on local circumstances. In Amsterdam it could look like rampant religious freedom. In Leiden it was hardly noticeable. In New Netherland it was more evident than in Massachusetts, but nothing like Amsterdam.

Connivance was arguably an effective force for restricting religious diversity in a world that lost its religious unity in the wake of the Reformation and revolt. It did not compel conformity, but it encouraged assimilation. Connivance provided just enough freedom for those not born and raised Dutch Reformed to appreciate the advantages of being a member of the church without alienating them by compelling them to join. From the very beginning of the Reformation the public church had sought limits on other religious groups precisely in the hopes that it would encourage conversions. It was not an unsuccessful policy. In the case of some, such as

English Presbyterians, there was no real need for connivance since they were recognized as essentially the same as the Dutch Reformed and perfectly capable of operating within the public church, as some did in Europe and America. All told, liberty of conscience entailed a degree of religious diversity in any Dutch population. It also created a strong public church in a world where the Dutch Reformed never were the majority. Combining a mixture of assimilative and marginalizing tendencies, connivance played a significant role in making Dutch society more resilient and expansive than it otherwise might have been, both at home and abroad. At the same time, it invited those who were not Dutch Reformed to push at its boundaries and transform it into something more akin to their needs and desires, as both Lutherans and English radicals would do in New Netherland, and Catholics, Jews, Chinese Buddhists, and Muslims would do elsewhere.

CHAPTER 3

TOLERATION

On the island of Manhate, and its environs, there may well be four or five hundred men of different sects and nations . . . No religion is publicly exercised but the Calvinist, and orders are to admit none but Calvinists, but this is not observed; for besides the Calvinists there are in the colony Catholics, English Puritans, Lutherans, Anabaptists, here called Mnistes, etc.

The Dutch reputation for trade and pragmatic compromise has obscured the extent to which the religious system of public church and liberty of conscience enabled them to avoid granting formal recognitions of toleration to other groups. The Lutheran petition campaign of 1653 had provoked a successful counter-campaign by the Dutch Reformed to ensure that the authorities in Amsterdam would grant no such formal recognition in New Netherland. The Lutheran campaign had confirmed the tenor of religious policy toward diversity in New Netherland was affirmed. As elsewhere in the Dutch world, religious diversity within the population was not prohibited. Neither Lutherans nor any other religious group (not even Catholics) were banned from the colony. However, they were expected to respect the public hegemony of the Dutch Reformed Church and keep whatever religious dissent they had to their domestic sphere. New Amsterdam resisted both the sort of connivance that enabled semipublic practice of other religions in Amsterdam, as well as formal recognition of the right to worship that existed elsewhere in northern Europe, such as Friedrichstadt and Gluckstadt—communities founded explicitly to foster trade by drawing specific groups of immigrants, like Jews and Remonstrants.

The Lutherans were not entirely mistaken in their hopes that they could be recognized. At certain times and places, the Dutch were capable of granting some form of toleration or recognition of other religions. By the 1650s the habits of connivance in Amsterdam had extended to the point of allowing Jews and Lutherans to build houses of worship, albeit on the commercial fringes of town. Elsewhere, the Dutch occasionally made a formal grant of toleration, with Brazil being the most extraordinary case. There, Catholics and Jews had recognized rights of worship alongside the Dutch Reformed. Significantly, though, what happened in Brazil was a response to the specific circumstances on the ground. The colony was not imagined as a haven of religious freedom like Pennsylvania or Rhode Island. No other Protestant churches obtained privileges of worship in Brazil. Operating a global trading system in which a variety of religious adherents participated was of course a consideration in Dutch religious policy, but the general consensus was that their system of liberty of conscience sufficed. When formal grants of toleration were made to other churches, it was always in response to political pressures, especially the exigencies of war. New Netherland's Lutherans did not have the weight in 1653 to achieve that, but in other times and places some groups did: Catholic communities in Maastricht, the Overmaas and Brazil as well as Lutherans in New Sweden. Such occasions were rare and never part of a systematic vision of religious liberty. Dutch tolerance was pliable, but it was not inveterately flexible. The Dutch and others could still claim it was tolerant because those of different faiths were not persecuted for what they believed. Others could claim it was intolerant if they were not allowed to worship as they saw fit. The apparent contradiction was constitutive of Dutch tolerance. It was this seeming contradiction that permitted the Dutch Reformed to live surrounded by religious diversity without having to endorse it, just as it permitted others to live with the Dutch without having to accept the Dutch Reformed Church.

The Dutch method of coping with religious diversity often brought charges that they cared little about religion (meaning Christianity) overseas, preferring trade profits to spreading the faith. As in so many areas, the Dutch suffer by comparison with their European rivals when one examines their efforts to spread their religion overseas. They had virtually no lasting missionary impact, unlike the Spanish, Portuguese, and French. Their settler churches were few, scattered, and rarely had anything like the cultural monopoly of, say, the New England churches. The churches that were built are sometimes referred to by scholars as "trade churches" (*handelskerken*), churches built to service Dutch merchants abroad but without any ambition to spread the religion, reinforcing the impression that Dutch religion was the handmaid to Dutch trade. Such interpretations misread the Dutch abroad as much as they've been misread, through foreign propaganda, at home. When treated on their own terms, the Dutch colonial enterprises did care quite a bit about religion, meaning the Dutch Reformed Church, and consequently imposed restrictions on or even tried to convert those of other faiths they ruled over in the colonies. They simply avoided the coercive mechanisms and aggressive proselytizing of their fellow Europeans. Their toleration was targeted, never indiscriminate.

Given the makeshift quality of Dutch nation-building and expansion, one looks in vain for a guiding light of clear national policy or influence. The Dutch colonies were not national enterprises but rather company enterprises undertaken with the blessing (and occasional support) of the emerging Dutch State. By 1620, the Dutch had divided the world into two separate spheres of influence and assigned to each a company monopoly. The VOC ruled over the Dutch in Asia, with posts of varying size from Japan through Indonesia, India, and the Red Sea to South Africa. The WIC oversaw an empire that, at its peak, stretched from Angola and West Africa to Brazil, the Caribbean, and North America. In between, particularly in Guyana and parts of the Caribbean, smaller companies and private enterprises played a role as well.

Colonialism was a regional endeavor in the republic. Without a national religious or political power center to provide consistency of purpose or direction, decentralization was intrinsic to the phenomenon of Dutch tolerance abroad as much as at home. For example, Brazil, which absorbed the vast majority of WIC's energy and resources, was overseen by the strongly Calvinist province of Zeeland. Zeeland's economy had become dependent on the war with Spain, giving an economic and political edge to its religious militancy. New Netherland, a small, insignificant colony receiving only a fraction of the resources devoted to Brazil, was delegated to the Amsterdam Chamber of the WIC. The same year the first handful of colonists sailed for New Netherland in a single ship, 1624, over three thousand men in twenty-six ships sailed to Brazil and conquered its capital city, Salvador da Bahia. Like many of the Dutch colonies, Brazil was conquered from the Spanish and Portuguese. New Netherland's colonists, on the other hand, moved into an indigenous world, far beyond the reach of Iberian power, to trade for furs. The contrast is worth remembering when making generalizations about the Dutch colonies.

Reformed Protestantism accompanied the Dutch everywhere they went overseas. When the first Dutch arrived on the island of Mauritius in 1598, en route to Indonesia, they carved "Cristianos Reformados" on a tree and attached a wooden cross to it.[1] Although the East and West India Companies were first and foremost trading corporations, and there was no mention of religion in their original charters, R. B. Evenhuis, historian of Amsterdam's religious life, argues that this did not mean they were free of religious influence. On the contrary, it was self-evident that the companies should support religion. "Religion" in this context of course means the Dutch Reformed Church. Already in February 1603, the VOC asked Amsterdam's consistory for capable men "to carry forth God's Word and to admonish the people with the Holy Scripture against all superstition and seductions of the Moors and Atheists."[2] Religion was expressly included in the VOC's second charter of 1622, which claimed the company had been created "for the preservation of the public faith." Just because many men got very rich from the VOC does not mean the advancement of the Dutch Reformed Church was inhibited.[3]

In the case of the WIC, the Amsterdam consistory was more proactive in setting the religious tone from the beginning. At the end of July 1623, it sent a delegation to the *Heren XIX*, the Lords Nineteen, the directors in charge of the WIC, to clarify company policy. They confirmed that from "then on a minister and three comforters of the sick could be employed on ships bound for the West." Willem Frijhof agrees with Evenhuis that for these seventeenth-century Dutchmen there was no obvious conflict between profit and religiosity. On the contrary, "profit was God-given proof of well-directed missionary zeal." As the WIC directors expressed it in a petition to the stadholder in 1628, "'its people (almost all of whom profess the true Reformed religion) have had the following aims: First the glory of God; secondly the true Reformed religion, here, and the propagation of the same in other lands; thirdly, the welfare of the provinces, and principally of this city; and fourthly harm to the common enemy.'" Frijhoff remarks that, for the seventeenth century "this is the correct order of the four motives, even if it was usually reversed when it came to actual behavior." More important, there was no perceived separation between religious, economic, and political motives.[4]

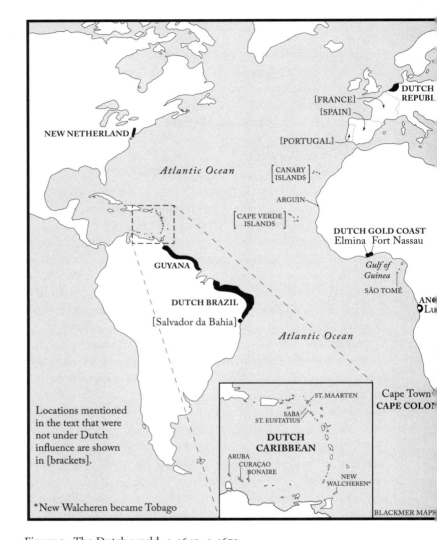

Figure 3. The Dutch world, c. 1640–c. 1670.

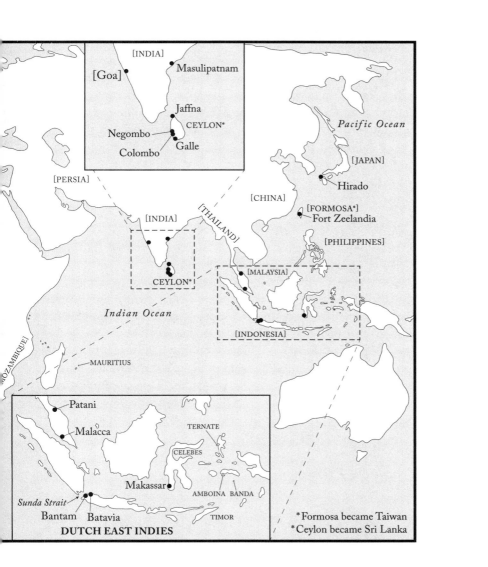

[INDIA]

[Goa] • Masulipatnam

Jaffna
CEYLON*
Negombo
Colombo • Galle

[PERSIA]

Pacific Ocean

[JAPAN]

Hirado

[CHINA]

[FORMOSA*]
Fort Zeelandia

[INDIA]

[THAILAND]

[PHILIPPINES]

CEYLON*

[MALAYSIA]

Indian Ocean

[INDONESIA]

MAURITIUS

MOZAMBIQUE

Patani

Malacca

TERNATE

CELEBES

Makassar

AMBOINA BANDA

Sunda Strait

Bantam Batavia

TIMOR

DUTCH EAST INDIES

*Formosa became Taiwan
*Ceylon became Sri Lanka

The Dutch colonies were a zone where the Dutch Reformed Church was often stronger and more thoroughly Calvinist than in Europe, at least among the European population. There had been an official religious presence on Dutch ships heading to the colonies since 1598 when Petrus Plancius, the prominent Amsterdam minister, astrologer, cartographer, foe of Arminius and advocate of Dutch overseas expansion, reported to the Amsterdam consistory that the city's Burgomasters wanted the next group of ships sailing to East India to "proclaim God's Word along the way and in the lands over there," and a reliably Calvinist word at that. He and his colleagues in the Amsterdam Church worked to ensure that, from the beginning, the range of unorthodoxy possible among the Republic's churchmen was stopped at the docks in Amsterdam before it could trickle overseas. Amsterdam's Reformed consistory examined men proposed for service in the colonies and required them to adhere to a stricter Calvinism than in Holland. The men had to be free "of the unclean teachings of the Remonstrants." If they exhibited signs of heresy such as "universal grace," they would be asked to sit out the voyage until their understanding could be corrected. Remonstrants remained a serious issue until the 1618 Synod of Dort ensured that they had no place in the Dutch colonies. One of the most famous pioneers of the VOC, Willem Ysbrantsz Bontekoe, whose narrative of surviving the explosion of his ship off the coast of Sumatra immediately became a classic of Dutch maritime literature, was a Remonstrant driven overseas in fall 1618 by the Counter-Remonstrant coup. By the 1620s, the classis of Amsterdam took over the task of examining most candidates for service overseas, ensuring a remarkable degree of religious conformity to the Dutch Reformed Church in the colonies, one dominated by the Counter-Remonstrant proclivities of the Dutch Reformed Church at the time.[5]

True, the VOC directors' inclinations were not always as reliably Calvinist as the Dutch Church would want them to be. Since Dutch religion overseas, as at home, was under civil authority, the directors could affect the composition of the colonial church. Before 1618, for instance, rather than ban men from the East Indies because of their alleged Remonstratism, they instead forbade ministers from engaging in religious disputes. Those who indulged lost a month's wages. One early admiral in the service of the VOC, Cornelis Matelieff de Jonge, gained fame for locking a Remonstrant and Counter-Remonstrant together in a hut on deck with nothing but water and bread until they came to an agreement.[6] Then there was the (for

Dutch Calvinists) notorious case of Joan Maetsuycker, governor-general of the Dutch East Indies from 1653 to 1678. Raised Catholic, Maetsuycker promised to join the Reformed Church on receiving his appointment. However, he never quite got around to it, to the great distress of the Reformed ministers, at least one of whom suspected he was a Jesuit, who were notorious among Protestants for their propensity to go in disguise and dissimulate their true, priestly nature. Nonetheless, a less than zealous relationship to Dutch Reformed Calvinism did not entail an endorsement of pluralism. Although he did not support the Dutch Reformed Church as fervently as its ministers desired, Maetsuycker never openly promoted Catholicism or any other faith in the Indies. Much the same can be said of Johan Maurits, the famous governor of Dutch Brazil. Though he is often credited with bringing toleration, it had begun before he arrived. He did not push it farther than it already existed and, like Maetsuycker, upheld the privileged position of the public church.[7]

Whatever their personal beliefs, colonial governors were expected to behave as godly magistrates, piously supporting the work of the Dutch Reformed churches under their authority. They could not do without the Dutch Reformed Church, which provided a significant cultural and political anchor to Dutch colonial expansion. The relationship is evident from the earliest sources on colonial religious policy, the directors' instructions for their colonial governors. Pieter Both, who was sent out in 1609 as the VOC's first governor-general, was reminded that he had been called to secure and expand the East Indian trade; to spread Christ's name; to enable the salvation of the heathens; to enhance the honor and reputation of the Dutch nation, all to the profit of the company.[8]

Wilhelm Verhulst's 1625 instructions for the much more humble post of director of New Netherland explained his religious role at length. They make clear that the freedom of conscience provided for in the Union of Utrecht was the law in all the colonies as well as the republic, but that this did not entail any formal grants of toleration to other religions. Verhulst was instructed that no one was "on any account" to be persecuted solely for his faith. Everyone was to be left with the "freedom of his conscience," yet there were clear limits on that freedom. Regulations firmly forbade any "other form of divine worship than that of the Reformed religion as at present practiced here in this country." Also, "if any one among them or within the jurisdiction should wantonly revile or blaspheme the name of God or of our saviour Jesus Christ, he shall according to the circumstances be punished by the Commander and his Council." Freedom of conscience allowed for differences of opinion. It was not freedom to criticize or challenge the supremacy of the Dutch Reformed Church.[9]

Freedom of conscience did not indicate indifference to religion. On the contrary, Verhulst was enjoined, like subsequent directors, to "take care that divine service be held at the proper times both on board ship [on the way to America] and on land." The directors had to ensure that those in charge of religious services performed their duties properly. Verhulst was even asked to see to it that the Indians were instructed "in the Christian religion out of God's Holy Word." Finally, he was enjoined to "prevent all idolatry, in order that the name of God and of our Lord and Saviour Jesus Christ be not blasphemed therein by any one and the Lord's Sabbath be not violated, but that by the example of godliness and outward discipline on the part of the Christians the heathen may the sooner be brought to a knowledge of the same."[10] The expectation is that the indigenous should and would convert and anything that could be construed as "idolatry" would be banned. Far from religious indifference or tolerance of religious difference, Dutch liberty of conscience was an assimilationist urge.

The prevention of "idolatry," a vague concept, originally implying the Catholic mass, was one that in the colonies could be extended to Chinese Buddhist temples or indigenous ceremonies, and it was a standard expectation of all Dutch magistrates. Suppressing idolatrous competition rather than enforcing conformity was the lynchpin between the strategy of permitting and discouraging diversity on which Dutch Reformed hegemony was based. The Dutch confession of faith (the Confessio Belgica of 1561), one of the cornerstones of the Dutch Reformed Church, contained within it a basic tension over the proper spheres of secular and religious authorities that would be worked out in a variety of ways across the Dutch world. Article 36 described the role of magistrates as having the sword to protect the pious and punish the wicked. They also were to protect divine worship from all idolatry and false religion, and to ensure that the Word of God was preached and honored. The men of the church, meanwhile, were to obey the authorities in all things that did not go against God's Word. How far did a magistrate have to go to protect the public church from "idolatry and false religion"? When did a minister's religious duties compel him to stand up to a magistrate? These issues had been a driving force of the Dutch Revolt; even after the Synod of Dort there could be questions about how far magistrates and ministers should or could meddle in each others' business.[11]

The limits imposed by Dutch tolerance require us to rethink New Netherland's reputation in American history as a place where people of many faiths, languages, and nationalities peacefully coexisted. As in the case of Amsterdam, that image owes much to the remarks of foreign visitors. A Frenchman who passed through the colony in the 1640s observed, on "the island of Manhate, and its environs, there may well be four or five hundred men of different sects and nations: the Director General told me that there were men of eighteen different languages." As for the religious allegiance of the inhabitants, "besides the Calvinists there are in the colony Catholics, English Puritans, Lutherans, Anabaptists, here called Mnistes [Mennonites], etc." The quote is one of the most frequently deployed descriptions of religious diversity in American history texts. American historians find in it welcome evidence for the role many believed the Dutch played in colonial American history—a source of diversity and a sort of informal, pragmatic tolerance that put business ahead of ideology. Another line from the same text seems to support this impression: "No religion is publicly exercised but the Calvinist, and orders are to admit none but Calvinists, but this is not observed."[12] The visitor did not entirely understand how Dutch tolerance worked, but he captured the result, a Dutch colony in which not everyone was Dutch Reformed.

A closer look at this influential source should give us some pause before we accept it as an authoritative description of New Netherland's religious landscape. First, although the author was correct that only the "Calvinist" religion could be exercised publicly, he erred in his claim that there were "orders" to "admit none but Calvinists." This may well have been the preference of some, but it never was the policy in New Netherland or any other Dutch colony. The author of the source clearly does not have an insider's understanding of how Dutch tolerance worked. This comes as no surprise when we consider who he was: Isaac Jogues, a Jesuit missionary and future martyr for the Roman Catholic cause in North America.[13]

Jogues's identity as a Jesuit is significant. As the embodiment of the archenemy of the Protestant Reformation, there is no way he could be a neutral observer of New Netherland's religious world. Even in Brazil, where a range of Catholic priests and monks were permitted to operate, Jesuits were explicitly excluded. Jogues was the first of several Jesuits able to enter the colony—often as ransomed prisoners from the Iroquois, as in Jogues's case. However, none were permitted to stay for long. There were Catholics living in New Netherland, but their numbers were few, no more than a

handful. When Jogues emphasized the religious diversity of New Netherland and listed Catholics first, he was conveying a certain impression of the
colony, one more open to Roman Catholics than the Dutch intended it
to be.

Exaggerating the religious diversity within the Dutch world was a long-
established Catholic strategy to justify extending toleration to themselves.
After all, it was "well known and notorious that in these lands the free
exercise of so many different sorts of Mennonites, Jews, Martinisits
[Lutherans] and other teachers is publicly allowed, only the Romish religion" was not permitted, a Catholic woman in the North Holland city of
Hoorn once remarked. She was well aware of the special cause. Roman
Catholicism was the religion of the Spanish enemy and if it was tolerated it
might encourage "correspondence and communication with enemies, leading to sedition and rebellion." That was the justification given in the placards that had originally forbidden the practice of Catholicism. Would not
the return of peace or, as in this case, the Twelve Year Truce beginning in
1609, then logically remove the only reasonable restriction on tolerating
Catholic worship? The Dutch authorities disagreed. Neither during the
truce nor even after peace was finally made in 1648 was Catholic worship
openly tolerated, though the Spanish repeatedly requested it.[14]

Given the fraught relationship between Catholics and Protestants, Catholic comments about Dutch religious diversity should be treated with an extra
dose of caution. A basic Catholic criticism of Protestantism claimed that the
religious pluralism that developed in Protestant countries was a sign of both
the lack of True Religion and the inevitable disorder and confusion that
Protestant heresy caused. Elements of these criticisms appear in a pamphlet
dated May 1673 entitled *Letters from a Protestant Officer in the French Army*.
Ostensibly Protestant, this pro-French (and rather pro-Catholic) account of
the "Religion of the Dutch" offers a vibrant description of Dutch pluralism,
noting "besides those of the Reformed Religion, there are Roman-Catholicks,
Lutherans, Brownists, Independents, Arminians, Anabaptists, Socinians,
Arrians, Enthusiasts, Quakers, Borrelists, Armenians, Muscovites, Libertines,
and others." Those were just the Christian sects. Though he barely mentioned "the Jews, the Turks, and the Persians," he went on at length against
the philosopher Spinoza.[15]

The explicit purpose of the officer's letters (published in French and
then English) was to prove to a Swiss "pastor and Professor of Divinity at
Bern" that "the States-General are not of our Reformed Religion," and that

the war then being waged by France against the Dutch was not a religious war of Roman Catholics against Reformed Protestants. The officer was writing from French occupied Utrecht in the midst of a formidable campaign that almost wiped out the republic (it was during this self-same war that the Dutch were compelled to finally turn New Netherland over to the English). Swiss Protestants had resisted French efforts to recruit Swiss men into their army, saying they should fight for the Dutch instead, referring to it as "that Sanctifi'd Republick, which has always been the Refuge and Sanctuary of those of the Reformed Religion." Echoing English anti-Dutch propaganda, this pro-French pamphlet claims the Dutch state was not Reformed because it had not established the Reformed Church. Instead, its liberty of conscience meant it could be considered to "be of all Religions" and thus "it has not any particular Religion" save one, "very common to most Inhabitants of the Country, to wit, that of Avarice, which the Scripture calls Idolatry. Mammon has a vast number of votaries, in these parts, and, there is no question to be made, of his being better serv'd here, than the true God is by most Christians." Reverberations of this trope can be found in Jogues's otherwise rather laconic account. Describing the Dutch trade with the Indians, he notes that free trade made things cheap for the Indians with "each of the Hollanders outbidding his neighbor, and being satisfied provided he can gain some little profit." While to an extent this was true, the implication that the love of profit could overcome support for the public church was not.[16]

Like the letters from the officer in the French occupying army, Jogues's brief but influential description of religion in New Netherland in 1643 creates an impression of pluralism for a purpose. Yet in neither the republic nor New Netherland was such pluralism quite the case. For example, Jogues was correct that there were Catholics present in Dutch North America, but they were extremely rare. On closer inspection, he only met two: the Portuguese wife of a colonist from Brazil and an Irish Catholic servant from Virginia. Many of the English Puritans were Presbyterians or otherwise Reformed and thus conformable to the expectations of the Dutch Reformed Church. The Lutherans were few in number and the Mennonites even fewer. No one who could not conform to the public church was allowed to worship openly. What Jogues described was nothing other than symptomatic of the Dutch world. There was diversity, but there were limits. The contained religious diversity was not a hypocritical religious freedom founded on a love of profitable commerce but endemic to the condition of a dynamic faith, Dutch Reformed Protestantism, battling its way up through a hostile world.[17]

Since the sixteenth century, individuals have written about the degree of religious diversity in the Dutch world for any number of reasons. My goal in pointing out the bias of accounts like Jogues's is not to dismiss his claims but to underline the fact that simply evoking religious diversity, especially in a contested ground like New Netherland, is not a neutral act. As with the French officer's depiction of religious diversity in the republic, contemporary descriptions of Dutch religious diversity cannot be taken at face value. They had political implications. They played up the degree of religious difference in the Dutch world for a reason. For some, like Jogues, it was to carve out space, ideological as well as physical, for people who otherwise had little purchase in New Netherland, like Catholics. For others, like Dutch Reformed ministers complaining about the threat of religious diversity, it was to restrict the limited pluralism even further.

Compared to the extraordinarily homogeneous religious environments of New England and New France, New Netherland certainly had a remarkable degree of religious diversity. However, it was nothing like in Amsterdam. Set against other Dutch colonial enterprises, New Netherland looks even less colorful. There were far fewer Catholics and Jews than in Dutch Brazil or the Republic; no Chinese or Muslims or Japanese as in East India; and no Remonstrants, Collegiants, or Spinozists as in Holland. From the perspective of virtually all other parts of the Dutch world, the really unusual aspect of New Netherland was its lack of Roman Catholics and, through the 1640s, Protestant dissenters. The colony Jogues described was an almost exclusively Protestant society, and most of those Protestants fit quite comfortably within the parameters of the public church.

Much of the religious diversity Jogues witnessed came from English Puritans, who began arriving just a few years before his visit. As the theological kettle of New England boiled over in the late 1630s, hundreds of English unable or unwilling to live according to the religious standards of Massachusetts Bay left for Connecticut, Maine, New Hampshire, and Rhode Island. Some were actively driven out, like Anne Hutchinson and Roger Williams. Others, like Thomas Hooker, simply found it more congenial to put some distance between themselves and the Bay colony. By 1641, a number began moving to New Netherland. A fragmentary source, possibly but not certainly written by the then director of the colony Willem Kieft, offers his government's view of this influx. They were "families and finally entire colonies, forced to quit that place both to enjoy freedom of conscience and to escape from the insupportable government of New England, and because many more commodities were easier to be obtained here than there."[18] Kieft, who considered it "necessary, to assist people coming over, for otherwise the country would come to nought and the people would remain in a pitiable state," was happy to grant them the same "Freedoms as the other inhabitants residing here."[19] Those freedoms included freedom of conscience and the right to practice the Reformed religion publicly, in other words, an extension to the New World of the decades old system of taking in English dissidents. No change or adaptation in the laws of New Netherland was necessary. The immigrants were the same sorts of people the Dutch public church had been absorbing since the 1590s. There was no reason to think the Dutch could not continue to do so in America.

New Netherland's public church had the strength and self-confidence to accommodate a spectrum of Reformed opinion that the fledgling churches of Massachusetts Bay could not. The first to apply to settle in New Netherland were Presbyterians: "a considerable number of respectable Englishmen with their clergyman," as the Presbyterian Reverend Francis Doughty was described. The Dutch Reformed minister immediately recognized Doughty as a colleague, much as Paget was in Amsterdam. When Kieft allowed the Presbyterians to "enjoy free exercise of religion," he was not granting toleration to a dissident group. He was acknowledging a group of fellow Reformed Protestants.[20] The Antinomian refugees Anne Hutchinson and John Throckmorton "with his associates" arrived that same year. Untroubled by the Antinomian allegations, Kieft granted them land and the same right of free exercise of religion. Several of these immigrants, including soldiers Daniel Patrick and John Underhill (expelled for moral offenses), had actually lived for some years in the Netherlands. Underhill even had a Dutch wife. In short, the New Englanders seemed perfectly compatible with New Netherland's public church just as many English immigrants to the Netherlands had been.[21]

Kieft's policies fostered the Reformed religion, not religious freedom. The only real difference between what Kieft was doing and what Dutch magistrates had been doing since the 1590s was that he granted whole towns to English colonists rather than welcoming them into existing Dutch communities. English Baptists could benefit from the colony's policy of liberty of conscience that offered freedom—as long as they practiced their beliefs privately. Such was the case with the second and third English towns founded in New Netherland, Vlissingen and 's-Gravesande (the Dutch name for Gravesend, meaning the Count's Sand), both incorporated in 1645. Neither group of settlers had a minister, nor wanted one. Lady Deborah Moody, who had been at 's-Gravesande since 1642, had been excommunicated from her church in Massachusetts for her Anabaptist views. Kieft, who was inclined to the Remonstrant vision of the public church if not Remonstrant theology, granted both towns liberty of conscience.[22] Prohibited from worshiping openly unless in accordance with the Reformed Church, they lived without a church and kept their beliefs to themselves. Ultimately, six English villages were founded in New Netherland, with names evoking towns and cities in Holland and Zeeland as well as local geography. Five were on Long Island: Vlissingen (Flushing), Middelburgh (Newtown), and Rustdorp (Peace Village, now Jamaica) in what is today Queens; 's-Gravesande (Gravesend) in what is now Brooklyn; and Heemstede (Hempstead) in today's Nassau County, near the border with Queens. A sixth, Oostdorp (East Village), was established in what is now Westchester. A few English also lived in New Amsterdam and the Dutch Hudson Valley settlements.

Kieft's successor Petrus Stuyvesant continued his affinity for New Englanders, but displayed a clear affection for the Presbyterians and Congregationalists over the Baptists. He had reasons to believe in a close compatibility between English and Dutch Calvinists. The son of a Dutch Reformed preacher, Stuyvesant had studied at Franeker when the famous English Puritan theologian William Ames was a theology professor there. From his days in Brazil, he may have been aware of an Englishman the Dutch called Samuel "Bachiler," who was "preaching to the Dutch" in Paraíba in the 1630s. In 1660, he actively solicited the settlement of the notoriously strict Calvinists from New Haven, reminding them that, regarding "the fundamentall points off Religion, the difference in Churches orders and gouvernment" in New Haven and New Netherland was "so small that wee doe not stick at it." He even voiced hope "that by a neerer meeting and Conference between oure & theire Ministers further Obstructions in this poinct shall be removed and that all Loving unity shall be observed." When the New Havenites balked at conforming to Dutch political and ecclesiastical norms, Stuyvesant conceded them virtually complete religious and civil autonomy. He even agreed to deprive defendants convicted of capital offenses by their own confession the right of appeal. Only

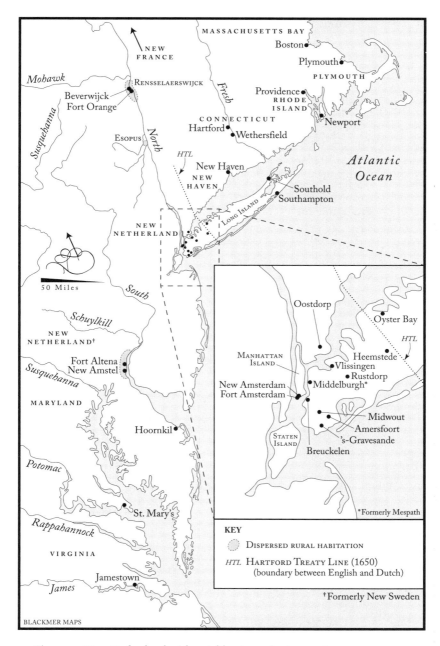

Figure 4. New Netherland with neighboring colonies, c. 1657.

in "dark & dubious matters, especially in Witch craft" did he retain Dutch authority. In short, New Netherland's governors displayed a willingness to incorporate English Protestants into New Netherland's religious environment and clearly believed it could be compatible with the public church, as was the case in Holland.[23]

Unfortunately for the Dutch colony, its rulers misread the power of Dutch tolerance over the English colonists. For Stuyvesant, the emerging series of Anglo-Dutch wars boded ill for the Calvinist collaboration he treasured. When England's Parliament declared war on the Dutch Republic in 1652, he confided to New England's governors his fear that "religion will become wounded & the gospell schandalised to the reioycing & triumphing of the ennemies thereof." Rather than join the war, he suggested a continuation of the peace between their colonies because of "our ioynt prfession of our faith in our Lord Jesus Christ not differeing in fundamentals."[24] After the Restoration of the English monarchy and consolidation of a stubbornly episcopal Church of England, the directors of the WIC believed that their offer of liberty of conscience would guarantee the political loyalty of the New England immigrants against their fellow Englishmen. In his report on why he surrendered New Netherland in 1664, Stuyvesant complained that he had not been able to prepare for the English attack in part because, a month before, he had received a letter from the directors noting that Charles II was sending commissioners to New England "there to install the Episcopal government as in Old England." The WIC directors knew the New Englanders had moved there to get away from episcopal government. They figured the English colonists "will not give us henceforth so much trouble, but prefer to live free under us at peace with their consciences, than to risk getting rid of our authority and then falling again under a government from which they had formerly fled."[25] Alas, instead of rushing to the defense of the Dutch colony, virtually all the English immigrants sided with the invasion force. Liberty of conscience let them into the Dutch world, but did not keep them there.

Dutch Brazil provides a dramatic contrast to the religious situation in New Netherland. In Brazil the Dutch went beyond liberty of conscience and extended toleration, the right to worship as a distinct congregation, to Catholics and Jews, neither of whom were as amenable to the public church as English Protestants. One Dutch report noted that there was "little hope of converting the followers of Roman Catholicism, owing to their stubborn opinion of its truth, which is difficult to dispel." Here too, Dutch tolerance

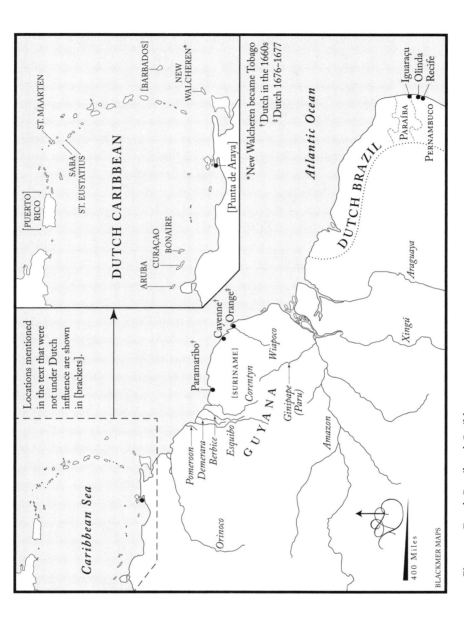

Figure 5. Dutch Brazil and Caribbean, c. 1645.

failed to ensure political loyalty to the Dutch regime. However much toleration the Dutch granted, it was always clear to those tolerated that they lived
in a world dominated by the Dutch Reformed Church, and this was not
something they happily embraced. Though open toleration was not a guiding light of the Dutch colonial agenda, the Brazilian experience demonstrates
how circumstances could draw it out. As with all the other territory the
Dutch captured from Catholic rules from Europe to Asia, the conquest was
not seen as a chance to create a haven of religious freedom for Catholics and
Protestants. On the contrary, the early writing and propaganda about Brazil
dwells on the Dutch Reformed hopes for a Protestant triumph. Usually,
when the Dutch conquered Catholic territory, the public aspects of the Catholic religion as well as Catholic priests, especially those in religious orders
and always the Jesuits, were banned. Of course, individual Catholics were
permitted to stay. Just the public and formal manifestations of their faith
were suppressed, not Catholic people per se. After Salvador da Bahia was
lost to the Spanish and Portuguese in 1625, the WIC directors granted slightly
more liberal conditions than usual in anticipation of the 1630 conquest of
Pernambuco. To the standard provision according liberty of conscience to
all inhabitants was added the extra step of specifying that this would be for
the "'Spaniards, Portuguese, and natives of the land, whether they be Roman
Catholics or Jews,'" for whom the "'exercise'" of their religion could be
permitted, though to what extent or how publicly was not clear. Jesuits and
members of other Catholic religious orders were still banned. The one major
change brought by the famously tolerant government of Johan Maurits
(1636–1644) was to allow back all the religious orders—save the Jesuits, who
Dutch Protestants never could trust. Even then, the returned monks and
friars remained objects of suspicion and occasional proscription.[26]

By the 1640s, Dutch Brazil had become a place of unusually wide-
ranging tolerance. Catholics and Jews worshiped quite openly, though still
with some restrictions, alongside the Dutch Reformed (non-Reformed
Protestants, however, had no such luck). This unique situation was the
result of the long, hard struggle to gain control of Brazil, and the special
role Jews played in the colony's economy. Tolerance was not the first item
on the Dutch conquerors' agenda. When they captured Olinda in 1630 they
promptly sacked and burned the churches and monasteries. In the early
years, the Dutch stuck to the usual grant of liberty of conscience to conquered Catholics; for example, after occupying the village of Iguaraçu, just
north of Olinda, in 1633 the Dutch promised the inhabitants who stayed

that their religion would "remain free," without specifying what that might look like. At the end of December 1634, the Dutch conquered the province of Paraíba and offered a more explicit set of terms to back up the religious tolerance promised the Portuguese Catholics. The Dutch promised "we shall let them live in the freedom of their conscience to the degree and manner that they have thus far lived, using their churches and performing their divine sacrifices in conformity to their laws and ordinances; we shall also not plunder their churches or permit them to be plundered, nor disturb their images or priests, both during their sacrifices and outside of them." The Dutch in Brazil were mimicking their comrades in Europe, who were offering similar grants of toleration to Roman Catholics during the same years in newly conquered lands on the eastern frontier, including the Overmaas, and cities like Venlo and Maastricht.[27]

The WIC directors finally provided more details of what freedom of worship and liberty of conscience for Catholics in Brazil should mean in 1642. They sent a list of instructions to the governing High Council based in Recife, the goal of which was clearly to limit the power of priests and the higher church authorities while avoiding the impression that Catholics would be forced to convert. Catholics could not acknowledge the "authority of any vicar, bishop or suffragan whatsoever, nor owe obedience to anyone of these outside the country, nor strategize with them or surreptitiously remit money to them." Priests had to "swear an oath of loyalty to the count [Johan Maurits] or to the High Council." Priests who entered Dutch territory without a "safe conduct will be held as prisoners." Colonists were not to be married by a priest. Catholics could "observe the rituals of their religion only inside their church buildings, and not outside on streets and roads." Finally, the directors emphasized that Catholics "shall be free to think as they please, and to speak what they think, without insulting" the Dutch Protestants.[28]

No grant of toleration went uncontested in the Dutch world. Agitation by Reformed ministers ensured the government kept limits on the Catholics' liberty to exercise their religion. After the grant of toleration to Catholics in Paraíba, the Dutch governing council "forbade" the province's governor "to permit a solemn procession or cortège of Catholics along public roads, for these were to take place only within the church or the cloister colonnades," and "the Catholic community was forbidden to build new churches without permission of the Council," among other restrictions. The tensions over the Catholics' privileges emerge in a 1639 report, which notes that the "papists have freedom to practice their ceremonies, but sometimes they become so excessive that they provoke the indignation of the Reformed." Reformed ministers, of course, complained the loudest. For example, the minister to the French Reformed Church in Brazil, Vincent Soler, lamented that the "papists enjoy the same freedom as they do in Rome and practice their superstition in five temples in the village of Olinda" while the Reformed "have only got one, because it costs quite some money."[29]

The Dutch regulations on tolerance for Brazilian Catholics reflect the deep suspicion with which Dutch Protestants regarded Catholic clergy. To a degree that suspicion was justified. Catholics were painfully aware of the constraints liberty of conscience put on them and many found it oppressive. As one seventeenth-century Catholic writer in the republic put it, " 'It has been declared that liberty of conscience is thriving in the United Provinces, though it should be understood in the sense that no one is forced to adopt the pretended Reformed Religion; as long as he does not blaspheme the chief dogmas of the Christian religion and duly venerates the supreme magistrate, he is permitted to have no religion at all or to hold a private belief. Nevertheless, the public exercise of any sect whatsoever is not permitted.' "[30] For Catholics, the inability to worship publicly in churches or perform processions was oppressive. One Brazilian priest complained that "the true law of Jesus Christ" was "greatly offended and impeded" by the Protestant heresies supported by the Dutch, who were "mortal enemies of Christianity, directing everything into commercial business, the one idolatry they agree on, without respect to God, the truth, not even reason, because" their government came from a company of merchants. This helps explain why, when the Brazilian Portuguese began their revolt against Dutch rule in 1645, they did so in the name of "freedom of religion." Of course what they meant was the restoration of the Roman Catholic establishment and suppression of Protestantism and Judaism.[31]

Dutch Brazil was an amazing place where pluralism was more open and wide-ranging than anywhere else in the Dutch world—even more so than Holland, where Catholics lived under far greater restrictions and Jews had few opportunities to expand outside of Amsterdam. However, neither the Catholics nor the Dutch Reformed found much to love in their coerced coexistence. In the end, the Brazilian experiment in coexistence lasted little more than a decade. The revolt quickly confined the Dutch to a small strip of territory, taking most Brazilian Catholics out of Dutch jurisdiction, and with them the issue of how they were to be tolerated. With the Dutch surrender in 1654 all of Brazil was lost to Dutch control (though the final peace treaty with Portugal was not signed until 1669). The Portuguese, rather than building on Dutch tolerance, restored the Catholic Church to its position as the established church of the colony, and suppressed heresy (meaning Protestantism) and Judaism. Nor did the Dutch find inspiration in the experience of toleration in Brazil. If anything, it reinforced the Dutch Reformed conviction that religious freedom for Catholics was not a good idea. As Jonathan Israel emphasizes, "At no stage . . . did the WIC regard the form of toleration established in its colony in Brazil as proscriptive for its other territories and conquests." He describes Dutch tolerance in Brazil as "essentially a pragmatic matter tailored to suit the harsh circumstances of an embattled colony." Once the colony was gone, so was the toleration.[32]

Perhaps more important than its famed toleration, Dutch Brazil provides an extraordinary example of the public church's potential for expansion overseas. Overseen by the classis of Walcheren (the Zeeland island on which Middelburg sat), Brazil's public church enjoyed far more institutional and ideological support than New Netherland's. Walcheren's classis sent out seven different men to serve as pastors in the colony's first year of existence (1624–1625). Eventually there would be twenty-two Dutch Reformed congregations in the colony. By 1636, when there was still just one Dutch Reformed minister and a few hundred colonists in all of New Netherland, Brazil's congregations organized into a classis, the classis of Brazil. In 1642 the classis of Brazil was split in two, with a classis of Pernambuco and a classis of Paraíba united under a Synod of Brazil. By contrast, New Amsterdam's first minister, Jonas Michaëlius, did not arrive until April 1628 (he was actually supposed to go to Brazil in 1625 but the loss of Salvador da Bahía prompted his reposting to North America). All told, ten ministers served in a grand total of seven Dutch Reformed congregations in New Netherland before the time of the English conquest. The institutional robustness of the church in Brazil reflected the size and importance of the Dutch colonial endeavor, a massive effort to dominate the sugar trade. The religious investment increased along with the mercantile involvement in the colony. For a company allegedly preoccupied with trade, the WIC did a remarkably good job of rooting the Dutch Reformed Church in its colonies, even those like Brazil with the most intense devotion to making money.[33]

Conquest pulled other territories into the Dutch orbit even as it took some out of their hands. The ongoing war enabled the Dutch to grab Portuguese territory in Ceylon and India, bringing the Dutch Reformed into increasing contact with two additional non-Christian groups, Buddhists and Hindus. Neither group was ever fully brought under Dutch authority, but by the late seventeenth century relations between them and the Dutch would grow close enough that it would start to raise questions, and the Dutch Church and governors had to come up with new responses to deal with the growing pluralism of their expansive empire. For example, they decided that Buddhists and Hindus could not be forcibly converted. However, initially, the only religious group they explicitly legislated for was Roman Catholicism, the remnant of the Portuguese presence. In Dutch Ceylon, the common prohibitions on the practice of Catholicism drove it underground but did not extinguish it. At the same time, in Ceylon as elsewhere in Asia, former Catholics proved a valuable source of converts to the Dutch Reformed Church.[34]

Political exigencies continued to produce formal grants of toleration, even in New Netherland, where a Lutheran church was permitted in what had been New Sweden. In 1655, Stuyvesant led an expedition that conquered the small Swedish colony on the South (or Delaware) River. The expedition was not a deliberate effort to increase religious and ethnic diversity in New Netherland. Nonetheless, it brought some two hundred Swedish and Finnish Lutherans under the WIC's rule. Now the Dutch in North America faced the question how much toleration to permit in the newly conquered territory, just as the Dutch in Brazil had twenty years earlier. Toleration of Lutheranism had not been originally part of Stuyvesant's plan. Had he been able to, he would have treated New Sweden much like the conquered Catholic communities in the Generality lands of Brabant and Flanders. In these "Churches Under the Cross," a minority of privileged Reformed lived amid a sea of disenfranchised Catholics.[35] However, the sudden outbreak of an Indian war at New Amsterdam forced him to offer lenient terms to obtain a quick surrender so he could return to deal with the crisis.[36] It is further evidence of the local distinctions that could emerge on an ad hoc basis in the Dutch world, and which were generally seen as necessary but unwelcome concessions by the Dutch Reformed.

As in Brazil, there were clear limits placed on the toleration extended to the Swedish Lutherans. Stuyvesant certainly did not take the grant of toleration in the peace treaty as a precedent for future policy. In the peace treaty, he granted the "many Swedes and Finns, at least two hundred" who stayed on after the conquest the right to "enjoy the privilege of the Augsburg Confession and a person to instruct them therein." Apart from that, he did all in his power to prevent Swedish Lutheranism from being nourished one iota beyond what the treaty required. The treaty of surrender explicitly allowed only one minister to remain and serve the tolerated church, even though there were three Swedish ministers in the colony at the time. The man who stayed on to uphold the Swedish Lutheran Church under Dutch rule was the Reverend Lars Karlsson Lock. Lock had arrived in 1648 and served as the only minister in the colony until 1654, when the two others arrived. They returned to Europe with the rest of the Swedish colonists. When another minister arrived with a group of Swedish colonists a year after the conquest, Stuyvesant kept the colonists and sent back the minister.[37]

The only figure of cultural authority left to the Scandinavians, Lock made an effort to preserve something of Swedish autonomy through his church. Weddings proved to be the battleground over which this struggle was waged. During the first year of Dutch rule he served as "ecclesiastical deputy in matrimonial cases" and defended the reputation of Niles Larsen against the declarations of a "woman of bad repute" in New Amsterdam. In 1660, Olof Stille abetted and defended Lock's right to marry a young couple in defiance of Dutch secular authority and "without proclamation in church and against the will of the parents." Stille and Lock argued that only the "Consistory of Sweden," not the Dutch court, had jurisdiction in the affair. When Lock's wife eloped in 1661, he found a young bride and married himself to her within five months. Nobody complained except the local Dutch commander. In April 1662, the Dutch court declared Lock's marriage "illegal, because he had married himself" without first asking the Dutch authorities for a decree of divorce from his absconded wife. In a petition to Stuyvesant, Lock protested that he had "proceeded lawfully therein and consent was given. I have followed the same custom, which others have followed here, who have not been called up on that account." Lock realized his position was precarious. Confronted, he took care to submit himself to Stuyvesant's authority and plead for mercy. He declared that he had not performed the marriage "with any bad intention," and offered to submit to "the usages of the Reformed church, which were not known to me," to settle his marriage. Stuyvesant eventually confirmed the divorce and approved Lock's second marriage. The authority of the Dutch magistracy over the Swedish church remained firm until the English conquest.[38]

As the experiences in Brazil and New Sweden indicate, the Dutch extended formal toleration to other groups only when they had to, and then only reluctantly and hesitantly. There was no guarantee it would happen just because there was a population to be tolerated. For example, the islands of Arbua, Bonaire, and Curaçao had also been Catholic territory when the Dutch captured them in 1634, populated by what the first governor called "popish Indians." Curaçao, the principal Dutch outpost in the Caribbean, began as a military base with virtually no settlers. When the Dutch took over, there were only three Indian villages with churches on the island that might have demanded toleration: Santa Barbara, partially abandoned and in disrepair, Ascension, and Santa Ana. The Spanish had burned down the main village of San Juan before abandoning the island. Many of the Indians who had not fled with the Spanish left soon thereafter. The year after the conquest, roughly seventy more were exiled from the island on suspicion of conspiring with the Spanish to retake the island. Ultimately, there was no pressure to extend toleration as in Brazil. Consequently, as in New Netherland before 1655, no religion but that of the public church was permitted to be openly practiced. As for the churches, the Santa Barbara church was used to garrison soldiers for a while. After that, there is no more mention of Catholic churches. The Fort Church was the only church on the islands from 1634 until the nineteenth century. No other form of Protestantism was permitted, and Catholic missionaries were kept off the island until the end of the seventeenth century, by which point the large enslaved population gave them ample material to work with. By the eighteenth century, the islands had a largely Catholic enslaved population, ruled by a small Protestant elite, along with a prosperous but small Jewish community dating from the 1660s.[39]

Connivance was one thing. Formal grants of toleration were something else. Both were possible, but neither was a necessary, or an obvious, manifestation of Dutch tolerance at home and abroad. The colonists in New Netherland knew they existed and could point to them as possible models or, in the case of the Dutch Reformed authorities, as anti-types. If the Dutch establishment of New Netherland had had its way, its religious climate would have been much more like the Cape Colony in South Africa than

Brazil. A settlement colony on an indigenous frontier without a subjugated population of Catholics, the Cape Colony provides the closest parallel to Dutch North America. Begun in 1652, when a fort was established at Table Bay, the VOC colony remained smaller even than New Netherland for the rest of the seventeenth century: barely four hundred Europeans lived at the Cape in 1662. Not until 1679 would they expand into the interior, with a new settlement at Stellenbosch and another, Drakenstein in 1687. These three villages made up the sum of Dutch settlements in 1700, by which time the population was still under two thousand European inhabitants. Here, as elsewhere, only the Dutch Reformed Church was permitted. There was no formal toleration for other faiths. There were individual Catholics and Lutherans, but they were included within the worship service and baptism of the public church, as was customary throughout the Dutch world.[40]

Until 1654, the religious situation in New Netherland was essentially like that of South Africa, albeit with more colonists and especially more Englishmen. However, circumstances pushed the religious arrangements of the two colonies apart. Stuyvesant's conquest of New Sweden brought a recognized, separate Swedish Lutheran congregation into the colony. The English colonists would soon pose challenges to Dutch liberty of conscience. More immediately, the loss of Dutch Brazil brought refugees, including a small group of Jews, who would then force New Netherland's authorities to address for the first time the question of how non-Christians could be incorporated into the colony. Cohabitating with non-Reformed Christians and even tolerating them under certain conditions was one thing. Living with non-Christians was another. However, non-Christians were a hallmark of the Dutch experience in Amsterdam and the colonies. New Netherland could not avoid it, but it did not have to entirely embrace it either. Once again, Dutch tolerance would prove itself flexible, within certain rigid limits.

CHAPTER 4

NON-CHRISTIANS

The merchants of the Portuguese Nation residing in this City respectfully remonstrate to your Honors that it has come to their knowledge that your Honors raise obstacles to the giving of permission or passports to the Portuguese Jews to travel and to go to reside in New Netherland, which if persisted in will result to the great disadvantage of the Jewish nation. It also can be of no advantage to the general Company but rather damaging.

The conjuncture of the Dutch nation, Dutch tolerance, the Dutch Reformed Church, the Dutch state, and the Dutch colonies emerging onto the historical stage virtually simultaneously created such a powerful impression that people ever since have had difficulty separating them out, particularly the connection between Dutch enterprises and tolerance. The Dutch built colonies and communities in situations of unprecedented religious and ethnic diversity from Asia to the Americas. Dutch tolerance, originally developed for a world full of non-Reformed Christians, proved remarkably adept at fitting itself to the new realities of a world full of non-Christians. In neither case did it actively promote religious pluralism. Rather, it was designed as a structure for Dutch Reformed Protestants to coexist with those who were not (yet) of their faith. Exactly what that meant varied from time to time and place to place. Beginning with the acceptance of the Jewish community in Amsterdam, Dutch tolerance recognized limits to the expansion of the Reformed faith. Across the Dutch world, initially fluid boundary lines between Christians and non-Christians gradually became set as local political struggles clarified what was and was not possible within each

particular iteration of Dutch tolerance. New Netherland was just one vari-
ant of this transglobal process.[1]

Pluralism was an inextricable part of the Dutch reality, but few desired
it. Generally interpreted as the coexistence, sometimes covert other times
overt, of more than one faith, exactly how and why pluralism happens varied
significantly across the Dutch world. From the moment they began setting
up posts and colonies overseas, the Dutch found themselves living alongside
Buddhists, Muslims, Hindus, and indigenous faiths of various sorts from
the Americas to Africa and Asia. At the same time, Jews began to live openly
as such in Amsterdam, Brazil, New Amsterdam, Curaçao, and later Suriname. However, it was never Dutch policy deliberately to encourage the
flourishing of religious diversity throughout their empire. For example,
although the year the Jews were granted permission to reside in New
Amsterdam, 1655, was the year that the Lutherans on the South River
received the toleration of their church, it was also the year the Lutherans on
the North River finally heard the discouraging word about the failure of
their petitioning campaign. The basic principle of liberty of conscience provided space for those of different faiths, both Christians and non-Christians,
to exist within the Dutch world, but exactly how depended very much on
the specifics of the time, place, and parties involved.

From the earliest days of the Reformation, the Dutch simultaneously
expected and combated religious diversity. Confronted by ethnic and religious pluralism at home and abroad, the Dutch did what they could to
reduce and restrain it. Though there were always men like Plancius who
dreamed of spreading the faith far and wide, it should not be surprising
that the Dutch Reformed religion never became the majority faith in the
colonies. They made no special plans or proposals for dealing with the
plethora of non-Christian faiths they came to govern. Instead, they simply
extended the practices of Dutch tolerance in Europe to non-Christians
overseas. While this did not compel Javanese, Chinese, Africans or Native
Americans to convert, it did allow Calvinist expansionists to extend their
reach farther than they had any demographic right to do. Given that initially there were no Protestants anywhere in what became the Dutch colonies, the degree to which they were able to spread their faith overseas is
impressive.[2]

The challenge of dealing with non-Christians first came to Amsterdam,
where a Jewish community began to emerge around 1600. Though by the

1640s the resulting tolerance was dramatic—a public synagogue—the legal underpinnings were often quite slim, more an absence of legislation than a formal endorsement. Jews had not existed in Amsterdam before they started arriving around 1590. They came initially as ostensibly Catholic "Portuguese." After they had lived some time in Amsterdam and realized it was safe, some began to convert and live as Jews. When the Amsterdam burgomasters found out, they took no action against it, yet they never formally granted Jews freedom of worship. Even as the first Jew was sworn in as a burgher of the city, Jews were informed that "'no other religion can nor may be practiced than that practiced publicly in the churches.'" Practicing Judaism in private, on the other hand, was another matter.[3]

Amsterdam's rulers maintained a vital distinction between what could happen and what should happen that could be a bit awkward for those subject to their tolerance. For example, they denied Jews the right to buy land for a cemetery until 1614. Even then they did not so much formally acknowledge the Jews' right to their own burial ground as deny the petition of the villagers of Ouderkerk aan de Amstel (where the land was purchased; Amsterdam did not permit it within its walls) to prohibit it. When Amsterdam's city council learned in 1612 that Jews had contracted with a Dutch carpenter to build a house large enough to serve as a synagogue, they proclaimed that no one of the Portuguese nation "'may live in that building and that no gathering may be convened there nor any ceremonies of the religion practiced, under penalty of demolition, to the ground, of that house or building and the prohibition to practice their religion in any other places within this city and its jurisdiction.'" Nonetheless, the building was built and even "used as a synagogue." However, ownership was technically transferred to "a member of the City Council." Jews could use it but not formally own it. They could be Jews in Amsterdam but were not fully accepted as or encouraged to be such.[4]

The evolution of the Jewish presence from Portuguese Christians in the 1590s to covert, domestic worship in the 1600s, to semipublic worship by the 1610s, and a full public presence by the 1630s can be seen as a classic case of connivance at its most liberal. As a recent historian of Amsterdam's Jewish community, Daniel Swetschinski, interprets it, the threat to prohibit worship in the synagogue under construction in 1612 was also an acknowledgement of Jews' rights to private worship. Therein lay the seeds of what a generation later became the acceptance of public worship by Jews. Despite the decision, Jews managed to use their building as a synagogue without incident, establishing a "*de facto* recognition of their right to practice Judaism publicly; and once *de facto* recognition had been granted, the right of public worship no longer needed to be translated into law." Thereafter "no other official statement, formal or informal, ever granted or denied the Portuguese, German, or Polish Jews the right to practice Judaism publicly." By 1616, there were three separate congregations meeting: one in a private home, another in a warehouse, and the third in the specially constructed building. When the three congregations united in 1639, the semi-clandestine synagogue from 1612 was expanded and renovated into Amsterdam's first public synagogue. In 1675, the synagogue was replaced by an even grander one, the beautiful "Portuguese" synagogue that still stands. Here, Amsterdam distinguished itself from other major trading cities with important Jewish populations, such as Hamburg, which never allowed Jews to proceed beyond the stage of private worship in their homes no matter how large their population grew.[5]

Known throughout the seventeenth century as "Portuguese," Jews benefited from the fact that they were foreigners and merchants who brought valuable trade connections and knowledge to Amsterdam just as the Dutch began expanding their trade networks overseas into the Iberian empires of Asia and the Americas. Initially not identified as Jews but as so-called "New Christians" or "conversos," descendants of Jews who had been forced to convert to Catholicism by the kings of Spain and Portugal, they were accepted as Catholics in a city that retained a sizable Catholic population. Their languages (Spanish and Portuguese) and customs underscored their immigrant, outsider status and kept the community out of the purview of the public church. Amsterdam's policy of denying them the right to pass on their burgher status from one generation to the next reinforced their position as permanent immigrants even after they had lived in the city for generations.

The connivance worked because the Jews cooperated in keeping themselves a separate and well-governed community. Unwilling to meddle in the Jews' internal affairs, Amsterdam's burgomasters left them a great deal of autonomy as long as no issue impinged on the public order. A statute of 1616, "the closest Amsterdam ever came to formulating a 'Jewry statute',", set the boundaries of this autonomy with three rules. Jews were not to speak or write anything " 'that may, in any way, tend to the disdain of our Christian religion' "; they could not "seduce any Christian person from our Christian religion" or circumcise a Christian; they could not " 'have any carnal conversation, whether in or out of wedlock, with Christian women or maidens, not even when such are of ill repute.'" Jews could remain Jews as long as they avoided intimate and intellectual mingling with Christians and Christianity.[6]

The case of the Jews in Amsterdam reveals much about the site-specific quality of Dutch tolerance. As with all cases of connivance, that of the Jews varied much over time and from place to place. Jews were not allowed access to any of the republic's colonies until Brazil in the 1630s gave them their first public foothold as Jews in the Americas (the republic never permitted them in VOC territory). In the Netherlands itself, Jews were not permitted to spread much beyond Holland until the eighteenth century. Utrecht kept them out until 1789. Most of the Generality lands (now North Brabant) did the same until the 1750s or later (1767 for Tilburg, 1785 for Maastricht). Even within seventeenth-century Holland, Jews were not allowed much beyond Amsterdam and Rotterdam. Professionally, Jews were excluded from a range of professions. Politically, they were denied full membership in Dutch society until the era of the French Revolution. Unwelcome as they were in much of the Dutch world, Jews were safer there than in the Hispanic world, where many continued to live. Historian of the Dutch Church in Brazil Frans Schalkwijk draws the contrast, noting how in 1642, "the year in which the king and queen of Portugal watched from a window as three men and three women were executed for their Jewish faith," the stadholder "of Holland, together with his wife and children made an official visit to the enlarged Portuguese synagogue" in Amsterdam. Dutch tolerance did not accept Jews as equals, but it did accept them as Jews. Sometimes. Some places.[7]

For the Dutch Reformed in New Netherland, the news that the WIC directors had rejected the Lutheran petition for recognition was small consolation for the news that in January 1654 Dutch Brazil had surrendered to the Portuguese. Brazil had been exceptional as the one colony where the Dutch allowed Jews to live and worship as Jews, but the arrangement collapsed along with the colony. Protestants and Jews fled the Portuguese takeover. The immediate impact on New Netherland was the arrival of a ship with "a few Jews," along with a Reformed minister of German extraction who had served for years in Brazil, Johannes Theodorus Polhemius. Dominie Polhemius was quickly appointed to serve the Dutch communities on Long Island, the first Dutch minister to do so. Based at "Midwout, which is somewhat the Meditullium of the other villages, to wit, Breuckelen,

Amersfoort and Gravesend," he started preaching "for the accommodation of the inhabitants on Sundays during the winter, and has administered the sacraments, to the satisfaction of all." The public church in the colony was getting stronger even as it confronted the challenge of a potential Jewish community.[8]

The Jewish arrival in North America was one small, accidental part of the flight and resettlement of Jews across the Atlantic world after the collapse of Dutch Brazil. Dutch Brazil was the first place in the Americas that Jews had lived openly as Jews. They had been able to carve out this unusual arrangement due to two factors: their position in Amsterdam and their long-standing presence as New Christians in the Hispanic world. Exactly when the first Jews appeared in Brazil is difficult to say. An account from the 1630s claimed that most "of the jewish inhabitants came here from the Dutch Republic. Some, who were originally Portuguese, pretended to convert to Christianity during the Spanish king's reign, but, freed from the fear of persecution under a more indulgent ruler [i.e., the Dutch], they now freely associate with the Jews." Some Dutch Protestants found in this phenomenon confirmation of their superiority over Roman Catholics. The account continued: "This proves clearly that such hypocrisy was the result of fear of persecution, induced by the worshippers of the purple [i.e., papal authority] rather than by God." Initially, they met for worship services in the house of a community leader, as they were still doing in Amsterdam and Hamburg. However, by 1636 the community had enough strength and influence to be able to build the first synagogue in the Americas, in the heart of Recife, the capital of Dutch Brazil.[9]

In some ways, Dutch Brazil offered Jews more opportunity than the Dutch Republic at the time. The Recife synagogue was built three years before the Portuguese synagogue in Amsterdam. Its rabbi, Isaac Aboab da Fonseca, "the first rabbi in the New World," presided over a congregation that rivaled in size and influence that of Amsterdam. Though initially, "Jews were permitted to hold their services and celebrate their feast days within a private space, but not in public areas," soon they had (according to a Dutch report) become "quite audacious in the performance of their religion and its rites, so that the papists and our followers of the Reformed Church complained that they should be expelled or returned to the Republic, where they are allowed to have their synagogues." After receiving a warning from the Dutch authorities, "they lessened the public display of their cult of Moses and their Jewish rites." Nonetheless, there were not the

restrictions on settlement that confined Jews in the republic. By 1644, Brazilian Jews were able to expand their religious presence to include a synagogue and rabbi in the neighboring province of Paraíba, though the local
Dutch council compelled them to worship on the outskirts of town rather
than the center. Population growth around Recife enabled the Jews to build
a third synagogue across the river on the island of Antônio Vaz. Another
existed for a brief time on Dutch Brazil's southern frontier, along the banks
of the River São Francisco in the shadow of Fort Maurits.[10] The importance
of Jews in Dutch Brazil as traders, tax collectors, translators, investors, and
more lent some substance to the Portuguese claim that the Dutch were
"half Jewish," an accusation the classis of Recife found particularly objectionable.[11]

The Jewish presence in Dutch Brazil was unwelcome to both Protestants
and Catholics. Their resentment actually provides much of the existing evidence on Jewish religious life in the colony. Laments from the Reformed
Protestant community, for example, provide the first documentary notice
of the synagogue in Recife. Vincent Soler, minister of the French Reformed
Church in Recife, complained regularly about Jews in his letters to Holland.
"The liberty granted the Jews exceeds the limits, which is the cause of scandal not only among the Portuguese Christians, but also the Indians and
blacks," he wrote in 1639. "They are protected to the detriment of the
Dutch, and the Christian Magistrate is so accommodating that it authorizes
their feasts and Sabbaths." Soler noted that Johan Maurits, often credited
with the extraordinary tolerance in Dutch Brazil that saw Reformed Protestants, Roman Catholics, and Jews all worshiping more or less publicly,
"declares to nurture a great hatred for" the Jews but found it politically
impossible to check them. Observing how the "Jews multiply, enjoy great
freedom and take on airs more than ever," Soler repeated the common
hostility of non-Jews to Jewish business competition: "they ruin the traffic,
suck the blood of the people, frustrate and violate the Company . . . to the
detriment of the Christian merchants." His comments are a reminder that
not everyone in the Dutch world saw trade and toleration expanding har-
moniously together.[12]

Fortunately, the Jews did not need the Dutch Reformed to love them in
order to prosper, for Soler's views on Jews were not atypical or isolated.
They very much reflected the views of many Dutch, particularly servants of
the public church. In July 1646, the classis of Amsterdam, which also oversaw New Netherland's church, turned in a rather vehement petition to the

Lords Nineteen of the WIC, protesting, "for the glory of God, and with the most cordial wishes for the prosperity of your company," their decision to allow the Jews "the free exercise of their religion in Brazil, although under some limitations" as something very "injurious . . . to the Christian Religion." The "heathen, and the newly converted Christians in those regions" would think that the Dutch were not truly zealous "for the doctrine and the glory of our Savior." What was the purpose of uniting "with such a sect, which so completely scorns and slanders the Christian Religion"? Was it simply "some temporary gain"? The Jews "are the sworn enemies of our Lord Jesus Christ." They should be converted rather than granted "freedom." After all, "Christianity and Judaism are not so incompatible and antagonistic to each other as would appear from the reading of the New Testament," a hint at hopes that Jews could be brought into the public church. Though no active campaign was waged to convert the Jews, there was steady pressure and constant desire to convert Jews whenever possible.[13]

The particular conditions of Dutch Brazil go far toward explaining why the political authorities supported the Jewish presence notwithstanding the opposition of the Dutch Reformed Church and the Christian merchants who objected to the Jewish competition, and the resentment of the Roman Catholic Portuguese who had long been accustomed to a state that suppressed Jews and Judaism through the Inquisition. The Dutch rulers knew they could count on the loyalty of Jews more than that of the Catholics. The Dutch also needed the skills, talents, connections, and capital of the Jews to run the former Portuguese territory and the sugar trade that sustained it. The High Council that governed the colony, like Amsterdam's burgomasters, upheld the supremacy of the Dutch Reformed Church, but could reduce its exclusivity as they saw fit. Historian Jonathan Israel claims "the degree of toleration accorded to this group by the late 1640s was, from any historical perspective, something wholly unprecedented in the Christian world since ancient times." It was an extraordinary situation, dependant on the unusual context that was Dutch Brazil.[14]

Dutch Brazil coincided with a pivotal moment in Jewish history. By the 1650s, opportunities for Jews were opening up across the Atlantic World. In 1650, Spanish king Phillip IV allowed Jews to trade in Spain and (via the port cities of Seville and Cadiz) with the Spanish empire, though they were not allowed to set foot on Spanish territory. One Jewish merchant almost received permission to settle near Antwerp in 1653–1654 for trading purposes. His proposal had to be shot down by the pope himself. By 1655, Jews were beginning to return to England for the first time in centuries. Though they still had to remain clandestine in London, they were openly welcomed to Barbados (then in the midst of its sugar revolution) and Suriname (recently colonized by Barbados). Meanwhile the Dutch opened up new territories for Jewish settlement. In 1651, Jewish leader João de Yllan received permission to settle Jews on Curaçao. His attempt, involving twelve families, failed, but another Jewish leader, David Nassi (Josef Nunes de Fonseca), a veteran of Brazil who had helped establish a Jewish presence in Dutch Guyana in the 1640s, received permission to settle fifty Sephardic families on Curaçao in 1652 before becoming an important figure in the Jewish community of Suriname in the 1660s. By the 1670s, Curaçao was the most important center of the Jewish community in the Americas.[15]

New Netherland, as in so many other things, remained a place apart from the rest of the Dutch world. Neither a Brazil nor part of the greater Caribbean, it had no sugar economy or immediate Spanish or Portuguese Catholic contacts to justify the recruitment of Portuguese Jews as brokers or specialists. Even for Jewish entrepreneurs it did not enter the horizon of possibilities until 1653, when several Amsterdam Jews came to New Amsterdam to trade, perhaps looking for new business prospects as Brazil's future darkened. The Jewish traders were part of an annual influx of merchants from the Netherlands who came to do business in the colony and then returned. In that respect they were little different from the occasional Jewish merchant or entrepreneur who would travel through the European countryside. They posed no threat to the religious order because they showed no signs of forming a local community.[16]

The chance arrival in 1654 of two dozen impoverished Jewish refugees from Brazil—men, women, and children, the possible nucleus of a community, was different from a trading visit. It put New Amsterdam on the map as a possible site of Jewish settlement. Or at least the local Dutch community feared this might be the case. Would the Jews treat New Amsterdam as they had Amsterdam and Recife? Rumors circulated in the colony "that still more of the same lot would follow, and then they would build here a synagogue." Minister Megapolensis reported in March 1655 a "great deal of complaint and murmuring" in his congregation, then expressed their sentiments in a burst of the sort of anti-Semitic invective common in the Dutch world: "These people, have no other God than the unrighteous Mammon, and no other aim than to get possession of Christian property, and to win all other merchants by drawing all trade towards themselves."

He asked the classis "to obtain from the Lords-Directors, that these godless rascals, who are of no benefit to the country, but look at everything for their own profit, may be sent away from here."[17] The objections to letting Jews into New Amsterdam were the same as those opposing their presence in Brazil. The ideas were the same. Would the circumstances produce a different outcome?

For the Dutch Reformed establishment, as represented by Dominie Megapolensis, the Jews were not simply a threat in and of themselves. They contributed to a growing challenge of religious pluralism that they saw as a threat to the fledgling colony. The minimal connivance that allowed non-Reformed Christians to immigrate to the colony was already too much in their eyes. As Megapolensis put it, "as we have here Papists, Mennonites and Lutherans among the Dutch; also many Puritans or Independents and many Atheists and various other servants of Baal among the English under this Government, who conceal themselves under the name of Christians; it would create a still greater confusion if the obstinate and immovable Jews came to settle here."[18] He was raising the argument that New Netherland's establishment would regularly employ in its struggle with religious diversity. The colony was too small and too vulnerable to absorb and cope with religious pluralism. Increasing religious diversity would only produce greater strife and divisions, weakening the small settlement's ability to withstand the challenges facing it in North America. New Amsterdam was not Amsterdam, after all.

The decisive moment came after the poor Jewish refugees sent word of their plight back to their fellows in Amsterdam. Exactly when New Amsterdam's Jews communicated with Amsterdam's Jewish community is uncertain, but it must have been sometime in the fall of 1654, shortly after their arrival. By January 1655, Jewish merchants had submitted a petition to the directors of the Amsterdam Chamber of the WIC, the men with immediate oversight over Petrus Stuyvesant and the governance of New Netherland. The petition contained several arguments, setting out a series of reasons for permitting Jews to live in New Amsterdam. First, they stressed the losses Jews had suffered in Brazil for the Dutch cause and the expenses the petitioners had gone to in order to maintain the refugees thus far. There was not enough opportunity for the Jews in the republic and "they cannot go to Spain or Portugal because of the Inquisition," thus they "must in time be obliged to depart for other territories" of the Dutch overseas. Where else could they find refuge? They reminded the directors that the Burgomasters and the States General "have in political matters always protected and considered the Jewish nation as upon the same footing as all the inhabitants and burghers" especially since the Treaty of Munster guaranteeing Dutch independence. Finally, they countered the argument of the Dutch Reformed colonists that New Netherland was too small, pointing out that the "land is extensive and spacious" and that the more "loyal people that go to live there, the better it is in regard to the population of the country," the "increase of trade," the "importation of all the necessaries that may be sent there," and "the payment of various excises and taxes which may be imposed there."[19] As will become clear later, the argument that the increase of colonists would lead to greater prosperity of the colony (regardless of their religious inclinations) was appealing to the directors of the 1650s and 1660s in a way it had not been to their predecessors.

The Jewish petition emphasized the connection between political loyalty and economic opportunity. They pointed out that "many of the Jewish nation are principal shareholders in the Company," yet more evidence of the Jewish investment in the Dutch cause. They then hinted that their loyalty and economic power could easily go to the Dutch rivals. After all, the French had allowed "the Portuguese Jews" to "traffic and live in Martinique, [Saint] Christopher and others of their territories, whither also some have gone from here, as your Honors know." Moreover, the "English also consent at the present time that the Portuguese and Jewish nation may go from London and settle at Barbados, whither also some have gone." In other words, much as the Jews were invested in the Dutch cause, they were also invested in their own, and this could lead them to take their business elsewhere. The petitioners tried to shame the directors and provoke their competitive instincts, asking "how can your Honors forbid the same and refuse transportation to this Portuguese nation who reside here and have been settled here well on to sixty years, many also being born here and confirmed burghers, and this to a land that needs people for its increase?" They asked that the Jews be granted "passage to and residence in that country," arguing that failure to do so "would result in a great prejudice to their reputation." They wanted Jews to have the same rights and liberties in New Netherland as "other inhabitants" and expected they would "contribute like others" in exchange for those liberties. In all this, they said nothing about religious rights.[20]

The Amsterdam Chamber was caught between sympathy for the Dutch Reformed colonists' views and the need to respond to the Jewish request. In the end, the Jewish emphasis on political loyalty and economic significance overrode fears of religious and ethnic diversity. "We would have liked to agree to your wishes and request that the new territories should not be further invaded by people of the Jewish race," they wrote to Director-General Stuyvesant in April 1655, "for we foresee from such immigration the same difficulties which you fear." Nevertheless, they claimed it would be "unreasonable and unfair, especially because of the considerable loss, sustained by the Jews in the taking of Brazil."[21] Sympathy for the Jewish suffering in the Dutch cause seems to have been a factor in a new transatlantic religious calculus extending more tolerance to Jews. Or was it?

There is an important dispute over the translation of the directors' letter to Stuyvesant, one of the crucial documents in the history of Jews in New Amsterdam and New York. Since the nineteenth century, Americans have translated the rest of the sentence as "and also because of the large amount of capital, which they have invested in shares of this Company," thereby affirming the view that Jewish investment power was able to sway Dutch authorities toward a more tolerant stance toward the Jews. However, Dutch historian Jaap Jacobs has recently revisited the Dutch original and claims that "de groot capitalen die sij alsnoch inde compagnie sijn heriderende" is better translated as "the large sum of money for which they are still indebted to the Company." In other words, it was less that the Jews owned significant in shares the WIC than that they owed it money that encouraged the directors to give them an opportunity in New Amsterdam.[22]

Jacobs's argument that it was debt rather than investment that prompted the WIC directors to favor Jewish settlement in North America rests on several points. First, while there were some Jewish investors in the WIC by the 1650s, they were too few to have "acquired a considerable number of WIC shares." At the same time, even if they had, the "West India Company did not have to pay much heed to its investors, a trait it shared with the East India Company." A more likely explanation, according to Jacobs, is that the Jews had been tax farmers, entrusted with collecting taxes and dues in Brazil—money the WIC needed to pay off its soldiers, sailors, and other employees. The Portuguese revolt had made it impossible to collect the taxes, which could be for huge sums—Moses Navarro was granted the tax farm in 1645, the year the revolt began, for ƒ74,000. The WIC needed the Jews in America to make up some of the tremendous losses the company had just suffered. Consequently, the directors decided that the Jewish petition "to sail to and trade in New Netherland and to live and remain there" would be granted. At the same time, it undertook no additional obligations for the Jews. The grant was valid only "provided the poor among them shall not become a burden to the Company or the community, but be supported by their own nation." Their orders to Stuyvesant were clear: "You will govern yourself accordingly," their phrase for a nonnegotiable command.[23]

The Amsterdam directors' admission of Jews to New Netherland purposefully said nothing about religion. It was concerned only with trade and residency. As they explained to Stuyvesant the following year, the "permission given to the Jews to go to New Netherland and enjoy there the same privileges, as they have here" was "granted only as far as civil and political rights are concerned, without giving the said Jews a claim to the privilege of exercising their religion in a synagogue or at a gathering." They chided Stuyvesant that "as long therefore, as you receive no request for granting them this liberty of religious exercise, your considerations and anxiety about this matter are premature." If anything did come up on that front, he was to forward the matter to the directors "and await the necessary order."[24] The following year, they clarified that the Jews could "exercise in all quietness their religion within their houses, for which end they must without doubt endeavor to build their houses close together in a convenient place on one or the other side of New Amsterdam—at their own choice—as they have done here."[25] New Amsterdam would not be another Amsterdam or Recife, but it would not be like Antwerp either. Actually, it would be a lot like Amsterdam in 1610.

The restrictions on Jewish life in New Netherland would not have been a surprise for the Jews. Restrictions on Jewish life existed in Protestant city-states of the Holy Roman Empire like Hamburg and Frankfurt that had Jewish communities. There were explicit restrictions on their interactions with Christians in Amsterdam. Even in Dutch Brazil, for all the opportunities available to Jews, the authorities still treated them as a separate people and tried to keep the Jewish community within certain bounds. In 1641, the WIC directors had drawn up a list of rules for Jews there just as they had for Catholics, though they were of a very different tenor, concerned with segregation and containment rather than subversion. The WIC ordered that "Jews shall not exceed a third part of the total" population, that any orphan of a Jewish-Christian union was to be raised Christian, and that Jews could not defraud anyone in their business dealings. Jews were not to construct any more synagogues. Jewish men could not marry Christian women or have a "Christian concubine," nor could they convert any Christians to Judaism. The directors described this as calling Christians "from evangelical freedom to the burdens of the ancient Law, from light to shadows," giving a clear indication of how they felt about the matter. Jews could not "revile the sacrosanct name of Christ." Indeed, one wealthy Jew was convicted of blasphemy in 1641 and fined 4,000 guilders (which was then used to build Soler's French Reformed Church), while another Jewish man was tortured for blasphemy the following year before the directors intervened to reduce punishments to the norms as practiced in Holland.[26]

In a sense, the orders regulating Jewish life in Brazil were an acknowledgement of the size and significance of the community. No similar set of rules was drawn up for the much smaller group of Jews in New Amsterdam, compelling the colonists to negotiate the boundaries of possibilities and prohibitions on Jewish lives in North America. Though the Dutch did not foresee religious worship for the Jews, the Jews of New Amsterdam agitated for community rights that had religious dimensions. In July 1655, soon after news arrived from Amsterdam that their petition to reside and trade in the colony had been granted, three community leaders, Abraham de Lucena, Salvador Dandrada, and Jacob Cohen, requested "to be allowed to purchase a burial place for their people." They were allowed to do so "on open land belonging to the Company," since "they did not wish to bury their dead in the common burial place (for which there has been no need as of yet)." Gaining a burial ground was of course one of the key early steps in setting up a community. In August, as Stuyvesant was preparing the expedition against New Sweden, a new issue was raised about the Jewish role in colonial defense. The "captains and officers of the militia of" New Amsterdam submitted a petition asking "whether the Jewish nation resident in this city should mount the guard under their militia banners." Stuyvesant and his council decided to exempt the Jews "from general expeditions and guard duties, according to the custom of the laudable government of the famous mercantile city of Amsterdam," using Amsterdam as an example to limit Jewish rights in New Amsterdam. The Jews were not entirely let off the hook for defense. Each "male above the age of 16 and under 60 years old shall contribute" a monthly payment of "sixty-five stuivers" for the "freedom of being relieved of general militia duties." Stuyvesant gave the "militia council" responsibility to collect the contribution and "to institute proceedings" if a Jew refused to pay. To justify the decision, the council noted "the aversion and disaffection of this militia to be fellow soldiers of

the aforesaid nation, and to mount guard in the same guardhouse" as well
that "the aforesaid nation is not admitted and counted among the militia
in the renowned mercantile city of Amsterdam or (to our knowledge) in
any other city in the Netherlands, whether in the trainbands or in the general militia guard." In exchange for "freedom in that regard" they "contribute a reasonable sum." When two Jews asked to serve rather than pay the
"contribution" they found unaffordable, Stuyvesant's council refused, saying they were free "to depart whenever and wherever it may please them."[27]
He could not force Jews to leave, but he could try to discourage them from
staying.

Stuyvesant refused to connive at the presence of Jews in New Amsterdam.
He did not persecute them in any way he would have recognized as persecution. However, he did try to make life for Jews in New Netherland as unpleasant as legally possible in hopes of encouraging them to move elsewhere. He
forbade Jews to trade outside New Amsterdam; he had Jews pay the fine
instead of serving in the militia, depriving them of a possible opportunity
offered by American conditions; he forced a Dutchman to auction his house
at a very low price rather than let a Jew buy it, and when still no Christian
colonist wanted it, he made up the difference with government funds. Jews
could take Christians to court, but if the court found for the Jews (as it
regularly did), the Christians could appeal to Stuyvesant, who sometimes
overturned the finding. In short, he did all within his power to encourage
Jews to leave without violating the basic injunction of the directors.[28]

Stuyvesant's treatment of the Jewish community was in part a response
to the striking determination with which Jews fought for privileges in New
Netherland. Some, like militia service, were unprecedented. Jews could not
serve in the militia in Holland, so trying to serve in the colonial militia
would have been a real innovation. Though the Jewish community in
Dutch North America was small, never exceeding the twenty-odd individuals who were there in 1654–1655, it secured a burial ground, engaged in
trade, and got two men licensed as kosher butchers, absolved from having
to slaughter pigs. They undoubtedly gathered in someone's house for worship, though they never lived together in adjoining houses as the directors
imagined they should. Amsterdam's Jewish community even sent over a
Torah. It seemed that the makings of a Jewish community in Dutch North
America were in the offing.[29]

Though Jewish mobilization for recognition of their community in New
Amsterdam was more successful than that of the Lutherans, in the end,

no Jewish community materialized. By 1663 virtually all the Jews in New Netherland had gone. With too few Jews in the colony to gather for worship, religious services terminated and the Torah was sent back. The only Jewish family remaining at the time of the English conquest was that of Asser Levy, an Ashkenazic (Germanic, not Portuguese) Jew who came from Amsterdam and was unconnected to the Brazilian Jews. For Levy, New Netherland offered enough opportunities to stay on even without a community. He gained an important position in the colony's mercantile class and was even able to hire a Christian maidservant—something usually forbidden in Europe. His family provided a slim thread connecting the Jewish community of New Amsterdam with that of New York.[30]

The combination of harassment and opportunity in shaping Jewish communities was typical of their experience of the Dutch world. Though Stuyvesant's harassment certainly made things unpleasant for the Jews, it was not the decisive factor in getting them to leave. The decline of Dutch North America's brief Jewish community owed more to the greater opportunities in the Caribbean than to the hostility of Dutch North America. Compared to Curaçao and Guyana, important nodes in the booming trade in sugar and slaves that the Portuguese Jews had long specialized in, New Amsterdam offered little in the way of business prospects. The Jewish communities there grew as that of New Amsterdam disappeared. In the grand scheme of things, New Netherland was more liberal than Utrecht but less appealing than Curaçao.

One final element should be stressed that set New Amsterdam apart from Amsterdam: the lack of interest expressed in converting Jews in any of the relevant sources. This is notable, for at precisely the time Jews were struggling to make a living in New Amsterdam, an eclectic range of learned Protestants in England and Holland dreamed of the imminent conversion of the Jews. For them, it was a crucial step on the way to the millennium. One aspect of this hope was the theory that Native Americans were descended from Jews. Some dreamed that both Jews and Native Americans could soon be converted and the millennium would arrive within a few years; 1650, 1655, and 1658 were possible candidates. By the 1660s, the expectations were dimming. Nonetheless, the hope and expectation that Jews would be converted was a persistent aspect of Christianity. Occasionally it produced a few individual converts, most if not all of them in Europe. None of the Jews in Dutch North America converted. They remained Jews and were never expected or urged to alter that condition, something that could be considered an extraordinary

degree of acceptance, even if it was the acceptance of men who simultaneously disliked having to live with Jews.[31]

Dutch tolerance contained a persistent tension between recognizing the dis-
tinctness of other groups, like the Jews, and Dutch Reformed efforts to
proselytize and bring in as many people as possible to their Church. These
contradictory impulses accompanied the Dutch overseas. In the early years,
the Dutch had hoped that Reformed religion could unite Dutch and non-
Dutch in a common bond, and in a number of places it did. The first Dutch
minister to Asia, Caspar Wiltens, displayed an impressive linguistic and
cultural adaptability after his arrival on Amboina in 1614. Building on the
work of two men who had already started learning Malaysian and teaching
local youths to read and write, Wiltens quickly learned the language well
enough to preach in it. Another minister, Sebastiaan Danckaerts, soon
joined him. By 1625, a church with a consistory of two elders and two
deacons was established on Amboina. Together with the existing school,
the church turned Amboina into one of the most successful missionary
terrains of the Dutch world. By 1700, there would be sixty-nine Dutch
Reformed communities with fifty-four schools and fifty-two churches serving a Reformed population of about seventeen thousand along with some
five thousand school children.[32]

Elsewhere in Asia, the position of the Dutch Reformed Church varied
depending on the local context. In Amboina, they had been able both to
prevent a mosque from being built and to develop a strong Dutch
Reformed community. In Ternate and other Muslim territories the VOC
negotiated agreements of mutual toleration, preventing either group from
proselytizing the other. On the important spice island of Banda, which had
been conquered in a brutal campaign of massacre and enslavement in the
1620s, missionary efforts unsurprisingly had little appeal, despite the vigorous efforts of the language genius Justus Heurnius in the 1630s. Heurnius,
like Wiltens, had learned Malaysian and begun preaching in it shortly after
his arrival in Indonesia. He went on to learn enough Chinese to translate
prayers, the Ten Commandments, and a profession of faith. His efforts
found fruit elsewhere in the Moluccas, but not on Banda. As late as 1750
only one hundred and thirteen natives were members of the Dutch
Reformed Church.[33]

On Formosa (Taiwan), the Dutch Reformed Church had one of its most
impressive success stories. The Dutch arrived in Formosa as a byproduct of

their effort to edge into the China trade. The island had the virtue of being close to China but outside of Chinese jurisdiction. The native Formosans were related to Filipinos in culture and language but had not yet encountered Hinduism, Catholicism, Buddhism, or Islam. Like Native Americans, they offered a thriving trade in animal skins, mostly deerskins. After establishing their base at Fort Zeelandia on the southern tip of the island in 1624, the Dutch rapidly gained control over the whole island, in part because of a vigorous missionary effort. Formosa's first governor had urged the VOC directors to send "2 or 3 competent ministers or readers of upright habits so that the name of God will here be spread, and the barbarous natives of the island may be brought to Christianity" soon after taking up his post and his request was soon filled. The first minister, Georgius Candidus, arrived in 1627. The second, Robertus Junius, joined him two years later. After learning the Formosan language, Junius used it to prepare a number of religious texts. Traveling all across the island and combining great resourcefulness with some flexibility on theological points, he is credited with bringing in over five thousand Formosans to the Dutch Reformed Church before leaving in 1643. Only a long, dramatic siege by a large Chinese army of Ming Empire loyalists in 1662 put an end to Dutch Reformed expansion on the island. After capturing Fort Zeelandia, the Ming general had the Dutch dominies crucified. Across the island, his men destroyed all signs and symbols of Dutch Christianity in a brutally successful effort to extirpate it. The Dutch were never able to recapture the island. The Chinese population continued to increase. The indigenous Formosans, who had proven so amenable to Dutch Protestantism, declined.[34]

Two final non-Christian groups were also, at times, subject to efforts at conversion: Native Americans and Africans. In Dutch America, Native Americans retained their independent status even as their population was declining through war and disease. Despite a persistent desire to bring them into the Dutch Reformed Church, New Netherland's Dutch did little to effect it. Unlike in Formosa and Brazil, where a number of indigenous allies of the Dutch had converted, virtually no missionary effort was made and the indigenous inhabitants had little incentive to learn the new religion. As New Amsterdam's ministers reported to the classis in 1654, "there is little appearance" that "knowledge of the Gospel is making great progress among the Indians here," as the classis had hoped. A sachem had stayed with them for a while, "who was diligent in learning to read and write, which he learned to do tolerably well." Instructed "in the principal grounds of the

Christian faith," he had "publicly joined in recitations on the catechism by Christian children." The ministers gave him a Bible, hoping that he would be able to convert his fellows. Alas, his knowledge was limited and, lacking "the practice of godliness," he was "greatly inclined to drunkenness, and indeed, is not better than other Indians." They did not think any would convert "until they are brought under the government of Europeans, as these latter increase in numbers." In the end, Native Americans did not join the Dutch Reformed Church until well after New Netherland was conquered. Until then, their communities were strong and independent enough to resist any temptation to become Christian, and the Dutch did very little to encourage it, a notable deviation from their efforts in Brazil and Formosa.[35]

Matters were different for the growing African population in the Dutch American colonies. For the enslaved, conversion potentially had more power and appeal than for indigenous Americans. Living in a radically subjugated position, they were as underneath the government of the Dutch as one could be. Some Africans saw in conversion and membership in the public church a chance for higher status, perhaps even freedom for themselves or their children, or at least some degree of social privilege regardless of its salvific powers. For this reason alone, Dutch churchmen, who initially expressed much interest in converting slaves, gradually abandoned that ambition as both the population and economic importance of the enslaved grew.

The Dutch entered the trans-Atlantic slave trade about a decade after the founding of New Netherland's church. Between 1637 and 1642, they captured Elmina and other Portuguese forts in West Africa, including Luanda in Angola. Thereafter the Dutch turn to African slavery was complete. Between 1641 and 1648, when the Portuguese recaptured Angola and São Tomé, fourteen thousand Africans were sent as slaves to Dutch Brazil. After 1648, the Dutch continued to ship slaves to the Americas through their remaining posts on the coast of West Africa. Curaçao, just off the Venezuelan coast, became a major slave trading center, marketing enslaved Africans to the Spanish and other colonies across the Caribbean. New Netherland did not become a slave society like Brazil or Curaçao, but African slaves formed an increasing part of the population, especially in and around New Amsterdam, where a few hundred arrived over the course of the colony's history.

Initially, Dutch churchmen had high expectations of African assimilation to the Reformed order. Most of the Africans brought over were not Christians, though a number had had some contact with Catholicism through the Portuguese slave system the Dutch usurped. Those who were not Christian (very few were Muslim) existed in a distinct space in the Dutch religious world. African religion was never recognized as a separate "church" of any sort. Instead, Africans were expected to conform to the public church. Or at least that is what Dutch ministers of the 1630s and 1640s hoped. A "principal" justification for enslaving Africans, the classis of Brazil proclaimed, was "in order to bring them to the knowledge of God and salvation." That same year, 1638, the Zeeland minister Godfriedus Udemans published his influential magnum opus *The Spiritual Helm of the merchant's vessel* (*'t Geestelyck roer van 't coopmans schip*). Udemans maintained that Christians could not enslave fellow Christians. However, Christians could enslave heathens justly brought into slavery, provided they were treated well. After all, slavery among the Dutch brought the benighted Africans closer to True Religion than they would have been otherwise. In the end, efforts to convert Africans to Protestantism were few. When it came to slavery, the public church found itself facing the great contradiction between its desires for comprehensiveness and the colonists' demands for exclusion and exploitation.[36]

The classis of Brazil addressed the challenges of spreading the faith among the colony's slaves in 1638. Troubled by what it called the "great disorder and godlessness common among the Negros," it itemized the elements keeping the "Negros" (they used the Portuguese word) in a godless state. First, they did not come to church. Second, the buying and selling of slaves frequently separated married couples. Third, adultery and "whoredoms" went unpunished among them. So common was this extramarital sex "that it was no wonder that the wrath of God is brought down upon the land by it." Fourth, slaves worked on the Sabbath. The classis urged the government to compel masters to bring their slaves to Reformed worship services on the Sabbath instead of forcing them to work or letting them indulge in their dancing. The classis continued to urge action on this front until the Portuguese revolt reclaimed the countryside, but there is no evidence that much was done. Far more effort was put into converting the "Brazilians," the Native American allies of the Dutch. Two ministers were delegated to work in the Brazilian villages; none were ever dedicated for service to enslaved Africans. The Africans were left with their "dances" and the "popish" rituals they used when harvesting and pressing sugar cane.[37]

On Curaçao, Dutch churchmen made some effort to bring the enslaved Africans into their church. In 1649, a minister baptized "twelve adult persons, all blacks or negroes, after they had been reasonably well instructed in the Christian doctrine, and who had good testimony as to their knowledge and life."[38] However, several reasons prevented a black Protestant community from forming on Curaçao. The connection between faith and social status was one. When the enslaved Africans started to become Christian later in the century, they generally adopted the Roman Catholic faith of the Spanish rather than the Protestant faith of their Dutch masters. The recurrent lack of a regular minister was another. A visiting French minister had performed the baptisms of 1649. The Dutch minister had left the year before and a new one would not arrive until 1659. Even then, all sorts of obstacles to conversion remained. For example, in 1660, the classis noted a report that a "negro" had given "some instruction in the Spanish language; but his wicked life gave occasion rather to the blaspheming of God's name than to its glorification." When the new minister asked the classis whether he could baptize the Africans, they replied that "you observe the good rule of the church here in this land, where no one, who is an adult, is admitted to baptism without previous confession of faith." As for their children, "as long as the parents are actually heathen, although they were baptized" en masse by Catholics, "the children may not be baptized, unless the parents pass over to Christianity, and abandon heathendom." Confronted with the chance to offer this token of membership in the public church, the Dutch religious authorities withdrew it. There was precedent for this in the republic and Asia. Most Europeans born in the Dutch Republic were entitled to be baptized in the public church. The one group in Europe denied baptism was the gypsies. In the East Indies, baptism was also denied to native inhabitants, even those born and raised in a Christian household who had a member of the Dutch Reformed Church willing to stand as surety. They were denied membership until they became adults and made a proper confession of faith.[39]

Compared to elsewhere in the Dutch Americas, the Dutch in New Netherland made extraordinary efforts to incorporate Africans into their church. Already in 1636, Governor Wouter van Twiller asked for a schoolmaster who could teach the Dutch and black children religion. By 1639, there were about one hundred blacks in New Netherland. In 1641, New Amsterdam's church reported on "the good conditions and daily increase of their congregation. The Americans come not yet to the right knowledge of God; but the negroes, living among the colonists, come nearer thereto and give better hope." At least fifty-six people of African descent had been baptized by 1656.[40]

However, even in New Netherland, efforts to baptize Africans waned by the 1660s. The ministers suspected that the Africans were more interested in freedom than in Reformed Protestantism. Dominie Henricus Selijns reported in June 1664 that he and his colleagues were refusing the "negroes'" requests for baptism, "partly on account of their lack of knowledge and of faith, and partly because of the worldly and perverse aims on the part of the said negroes. They wanted nothing else than to deliver their children from bodily slavery, without striving for piety and Christian virtues." Selijns still tried to catechize them and had "some hope for the youth" but "among the elder people who have no faculty of comprehension" his work bore "but little fruit." Cultural, political, and other obstacles made it increasingly less likely for enslaved Africans to become Reformed Christians, even in New Netherland where that had been the case more than anywhere else.[41]

The most extraordinary case of religious diversity in the Dutch world was Batavia, the most powerful Dutch outpost in Asia. From the moment of its founding, it was never a very "Dutch" society. Muslim Javanese peasants inhabited the surrounding countryside and sometimes came to live and work in the town. Slaves, servants, mercenaries, and employees drawn from India to Japan filled the streets. The European presence was mostly restricted to men who, as employees of VOC, were not allowed to marry. Nonetheless, there was a public church, the largest and most important in Dutch Asia, just as Batavia was the largest and most important Dutch outpost in Asia. Set up in 1616 by Batavia's first minister, Adriaen Jacobz Hulsebos, the church became the center of the colony's privileged social life and the coordinator of the Dutch churches elsewhere in Asia. As elsewhere, the public church did not adopt a new strategy for dealing with the exotic faiths it presided over, from Chinese Buddhists to Javanese Muslims. They were simply incorporated into the habits developed in Europe to protect the Protestant public church from Catholics and idolatry.[42]

The greatest challenge to the hegemony of the public church in Batavia came from the Chinese. When the Dutch arrived, several hundred Chinese already lived in the city of Jakarta, on whose ruins Batavia was built. Long an essential part of Southeast Asian trade networks, some stayed on in Batavia. Knowing their Asian trade would not go very far without Chinese participation, the Dutch did what they could to attract even more. By 1632, the roughly two thousand four hundred Chinese inhabitants comprised the largest single ethnic group in the city of eight thousand. They were not a majority. No one was. The Europeans population was slightly less than that of the Chinese. Of the remaining Batavians in 1632, slaves accounted for about fifteen hundred; "mardijkers," former slaves, generally of southern Indian origin, who had been baptized—usually as Catholics but some became Dutch Reformed—made up around six hundred and fifty; Japanese about one hundred.[43]

Batavia was as much a Chinese city as a Dutch one and remained so into the eighteenth century. Religiously, the Chinese posed a peculiar challenge to Dutch authorities because their religion arguably fit within the category of "idolatry" they were supposed to suppress. Yet to prohibit Chinese religion and culture, or, in the terms of the Dutch churchmen, their "heathenish superstitions and devil worship," risked alienating and driving out a major group on whom Batavia's economic and social stability depended. The result was a persistent tension that came to a head in the same years as the struggles over tolerance in New Netherland. Occasionally the authorities would prod the Batavian dominies to spread the word among the Chinese. The dominies had little faith that the Chinese could be converted. The obstacles of language and culture daunted all but a very few of the Dutch. Worse, as the dominies complained in 1651, the few Chinese who did convert did so purely for worldly reasons.[44] This complaint echoed criticisms of enslaved Africans who seemed to hope that conversion could better their condition. Rather than dedicate themselves to converting the Chinese, the dominies repeatedly urged the government to suppress Chinese religious culture, much as it did Roman Catholicism.

The Chinese pushed at the bounds of connivance. Over the years, their processions and street theater took place ever more openly. The temples set up in private homes gradually evolved from modest domestic shrines to substantial pagodas located in the largest houses. Reformed churchmen objected to these encroachments on the public domain, which was supposed to remain the prerogative of their Church. They demanded that "the idolatrous Chinese temples be demolished and their public and private sacrifices and offerings of swine, the fruits of the earth, pastries and all sorts

of edible commodities be once and for all extirpated, banned and suppressed as a pestilential cancer along with the burning of lamps, candles,
incense and the performance of comedies and plays and especially their
solemn processions, the regal display and carrying about of their idol."
Initially the authorities did not act, but eventually they responded.[45]

Dutch authorities were not always willing to suffer the idolatry that
their churchmen decried. For a few years, 1647–1656, those Dutch who saw
in Chinese practices an intolerable idolatry waged an active campaign to
suppress all manifestations of Chinese religion, which illustrates how uncertain colonial connivance could be, and just how far some Dutch could go
in the direction of suppression even in a cosmopolitan city like Batavia.
Heeding the dominies' complaints about the "hidden temples" of the Chinese, a determined bailiff, Ambrosius van der Keer, launched the campaign
by breaking up several private Chinese ritual celebrations and seizing religious images and statues in the name of suppressing idolatry. But was it
really idolatry? The officer who would have been in charge of prosecuting
the offense, Gerard Herberts, did not think so. According to him, the Chinese images were not idols. For Van der Keer and the church consistory,
they were. Any images before which lamps were lit, offerings made, incense
burned, and open respect shown through the raising of hands and bowing
of the body were idols, and the manner in which they were treated was a
"false and horrific idolatry" to be suppressed.[46]

Van der Keer's raids outraged the Chinese community and alarmed his
superiors. The immediate reaction of the Dutch authorities was to sweep
the problem under the rug to avoid further controversy. Batavia's governing council seized the images, replaced Van der Keer with a less zealous
officer, and swore both sides of the idolatry debate to "eternal silence" on
the matter. However, the iconoclasts' failure to get the local government
on their side simply persuaded them approach the highest levels of the
VOC. They launched a letter campaign and worked on individual members
of the governing council in Batavia. By 1650 the combination of influences
compelled local authorities to effectively suppress all Chinese public ceremonies. The campaign reached a climax in 1651 when the governor was
compelled to force the Chinese to tear down a temple he had earlier connived at. However, he did nothing when the Chinese simply dismantled
the temple and immediately rebuilt it outside the city wall, in view of "anyone who just sticks his head out of the gate," the dominies complained.
The Dutch churchmen continued to agitate to have this temple destroyed

as well. The beginning of a war with Bantem in 1656 provided then governor-general Joan Maetsuycker with a solution. Touring the city's defenses, he noted that the temple was located on a prime defensive spot. At his command it was covered in dirt and turned into a redoubt with eight cannons. It was only a temporary resolution to the conflict.[47]

The Calvinist campaign against Chinese idolatry was not a lasting success. The Chinese population continued to grow. Their street theater and processions returned. By 1670, they had two public temples. The Chinese in Batavia existed in a space that shared aspects of both the Jewish and Catholic experiences under Dutch rule. As with the Jewish synagogue in Amsterdam, the Dutch government never formally permitted Chinese religious practices. As with Catholic services in the republic, a system of semi-bribery made them possible. If notice of a street performance was given in advance and a fee paid, it could usually proceed unmolested. It was not always a smooth process, involving a certain amount of awkwardness as the government tried to limit the number of public events while the Chinese tried to limit the payments they had to make.[48]

Extortionate as the Dutch system of restrictions on Chinese worship was, it was something of a privilege for the Chinese. They were the only non-Reformed group able to practice their religion openly in Batavia. Like Amsterdam's Jews and Lutherans, the Chinese benefited from their status as foreigners, valued traders, and workers. The size and strength of the community were feared and respected. Likewise, Dutch dependence on the Chinese never translated into acknowledgment or acceptance of anything like equality between Chinese and Dutch. It was precisely the degree of difference that made the level of tolerance possible. And, as ever, it was very specific. Batavia's connivance of the Chinese did not extend to local Catholics or Muslims, never mind Jews, Mennonites, or Lutherans.

Batavia's Muslims never gained formal recognition of a right to worship. In 1636, they were explicitly forbidden to build a new school, where, of course, in addition to reading and writing, the Koran was taught. However, they avoided a campaign of suppression because they excelled at keeping their worship away from the prying eyes of the Dutch Reformed Church. As a result, little is known about their religious lives under Dutch rule. Originating in the territories and islands around Batavia, they formed an important part of the city's workforce. At least two religious leaders operated surreptitiously in the Muslim part of town in the 1630s, marrying people in Islamic fashion, opening up a clandestine school, and holding secret worship services of some sort. Despite occasional complaints from the church and a vigorous promise from Governor Maetsuycker to "throw in chains" any "pope of the Moorish idolatry" caught leading a worship service, no conventicles were found or broken up. Indeed, by the middle of the century, even the church consistory admitted that the Islamic schools performed an important educational function, restricting its demands to ensuring that the schools remain closed on Sundays and that any new religious leaders who came to the city be deported. Of course, those already present could stay. By the second half of the seventeenth century, Muslims had become such an important part of the city's life that the governing council called in a mullah to explain the workings of Islamic law to them. Nevertheless, no public mosque or Islamic worship was permitted within the city.[49]

The expansion of Dutch trade and rise of colonialism brought the Dutch into contact with an unprecedented amount of religious diversity: Jews, indigenous faiths from Formosa to North America, Muslims, Buddhists, Hindus, and Confucians. Dutch colonists found themselves living in a much more pluralistic world than anyone had suspected when the Union of Utrecht was formed. Though liberty of conscience prevented the Dutch from compelling non-Christians to convert, many hoped they would. At the same time, they had a framework in place for coexisting with those who would not. In most cases this meant that the Dutch did not intervene in their private religious worlds. Only when they pressed onto the public sphere of the Dutch settlements, as the Jews did in New Amsterdam and the Chinese did in Batavia, did they run the risk of suppression.

Colonization did not prompt the Dutch to adopt a new attitude towards religious diversity. They simply calibrated their existing habits and expectations onto a vastly different reality, applying the terms and concepts of European Christianity—heathenism, idolatry, superstition, and so on—to a range of different peoples across the world. The main story of Dutch tolerance in its relations with non-Christians at home and overseas is thus less about the tremendous religious diversity the Dutch lived with than how they constrained the new faiths with their established European model. The presence of Jews in Dutch Brazil simply imported to America an arrangement that had recently been worked out in Amsterdam. The restrictions on Chinese processions and Muslim religious leaders echoed similar restrictions on Catholics.

Dutch North America fit into the spectrum of relations with non-Christians in a distinctive way, primarily through the comparative lack of contact. The indigenous inhabitants lived largely beyond the purview of the public church. Africans were few enough in number, and surrounded by a strong enough church, that New Netherland developed an unusually large Afro-Dutch Reformed community. For the small Jewish community, New Amsterdam was an unlooked-for way station in a time of need. Though by 1660 they had gained far more rights there than virtually anywhere in the republic outside Amsterdam, there was little to keep them in the colony once opportunities opened up in the Caribbean. In the diverse sweep of Dutch colonies across the globe, New Netherland was an unusually Protestant society. Its church took on pretensions of comprehension over the colonial population that hardly any other colonial church could do. In Batavia and Brazil, the Dutch had to develop strategies for coping with demographic majorities that remained outside of the Reformed Church. In New Netherland, the struggles over tolerance had a very different cast, as Protestants tried to break out of the public church that claimed jurisdiction over their religion in a way it could not over the Chinese or Jews. It was a fight between close relatives rather than distant strangers.

CHAPTER 5

BABEL

If the Lutherans should be indulged in the exercise of their worship, the Papist, Mennonites and others, would soon make similar claims. Thus we would soon become a Babel of confusion, instead of remaining a united and peaceful people.

In a May 1656 letter to New Netherland's dominies, the classis of Amsterdam expressed its fears about religious diversity in the colony. The quashing of the Lutheran effort to form a congregation was "an affair of great consequence." Had the Lutherans succeeded, "the Mennonists and English Independents, of whom there is said to be not a few there, might have been led to undertake the same thing in their turn, and would probably have attempted to introduce public gatherings. In fact we are informed that even the Jews have made request of the Hon. Governor, and have also attempted in that country to erect a synagogue for the exercise of their blasphemous religion." If this were permitted "there would have arisen a very Babel."[1] The biblical story of Babel told of how the people of the earth had been transformed from a powerful, unified, monolingual society into scattered, divided, multilingual peoples. In Genesis it helped explain the diversity and dispersion of humankind. For defenders of the public church it represented the danger of destroying the unity and strength of colonial Dutch society by replacing it with what scholars might call pluralism, an open recognition and coexistence of more than one faith. To the horror of Dutch ministers on both sides of the Atlantic, pluralism—what the Amsterdam classis called a Babel—became a frighteningly viable possibility even as their letter made its way to America.

Like many other parts of the Dutch world, people of several different faiths inhabited New Netherland. However, this latent pluralism need not lead to permission to practice a religion other than that of the public church. Though occasionally Dutch authorities granted formal toleration, as in Brazil and New Sweden, they preferred not to. Connivance, the gradual, informal process that had allowed Jews and Lutherans to build public communities in Amsterdam over decades of careful maneuvering, was the preferred route even for the most ecumenically minded magistrates. But connivance required a degree of subtlety and patience noticeable in the colonies primarily by its absence. Until 1655 the hegemony of the public church had been maintained without serious challenge. The Lutheran petition campaign for a separate church had failed, merely provoking a restatement of the official policy favoring the public church. However, when the colonial council drove home the supremacy of the public church in winter 1656 by passing an ordinance against separate religious gatherings, or conventicles, it provoked a crisis that almost resulted in precisely the official grant of toleration it was designed to deny.

By 1656, the Dutch Reformed felt themselves to be on the defensive for a dominance threatened by recent events. The religious complexion of the once predominantly Reformed colony was altered, with Jews living in New Amsterdam and a Lutheran church tolerated on the South River. Over the next two years, a series of incidents confronted the colonial authorities with the prospect of an assertive religious pluralism. English Baptists entered the colony from Rhode Island and made converts. Amsterdam's Lutherans sent over a minister to get a clandestine congregation underway and begin a process of connivance that would hopefully lead to the creation of a separate church in New Amsterdam, much as had happened in Amsterdam. For the first time since the colony's founding, local authorities had to come up with a strategy to defend the public church's official monopoly on religious worship. Paradoxically, the more they suppressed separate religious gatherings, the more they faced demands from both sides of the Atlantic to accept them. The struggles for toleration were inseparable from the struggles against it.

The plastic character of Dutch liberty of conscience both made confrontations possible and prevented them from ever being fully resolved. As long as there were those willing to defend one position or the other, the struggle could persist, for there was no single Dutch strategy for managing liberty of conscience, but rather a range of options and authorities to negotiate with. Liberal-minded magistrates and WIC directors in Amsterdam represented one end; Amsterdam's zealous Dutch Reformed Church the other. Both would affect developments in New Netherland. In between was a zone of nuance and negotiation that kept hopes, fears, and possibilities alive. Ultimately, neither those who wanted official recognition of their different faiths nor those who wanted to suppress them triumphed. Instead there was a persistent struggle over the limits of liberty of conscience that lasted until the English conquest. Rather than simply defend the position of the Dutch authorities or support the aims of those who challenged them (the tendency of much scholarship on the matter), the goal here is to show the interactions between the two, revealing the process by which both authorities and those who challenged them added texture to Dutch tolerance in the colony even as, officially speaking, little actually changed.

Typically, scholars working on toleration in New Netherland have collated the efforts of the various religious groups into a broader struggle for toleration. However, this may not be the best way to characterize what was happening. The most paradoxical aspect of this history is that, while there was a definite struggle *against* tolerance and the Babel the Reformed Protestants feared it threatened to bring, there was no explicit struggle *for* tolerance. All evidence shows that the Jews, Lutherans, Baptists, and Quakers waged individual struggles with no reference to each other. It is unclear whether they were even aware of what the others were doing, although they agitated virtually simultaneously. Nor did the directors of the Amsterdam Chamber who favored positions we might classify as tolerant conceive of what was happening as a struggle between tolerance and intolerance. For them, as for Amsterdam's burgomasters, the issue was not about a uniform practice but rather a series of individually negotiated arrangements; residential privileges of particular groups, as in the case of the Jews; rights to worship separately, as in the case of the Lutherans; or permission to proselytize, as in the case of the Quakers. For the Dutch Reformed authorities, however, it all portended the same thing—a disastrous Babel. While there was not a united struggle for toleration in New Netherland, there was definitely one against it.

The domino theory expressed by Dutch Reformed churchmen—that Catholics, Mennonites, and more would demand toleration if the Lutherans attained it—was both hyperbole and logic. After all, if one group was tolerated, how in fairness could others be denied it? Consequently, the only individuals to reason that the toleration of Lutheran worship granted the Swedes on the Delaware meant that "on account of the contrast, it could hardly be disallowed to" the Lutherans in New Amsterdam, were members of the classis of Amsterdam.[2] No Dutch Lutherans ever invoked the idea. Amsterdam's Lutheran consistory did not even seem to notice that the Swedish church on the South River existed. The compelling logic of this nightmare vision helped mobilize the Reformed establishment into action by putting matters into an all or nothing calculation to keep on guard against any challenge to their hegemony. They were acutely aware of the troubles pluralism would cause in America. "One cannot contemplate, without great emotion of soul, how greatly a pastor's labor would have been increased under such circumstances, and beset with obstacles, and what difficulties would have arisen to interfere with their good and holy efforts for the extension of the cause of Christ," Amsterdam's Reformed classis lamented. "Let us then—we here in this country and you there—employ all diligence to frustrate all such plans, that the wolves may be warded off from the tender lambs of Christ."[3]

Change was provoked by the English community. Stuyvesant had continued Kieft's policy of favoring migrants from New England, though he displayed a marked preference for Calvinists in a way Kieft had not. Unfortunately for Stuyvesant, not all English immigrants were reliably Calvinist. The English world was in the midst of a religious and political revolution in the 1640s and 1650s. Many who had begun as Calvinists now held a variety of religious opinions, some of which filtered into the English towns under Dutch authority. In the republic, English Reformed ministers played an important role in drawing English immigrants into a Reformed orthodoxy the public church could live with. In New Netherland, lack of funds and religious agreement drove away the few English Reformed ministers who could have performed a similar function, leaving Dominie Megapolensis perturbed by the "many Puritans or Independents and many Atheists and various other servants of Baal among the English under this Government, who conceal themselves under the name of Christians."[4]

The divided English towns both challenged the Dutch and cooperated with them in suppressing religious innovations. Many of the English, Presbyterians and Congregationalists, were as hostile to Baptists and other radicals as the Dutch Reformed were. They took the lead in defending Reformed hegemony in their towns and pulled in the Dutch Reformed establishment as allies. A rare portrait of religious life in the English towns composed by Megapolensis and his colleague Drisius in August 1657 proffered a sort of rough religious census of the English, indicating at the same time the dominies' sympathies for Reformed Englishmen. There were "Mennonites" in 's-Gravesande. Vlissingen had had a Presbyterian preacher (Francis Doughty) "who conformed to our church," but in recent years "many of" Vlissingen's inhabitants "became imbued with divers opinions and it was with them *quot hominess tot sententiae*" (as many opinions as men). They "absented themselves from preaching, nor would they pay the Preacher his promised stipend." Unable to make a living in Flushing, Doughty left for "the English Virginias" in 1655. In Middelburgh, the English were "mostly Independents, and have a man of the same persuasion there named Johannes Moor, who preaches there well, but administers no sacraments, because (as he says) he was permitted in New England to preach but not authorized to administer sacraments." In other words, he had not yet been ordained as a minister. There were still a number of Presbyterians in Middelburgh (some of the original settlers having arrived with Doughty in 1641), but they had not been able to afford "to maintain a Presbyterian Preacher." In Heemstede "there are some Independents, also many of our persuasion and Presbyterians. They have also a Presbyterian Preacher named Richard Denton, an honest, pious and learned man." Denton particularly pleased the dominies because he "in all things conformed to our Church." This did not quite please the Independents in the village, who "listen attentively to his preaching, but when he began to baptize the children of such parents as are not members of the church, they sometimes burst out of the Church." Denton had actually left Connecticut for New Netherland because he opposed the limits on baptism placed by New England Congregationalists, who were in the midst of the so-called Half Way Covenant controversy over whether children of church members who had not had the conversion experience expected for full membership could be baptized into the church. Presbyterians like Denton and the Dutch Reformed felt that everyone who lived in their jurisdiction could and should be baptized, whether they were full church members or not. Finally there was the English village at Oostdorp. "The Inhabitants of this place are also Puritans *alias* Independents." Without a preacher, they read "from an English book a sermon" and prayed together. Out of this turbulent mix of religious preferences emerged a powerful series of confrontations over Dutch tolerance.[5]

The existence of the diversity itself did not spur the Dutch into action. It was, after all, what they were accustomed to and perfectly constitutional under liberty of conscience. Only when it upset the public religious order did they move. For example, in February 1652 Megapolensis turned in a petition to the governing council asking that Anna Smith, "Anabaptist, should be restrained from using slanderous and blasphemous expressions against God's word and his servants." The response of Stuyvesant and his council was telling. Smith was not fined or thrown in jail but ordered to "appear on the following Wednesday at the school of David Provoost, where the alderman are accustomed to meet, and that the director and council, together with the petitioner and church council, shall appear there in order to hear what the aforesaid Anna Smits has to say against the teaching of the petitioner."[6] No record of the meeting exists, but she was probably admonished and urged (but not compelled) to leave her Anabaptist views and join the Dutch Reformed Church. The reprimand was a facet of Dutch tolerance in a time and place where the public church was strong and confident. The authorities did not conceive of it as persecution.

Why, then, did the Dutch colonial government begin a forceful suppression of additional manifestations of religious difference in 1656? Petrus Stuyvesant has received much of the historical blame for this, for he oversaw the passage of the ordinance against conventicles by which religious pluralism was quashed and presided over all the punishments of those who violated it. However, he never operated alone. In fact, English Calvinists from Middelburgh spurred him into action. Middelburgh's minister, John Moore, had become "dissatisfied with the meager and irregular payments from his hearers," and at some point in 1655 he "went to Barbadoes, to seek to find another place," perhaps inspired by news of Cromwell's Western Design. In his absence, a religious conflict in the town between "Independents" like Moore and a minority of "Presbyterians" became public. At the end of 1655, the Presbyterians evidently complained to New Amsterdam's dominies that "some unqualified persons" had begun "to hold conventicles and gatherings, and assume teaching of the doctrine." In early January 1656, Megapolensis and Drisius submitted a petition to the colonial council warning that "there is nothing else to be expected than strife, confusion, and disorder in the church and administration; not only in those places but also as a bad example for others belonging to this province." They asked that an English colonist, "a capable person be appointed temporarily who on Sundays can observe some form of the divine service, with readings from the bible and from some other edifying and orthodox author" until further action could be taken.[7]

Stuyvesant and his council agreed with the judgment of the dominies. They ordered the petitioners to return to Middelburgh and, in consultation with "the magistrates and some of the most qualified persons" find "a person capable to serve as a reader." In the meantime, they announced "ordinances shall be issued against" the "conventicles and the assumption of teaching the doctrine by unqualified persons."[8] With this, Stuyvesant also had in mind the Lutherans who had begun to follow the "advice and counsel" of their Amsterdam consistory to "assemble secretly for the observance of your religion, to edify your honors mutually with the reading of some sermons, and to strengthen yourselves in the faith to the glory and honor of God."[9] On February 1, 1656, the governing council issued the new placard, or ordinance, "against practicing any religion other than the Reformed." The law was justified as a response to both Lutheran and English activities: "not only are conventicles and meetings held here and there in this Province," a reference to the Lutheran gatherings, "but also that some unqualified persons in such meetings assume the ministerial office, expounding and explaining the holy word of God without being called or appointed thereto by ecclesiastical or secular authority," a reference to Middelburgh's church. Such unsanctioned preaching was "in direct contravention and opposition to the general civil and ecclesiastical order of our fatherland." If that order was subverted, religious chaos, "many dangerous heresies and schisms" was "to be expected."[10]

It is worth taking a closer look at what this law did and did not do to appreciate the fine distinctions that could be made within Dutch tolerance, keeping it both tolerant and intolerant at the same time, depending on one's point of view. The ordinance forbade "all such conventicles and meetings, whether public or private, differing from the customary and not only lawful but scripturally founded and ordained meetings of the Reformed divine service." The council rested the authority of its action on Scripture, the Synod of Dort, and the practice of "other Reformed churches in Europe." Justifying the law through an appeal to the orthodoxy and legitimacy of the Dutch Reformed Church as well as its international brethren was a clear statement that matters should *not* be handled differently in the colony and Europe. As in the republic, the primary punishment was a fine. One hundred Flemish pounds were charged to any "unqualified" person who assumed "either on Sundays or other days, any office whether of preacher, reader or singer, in such meetings whether public or private, differing from the customary and lawful." Twenty-five pounds was the fine for those caught attending such a meeting. In the republic, fines could be transformed into bribes to the magistrate not to enforce the law. There is no sign of that ever happening in New Netherland.

Stuyvesant's anticonventicle ordinance was a classic statement of Dutch tolerance, forbidding any sort of religious gathering or service that was not Reformed Protestant while simultaneously taking pains to guarantee liberty of conscience, at least as Dutch Calvinists like Stuyvesant understood it. Though all "public and private conventicles and meetings, whether in public or private houses, differing from the oftmentioned customary and ordained Reformed religion" were forbidden, the ordinance did not "intend any constraint of conscience in violation of previously granted patents," a reference to the charters Kieft had granted the English towns. Nor did it "prohibit the reading of God's holy word, family prayers and worship, each in his household." All of these were desirable aspects of behavior for good Reformed Christians and could possibly include some, like Mennonites or Lutherans, who were not Reformed but willing to respect the primacy of the Reformed Church and keep their dissent within the family. Only when they joined with worshipers from beyond their family or household did they risk punishment. No one was required to conform to the Reformed Church. They simply could not pose any visible challenge to it outside the most domestic of spheres. In other words, the ordinance proclaimed that it did not violate the colony's fundamental law of liberty of conscience.

For those, like Stuyvesant, who had been serving in the WIC colonies since the 1630s, the anticonventicle ordinance was not an innovation. It merely gave legal form to what had been the prevailing attitude toward religious diversity everywhere in the WIC's administrative hierarchy as well as the States General before 1650. As Jaap Jacobs points out, the language and dimensions of the 1656 law goes "back to policy documents" drawn up by the Amsterdam Chamber in 1638 to promote colonization in New Netherland, when the directors asserted that it was "of the highest importance, that, in the first commencement and settlement of this population, proper arrangement be made for Divine worship, according to the practice established" in the Dutch republic. The religion that would be preached and taught would be that of the Synod of Dort, "with which every one shall be satisfied and content." Of course, no one was to infer that the official support for the Dutch Reformed Church entailed "that any person shall be hereby in any wise constrained or aggrieved in his conscience." On the contrary, every "man shall be free to live up to his own in peace and decorum; provided he avoid frequenting any forbidden assemblies or conventicles, much less collect or get up any such." The magistrates were given the responsibility for enforcement, and to restrain colonists "from all public scandals and offenses" and to keep the directors abreast of developments "so that confusions and misunderstandings may be timely obviated and prevented."[11] Stuyvesant was thus reiterating a long established official view. How could there be any controversy over his law?

The ordinance was proclaimed immediately—in Dutch. It remained in force until the colony's conquest by the English in 1664. In 1662 it would be reissued in English as well. The sequence is telling. In 1656, the government was concerned with challenges from the Dutch world. By 1662, English Dissenters posed the more serious threat.[12] The English in places like Middelburgh certainly obtained or translated the ordinance into English for use at the local level, but the first to act on it seem to have been the magistrates of Fort Orange and Beverwijck, which had Lutherans but no English Dissenters. They sent to Stuyvesant in early March 1656 "a copy of a certain placard against the congregation of certain persons of the Lutheran sect, published and executed by us against the transgressors and disobedient." By May, new magistrates in Beverwijck had to swear a revised oath adding to the usual pledges of loyalty to the States General, the WIC directors, and the director general that they would "help to maintain here the Reformed Religion according to God's Word and the regulations of the Synod of Dordrecht *and not publicly tolerate any sect*" (the emphasis is from Jacobs). Soon thereafter they fined one Tjerck Claesz six guilders for conducting a Sunday religious service with the Lutherans. Was this a new intolerance, or simply making explicit what had always been implicit?[13]

The WIC directors, prompted by the Lutherans, objected to the placard against conventicles. Several factors fed the Amsterdam directors' reaction, which historians have tended to classify as tolerant, though the term obscures more than it reveals in this case. First, by putting assumptions about orthodoxy into a law and then enforcing that law, Stuyvesant had taken matters to a level that made any sort of connivance much more difficult. Even the pro-Calvinist directors of 1638 had insisted that the director act in consultation with them. Second, the composition of the directors had changed, as had the trans-Atlantic context. In a March 1656 letter to

Stuyvesant, before they knew about the conventicle ordinance, they had chided Stuyvesant for having drafted a capitulation agreement with the Swedes when he conquered New Sweden. They "would have preferred to see, that no such formal capitulation had been made for the surrender of the fort," explaining their "reason for it is specially, that what is written and given in copy can be preserved for a long time and appears occasionally at the most awkward moment, while on the other side the spoken word or deed is forgotten in the course of time or may be interpreted and smoothed over one way or another, as the occasion may seem to demand." Careful not to antagonize Stuyvesant, they explained "we have only wished to make this remark as a rule, if similar situations present themselves in the future." The clash between this attitude and the one that prompted the placard against conventicles explains much of the subsequent story of Dutch tolerance in New Netherland.[14]

The new experience of what the colonial Lutherans would call persecution led them to exploit their transatlantic connections more vigorously than ever before, bearing fruit by the end of spring. Writing in March 1656 to their consistory in Amsterdam, the Lutherans complained that they "were not only actually disturbed and molested" in their meetings, but two of them had been "held in civil detention" (probably the men arrested by Fort Orange's magistrates). Amsterdam's Lutherans now lobbied actively as they had not three years earlier, making their influence felt by June 1656. Changing circumstances in Europe meant at least "some of the Directors of the West India Company" were now more inclined to be friendly to Dutch Lutherans than in 1653. Just days after delegates from the Lutheran consistory brought the law to their attention, the directors protested Stuyvesant's "placard against the Lutherans." Ignoring the other groups and broader principles Stuyvesant also had in mind when he created the ordinance, the directors treated it as a partisan matter directed at the Lutherans, telling him they would "have been better pleased, if you had not published" the placard and imprisoned the Lutherans.[15]

By giving legal form to longstanding assumptions, Stuyvesant's council raised a set of issues that had previously been unspoken and now needed to be addressed. The Amsterdam directors articulated their policy on Lutherans, claiming to Stuyvesant, "it has always been our intention, to treat them quietly and leniently. Hereafter, you will therefore not publish such or similar placards without our knowledge, but you must pass it over quietly and let them have free religious exercises in their houses."[16] At the same time, they told the Lutheran delegates that "in future in the West Indies and New Netherland our religion . . . shall be tolerated by connivance, in the same way it is at the present time tolerated here in this country."[17] The directors could not disapprove of the law in theory, but they were urging Stuyvesant to resist enforcing it. Such was the cornerstone of connivance in Amsterdam.

The Amsterdam directors' rebuke of Stuyvesant was significant. Even if they did not disallow the anticonventicle ordinance or draw up a new, publicly tolerant one, they began to chart a new course of toleration for the colony. By summer, the Reformed classis of Amsterdam was worried "that the Directors of the West India Company had given consent to the public exercise of the Lutheran religion in New Netherland." The directors denied that "they knew of any such complete toleration of the Lutherans there, but neither did they know what more there might be of such designs," refusing to uphold the privileges of the public church as they had earlier.[18] The Amsterdam directors found themselves trying to manage an awkward balancing act between the various parties, none of whom they wanted to offend. Connivance was the hope of at least some of the directors to resolve the dilemma; they gave the Lutheran consistory the distinct impression that through connivance "the door and the way was opened for your honors [the Lutherans] and other Christians living in the territory under the dominion of the said Company, to come and enter upon the free and public exercise of religion." The Lutheran consistory seized on the possibility and offered their help to the Lutheran colonists to find a "regular preacher and spiritual leader." In the meantime, it encouraged the colonists "to hold mutual gatherings in the manner most acceptable to the others, and to conduct themselves in everything quietly and modestly."[19] Such, in brief, was a definition of a successful conventicle. One that was not so obnoxious to the authorities as to be suppressed. Exactly how one could pull that off with magistrates and ministers as vigilant and demanding as in New Netherland was another matter.

The directors and the Lutheran consistory drew an important distinction between formal and informal agitation for tolerance that worked well in the big city of Amsterdam but not so well in the small communities of America. The directors explained to Stuyvesant that only if the Jews made a formal request would they take seriously any complaints about their religious worship. Otherwise they should be allowed to "exercise in all quietness their religion within their houses."[20] Over time this might lead to the construction of hidden houses of worship, as had happened in Amsterdam. Unfortunately, none of the colonists had the subtlety or patience to re-create the roughly forty-year process Amsterdam's Lutherans and Jews had gone through before they could worship in their own buildings. The colonial Lutherans reverted to their frank habits in October, presenting Stuyvesant and his council with a petition "to be permitted to enjoy their own public worship." They misinterpreted the directors' encouragement of con-nivance as an endorsement of public rights, claiming the directors had openly affirmed that Lutheranism "should be tolerated in the West Indies and New Netherland under their jurisdiction, in the same manner as in the Fatherland." They even told Stuyvesant what they intended to do: gathering for "prayer, reading and singing until, as we hope and expect, a qualified person shall come next spring from the Fatherland to be our minister and teacher, and remain here as such." This was not the quiet and humble manner the Lutheran consistory had been urging. Stuyvesant and his coun-cil stalled, agreeing to send the petition to the Amsterdam directors, but proclaiming they would enforce the law against conventicles until they were explicitly ordered not to. The Lutherans then sent Paulus Schrick back to Amsterdam with a copy of their petition and reiterated their request for help from the consistory. They wanted a pastor but they wanted him sent "by order of their High Mightinesses [the Lords Nineteen] as our sover-eigns and the honorable Directors as our patrons, otherwise the governor of this place would send" him "back to Holland."[21] The colonial Lutherans were still operating on the Holy Roman Empire's model of official public tolerance and could not grasp the nuances necessary for connivance in the Dutch world.

In the meantime, Stuyvesant was discovering that not all his local mag-istrates were as compliant with the anticonventicle ordinance as those of Fort Orange. In Vlissingen, one magistrate even contravened it. At some point in summer or early fall 1656, William Wickenden, "a cobbler from Rhode Island" and a "troublesome fellow" (in the words of the Dutch dominies), stepped into the gap left by minister Doughty's departure, say-ing "he had a commission from Christ." William Hallet, the town's schout, a rough equivalent of an English sheriff or the local magistrate in charge of upholding the laws, rather than enforce the ordinance against conventicles, did precisely the opposite. In the words of his later indictment, he "had the audacity to call and allow to be called conventicles and gatherings at his house," allowing Wickenden to preach an "exegesis and interpretation of

God's Holy Word" before accepting communion from him and going down to the river with several others to be baptized by him. The information was provided to New Netherland's council by one of Hallet's English neighbors, prompting them to send out the fiscaal (the Dutch prosecutor and chief court officer) to arrest Hallet and Wickenden and bring them to New Amsterdam for trial. Hallet, "bound to uphold and strictly enforce" the law against conventicles, "not only failed to do" so, but "transgressed and disobeyed" it.

The council dismissed Hallet from his office, charged him with a double fine for setting such a bad example, and sentenced him to be banned from the colony. Wickenden was fined and banished alongside Hallet, though after learning that Wickenden "is a very poor man with a wife and several children and a cobbler by trade, to which he does not properly attend, so that nothing can be obtained from him," the council suspended the fine. However, if Wickenden was "caught here again, he must pay it." Hallet, meanwhile, was "detained in prison, until" his fine and court costs were paid. In December, a repentant Hallet appealed to have the sentence of banishment withdrawn. The council granted the appeal, giving him "permission to earn his living as a private inhabitant quietly and properly within this Province, provided that" he pay the fine and court costs "to which he was condemned." One can interpret the treatment of Hallet and Wickenden as persecution of Baptists, enforcement of a law against subversive gatherings, or both. Either way, it was obvious that the Reformed hegemony of the colony's public church had cracks in it.[22]

Matters brewing in Europe over the winter and spring of 1657 brought more trouble for the public church. The Dutch Reformed classis of Amsterdam anxiously continued to lobby the "worthy burgomasters of the city of Amsterdam as well as the committee of the Directors" of the WIC "to check at the beginning this toleration of all sorts of religions, and especially Lutherans, lest God's Church come to suffer more and more injury as time goes on." Though there is no evidence the directors had anything like it in mind, the members of the classis feared that a toleration of the Lutherans would lead to "toleration of all sorts of religions."[23] Again, the real vision of pluralism in the colony came from those who feared it rather than those who might have favored it. In April 1657, the classis's deputies could "report that they have fulfilled their commission of opposing the free and public exercise of worship by the sects, and in particular, by the Lutherans in New

Netherland" with both the burgomasters and the directors. According to them, "not only have requests to that end been addressed to the Directors," but the directors had been about to adopt a resolution "tending to permit free worship of the sects, by connivance" when the deputies intervened. Through "diligence and labor" they had induced "the gentlemen, by many arguments, and powerful motives, never to consent to the permission by connivance, or in any other way." It worked, "but not so perfectly that it should heal together out of existence." The directors resolved "to abide by the resolution of the preceding year," which they had outlined to Stuyvesant in their June 14, 1656, letter, that the "Lutherans are to be permitted quietly to have their exercises at their own houses." Further importuning of the directors in May and June elicited the promise "to be on their guard against their exercising public worship, and not permit it, but endeavor to prevent it." The directors manifested their resolution through a significant absence, mentioning nothing about religion, tolerance, or connivance to Stuyvesant in their correspondence the entire year of 1657.[24]

Amsterdam's Lutheran consistory, though disappointed that it did not receive a formal grant of toleration, continued to believe that connivance could work in New Amsterdam. Encouragement from certain of the WIC directors seems to have given them hopes. On April 10, 1657, the same day the classis recorded its success in preventing a full toleration for Lutherans in New Netherland, the Lutheran consistory wrote to its fellows in the colony announcing that they were sending Johannes Ernestus Gutwasser (a German, whose name the Dutch rendered Goetwater) to serve as their clandestine minister until a formal approval was granted by the directors. By the beginning of July, Gutwasser was in New Amsterdam.[25]

The Dutch colonists were nowhere near as indulgent of religious diversity as the Amsterdam directors. As soon as the Lutheran minister Gutwasser landed in New Amsterdam, someone informed Megapolensis and Drisius. The dominies sprang into action, drawing up a petition for the recently created town council of New Amsterdam. Protesting that Gutwasser intended to settle "in his official capacity, in this important place," they correctly deduced it was part of a Lutheran plot whereby, "if they obtain a foothold in this place, to extend themselves, which they may then do the more easily, to other parts of this province." If the plot was not "successfully opposed at the beginning," connivance would take hold. If that happened, the colony would face six major problems. First, since Lutherans already had "obstinately and perseveringly" persisted in holding "their separate conventicles" even though it was forbidden, it would lead to lack of respect for the law. Second, it would cause "great contention and discord . . . not only among the inhabitants and citizens in general, but also in families." Already in the previous year, Lutheran husbands of Reformed wives had "forced their wives to leave their own church, and attend their conventicles." Third, it would set a bad precedent for colonial policy. Though there were many Lutherans "in the East Indies, and also, formerly, in Brazil," they had not been granted "the public exercise of their religion." Doubtless, the ministers surmised, this was "because strife in religious matters would produce confusion in political affairs." Fourth, "the number of hearers in our church would be perceptibly diminished." Until now many Lutherans had attended Reformed services and "several" had converted. If Lutheran worship were allowed, they "would separate themselves from us." Fifth, the "treasury of our deacons would be considerably diminished, and become unable to sustain the burdens it has hitherto borne." At present, the Reformed deacons used their poor funds to support all the colony's poor "whatever may be their religious persuasion" (they had done so dutifully, even supporting the poor Jewish refugees when they first arrived). This important social welfare function would be impossible if the Lutherans' money went to a separate Lutheran church. Finally, they reiterated the domino theory: to tolerate the Lutherans would mean that everyone else, "the Papist, Mennonites, and others, would soon make similar claims." New Netherland would become "a Babel of confusion, instead of remaining a united and peaceful people." That would be not just disagreeable but "a plan of Satan to smother this infant, rising congregation, almost in its birth, or at least to obstruct the march of truth in its progress." The use of Satanic imagery was a telling difference between the discourse of the colonial ministers and those in Amsterdam, who always spoke more moderately. They sounded much more like their colleagues in New England.[26]

New Amsterdam's town council responded in a manner to make the Amsterdam classis proud. They immediately summoned Gutwasser and interrogated him, asking with "what intentions he had come to this country." True to the Lutheran type, Gutwasser "frankly answered, he had been sent on behalf of their Consistory, to occupy the position of a preacher here, as far as it would be allowed." He believed a letter of authorization from the directors would arrive any day on the next ship from Amsterdam, giving Lutherans "freedom of religion as in the Fatherland." The magistrates retorted that they "could not believe that" the directors "would tolerate in this place any other doctrine, than the true Reformed Religion." After all, they had all taken an oath "to help maintain the true Reformed Religion, and to suffer no other religion or sects." They accordingly ordered Gutwasser "not to hold public or private exercise in this city, and not to deliver to the congregation, as he called it, the letters" he said he had brought from Amsterdam's Lutheran Consistory "until further orders."[27] Disputing Gutwasser's use of the term "congregation" was not petty. To acknowledge that a Lutheran congregation even existed would be the first step toward recognizing them as a group deserving of toleration.

The town government immediately sent a report to Stuyvesant and his council, along with the petition, as "this is a matter which concerns not only this place, but the whole Province." It requested that "measures may be found, by which the true Reformed Religion will be maintained, and all other sects excluded, that the blessing of the Lord may increase in its flow upon us." In brief, New Amsterdam's magistrates were not the same as Amsterdam's. They wholeheartedly shared the Reformed establishment's vision of a colony united under one church. Stuyvesant and his council agreed "in every particular with the report," ordered magistrates across the colony to republish and continue to enforce the ordinance against conventicles, and ordered Gutwasser "not to hold any conventicles within this province, either directly or indirectly, nor within the same to perform any manner of religious services, whether by preaching or by administering the sacraments."[28] Within days of the Lutheran minister's setting foot on shore, the consolidation of local forces against Lutheran worship was complete.

Having secured the support of the colonial magistrates, the dominies then reported to the classis at the beginning of August. Gutwasser's arrival had been "to the great joy of the Lutherans, but to the special displeasure and uneasiness of the congregation in this place; yea, even the whole country including the English, were displeased." As long as Gutwasser was in town "we had the snake in our bosom." The ministers had urged the magistrates to "send back the Lutheran preacher" on "the same ship in which he had come" to prevent him from forming a Lutheran congregation in the colony. However, Gutwasser had not yet broken any law. Being Lutheran was not illegal in New Netherland. He was allowed to stay, as a private citizen, not a recognized Lutheran minister.[29]

Gutwasser had not expected such a hostile reception. In his version of events, it is clear that he was ignorant of the range of individuals and institutions mobilized against him on both sides of the Atlantic. Gutwasser portrayed Director-General Stuyvesant as the chief obstacle to the toleration of Lutherans in the colony: an interpretation adopted by many historians since. The laws against conventicles designed "to throw a scare among the congregation," that is, the Lutherans. Both the council and "especially" Stuyvesant "listened very little to reason" on the matter. Stuyvesant would not relent until he had heard from both the WIC directors and the States General and "if orders came from both not to molest us here, he would quit his post, as such orders would conflict with his oath." Gutwasser accused the Reformed of having a plot of their own, namely "in time, by sweet whistling, to convert to their religion the children who have been baptized by them" and to prevent the loss of "many incidental benefits" should there be a "separation" from the public church. He was right on both accounts. It was clear that the Lutherans' chances at gaining formal toleration were becoming slim. The sort of connivance through quiet, local persistence that both the consistory and certain directors had hoped for was impossible. None of the colonists on either side would cooperate with it.[30]

Gutwasser's emphasis on the importance of Stuyvesant in shaping colonial policy has been echoed by virtually all historians analyzing the struggles over toleration in New Netherland, and with some reason. According to Joyce Goodfriend, "the distribution of power under the colonial system of governance" helps explain why toleration "was stunted" in the colony. Unlike the Netherlands, where "power was decentralized" and "provincial and municipal authorities held the largest shares in government," in New Netherland "authority was centered in the director and his council. With power essentially vested in one individual (though council members could disagree with him), the religious views of the man who filled the director's office counted disproportionately in determining the degree of toleration present in the colony." A "man of extreme Calvinist views" like Stuyvesant thus could assert his "determination to maintain the dominance of the Reformed church" quite effectively. She claims the burgomasters of New Amsterdam occasionally "tempered" the "anti-Jewish policy" of Stuyvesant and treated Jews in their courts with a "notable" degree of "impartiality." However, being only "recently empowered, they were not in a position to emulate Amsterdam's magistrates in shielding alternative forms of worship in the city."[31] To those on the receiving end of Stuyvesant's justice, like Gutwasser, he must have seemed extraordinarily powerful. However, looking at the great network of allies Stuyvesant had in both the colony and the

Netherlands makes it clear that he was not imposing his own views so much as enforcing a widely held conception of how things should be done in the Dutch world, a Counter-Remonstrant vision that was losing its purchase in Holland by the 1650s but remained strong in the colony.

Johannes Gutwasser tried to work from within the Dutch system, not launch a frontal assault on it. For him it was purely a struggle for privileges for his fellow Lutherans, much as Lutherans had been attempting in the Netherlands for decades. He betrays no awareness or interest in the cause of other non-Reformed colonists, whether Jews or English radicals. His dependence on an explicit grant of toleration from higher authorities meant he could do little more than anxiously await news from Holland. It never came. Instead a letter from his brother arrived, "bearing the superscription 'Lutheran pastor in New Netherland.'" When Gutwasser showed the letter to Stuyvesant and his council on September 4, they were outraged by the superscription's ecclesiastical pretensions to divine office. Now Gutwasser could be accused of claiming to be a pastor and not just a private citizen. They ordered him to "return to the fatherland" on "the first ships" available. His explanation that he had come with the tacit endorsement of the directors was dismissed for lack of "proof from political or ecclesiastical authorities in our fatherland." Gutwasser penned another desperate plea to the consistory, deploring the "continual tragedy which is inflicted upon us by the magistrates of these New Netherland places." He stressed that the Lutherans obeyed the law and "thus far neither hold nor intend to hold any meeting or religious services contrary to the published ordinance." Accustomed to the ways of the Holy Roman Empire, Gutwasser was frustrated by how "in an oligarchical republic the good of all must always mean the loss of the individual." He managed to prolong his stay in New Amsterdam until the beginning of October, maintaining that the ultimate target of Stuyvesant's campaign was not himself, but "the children and young people, who have been baptized by their ministers and whose parents are forced to promise to bring them up in the Reformed Faith." His alternate reading of what the dominies had presented as the advantages an unchallenged public church reflected the Lutherans fears of losing their religion.[32]

The Lutherans tried to play for more time, submitting a petition to Stuyvesant and his council to keep "suspended" Gutwasser orders to leave the colony "until we shall have received further and more definite orders from the fatherland," which they still expected. Five days later, Gutwasser turned in his own petition, in "answer to the repeated verbal and written denunciations or orders to me, to depart from here within three times twenty four hours." Both petitions stressed Gutwasser's obedience to the anticonventicle ordinance, emphasizing how decently and law-abidingly he behaved. He was worried that his "reputation and conduct" would be "endangered" if he followed the order to suddenly leave. He clearly felt he had something at stake in his mission. However, Stuyvesant's council would not indulge the Lutherans. It rejected the petitions, saying the council did "not recognize the Unaltered Augsburg Confession, much less any of the adherents of it" and telling Gutwasser that he "forgets himself and the truth," he should already have left, and ordered him to leave immediately "in one of the two ships about to sail." The colony's governing council reiterated that his departure was "necessary for the honor of God, the advancement of the Reformed Religion, and the common quietness, peace and harmony of this place." Four days later, on October 20, Gutwasser went into hiding.[33]

Shortly after the final encounter with Gutwasser, New Amsterdam's ministers sent another report to the classis. They disparaged the Lutheran petitioners, calling them "the least respectable of that body." As for the respectable Lutherans, "the most influential among them were unwilling to trouble themselves with it." Without certain news from Holland, the ministers were worried by reports that the Amsterdam directors "gave him permission to come over" and asked the classis to ensure that no more Lutheran ministers "be sent over, as it is easier to send out an enemy than afterward to thrust him out." The "magistrates here" promised to "compel him to leave" but when the fiscaal went to remove him, he had "left our jurisdiction." Megapolensis and Drisius believed "that he remains concealed here, in order to write home" for authorization. They feared he would reappear if authorization arrived and in the meantime would "persevere with the Lutherans in his efforts." They looked to the classis to prevent such an authorization from being sent.[34]

Unfortunately for the colonial Lutherans, Stuyvesant's government proved effective at hounding them with the conventicle ordinance. Gutwasser remained in hiding for a year. Had he not fallen ill, he might have stayed in secret much longer. Instead, the Lutherans had to petition to bring him into New Amsterdam for treatment. Stuyvesant agreed, but had the fiscaal watch over him.[35] Gutwasser still managed to escape. This time he gave up his policy of patience and began "to hold meetings and to preach . . . anxious to trouble the waters . . . and with his adherents determined to persevere," according to the Dutch dominies. Not until spring 1659 did colonial officials find, arrest, and pack him off on a ship back to the Netherlands. The Reformed ministers breathed a sigh of relief. "There is now again quietness among the people, and the Lutherans again go to church, as they were formerly accustomed to."[36] Back in Amsterdam, Gutwasser pressed his consistory to petition the directors "as well as others, to obtain as yet, if possible, at least by connivance, the *exercitium nostrae religionis* [exercise of our religion]."[37] Nothing came of it. The supportive words the Lutherans had received from some WIC directors were hollow without cooperation from local authorities. There would be no organized Lutheran Church in New Netherland or anywhere else in the Dutch colonies beyond the Swedish minister Lock on the South River, only "persecution and distress," as one colonist reported back to the consistory in August 1663.[38]

Had New Netherland become intolerant? The defenders of the Reformed establishment could easily argue that they were doing no more than enforcing the laws, including the conventicle law of the previous year. The Amsterdam directors were not pleased with the law, but they did not disallow it. What is clear is that neither the colonial dissidents nor the colonial government was willing or able to engage in the delicate dance of clandestine acceptance and connivance that made Amsterdam seem so openly pluralistic. The Amsterdam directors hoped that something like what they were familiar with could happen in America, but they and the Lutheran consistory had a very difficult time teaching the colonists how to carry it out. Most colonists either did not understand how to do so or deliberately refused. In the view of the Reformed authorities, a single concession would of necessity have to lead to all sorts of concessions. Ironically, they had the greatest vision for toleration and pluralism in Dutch America, and it was their nightmare. It proved a powerful tool for mobilizing against any and all threats to the hegemony of the Reformed Church.

The most extraordinary aspect of the Reformed Protestants' fear that to tolerate one group would by logical necessity lead to the toleration of all groups is that it was not shared by the men most favorable to tolerance in the Dutch world: Amsterdam's magistrates. On the contrary, the whole system of toleration that had evolved in Amsterdam was predicated on making subtle distinctions between different groups, between the Lutherans and the Mennonites and Remonstrants, and among Protestants, Catholics, and Jews. Above all, it depended on putting as little as possible in writing.

Oral promises could be made and retracted, giving magistrates the room for maneuver they liked. Connivance was to a significant degree a sign of their power. They spoke of privileges to worship, not rights to toleration. Thus Lutherans and Jews could have public houses of worship in the city while others had to be satisfied with hidden churches, all depending on the will and favor of the magistrates. The pattern of individual groups attaining specific forms of toleration was typical for the Dutch Republic, where tolerance was not something uniformly, logically, or equally extended to all groups. It was something every group had to fight for on its own, some receiving it and others not, depending on the particular constellation at play in the locality. Scholars repeatedly remark on the lack of consistency in Dutch tolerance, calling it pragmatic rather than theoretically grounded. Yet there were those who perceived and expected a logic and uniformity to Dutch tolerance. They were not those who extended or granted tolerance in any particular instance but those who opposed it. Is that ironic? Or should it give us pause before charging ahead with a narrative about the rise of tolerance? Perhaps it is time to start thinking differently about what we mean by tolerance and how it evolves. The old, Whiggish images of toleration growing over time do not apply in a case like New Netherland. At the same time, one cannot simply dismiss it as intolerant.

Before judging the quality of tolerance in New Netherland, it should be noted what aspects of Dutch tolerance did not exist in the colony. Scholarship on the everyday practice of tolerance in the Netherlands finds that a variety of financial arrangements—loans, bribes, debts, business dealings, blackmail, social welfare—played a rather large role in the experience and progress of tolerance across the Dutch Republic. Depending on who was in charge, the prevailing political and religious atmosphere, or any number of other factors, dissenters from the public church—be they Catholics, Mennonites, Lutherans, or otherwise—could and would be pressured into some sort of financial arrangement to stave off the full power of the law or persecution. There is evidence for this at different times and to varying extents across the Dutch Republic.[39] However, no evidence has yet turned up in New Netherland. If that is indeed the case, New Netherland can be seen as not only an unusually strongly orthodox province, but an unusually principled one as well. It opposed bribery and corruption as much as connivance. Then, in August 1657, its public church was tested by a dramatic new power: the Quakers.

CHAPTER 6

LIBERTY OF CONSCIENCE

The law of love peace and libertie in the states extending to Jewes Turkes
and Egiptians as they are Considered the sonnes of Adam which is the
glory of the outward State of Holland, soe love peace and libertie
extending to all in Christ Jesus Condems hatred warre and bondage.

By the 1650s, the Dutch arrangements that had seemed so progressive to
English radicals fifty years earlier looked conservative compared to what was
then available in the English world. Liberty of conscience, a conservative but-
tress of the Dutch public church, had become a force for revolutionary
change in the hands of radical English Protestants. The sudden arrival of
Quakers in August 1657 provoked the only open debate over the nature of
Dutch tolerance in New Netherland history. For the first time, a new and
positive vision of tolerance was proposed in a document that has gone down
in history as the Flushing Remonstrance. It offered a broad, if idealistic vision
of what pluralism in the Dutch world was and should be, one also tailored to
the needs of Quakers, a new evangelical religion bred in the revolutionary
turmoil of 1640s England. With the Flushing Remonstrance, colonial English
radicals held the Dutch up to these heightened expectations. It was a local
culmination of the longstanding history of religious interactions between the
Dutch and English. Of course, their understanding of what the Dutch were
capable of drew on their knowledge of Amsterdam and Holland, not the
other Dutch provinces. The ensuing clash reflected persistent tensions
between cosmopolitan and provincial approaches to Dutch tolerance as much
as between radical and conservative or even English and Dutch visions.

Since New Netherland was closely connected to and supervised from
Amsterdam, it could not avoid being held up to its example. Yet New

Amsterdam was not like Amsterdam. It was, however, more typically Dutch than that cosmopolitan center of global trade, resembling a small provincial city like Kampen on the republic's eastern frontier. In Kampen, Lutheran ministers were kept out until 1669, dissenting conventicles were repeatedly suppressed, and a strong-willed Calvinist minister, Simon Oomius, dominated the local church. Under Oomius, Kampen's Reformed Church consistently resisted all liberalizing trends that would diminish the position of the public church, much as Megapolensis and Drisisus did in New Amsterdam. Only in the second half of the seventeenth century did Kampen's magistrates gradually adopt a broader connivance, but even then it was reluctant and never on the scale of Amsterdam. Had New Amsterdam remained Dutch after 1664, Kampen provides an example of how religious pluralism could have evolved in the colony: slowly and irregularly.[1]

Of course the eastern provinces of the republic had nothing like the strong English influence that pervaded the lands around New Amsterdam. The case of the Quakers and the Flushing Remonstrance is a reminder that Dutch tolerance was never something fully determined by the Dutch authorities on the ground, regardless of how much legal and political power they wielded. The ideals and aspirations of all the inhabitants played a role as well, keeping it dynamic, contested, and shifting. Unlike the many pamphlet wars and public disputes that fill the history of toleration in Europe, the American struggle took place on a much smaller scale. On the one side was the Dutch Reformed establishment, embodied in the persons of Stuyvesant, the Reformed ministers, local magistrates, and the laws they enforced. On the other side were Quaker missionaries, Quaker propaganda, and a petition, or remonstrance, drawn up by a number of English colonists in Vlissingen in December 1657. The Flushing Remonstrance, as it has come to be known, was never printed. It was transcribed into the court records after Tobias Feake presented it to the Dutch court. Without that copy, there would be no direct evidence of the thinking of at least some of the English colonists in New Netherland about Dutch tolerance. It is a short but invaluable document that opens up a window onto some of the intellectual and religious currents running through Dutch America, even if it was in English.

Minister Gutwasser had anticipated that the next ship in port would bring news from Holland about a grant of toleration for the Lutherans. Instead, it brought Quakers.[2] The Quakers' arrival on August 6, 1657, was a dramatic challenge to the Dutch religious order. As with all aspects of their radical missionary work, there is more than one interpretation of what happened. One gets a sense of the problem from the contrasting accounts of their initial appearance in New Amsterdam. For New Amsterdam's dominies, the Quakers' arrival was full of foreboding. Their ship carried no flag and did not fire a salute on arrival. Its captain refused to pay his respects to Dutch authorities as he dropped off his passengers. The ship continued to New England, probably Rhode Island the ministers guessed, "for that is the receptacle of all sorts of riff-raff people, and is nothing else than the sewer (latrina) of New England. All the cranks of New England retire thither." Rhode Island's reputation for tolerance was clearly not something New Netherland churchmen wanted to associate with. The ministers figured the Quakers would go there because "they are not tolerated by the Independents in any other places." With a sense of approval, they noted that several Quakers had landed in Boston the previous year, "but they were immediately put in prison and then sent back in the same ship." Perhaps this was why they were entering New England through New Netherland, the ministers reasoned. However, "they did not pass from us so hastily, as not to leave some evidences of their having been here."[3]

What came next, according to the Dutch authorities, was a shock and threat to public order. Two "strong young women," Mary Witherhead and Dorothy Waugh, disembarked and "began to quake and go into a frenzy, and cry out loudly in the middle of the street, that men should repent, for the day of judgment was at hand." The Dutch, "not knowing what was the matter, ran to and fro, while one cried 'Fire,' and another something else" until the fiscaal "seized them both by the head" and dragged them off to jail. They "continued to cry out and pray according to their manner" until they were expelled from the colony, restoring peace and order.[4] Such was the Dutch Reformed account, emphasizing chaos, confusion, and fanaticism. The Quaker mission was indeed very public, dramatic, and confrontational. It produced the closest thing to martyrs in New Netherland history in the persons of Robert Hodgson and John Bowne. Indeed, Quaker accounts have done more than any other source to create New Netherland's reputation for persecution.

Quaker accounts convey the religious power and purpose that inspired them to act, as well as a sense of persecution. The "servants of God come for New-England" had not planned to approach the region through New Netherland, as the Dutch thought. Instead, they had been carried by "his providence" to New Amsterdam. Three Quakers (the third was a young man named Robert Hodgson) disembarked because they had "drawings forth into the Town and Countrey to seek the scattered seed." Two "declared in the streets," New Netherland's first experience of what Quakers called a proclamation of religious "Truth in the Streets." The Dutch arrested them and cast them "into miery dungeons apart each from other, where was much Vermine." After about eight days, they were taken out of jail, "having their arms tyed, and rods made fast to them, and two Negroes going with them, until they came at a Boat, which was to go to Road-Iland into which they was put and carried away." The Dutch accounts of course omit these details, but the associations, from the separation to miserable cells to the use of rods, ropes, and "Negroes," all convey the Quakers' sense of mistreatment.[5]

The shock of the Dutch encounter with the Quakers was significant. However, Quakers and their deeds would not have been completely unknown to the colonists. Even if they had not yet actually met a Quaker, they had heard about them. The Quakers themselves were active publicists of their cause, making extraordinarily sophisticated use of printing presses, letters, and petitions to promote their message and advance their movement.[6] News of their actions and tactics had spread to North America before any actual Quakers had. Hence the Dutch ministers could describe the way the first Quakers in New Netherland continued to "cry out and pray" from their prison cells as "according to their manner."[7] One way or another, they had heard of the Quakers' antics. Quaker propaganda was effective among friend and foe alike.

The dominies' response to the Quaker assault highlights their strong sense of connection to Europe. They saw themselves locked in a common struggle with their European counterparts against a diabolical conspiracy, the "machinations of Satan" against "the truth." In the ministers' judgment, the whole incident was a reminder that "the devil is the same everywhere. The same instruments which he uses to disturb the churches in Europe, he employs here in America." This was not a fight between people of more or less religious conviction, nor was it between those who favored tolerance and those who opposed it. God was on all sides in this struggle. In that August of 1657, while the Lutheran minister Gutwasser looked to God to assist "the edification of his believers" and the Quakers let themselves be guided by God's providence, the Dutch ministers trusted "that our God will baffle the designs of the devil, and preserve us in the truth."[8]

In none of these expectations was anything like the word "tolerance" used. Everyone was struggling for the primacy of religious truth, albeit competing truths. Any tolerance that occurred was subsidiary to that goal.

How could toleration even figure in such a fight between conflicting interpretations of the same divine will? The president of Rhode Island's Court of Tryals offered a suggestion in October. As the rest of the Quaker missionaries on Witherhead and Waugh's ship spread across New England, facing a sharpening application of laws designed to keep them out or suppressed, the Rhode Island judge advised a different course. He wrote to the other New England governments that the best way to cope with the Quaker invasion was simply to ignore them, for "they delight to be persecuted by civil powers." He was onto something. Persecution had not yet figured in any of the religious discussions related to New Netherland. The third Quaker who landed with Witherhead and Waugh, Robert Hodgson, brought it out.[9]

Before assessing New Netherland's treatment of the Quakers, it is important to set it in the perspective of the Quaker missionaries' experience elsewhere. Even in Holland with its famed liberty of conscience, Quakers could be mobbed, imprisoned, and banished. In New England, the reception ranged from the murderous extreme of Massachusetts to the benign neglect of Rhode Island. Every New England colony except Rhode Island had laws designed to keep Quakers out. Penalties ranged from fines or imprisonment for those who harbored Quakers or Quaker literature, to banishment, whipping, and branding of Quaker missionaries. The laws were new, responding to the sudden arrival of Quakers in the area. Connecticut was the first colony to legislate against Quakers, in October 1656, before the arrival of any Quakers in the colony. Massachusetts followed, reacting to the arrival of the first Quakers that summer, then Plymouth in 1657 and New Haven in 1658. Ultimately the Quakers were able to establish themselves in places where the church order was weak, like Plymouth and Rhode Island, or where there was a tradition of radical Puritanism, like Salem, Massachusetts, where Roger Williams had been active before going to Rhode Island. Connecticut and New Haven managed to keep Quakers out. Massachusetts kept them contained. There, Quakers were fined, imprisoned, banished, and whipped, had their ears cropped, and finally, most famously and notoriously, executed for returning to the colony after having been banished. Understandably, the struggle in Massachusetts is the focus of most of the sources available for the Quaker mission in America and much of the subsequent scholarship.[10]

The struggle against the Quakers was thus not simply Stuyvesant and the Dutch establishment fighting off a foreign intrusion. They had strong allies among Reformed English colonists. At the same time as Rhode Island's magistracy was advising against taking action in fall 1657, an English magistrate on Long Island was enforcing Stuyvesant's anticonventicle ordinance against Robert Hodgson. From his experience would flow the most notorious story of persecution in New Netherland history, a persecution at English hands as much as Dutch.

Hodgson had not felt compelled to immediately proclaim the truth in the streets along with Witherhead and Waugh. Instead, he "was moved forth amongst the English in these parts, to make known unto them the Gospel of God." He quietly made his way over to Long Island and began meeting with people in the English towns, where a number "gladly received and believed" the Gospel as Hodgson preached it. For about a month and a half, Hodgson operated undisturbed by the Dutch authorities. On September 15, Henry Townsend of Rustdorp was convicted (but not arrested) by his local (English) magistrates for having "called together and been present at the conventicles of Quakers." The "Heathen raged, and the people imagined mischievous things," reported one Quaker account. Around the beginning of October Hodgson was in "Hempsteed" (Heemstede), where he had arranged an outdoor conventicle. He was "walking in an Orchard belonging to such as was willing to receive a meeting" when an officer "laid violent hands upon him, and carried him before" an English magistrate named Richard Gildersleeve. Gildersleeve "committed him prisoner," then "rode to the Dutch-Governor, it being in that Jurisdiction." Here was a fight between conservative and radical English Protestants, one being waged on both sides of the Atlantic. In the Quaker account Gildersleeve had taken "counsel at the baser sort of people," in other words, English colonists who opposed the Quakers. Demeaning the status of those who most strongly opposed them was a common tactic of both sides in the struggle over toleration, but it also betrayed a degree of popular support.[11]

Imprisoned in Gildersleeve's house (actual prisons were rare in New Netherland), Hodgson stood at the window and preached to a crowd gathered outside. Now, instead of a secret conventicle meeting in an orchard, Gildersleeve had a public gathering outside his very house. Assistance came from New Amsterdam in the form of twelve soldiers and the fiscaal. The "guard of Musquetiers" took charge of Hodgson, "searched him and took away his knives, and papers, and Scripture-book, and pinioned him all the night and the next day, so that he had hardly liberty to refresh or rest himself any way." While Hodgson sat in custody, the soldiers "searched strictly for those that had entertained him." Two women were seized, each with children, and put into a cart. Hodgson was tied to the back of it and dragged to New Amsterdam "through the woods in the night-season, whereby he was much torne and abused." The women were soon released from custody and banished to Rhode Island. Hodgson, on the other hand, was thrown into prison ("a nasty Dungeon wherein were many Vermin") to await his trial for violating the conventicle ordinance.[12]

In the Quaker accounts, Hodgson's main struggle was not portrayed as being with Stuyvesant (as it had been for the Lutheran Gutwasser) so much as other Englishmen. The Quakers never mention Stuyvesant by name, nor do they assign him primary blame for Hodgson's suffering. Indeed, the "Dutch Governeur" did not have much of a will of his own. Instead, he was "incensed against" Hodgson "by one Captain Willet of Plymouth," Thomas Willet, one of the English Separatists who had lived in Leiden before settling in Plymouth. In America, Willet had taken advantage of his knowledge of Dutch ways to develop a thriving trade between the English and Dutch colonists. He resided frequently in New Amsterdam and was well integrated into the Dutch colonial elite. After the English conquest of 1664, he would become New York City's first mayor. How much Willet actually influenced Stuyvesant is hard to say. Another Quaker account simply says that Willet "interpreted to" Hodgson the accusation and sentence of the Dutch court. Yet another claims Willet had long held "an implacable enmity against the power of godliness," explaining further that "severall moderate people" thought that Willett, who was a Plymouth Magistrate and thus connected to that colony's persecution of Quakers, "was the cause of" Hodgson's "sufferings." The Dutch sources, on the other hand, offer no light on the matter of whether Willet had anything to do with the Hodgson affair at all.[13]

Hodgson's fate at the hands of Dutch colonial justice formed the material for one of the longer tales of persecution in the Quakers' famous collection of "Sufferings" detailing their early missionary efforts around the Atlantic. Since the Dutch evidence of the proceedings is no more than laconic court sources and the disapproving rhetoric of the Dutch ministers, Hodgson's narrative, transmitted through several Quaker sources over the years, provides a rare personal and visceral account that has played an influential role in forming many historians' assessment of Stuyvesant's character as a persecutor (indeed, that was one of the aims of the Quaker "Sufferings" genre) or as merely an enforcer of law and order. Stuyvesant's current biographer, Jaap Jacobs, is skeptical of Hodgson's version of events. He finds that, though the Quaker story agrees with the Dutch version of events in its broad outlines, "some details in the Quaker publications give the impression that the account has been embroidered upon to emphasize the parallel with Christ's Passion." Given the event's importance in shaping many American historians' understanding of toleration in New Netherland, it deserves close examination.[14]

Was Hodgson persecuted? The nub of the controversy lies in the fact that he was convicted for violating the conventicle ordinance of February 1, 1656, not for being a Quaker. The ordinance explicitly did not "intend to force the consciences of any, to the prejudice of formerly given patents, or to forbid the preaching of God's Holy Word, the use of Family Prayers, and divine services in the family." It only forbade "all public and private conventicles and gatherings, be they in public or private houses, except the already mentioned usual, and authorized religious services of the Reformed."[15] In this, it could claim to be in agreement with existing Dutch law upholding liberty of conscience on both sides of the Atlantic. According to Dutch authorities, then, it was not Hodgson's beliefs that were in question but his inability to keep them to himself. Indeed, he had been allowed to circulate in the colony for weeks before he was caught holding conventicles. As with the Lutheran Gutwasser, the court only took action after he could be accused of forming a separate group for worship.

It is difficult to separate Hodgson's determination to publicly proclaim Quakerism from the court's treatment of him. Stuyvesant was not endeared by Hodgson's manner, which indicated a lack of respect for his authority. When the Quaker refused to remove his hat (a conventional European sign of respect and deference), Stuyvesant had it knocked off. He then gave Hodgson a harsh, but not violent, sentence: "to work two years with a Negro at the Wheel-barrow, or pay a Fine" of six hundred guilders. Hodgson protested. He did not pay the fine. Nor did he work, complaining that he "was not brought up nor used to such Work." Then the violence began. He was whipped "with a pitched Rope." After several days of being whipped and held in prison on a meager diet of bread and water, Hodgson suddenly found himself "marvelously restored to his Strength, and free to labour."[16] In other words, Hodgson started doing the work he had been sentenced to do. The whipping stopped.

Why was Hodgson treated so brutally? Historian George Smith claims it was the "the most barbaric act of religious oppression perpetrated by the Dutch during their time in New Netherland-in fact, their only use of physical force to coerce conscience." Jacobs disagrees. The "excessive violence was applied in the attempts to carry out the sentence, not to make him abandon his Quaker persuasion." It worked. Hodgson started to labor. Nevertheless, there was a religious aspect to the punishment as well. Jeremy Bangs notes that "Reformed governments in Switzerland, while persecuting Mennonites, similarly denied that anyone was ever punished for belief or matters of conscience; obstinate refusal to adhere to civil laws—such as the requirement to swear oaths or the prohibition of religious conventicles outside the official church—had to be punished lest the authority of the magistrates fall into disrepute and civil unrest result." For Bangs, claims that liberty of conscience could coexist with this sort of treatment of ostensible threats to public order are "disingenuous."[17] In such ways Dutch tolerance was and remains contested.

The experience of the Quaker missionaries in New Netherland had parallels, but also important contrasts, in the Dutch Republic, where Quakers had been active for the previous two years. The Quaker mission to Dutch America was an offshoot of the strategy of targeting the English Puritan Diaspora, where the Quaker message found its greatest resonance. Aflame with the missionary zeal of a new religion, Quakers had emerged from a variety of impulses and tendencies unleashed by the English Civil War and Revolution of the 1640s that coalesced around the person of George Fox by 1650. Supported by influential and charismatic allies, Fox's vision had taken root in the north of England by 1653, spread to the south in 1654, then overseas the following year. Holland, with its large community of English and Scottish refugees and immigrants, was one of the first places Quaker missionaries targeted in Europe, while Barbados was their first in the Americas.

That the first Quaker missionaries in New Netherland were two young women and a young man was typical of Quaker missions. Two women, Ann Austin and Mary Fisher, had begun the mission to Barbados and then Massachusetts, where they arrived in the summer of 1656. Promptly expelled from the colony, they were followed two days later by eight other Quakers who came directly from London, who were also quickly expelled. However, men pioneered the Quaker mission to the Netherlands. In fall 1655, two men, John Stubbs and William Caton, moved by the spirit to preach to the Dutch, arrived in Vlissingen, Zeeland, long an important base of the English community in the Netherlands. They proclaimed God's "eternal truth in and through the streets, whether they could understand or no" (the men did not speak Dutch), then moved on to Middelburg and Rotterdam, preaching to English and Scottish congregations in particular, before returning to England. The next year another Quaker (and former Baptist), William Ames, went to Rotterdam and Amsterdam. Ames had learned Dutch while serving on a privateer with Dutch sailors. In Amsterdam, the minister of the English Separatists physically shut him out of the church. Stubbs and Caton soon joined Ames in Amsterdam, which became the base of Quakerism in the Dutch Republic. Though most converts were English and Scots resident in Holland, some Dutch converted, usually Mennonites and Collegiants. Gradually Quakers carved out a small presence in a few Dutch cities, but they did not take the country by storm as they had England.[18]

The arrival of Quakers in New Amsterdam was part of the Quakers' second (and successful) mission to New England in 1657. Whereas the first had aimed straight at the heart of Puritan New England, this time the Quakers worked their way in from the radical fringe. Ten missionaries (four women and six men) were in the ship that dropped off the first Quakers in New Amsterdam. The rest moved on to Rhode Island and Massachusetts. Sources on the Rhode Island mission are few. Many local records were destroyed during King Philip's War in 1676–1677. Nevertheless, the silence is telling. Even in cases where there are few local records the Quakers themselves produced narratives of their "sufferings," as they termed them, at the hand of local persecutors. There are no such "sufferings" recorded for Rhode Island. There are many for Massachusetts.[19]

In Rhode Island, local magistrates interpreted the provincial policy of liberty of conscience as allowing Quakers to preach and convert at will. Though Roger Williams personally despised their doctrines and spoke out against them when he could, Quakers were not fined, imprisoned, banished, or physically punished as they were elsewhere. By 1660, Rhode Island had become the most important Quaker colony in North America. In the words of ministers Megapolensis and Drisius in 1658, Rhode Island, "the caeca latrina of New England," was the "one place in New England where they are tolerated," and it was from there that the Quakers "swarm to and fro sowing their tares." The affinity between Rhode Islanders and a number of the English in New Netherland, some descended from the same group of New England religious refugees (including former supporters of Anne Hutchinson) ensured that events in Rhode Island would have a bigger impact on New Netherland than would Massachusetts, Connecticut, or New Haven.[20]

By contrast with most of their missionary encounters outside Rhode Island, the Quaker experience in New Netherland was quite mild. Hodgson's case was exceptional, with reason. As the first Quaker to organize conventicles, and to refuse to pay the penalty for doing so, the Dutch authorities wanted to make an example of him for the other colonists to "repress the evil in the beginning."[21] The Dutch authorities clearly feared that Hodgson might convert some English colonists through his words and, according to his account, did all they could to prevent him from communicating with them. The court did not allow any English "to come at him for several dayes," telling him "that if he spake to any one he should be punished worse." Nonetheless, "his mouth was opened to such as came about him." Realizing "that he could not be silent," Hodgson claimed "they put him up into the Dungeon, and kept him close several dayes" before having "a strong Negor with rods" flog him. Only after the beatings left him so faint that he was "doubtful of his Life" did the authorities allow "some English" to visit him. An English woman washed his wounds and feared "he could not live till next Morning." The authorities seem to have realized that they were on the verge of creating a martyr. Rather than rendering Quakerism distasteful and unappealing, Hodgson was positioning it as a heroic faith, much as had happened with the early Protestants tormented and executed by the Inquisition in the Netherlands. The principle of carrying out the penalty became less urgent than the need to distance Hodgson from a growing band of supporters. Hodgson worked for a time (no more than a few weeks) and then was set free on condition that he leave New Netherland. He did, going to Plymouth until the prospect of confronting the authorities there persuaded him to settle in Rhode Island. He would, however, return. So would at least one of the women who had pioneered the New Netherland mission with him.[22]

Exactly why Stuyvesant released Hodgson has long been a matter of speculation. By the eighteenth century, Quaker accounts claimed that Stuyvesant was moved by his sister to exercise mercy. The trope is a common one in the Quaker "Sufferings," implying sympathy for, if not downright acceptance of, the cause of the suffering Quaker. None of the contemporary sources contain the anecdote. Megapolensis and Drisius reported that Stuyvesant received a letter about Hodgson "brought by an unknown messenger from a person unknown to the Director-General." The letter, in English, asked Stuyvesant to consider "whether it be not best to send him to Rhode Island, as his labor is hardly worth the cost."[23] Stuyvesant had already banned the other two Quaker missionaries to Rhode Island, along with the women who had attended Hodgson's conventicle. Sending Hodgson there as well could easily have seemed a better alternative than continuing the drama of persecution he was able to stage in New Amsterdam.

Hodgson's release marked a change in Dutch strategy to prevent the spread of Quakerism in the colony. Initially, the hope clearly had been to stop the spread of Quakerism by first expelling Quakers as soon as they made themselves a public nuisance, as with the two female missionaries. This tactic imitated that of Massachusetts's government from the year before. Next came the enforcement of the conventicle ordinance; then rendering Quakers despicable in the eyes of the colonists through exemplary punishment. Hodgson's obstinacy undermined both of these strategies, making more people aware of and sympathetic to his views. Social and legal ostracism within the colony having failed, the Dutch authorities decided that the best way to combat the Quakers was to simply not let them into the colony in the first place.

At some point in fall 1657, probably late October or November, around the time of Hodgson's release, Stuyvesant and his council issued an ordinance, the first and only one in New Netherland that specifically targeted a religious group. The law itself has since been lost. The closest mention of it in a Dutch source is a line from a September 1658 letter from Megapolensis and Drisius complaining about the "raving Quakers": "although our government has issued orders against these fanatics, nevertheless they do not fail to pour forth their venom." Our knowledge of the law comes primarily from the fierce opposition it raised.[24] Typically, the only people subjected to such legislation in the Dutch world were Jesuits and other Catholic priests. Remonstrants had come in for similar treatment for a few years after 1618, but that soon abated. To legislate specifically against another group of Protestants was unusual for the Dutch. Our best record of its content comes from the passionate protest it elicited. The Quakers complained that anyone who hosted a Quaker in his home was subject to a fine "of fifty pounds sterling, for every transgression, although it were but one person one night." Quakers particularly resented that the law encouraged locals to turn informant against them. It allocated "a third part" of the fine and promised anonymity "for the incouragement of base spirits to inform." Quakers and those sympathetic to them resented this last element in particular. For they would be informed on, "notwithstanding many of us did entertain them willingly, suffered them to speak in our houses, for which some were imprisoned, and some fined."[25]

Stuyvesant's council passed the law, but it was not originally their idea. The Dutch were adopting an English policy from their neighbors. Connecticut (in October 1656) and Plymouth (in June 1657) had recently passed similar laws fining those who hosted Quakers in the colony. Maybe the Quakers were right and Thomas Willet of Plymouth passed on the idea for the law, which very much resembled Plymouth's law. The Quakers certainly thought Willett was responsible for a transformation in Dutch policy by "incensing the Dutch Governor with several false reports of them that are called Quakers; for a little before this, Robert [Hodgson] was with the Dutch-Governor, and the Governor was very moderate to him. But since through misinformation, such a deadly enmity is grown up to him [Stuyvesant], that upon all occasions he doth seek to ruinate those that do receive or own the Quakers," singling out in particular the anti-Quaker law that fined those who "receive any Quakers into their houses" and rewarded the informants. According to the Quakers, the law even provided that "if any Vessel should bring a Quaker into their Jurisdiction, it should be forfeited with the goods." The Dutch sources are silent on the law and its origin.[26]

The anti-Quaker law was in effect by December 1657, when two local men, Henry Townsend and John Tilton, were convicted. The two were early and persistent supporters of the Quakers and provided them with a crucial entrée into the Dutch colony. Townsend, already convicted in September for organizing and attending conventicles, was presented to Stuyvesant's court by "twelve of the principal inhabitants" of his hometown of Rustdorp. They claimed, "that the Quakers and their followers are lodged and provided with meat and drink and have an unusual correspondence" in their town, thanks to the hospitality offered them at Townsend's house. Townsend "openly" acknowledged this but did not beg forgiveness. In fact he still had not paid his fine from his September conviction. Now he was condemned to pay an exemplary fine of three hundred guilders and ordered "to remain in prison until the fine has been paid with the costs and mises of law as an example to others." John Tilton, former clerk of 's-Gravesande, was arrested and imprisoned for having "lodged a Quakeress," one of the two who had been "banished from this Province of New Netherland" in

August. Mary Witherhead or Dorothy Waugh had thus returned to the colony and lived in Tilton's house with "some persons of her following, adhering to the abominable sect of Quakers," apparently "neighbors" of Tilton's and doubtless former Baptists. Tilton claimed that the Quakers "came to his house during his absence," begged forgiveness, and was given a reduced fine of twelve guilders. Townsend, like the Quaker missionaries, refused to pay the fines or let others pay the fine for him, "being fearful to wrong a tender Conscience." In the end his wife and friends, concerned for his health, being of "a weakly constitution and sickly" and imprisoned in wintertime, collected "a pair of Oxen, and a Horse although he had no more, and gave them to the persecuters to free him out of their hands." The Quakers had no doubt that they were being persecuted in New Netherland, even if it was just by fines, and imprisonment for the refusal to pay the fines.[27]

The Dutch Reformed did not see themselves as persecutors. They did not whip, brand, imprison, or execute people simply for the beliefs they were known to advocate. They were better than the Spanish Inquisition. Nonetheless, the liberty of conscience they offered was not enough for some of the English inhabitants. The law against hosting Quakers provoked the one great moral and legal protest for religious toleration in New Netherland's history: the Flushing Remonstrance. On December 27, 1657, not long after the convictions of Tilton and Townsend, the magistrates and inhabitants of Vlissingen met in a town meeting and drew up an extraordinary protest, or remonstrance, against the anti-Quaker law. Proclaiming themselves "your Humble Subjects" even as they declared their determination to "houlde to our pattent," thirty-one men signed the remonstrance and sent their schout, Tobias Feake, to read it to Stuyvesant and his council on January 1, 1658. They rested their case on "the Pattent and Charter or our Towne given unto us in the name of the States Generall which wee are not willing to infringe and violate." Feake was "immediately" arrested after presenting the remonstrance. Three other magistrates (Edward Farrington, and William and Edward Hart) were arrested two days later.[28]

The Flushing Remonstrance is a unique source providing an inside look at how at least some of the more radical English colonists conceived of Dutch freedom of conscience. Since the mid-twentieth century, the Remonstrance has attained a rather iconic status as an early testament to American religious freedom. However, there is virtually no acknowledgment of it in any English source from the time. One Quaker account points out that men

in Flushing "met also with hard Measure there from the Dutch Governeur." Here again, Stuyvesant's severity is blamed on "the Instigation of the
said Captain Willet." The account actually goes on to stress the comparative
mildness of New Netherland compared with New England: "this Governeur
soon relented, while those of New-England continued in their severity."
Another recorded that "Tobias Feake and Edward Hart, because they could
not prosecute the Dutch-Governors Order against the Quakers so called,
were cast into prison." Only one version hints at the Remonstrance, noting
that Flushing's magistrates could not "prosecute the Dutch governors
Order against the Quakers in that Town; there [sic] Consciences ingaging
them otherways which they certified by signing a letter to the foresaid Governor giving him grounds sufficiently for what they did." This mention of
"a letter" is perhaps the only direct contemporary reference (that does not
come from the Dutch trial records) to what has become a fabled piece of
New York lore.[29]

How important was the Flushing Remonstrance? Some say it convinced
Stuyvesant to relent in his persecution of the Quakers. Others see in it a
valuable precedent for American religious freedom. In fact, it had no such
impact. There is no indication that it in any way changed the practice and
enforcement of freedom of conscience in New Netherland or anywhere
else. Jacobs notes that the "Flushing Remonstrance was not endowed with
the honor of being a precursor of the Bill of Rights until after World War
II. Its current fame reflects twenty-first century rather than early-modern
ideas."[30] Though the Remonstrance did not change Dutch colonial policy,
it is still an important source of ideas about religious liberty circulating in
New Netherland and evidence of the struggle to expand it beyond what the
colony's Reformed establishment would allow.

The Flushing Remonstrance is of special interest because it was the product of a communal discussion, not an individual thinker. At least two of the
signers, Michael Milner and William Thorne, Sr., had moved to Gravesende
with Lady Deborah Moody in 1643 and subsequently resettled in Flushing,
along with Edward Hart, also an associate of Moody's. While still in Massachusetts, Thorne had been fined for sheltering Anne Hutchinson's son and
son-in-law after they had been banished from Massachusetts. Henry Townsend, already convicted for his Quaker sympathies, also signed the document,
along with his brother John.[31] When the Dutch wanted to find out whose idea
it was, it became clear that it represented the combined views of a number of
Englishmen predisposed toward radical Protestantism, though not a single

sect thereof. Hart, the town clerk, wrote it up, but claimed he merely "gathered the utterances of the people when convened in the town meeting" and wrote it "according to the intentions of the people." It represented "the general votes of the inhabitants," not, as the Dutch authorities feared, the "proposition" or "order" of a single individual.[32] The quality of joint authorship gives the Remonstrance its somewhat incoherent character, mixing an apocalyptic vision and moral theorizing with references to Holland's ecclesiastical policies, all laced with biblical precepts and allusions.[33]

The Flushing Remonstrance argues that liberty of conscience is more than simply allowing people to believe what they believed as long as they kept quiet and did not form conventicles. It claims that freedom of conscience actually prevented a magistrate from persecuting people if his conscience could not justify it. The Remonstrance's definition of persecution differed significantly from Stuyvesant's. For the men of Flushing, persecution was anything that impinged on the religious freedom of movement, expression, and organization of a group they deemed worthy of respect (they did not extend this benefit to all religious groups). In other words, the issue of conscience compelled Vlissingen's magistrates to limit how far they would comply with Stuyvesant's law against conventicles. In the case of Quakers, that was not at all.

The men of Flushing began their remonstrance by calling into question the Dutch Reformed establishment's representation of the Quakers, lamenting that "some" supposed that "the people called Quakers" were "seducers of the people." They doubted the Quakers exerted a malicious influence on the people, saying "wee cannot condem them in this case." They rejected the Dutch establishment's view of the new group and refused to enforce the laws aimed at them: "neither can wee stretch out our hands against them to punish bannish or persecute them." They would not treat Quakers as the first three Quaker missionaries to the colony had been treated.[34] Stuyvesant and his court agreed that it was primarily about the Quakers and not liberty of conscience. When they sentenced Tobias Feake for submitting the Remonstrance, it was in part for his refusal to combat the "sect called Quakers," which it called "heretical and abominable." Quakers "vilify both the political authorities and the Ministers of the Gospel and undermine the State and God's service." They were not to "be tolerated" or "admitted" into the colony.[35] The battle was not simply over the question of toleration per se, but over one's views about the Quakers. The two issues were linked.

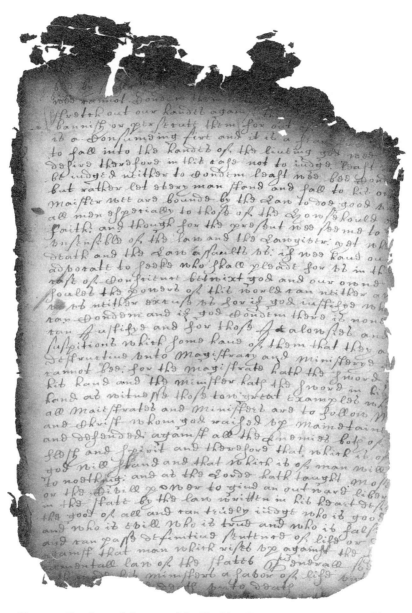

Figure 6. Portions of the text of the Flushing Remonstrance, as entered in the Dutch court records. Courtesy New York State Archives.

... extending to all
... hatred warrs and
... cause our Saviour saith it is
... but that offences will come but woe
... unto him by whom they commeth our desire
... not to offend one of his little ones in what
... wee name or title hee appeares in whether
... Presbiterian independant Baptist or Quaker
... but shall bee glad to see any thing of god in any
... of them: desiring to doe unto all men as wee desire
... all men should doe unto us which is at wee desire
... men both of Church and state for the true
... saith this is the Law and the Prophets
... therefore if any of these said persons come
... lent hands upon them but give them free
... ingresse and egresse into our Towne and houses
... god shall perswade our Consciences and in the
... wee are bounde by the law of god and state
... doe good unto all men and ill to noe man
... this is according to the Pattent and Charter of
... our Towne given unto us in the name of the state
... wee are not willing to infringe
... violate but shall houlde to our Pattent and
... shall remaine your humble subiects the
... inhabitants of Vlishing written this 27th of
... December in the yeare 1657 by mee

                    Edward Heart

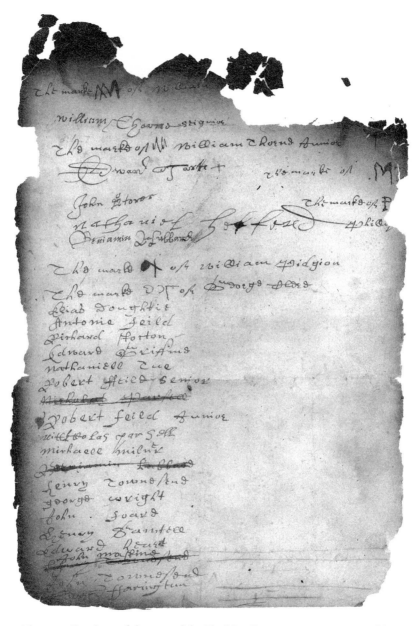

The mark [M] of William

William Thorne senior

The mark of [M] William Thorne Junior

Edward Tarne +   The mark of [M]

John Stover   The mark of [P]

Nathaniel Hefferd   Philip

Beniamin Hubbard

The mark [X] of William Pidgion

The mark [DW] of Edward Heart

Elias Doughtie

Antonie Feild

Richard Horton

Edward Griffine

Nathaniell Tue

Robert Ffield Senior

~~Michael Milner~~

Robert Feild Junior

Nicholas Parsell

Michaell Milner

~~Beniamin Hubbard~~

Henry Townesend

George Wright

John Soard

Edney Ffrantcee

Edward Heart

~~John Mastine~~

John Townesend

John Harrington

Figure 6. Portions of the text of the Flushing Remonstrance, as entered in the Dutch court records. Courtesy New York State Archives.

To justify their defiance, the men of Flushing invoked the higher authority of God. Their God was more intimidating than any Dutch magistrate: "for out of Christ God is a Consuming fire and it is a fearefull [thing] to fall into the handes of the liveing God." They also pointed to the religious uncertainty of the times, which was more an issue for the English, having just experienced a revolution and accompanying explosion of new sects, of which Quakers were just the most notable, than for the Dutch, whose truly revolutionary years in religion and politics lay decades in the past. In Flushing the solution was to leave all religious choice and authority to the individual, dropping all support for the prerogatives of the public church: "wee desire therefore in this case not to judge least wee be judged neither to Condem least wee bee Condemed but rather let every man stand and fall to his own." They justified this by an appeal to biblical "Law," which bound them "to doe good unto all men." This was "especially" the case for "those of the Household of faith."[36] They did not specify exactly who was of the "Household of faith," but the possibilities are not hard to identify. Certainly Protestants. Most definitely those of the "Seeker" sort looking for an improved Protestantism such as the Quakers had to offer; possibly the Dutch Reformed; definitely not Catholics or Jews.

What the Flushing Remonstrance did reveal was the revolutionary potential of conscience to justify disobedience to authority. For these Englishmen, conscience was not a matter of secular law or social peace, as it was for many Dutchmen. According to the Remonstrance, it was a sacred issue for which everyone would be held to account at the court of God. For even if at "present wee seeme to bee unsensible of the law and the Lawgiver: yet when death and the Law assault us: if we have our advocate to seeke who shall pleade for us in this case of Conscience betwixt god and our owne soules." It would not have been difficult for Stuyvesant's council to perceive how divine matters usurped the authority of mere men. After all, "the powers of this world can neither attack us neither excuse us for if god justifye who can Condem and if god Condem there is none can justifye."[37] With salvation at stake, worldly authorities carried little weight.

Authority figures would have easily recognized the Remonstrance's subversive thinking, and could claim it echoed the sort of logic that had brought revolution and regicide to England in the 1640s. Flushing's magistrates were aware of this. They knew that "some" had "Jealowsies and suspitions" of "them" (Quakers presumably) that "they are destructive unto Magistracy and Ministery." This "cannot be," they claimed. Then the signers of the Remonstrance laid out their understanding of the relationship between secular power and religious righteousness, each having distinct power that need not be in conflict: "for the Magistrate hath the Sword in his hand and the Minister hath the Sword in his hand as witnesse those two great examples which all Majestrates and Ministers are to follow, M[oses] and Christ whom god raised up Maintained and defended against all the Enemies both of flesh and spirit." Moses and Christ represented not just secular and religious rule. They also stood for the Old and New Testaments. With the full backing of God, the Christian alliance of secular and religious could not fail. As the Flushing magistrates put it, "that which is of god will stand and that which is of man will [come] to noething."[38] Their vision of a complementary yet separate relationship between church and state was unusual for the time, confined primarily to religious radicals.

The idea of separation of powers contained a very exalted view of the powers of the magistrate—within his limited, nonecclesiastical sphere. Religion, on the other hand, was the preserve of churchmen. Drawing on the Old Testament, the Remonstrance argued the "Lord hath taught Moses, or the Civill power to give an outward libertie in the State by the law written in his heart designed [for] the good of all." Just as the godly rulers of the Netherlands "can truely judge who is good and who is evill who is true and who is false and can pass definitive sentence of life or [death] against that man which rises up against the fundamental law of the States Generall," so did the Lord make "his Ministers a savor of life unto [life] and a savor of death unto death."[39] In other words, it was for the men of the church to decide on religious matters, for they were as weighty as any matter of state. This was quite contrary to Dutch tolerance, which had evolved through magisterial influence over the church (though Counter-Remonstrants in the Dutch Republic still dreamed of a church free of that influence).

Similar views of the separate powers of magistrate and ministers can be found in the writings of a number of early seventeenth-century radical Protestants. In the 1640s Roger Williams had written, "All Civil States, with their Officers of justice in their respective constitutions and administrations are proved essentially Civill, and therefore not Judges, Governours or Defendours of the Spirituall state and Worship."[40] Jeremy Bangs traces the idea's entry into radical English thought to the Dutch Mennonite and historian Pieter Twisck, who participated in a two-day conference with Separatist minister John Robinson in 1617, "after which Robinson supported the theological justification that Twisck had worked out in his book from

1609." According to Bangs, Twisck's was the first book to provide "a history of opinions and arguments in favor of religious toleration," even if it has not drawn the attention of many scholars (perhaps because it was published in Dutch). The title, as Bangs translates it, "says it all":

> *Religion's Freedom, A brief Chronological Description of the Freedom of Religion against the Coercion of Conscience, Drawn from Many Various Books from the Time of Christ to the Year 1609; From which One Can See Clearly . . . How One Should Treat Heretics; That the Steel Sword of the Worldly Government Does Not Extend over Conscience to the Compulsion of Belief; That Heretics and Disbelievers Must Not Be Converted with the Violence of the Worldly Government but with God's Word; That Variety of Religions Does Not Bring Decay or Disruption in a Country or City; That the Kingdom of Christ is Not of This World; And that the Gospel Does Not Have to be Defended with the Sword.*[41]

The men of Flushing were thus drawing on a longstanding tradition among English and Dutch radical Protestants of toleration in their argument for a separation of religious and political authority. It was the product both of very local circumstances, Flushing, New Netherland in 1657, and a transnational experience spanning decades. It contained some radical Dutch ideas, but was not an accurate representation of official Dutch practice.

As the English in Flushing understood it, God had given clear instructions to all secular authorities on the matter of religious freedom. The United Provinces' guarantee of freedom of conscience gave them a special appreciation for this divine dictate. They spoke of the republic's "law of love peace and libertie" and believed it extended beyond the Christian community to "*Jewes Turkes* and *Egiptians*," all meriting tolerance as "sonnes of Adam." The men of Flushing praised this pluralism as "the glory of the outward State of *Holland*." It was a Bible-based and justified religious diversity. They made no mention of the public church.[42]

Where did the Flushing petitioners get their understanding of Dutch tolerance? Jeremy Bangs maintains that it was denominationally biased and somewhat dated, being the ideals of Mennonites and Remonstrants from the days before the Synod of Dort changed the Dutch religious landscape. "No longer was it true, even as an ideal" in the republic by the 1650s. After 1618, "Dutch religious toleration had become at least for the meantime an evanescent, unrealized goal." Noting the States General had passed an edict against conventicles in 1619, Bangs concludes, "the law and custom of Holland applicable in New Netherland in 1645, when a charter was granted for Flushing, was no longer what had been conceived in 1579" in the Union of Utrecht. However, most English "were unaware of the changes." They continued to read Dutch publications on toleration, especially by Remonstrants and Mennonites, and were familiar with the Union of Utrecht as it was republished in the histories they read of the Dutch Revolt. "The religious toleration of the Dutch thereby remained famous in England, while toleration mandated by law had become a memory inconsistent with mid-seventeenth century reality."[43] Bangs underestimates the persistent workings of connivance and the flexible possibilities of liberty of conscience, however limited, but he rightly notes that there was a major shift in Dutch tolerance around 1618.

Bangs's point about the mediated and often decontextualized image of Dutch tolerance that prevailed with many Englishmen is important. Indeed, several additional aspects of the Remonstrance situate it within a very English set of concerns that were only loosely tied to Holland. First of all, it was not entirely accurate. There was a growing Jewish community in the republic, but paradoxically, it was precisely because they were regarded as strangers, outside the traditional Dutch community, that they could be granted the religious freedoms they had. They were tolerated not simply as Jews, but as foreign, Portuguese Jews.[44] Second, there was no Muslim community in the Netherlands, be it Turkish or Egyptian. In Western Europe, only Venice had a permanent community of Muslims, all merchants. They were allowed to worship as they saw fit within a particular space, not unlike the Jewish ghetto. Occasionally a Muslim visited the Netherlands and was generally well treated, but no permanent community existed or practiced Islam in the Netherlands in the first half of the seventeenth century.[45] In Dutch Asia, Muslims had to live their faith covertly, much like Catholics. Third, the term "Egyptians" is not exactly clear. Most contemporary Egyptians had been Muslim for centuries by the 1650s, in which case they generally fell under the European category of "Turks." Historian David Voorhees has suggested it is a reference to Gypsies, and that seems the best possible alternative. It was the term used for Gypsies in the Netherlands.[46] Perhaps, in the American colonial context, it was also intended as a reference to Africans or indigenous Americans. Whether Gypsies, Africans, or Americans, the referent was a group of people excluded from the public church, yet not recognized as having a separate church of their own.

Altogether, toleration of *"Jewes Turkes* and *Egiptians"* was a compelling idea, but not quite the Dutch reality. It is, however, reminiscent of a common phrase used by radical English tolerationists since the early seventeenth century. Separatists, Baptists, and, later, Quakers all adopted some combination of this interfaith vision when advocating toleration and denouncing persecution. In fact, it had become something of a stock phrase. For the past several decades, when they spoke of religious freedom, they regularly asserted that toleration should be extended to "Jews, Turks, and pagans" or "Heathens and Pagans, Turkes and Jews" or "Turckes, Jewes, Pagans, and Infidels." Exactly where the idea and phrasing originally came from is unclear, but by the mid-seventeenth century it was a pervasive part of English radical thinking.[47]

Something about Dutch tolerance had inspired certain English radicals to embrace an extreme pluralist vision, at least in theory. The early Baptist leaders Thomas Helwys, John Murton, John Smyth, and Leonard Busher first articulated the argument in print in the 1610s.[48] All these men had spent time in the Netherlands and used Dutch tolerance to criticize England's comparative lack thereof. In 1612 and 1614 they published tracts arguing that religious liberty should be extended to "Jews, Turks, and pagans, so long as they are peaceable, and no malefactors."[49] Baptists and radical Protestants would be the primary advocates of this sort of toleration during the English Revolution in the 1640s and 1650s.[50] Roger Williams wrote in his famous 1644 *Bloudy Tenent of Persecution, for Cause of Conscience* that it "is the will and command of God, that since the coming of his Sonne the Lord Iesus a permission of the most Paganish, Jewish, Turkish or Antichristian consciences and worships, bee granted to all men in all Nations and Countries."[51] In Plymouth colony, a 1645 petition for religious toleration asked for a law to "'allow and maintain full and free tolerance or religion to all men that would preserve the Civil peace, and submit unto Government. And there was no limitation or exception against Turk Jew Papist Arian Socinian Nicholaytan Familist or any other.'" Governor William Bradford and Plymouth's General Court discussed the issue for a full day, but in the end decided not to vote on it, fearing for the colony's reputation for piety if it passed.[52]

It was probably through this set of ideas that the men who signed the Remonstrance got the idea of tolerating "Jews, Turks, and Egyptians." It need not have been a direct inspiration of Roger Williams, who was himself drawing on a preexisting tradition. From the same intellectual and religious heritage, Flushing's inhabitants could come to a similar conclusion without having to rely on any inspiration from Rhode Island. In fact, since Williams occasionally included Catholics in his idea of toleration and the men in Flushing did not, they gave the idea a significantly different twist from Williams. Moreover Williams, who virulently opposed Quakers in print and preaching, strongly disagreed with the Flushing Remonstrance endorsement of Quakers.[53] Finally, both Williams and the men of Flushing differed from the even more radical ideas propounded in Plymouth.

The phrase had its uses. Much as Roman Catholics, like Jogues, exaggerated the degree of religious diversity in the Dutch world to argue for more privileges in a hostile world, so Quakers advocated toleration for all sorts of religions to carve out space for themselves in a world that had never known Quakers before. The Quaker leader George Fox would later advocate religious liberty even for pagans "such as worship sun or moon or stocks and stones." He claimed it was a sin to compel anyone's conscience, whether they were "Jew, or Papist, or Turk, or Heathen, or Protestant, or what sort soever . . . let there be places set up where every one may bring forth his strength, and have free liberty to speak forth his mind and judgment."[54] Radical Protestants, shut out from all official churches, found the concept of a more than Christian pluralism feasible if not appealing. However, it should be pointed out that when these arguments were first made, there were no Jews, Muslims, or pagans living openly as such in Britain.

The idea of tolerating "Jews, Turks, and Egyptians" was a very English one. Dutch writers did not use the phrasing. Of course, if one scans the entire Dutch empire, they were doing it to a certain extent, simply by extending the habits of liberty of conscience overseas, with a few awkward adjustments. For the English, with nothing like the degree of religious diversity of Holland, there was something fascinating about the diverse religious world presided over by the Dutch. Some, like the radicals in Flushing, wanted more of it. Others felt it was already too much. It had already been used to attack the Dutch in the propaganda associated with the first Anglo-Dutch war and was a recurring motif in anti-Dutch propaganda across Europe.[55]

For all its expansive claims, the vision of tolerance expressed in the Flushing Remonstrance was a very Protestant one. The "love peace and libertie" extended "to all in Christ Jesus," suggesting that those who were not or would not become Christians, or who placed the authority of the pope over biblical revelation, did not quite belong. There was almost something millenarian in the Flushing colonists' understanding of Dutch law and its application across the Atlantic. Revelation was not yet over. New improved forms of faith could still be found as God continued to send his messengers abroad. The Remonstrance conveys something of the power and excitement that the Quaker message had for the colonists. They felt that it "Condems hatred warre and bondage."[56] It resonated with their understanding of Scripture and resolved what must have been for some the lifelong quest that had brought them to New Netherland in the first place.

The Remonstrance is not a Quaker text, but it is a very pro-Quaker text. Less a statement about religious freedom in general, it is a clear refusal to condemn Quakers as dangerous and malicious people deserving punishment. The men's reading of the Bible told them that their "Saviour" knew "that offences will come." In other words, it had been predicted that men would continue to offend the word and rule of God. However, God had also warned "woe bee unto him by whom" the offenses "Commeth." They did not want to be those offenders. Their "desire" was to not "offend one of his little ones in what soever forme name or title hee appears." His little ones all appeared in Protestant form, with roots in the Reformed and radical Reformation traditions: "presbiterian independent Baptist or Quaker." No Catholics, Jews, Turks, or Episcopalians. Not even their Lutheran neighbors. In other words, these men knew more or less the direction from which God's truth would come, but they did not believe it would necessarily be confined to a single faith. To play it safe and benefit their own salvation, they would "bee glad to see any thing of god in any of them." These were the sentiments of a Seeker. That a number of the men who signed the document, along with their neighbors, later became Quakers themselves is not surprising.[57]

The men of Flushing favored evangelization—the spreading of religious faith and zeal—as long as it was Protestant and met their requirements of truth. They did not see themselves simply as passive recipients. They actively engaged with whatever was proposed to them. After all, just the year before, several members of the town had been persuaded by Wickenden to become Baptists. Now some were contemplating a move to Quakerism. Invoking the Golden Rule, "desireing to doe unto all men as wee desire all men should doe unto us," they proclaimed "wee cannot in Conscience lay violent hands upon" anyone who comes "in love unto us." On the contrary, hospitality (precisely that which Stuyvesant had outlawed) was obligatory. They must "give them free Egresse and Regresse into our Towne and howses as god shall perswade our Consciences." In their minds, this was "the true law both of Church and State for our Saviour saith this is the Law and the Prophets." Their disobedience of Stuyvesant's ordinance against hosting Quakers was actually a sign that they were profoundly obedient. They were "true subjects both of Church and State" because they followed this Golden Rule, "bounde by the law of god and man to doe good unto all men and evill to noe man."[58] It was not exactly the sort of obedience Stuyvesant had in mind.

The Flushing Remonstrance did include some important new thinking about toleration. Running contrary to the received wisdom of the time (both Catholic and Reformed), it maintained that heresy and religious diversity are not the real offences in God's eyes. Rather, it is persecution that angers God. Though Protestants had long criticized Catholics as persecutors, this was a new twist. Quakers and others would advance it in later years, but in 1657, there were very few people making the case that any sort of religious coercion was offensive to God.[59] Persecution was thus not only cruel and ineffective (the usual argument, made by Coornhert and others in Holland, as well), but it actually caused the wrath of God. In brief, God could accept heresy and religious disunity—something the many Protestants who denounced Catholic persecution and the Spanish Inquisition had yet to accept. Persecution—also known as the enforcement of conformity and unity—was tied up with the many justifications for both an established church in England and the public church in the Netherlands. It also marks a difference from Roger Williams, who advocated separation of church and state not because he wanted a free market for religious beliefs, but because he believed that true religion was spoiled as soon as the state got involved. He wanted to keep the state out so as to keep his religion pure. In Flushing, on the other hand, people clearly are not sure what the true faith is or who God's genuine messenger is. They claim it could be almost anybody—and quite possibly a Quaker. The men in Flushing wanted the chance to be open to a variety of possible truths—and deciding which truths were acceptable was individual choice, perhaps done in consultation with neighbors but free from all other constraints and coercion.

To support their argument, the men of Flushing had cited the Golden Rule, Biblical Law, and the laws of the Dutch Republic. Finally, in more legalistic and political terms, they rested their case on "the Pattent and Charter or our Towne given unto us in the name of the States Generall which wee are not willing to infringe and violate." Proclaiming themselves, "your Humble Subjects," even as they declared their determination to "houlde to our patent."[60] It was a localist argument, indicating that whatever religious freedom it might have implied would be restricted to the bounds of Vlissingen, making it both a liberating document for the town while suggesting it would not threaten the status quo elsewhere in New Netherland. Europe had a number of such localized exceptions to the prevailing religious order—Gluckstadt, Friedrichstadt, and Maastricht to name a few—why not America?

The patent protected liberty of conscience within Vlissingen, but what did that mean for local law enforcement? Edward Farrington together with William and Edward Hart were rather creative in their interpretive reconciliation of liberty of conscience and the obedience due the Dutch government. They actually denied they had disregarded the law. Rather, they had prosecuted it "unto our powers." They did not act out of deliberate "disobedience," for the patent granted them "libertie of Consience: without molistacion either of Majestrat or Minnester." They claimed their Remonstrance had been merely a "petition . . . toe know if that liberty might be granted which was desired," in other words their own understanding of freedom of conscience. They claimed they had expected no more than a "ye or nay" answer from Stuyvesant to their extraordinary document. In the end, they were not revolutionaries. They submitted to the authority of the Dutch court. Begging forgiveness, the three were pardoned and freed upon payment of the court costs.[61]

Stuyvesant and his council understood the Remonstrance very well. Ironically enough, in their rejection of it, they came close to the twentieth-century understanding of its significance, though they did not endorse it. The Dutch magistrates denounced the Remonstrance as a "seditious, mutinous and detestable letter of defiance" that dared to "justify and uphold the abominable sect of Quakers who vilify both the political regents and the teachers of God's word." The next logical step was obvious to a council that knew the Lutheran minister Gutwasser was then in hiding somewhere, waiting for the chance to establish a Lutheran congregation. The Remonstrance "absolutely demanded, that all sects, especially the said abominable sect of Quakers shall and must be tolerated and admitted."[62] Once again, as with the Dutch Reformed reaction to the Lutheran petition campaign, it was those who opposed granting toleration who saw it as inevitably leading to religious pluralism, if not religious freedom.

For the Dutch authorities, what was at stake in this case was less the nature of liberty of conscience than obedience to the law, though, as the Englishmen had pointed out, it could be hard to distinguish between the two. Just as the court had sought to make an example in its punishment of the prior schout of Flushing, William Hallet, for joining Wickenden's Baptist conventicle, it did the same with the new schout, Tobias Feake, accusing him of having "misled" the other magistrates. He was fingered as the "leader and instigator in the conception of" the petition. Like Hallet, his offense was to have advocated acting "directly contrary and repugnant to the . . . orders and placates of the Director-General and Council." The offence was all the greater given "his oath, official position and duty, as a subordinate officer of the General." With his failure to enforce the laws as he was supposed to, he deserved "severe punishment." Feake confessed "his wrongdoing" and promised "hereafter to avoid such errors." Considering this the court dismissed him from his office and sentenced him to be either banished or charged a fine of two hundred guilders in addition to court costs.[63] For Stuyvesant this was a matter of authority and obedience, and he had won. The recalcitrant magistrates of Flushing had recognized the legal authority of Stuyvesant and his council. Scholars familiar with the Dutch practice of law and toleration agree that Stuyvesant was in the right to punish the magistrates who presented him with this petition. They emphasize that it was only the magistrates who were punished, and that punishment was for failing to uphold Dutch law. It was not for their beliefs. Nor was it a refusal of freedom of conscience, which it "was never the intention of director general and council to hamper," according to Jacobs.[64] The problem, of course, was that their beliefs were leading them to defy Dutch law. Not everyone shared the governor's narrow definition of liberty of conscience.

The confrontation with Quakers and their supporters in the final months of 1657 pushed Dutch tolerance in New Netherland to its extremes. It is important to remember that the Dutch distinction between liberty of conscience and public order was not the English way. For an individual to have heretical ideas was not a threat to the Dutch system, as it was for an established church like that of Massachusetts or New Haven, which demanded conformity of belief as well as action. What was a threat was when someone used their belief as license to engage in activities that subverted the dominance of the public church: preaching, ministering sacraments or otherwise performing functions reserved to a properly installed Dutch Reformed minister; gathering in groups small or large as congregations separate from the public church; or proselytizing in public. The Quakers did all three of these things and claimed their conscience drove them to it. In this they pushed up against the various grey zones with which the Dutch Republic cushioned itself from confessional conflict. Not everyone in the Dutch Republic defined liberty of conscience as narrowly as Stuyvesant. However, no more than a few radical Dutch Protestants would advocate the radical vision promoted by the Flushing Remonstrance.

The crackdown on Flushing's magistrates did not put an end to the Quaker campaign for souls in New Netherland. The Dutch Reformed establishment may have gained an immediate point, but it was clear that many of the English were willing to accept, if not join the Quakers. There was little the Dutch could do to stop them. The English towns sat along New Netherland's eastern border with no Dutch settlement or post to guard the frontier. Quakers continued to enter the colony from Rhode Island and colonists continued to aide them. In the meantime, in response to the challenges from dissidents within the colony, WIC directors were about to actively intervene for the first time to shape the nature of the public church.

CHAPTER 7

PUBLIC CHURCH

... henceforth you will use the least offensive and most tolerant means,
so that people of other persuasions may not be deterred from the public
Reformed Church, but in time be induced to listen and finally gained
over to it.

After the hullaballoo over Lutheran conventicling and Quaker proselytizing, the directors of the West India Company shifted their policy for managing religious diversity in New Netherland. Their encouragement of an
Amsterdam-style connivance of a Lutheran conventicle having failed, they
turned to a capacious vision of the colonial public church that diluted its
Calvinist character enough to reduce the provocations driving Lutherans
into a separate congregation. Over the next two years (1658–1660), the
struggle for connivance turned on a crucial function of the public church:
baptism. The directors took a remarkably determined stance on a seemingly
trivial issue. At their insistence, the baptismal formula, the series of questions asked of those who presented a child for baptism, was altered so that
one word in the second question, "alhier," meaning "of this place," was
dropped. Without it, the question asked the parents to accept the Christian
Church as the True Church. Since Lutherans considered their church the
true Christian Church, they could say yes without compunction. With it,
the parents had to acknowledge the Dutch Reformed Church as the one
true Christian Church, something they could not do without betraying
their Lutheranism. Underlying the controversy over this one word (in
Dutch) was a struggle over the overt confessional affiliation of the public
church and all who participated in it. It was also a struggle unique to New
Netherland. The trans-Atlantic Lutheran community had not succeeded in

getting a congregation of its own in America, but in this colony it was forcing the Dutch Reformed to adjust their Calvinist zeal. Unlike the men of Flushing, who had sought to do so by emphasizing local privilege, the Lutherans carved a space for themselves by stressing generic qualities over the specifics of the colony's church.[1]

Baptism was vital because it represented the religious future of the colony. The population was growing rapidly through immigration and birth. Though the vast majority of adults in the colony in the 1650s had been born and raised in Europe, they were beginning to have children. How those children were raised would affect the religious composition of the colony in the second half of the seventeenth century. In the provinces of the republic, like Drenthe and Friesland, where a majority of the population were Reformed, it was in no small part because of the lack of religious alternatives. The public church with all its privileges and opportunities for instruction ensured that Reformed way was the prevailing religious path. In localities without a strong local Mennonite community or Catholic missionary presence, within a generation or two it was very difficult for the inhabitants to be something other than Reformed Protestants. The areas where significant portions of the population were not Reformed lay along the military borderlands in the south and east—Overijssel, Gelderland, and Brabant. All were open to infiltration from neighboring territories. Zeeland was something of an exception in being overwhelmingly (some 95%) Reformed, while Holland was exceptionally mixed, though never equally across the province. If the Calvinists were to prevail in New Netherland, then its religious future could be much more like that of Zeeland or Drenthe than Holland or Gelderland.[2]

The immediate effect of changing the baptismal formula was a temporary quieting of confrontations between Lutheran and Reformed ministers at a time when Amsterdam needed to be on good terms with as many Lutherans as possible—precisely what the directors most desired. For in the same years as the colony's baptismal controversy, the Dutch Republic found itself pulled into a war against Sweden as an ally of Denmark to secure freedom of trade in the Baltic. Lutherans had dominated the Baltic since the early Reformation. In addition to the Lutheran kingdoms of Denmark and Sweden, crucial Hanseatic cities, from Hamburg to Lubeck and Danzig, were dominated by German Lutherans. Since most Lutherans in both Amsterdam and New Netherland were of German and Scandinavian origin, their connection to these powerful patrons and important trading partners of Amsterdam suddenly made them an issue of special consideration for the directors.

Exactly what the directors' intervention on behalf of the Lutherans amounted to was and is debatable. Many have seen in it evidence of the directors' inclination toward tolerance. When the baptismal controversy has been discussed in the past, it tends to be as a brief coda to the Lutheran struggle to establish a congregation, interpreted as a small compensatory concession to the Lutherans. Perhaps it was. It relieved Lutherans of the burden of confronting a confessional choice over what minister Gutwasser identified as the key source of conflict: the children. With the shift in baptismal practice, Lutherans could remain Lutheran even as they participated in the public church, restoring the everyday ecumenicity Frijhoff has suggested existed before the agitation began in 1653, that Lutherans could participate "*as Lutherans* in the life of the Reformed congregation" (his emphasis). The public church after all was the church of everyone in the colony, not just the Calvinists. Frijhoff points out that technically, "the community ritual" of the public church "was recognized *as a full community ritual*, not as a denominational confession of faith" (his emphasis). It was a difficult balance to strike, especially in a place like New Netherland where neither the local magistrates (personified by Stuyvesant) nor the ministers nor even the Lutherans accepted the arrangement, each instead pulling matters toward a denominational end.[3]

The directors did not claim to be promoting toleration of Lutherans in the colony. They repeatedly affirmed that their goal was to make Lutherans more comfortable in the public church and thus more likely to join it eventually. The question remains, why did they zero in on baptism? The fight, in the eyes of Dutch churchmen in Amsterdam and New Amsterdam, was over the degree to which New Netherland could and would be properly Calvinist. For the directors, however, it seems to have been primarily an effort to strengthen the public church. To do so, they had to change its confessional tenor from overtly Calvinist to more generically Protestant, harking back to a Remonstrant, pre-Synod of Dort approach that made the church inclusive and theologically flexible rather than exclusive and theologically strict, as the Counter-Remonstrants had done. That at least one of the directors in charge of implementing the policy had Remonstrant sympathies if he was not (yet) actually Remonstrant lends weight to the claim that this was perhaps not simply a gesture to placate the Lutherans, but also a different vision for the colony's public church, one less Counter-Remonstrant. The directors claimed they were doing no more than bringing the church in line with current thinking and practice in the republic.

What is most striking about the baptismal controversy is the way the directors for the first and only time directly intervened in the management of religious affairs in New Netherland. Hitherto they had allowed the classis and colonial clergy to set the tone for religious life in the colony. Now, for once, the directors rejected the advice of the classis and forced a policy change on Stuyvesant and his ministers, setting a course for a church of a slightly different texture in the future. How and why they did what they did can only be inferred from the existing correspondence. It is clear that the WIC directors, the key players in this part of the story, were not fully unified or consistent in their approach to dealing with the Lutherans, despite the tone of unity they struck in their correspondence with Stuyvesant. Some gave the Lutherans hints that freedom of worship would eventually be a possibility through some sort of connivance. Others told the Reformed classis of Amsterdam that there would be no official recognition of a Lutheran congregation. Exactly who was saying what is still unknown. Discretion and lack of public commitment to a clear course of action was, after all, the style of politics they urged on Stuyvesant. It was characteristic of much Dutch politics, with its constant negotiations and consultations. However, as a group, legally and formally, the directors never embraced open freedom of worship. Instead, they opted for a single, unified public church that included as many colonists as possible. In other words, they favored a Remonstrant-style (albeit not theologically Arminian) public church in a colony where the clergy, administration, and a significant portion of the population clung to the Counter-Remonstrant dream of a strict Calvinist consensus, even if that meant alienating those who had qualms about it.

The broader European context played an important role in this story, which has so far been treated as a debate exclusively between Amsterdam and New Amsterdam. Lutherans and Lutheran powers were very much on the minds of Dutch diplomats and Amsterdam regents and merchants in 1658–1660. A new war between Sweden and Denmark threatened Dutch access to the Baltic Sea, Amsterdam's most important trading zone. Given the Lutheran Church of Amsterdam's connections to Lutheran powers in the Baltic, both German and Scandinavian, and its heightened concern for New Netherland, it seems that the directors wanted above all else to prevent controversy about their treatment of Lutherans. Whether this was tolerance of some sort is debatable. The colonial Lutherans certainly did not think so. The whole affair was very Dutch—a magisterial involvement in church affairs to blunt confessional antagonism, of limited scope in both time and place and an uncertain future. However one chooses to label it, it undoubtedly falls within the realm of Dutch tolerance and deserves a closer look.

The struggle over the baptismal formula was the most obviously political element of the story of Dutch tolerance in America. It brought Amsterdam's secular authorities to intervene openly in colonial church policy for the first time and produced a shift in the tenor of the colonial church. A few years earlier the various trans-Atlantic elements in charge of the colony's religious life had cooperated smoothly to deny the Lutherans' petition for freedom of worship. Now, to make the church of New Netherland a truly public church (in Frijhoff's sense of a community institution), not simply a Reformed congregation with the capacity to coerce conformity (the direction it was headed), the directors had to reduce the extraordinary autonomy the colonial ministers and Amsterdam classis had enjoyed with the colony's religious life thus far. In doing so, they had to pull the Dutch colonial church out of the Counter-Remonstrant-dominated 1620s past and into the more ambiguous present of c. 1660.

In the Netherlands, the public church was becoming more liberal, if only because magistrates were backing away from the Counter-Remonstrant activism of the 1620s. Conventicles and connivance were growing, albeit unevenly and always contested. The situation in the colony, where magistrates (in the persons of Stuyvesant and his council) and ministers agreed on the religious policy to be pursued in their province, and all favored as strict a Calvinist policy as possible, was something that had not been seen in Amsterdam since 1622. In that year, the elections for burgomaster and the city council drove out the strict Calvinists who had placed Amsterdam on the side of the Counter-Remonstrants and the Synod of Dort, and replaced them with several men of more liberal—or Remonstrant-like—sentiments. Thereafter the magistrates of Amsterdam increasingly crossed swords with the fiery Calvinists of the city's Reformed Church consistory and classis. Matters came to a head in 1630. Adrianus Smoutius had long resisted any liberal sentiment in religious policy. He and his colleagues in Amsterdam's church had supported a riot against a Remonstrant conventicle and spoke out harshly against all other conventicles as well. In 1629, when the war against Spain was not going well, Smoutius preached a jeremiad against the political leaders of Amsterdam, suggesting the republic's cause was suffering because the magistrates were not doing enough to support the Calvinist cause. Smoutius had a popular following in the city. His challenges to the authority of the magistrates implied a threat of popular uprising at worst and disrespect of the city's magistrates at least. In January 1630, the city council decided to ban Smoutius from the city. He left at night in a carriage, escorted by thousands of supporters. Two years later, the burgomasters began sending a representative to the meetings of Amsterdam's Reformed Church Consistory, ensuring that it could take no action—especially in hiring or dismissing ministers—that the burgomasters would not approve of. They did not want any more defiant Calvinists.[4]

By 1658 New Amsterdam's church was in a distinctive position compared to most public churches across the Dutch world. Circumstances had conspired to keep it supplied with nothing but strict Calvinist ministers ever since its first minister, Jonas Michaëlius, a correspondent of Smoutius. If anything, the strict Calvinist character of the colonial church had grown even as Calvinist inclinations were curbed in the republic. Michaëlius's successors (Everardus Bogardus, Johannes Megapolensis, Gideon Schaets, Samuel Drisius) carried on the legacy of 1618 in Dutch America until after the English conquest. All four had matured into their faith during the 1620s, the heyday of Counter-Remonstrant influence in the Netherlands. Each manifested an evangelical streak. Zeal for the faith, not careerism, had pushed them out into the Atlantic world. With the support of Director-General Stuyvesant, they kept liberty of conscience within very limited bounds in New Netherland. A strong Calvinist consensus between ministers, magistrates, and a number of New England immigrants provided a powerful unity of purpose for the colony, even if not all the inhabitants fully accepted it.

When the WIC directors began intervening in the management of the colony's church in 1658, their actions had parallels with what had happened in Amsterdam after 1622. They first restricted the extreme Calvinist tendencies of the Dutch churchmen in both the colony and the Amsterdam classis. Eventually, in 1660, they ensured the appointment of ministers who lacked the fiery Calvinism of the older generation and proved more amenable to the directors' demands. As in Amsterdam, the directors never challenged the hegemony of the Reformed Church in society. What they did do is make the "public" character of the church more of a reality than before. To do so they revived aspects of the pre-1618 Remonstrant public church. No mention was made of the question of predestination, the theological issue that had caused the schism in 1618, driving determined Arminian Remonstrants to form a church of their own. Nonetheless, the ability to distinguish between issues that mattered and those that were "indifferent" and thus could be compromised on recalled the spirit of the Remonstrant Church, as did the desire to include as many people as possible within it.

Once again, New Netherland's experience harked back to the republic's earlier history. Under the Remonstrants, the public church had still been a Reformed Protestant institution. The great difference was that it was not exclusively restricted to Calvinists. This had been an effective policy in the first generations after the Reformation, when only a minority of the population were Reformed and not all the Reformed were strict Calvinists. A certain ambiguity in the church's theology and expectations made it easier for a range of people to enter the Dutch Reformed Church without having to commit to a rigorous confession of belief. When Amsterdam's WIC directors diluted the remarkably strict Calvinism of the colonial American church, they did so with an old Remonstrant-era baptismal ceremony. They did so not in the name of tolerance but in the name of public peace, order, and assimilation. If separate congregations would not be connived at by the colonial establishment, then the public church would really have to take on a more public role to keep as many colonists as possible within its orbit. The proposed transformation would be, like the Remonstrant Church had been, more theologically flexible but more ambitiously comprehensive.[5]

The public church was recognized by many on both sides of the Atlantic as an important cultural and social institution, from Stuyvesant, who never ceased to support the recruitment of ever more Reformed ministers, to the directors and many colonists. In the spring of 1660, as Quakers circulated through the English towns, several inhabitants of 's-Gravesande wrote to Stuyvesant asking for a minister for their town. They claimed that "the licentious mode of living, the desecration of the Sabbath, the confusion of religious opinion prevalent in this village" led "many" to grow "cold in the exercise of Christian virtues and almost surpass the heathens, who have no knowledge of God and his commandments." They invoked "the words of the wise King Solomon" that "where prophecy ceases, the people grow savage and licentious." Pointing out that "the fear of the Lord alone holds out promises of temporal and eternal blessing" and confessing that they saw "no means, by which to make a change for the better" the ten men requested Stuyvesant to send "a preacher or pastor . . . that then the glory of God may be spread, the ignorant taught, the simple and innocent strengthened and the licentious refrained. Then we shall be able to live in greater peace and in the fear of the Lord under your Honors' wise administration and government." Stuyvesant and his council were "well pleased with the remonstrance" and promised to find a preacher as soon as circumstances permitted. This request was particularly significant, for it was the town founded by Lady Deborah Moody the Baptist, who had died about a year earlier. Perhaps taking advantage of her passing, these men decided to acquire a minister where they had not yet had one. Unfortunately for them, the moment never arrived. Only well after the English conquest did 's-Gravesande receive a preacher. Nevertheless, the petition reveals a possibility of religious change in New Netherland, of bringing what had been a largely Baptist town into the Dutch Reformed orbit.[6]

The cantankerous response of the colonial ministers to the Lutherans and Quakers in 1657 seems to have convinced the directors that, if the colony's church was to be truly public, it had to be more open to those who were not as strictly Calvinist as the colonial ministers. The current ministers were simply too prone to controversy and confrontation. By April 1658, the Amsterdam directors had stepped in. Since the ministers had hitherto reported to the classis but not to the directors, they asked the classis to "have the perusal of them, or a copy" when their letters arrived in Amsterdam. This was their first serious intervention in the operations of the churchmen. The classis decided to "inform them of the contents of the letters orally; but if the perusal of the letters be insisted on, to grant this to the Directors." When the classis's deputies gave an "account of the letters" to the WIC directors at the beginning of May, the directors "expressed themselves surprised at the character of the correspondence of the church" in the colony. They clearly did not approve and "insisted strongly upon the perusal of the letters." They assured the representatives of the classis that they were inclined to "take action against" the "Lutherans in New Netherland."[7] The result was a new articulation of their policy of tolerance.

The directors' updated policy for the colonial Lutherans came in a letter dated May 20, 1658. Gutwasser was still in hiding (and would be for almost another year), but they believed Stuyvesant had successfully "sent back here the Lutheran preacher." This, they explained, was "not contrary to, but rather in accordance with our good intentions." Their one criticism was that "you might have proceeded less vigorously." In the eyes of the directors, the principal reason the Lutherans in the colony wanted "to separate

from the Reformed Church" was because of the explicitly Calvinist baptismal formula the ministers used in the public church and, "so people of
their persuasion here complain" because the parents "were compelled to
be present at the baptizing of their children." Here the directors wanted the
colonial church to change.[8]

The directors said nothing about tolerating Lutherans by connivance,
which the Lutheran consistory had hoped would be the case. Instead, by
being less strict in the baptismal rite, using an older, "less offensive and
more moderate" formulary than the newer Calvinist one, the directors
hoped the colonial church would be able "not to alienate, but to attract
people of different belief." The urge for Stuyvesant to "use the least offensive and most tolerant means" was not intended to leave those "of other
persuasions" in peace. Rather, it would ensure that they "may not be
deterred from the public Reformed Church, but in time be induced to listen
and finally gained over to it." It was tolerant in the sense of being a less
confrontational approach than that of Stuyvesant and his ministers. However, the goal of an all-encompassing, albeit less doctrinally precise church
also denied Lutherans the right to organize a separate congregation. The
directors wanted Stuyvesant to take it easy on the Lutherans the better to
assimilate them into the Reformed Church. This and nothing further would
be the extent of their formal urgings for tolerance in New Netherland.[9]

Nonetheless, the ambiguity in the Amsterdam directors' stance toward
Lutherans persisted. Certain WIC directors do not seem to have given up
encouraging Lutherans' hopes for formal toleration. On October 23, 1658,
the Lutheran consistory in Amsterdam recorded that it had been granted
"freedom of worship in America" in a September 2 meeting of WIC directors. It was geographically restricted. Lutherans would be allowed to worship along the middle coast of the American mainland "north of the line
from one to ten degrees." One to ten degrees latitude encompasses the area
roughly between the Amazon River and the island of Trinidad, where the
Dutch had some settlements in what is now Guyana. The specification that
it was only for the mainland meant that the grant did not include Curaçao
or any of the other Dutch Caribbean islands. If Lutherans in a Dutch colony
from that part of America asked the Amsterdam consistory for a "competent and devout person" who they would pay for, it was encouraged to
send one out.[10]

News of an alleged grant of religious freedom to Lutherans seems to
have made it to New Netherland by 1660, giving some colonial Lutherans

hope even after Gutwasser had been sent back to Amsterdam. Fort Orange and neighboring Rensselaerswijk had always been an important part of the Lutheran community, even if Gutwasser was never actually able to visit. In September 1660, the minister at Fort Orange warned the classis that the Lutherans were organizing. They had begun "making up subscriptions for the salary of a Lutheran preacher," claiming "that this has been allowed to them by the gentlemen of the West India Company." Rumors of the promises of certain Amsterdam directors evidently still circled in the colony. The minister, dominie Gideon Schaets, implored, "may God prevent" it.[11]

The reasons Dominie Schaets gave for opposing Lutheran gatherings were the same ones his colleagues Megapolensis and Drisius had given earlier. It would divide and weaken the public church and undermine the progress made in absorbing the Lutherans into it. It "would create a great schism among us here in our congregation, which is now at peace." Several Lutherans "are members of our church" and others "are gradually being led to us." The colonial American experience had the potential to break down the confessional independence of the Lutherans, a boon for the Reformed and a horror for the Lutherans. "Some of these are on the point of becoming members, who were at home of different opinions." The "hope of obtaining a Lutheran preacher" only encouraged certain "unstable Lutherans, who do not seem to like any other form of baptism than that according to Luther, and his religion." Without it, "they come again to church." Schaets urged the classis, "faithful guardians of the Israel of God," to "do their best in this matter to protect Christ's sheep against the wolves and foxes, and catch also the young foxes, that they may not injure the vineyard of the Lord," the vines of which were "still very young and tender in this country, and especially in this place." For Schaets as for the rest of the Dutch Reformed establishment in New Netherland, being in a new colonial situation was a chance to maintain unity, not foster diversity.[12]

The directors actually agreed with the colonial ministers on the issue of unity. However, they believed the ministers were responsible for undermining it with their insistence on the purely Calvinist character of the church. The place the directors ultimately determined to intervene, as upholders of the colonial public church, was in its basic function of baptizing children into the Christian community. As everywhere in the Dutch world where Lutherans were not allowed a church or minister of their own, the colonists in New Netherland had to have their children baptized in the Reformed

Church. However, the formulary used in New Netherland had a special Counter-Remonstrant twist not present in all Dutch churches. The second question to the parents or witnesses asked whether they acknowledged the dogma of the Christian Church. However, the New Netherland ministers had been using newer texts that added "of this place" ["alhier"] to empha-size that the child was being baptized in that specific and thus Calvinist Dutch Reformed Church.

Interjecting "alhier" into the baptismal questions was an old Calvinist trick, going back to the struggle with the Remonstrants. In 1613, the Calvin-ist minister of Amsterdam, Petrus Plancius, had used the same formula with "alhier" at baptisms attended by prominent Remonstrants, including leading Remonstrant churchmen Uitenbogaert and Episcopius. If they repeated the formula with "alheir" it was perceived as an admission that they had given up their Remonstrant views in favor of the Calvinist practice of Plancius's church. Uitenbogaert, not suspecting anything, unwittingly reiterated the phrase with the "alhier" once. Rumors quickly spread that the leader of the Remonstrants had gone over to the Calvinists. Uitenbo-gaert had to write a letter to Plancius explicitly denying that this was the case. Episcopius, forewarned, recited from memory a different formula without the "alhier."[13]

At some point, the Lutherans, like the Remonstrants, realized the use of "alhier" was an attempt to surreptitiously incorporate them into the Dutch Reformed Church. One way to get around this was to stay away from the ceremony and send in friends as proxies. At times in Holland parents had sent children as the proxies to accompany their child to be baptized.[14] The colonial authorities did not permit even this bit of connivance. The Luther-ans resented being "compelled to be present" at their children's baptism as much as the new formulary that forced them to say "alhier" and not just of the Christian Church.[15] They wanted to take advantage of the public church as just that—a public church, not a strictly Calvinist one. New Netherland's Reformed establishment rendered it impossible to do so.

The Lutherans were able to draw the attention of the Amsterdam direc-tors to their plight through their stronger contacts with Amsterdam. The directors reacted sympathetically, with a characteristic desire to prevent controversy from flaring up. They pointed out to Stuyvesant, with some pretended humility, that they did "not know how this is, but we are aware, that the Church here does not lay such great stress upon the presence of the parents and witnesses; we think also that the old formulary of baptism is still used in many churches here, as being less offensive and more moderate than the new, and therefore adopted at the beginning of the Reformation as necessary under the circumstances, in order thereby not to alienate, but rather to attract people of different belief."[16] In classic Dutch Republican style, the directors wanted to avoid a confrontation by not pushing things too far. This was not simply a reflexive stance. It grew out of a fondness for how things had been done before 1618 as well as the delicate diplomatic situation in the Baltic. The Lutherans' powerbases abroad were putting strong claims on Amsterdam's attentions. While the directors had not supported the Lutherans' bid for a separate church a few years earlier, now the Lutherans' complaint about the baptismal practices provoked a response.

At this point, it is necessary to examine the Amsterdam directors in more detail than they usually receive in histories of New Netherland. Understanding more about their religious and political inclinations and the context in which they were operating helps explain what they might have been thinking when they urged the colonial church to change its baptismal policy. The directors were men of Amsterdam's elite, living at a very particular time and set of circumstances, and the 1650s and 1660s was a unique era in Dutch history in many ways.

The exact composition and political and religious inclinations of the Amsterdam Chamber of the WIC is virtually impossible to determine. Most of the records that could have helped on this matter were thrown out in the nineteenth century. However, there is one telling factor, and that is who signed the letters from the Amsterdam Chamber to Stuyvesant. In several of the key letters in the unfolding dispute between the directors and Stuyvesant over how to respond to the assertive pluralism in New Netherland, one name stands out: Hans Bontemantel. Bontemantel was one of the wealthiest and most influential members of Amsterdam's elite. A confidant of the great leader of the "True Freedom," Johan de Witt, Bontemantal served as a burgomaster of Amsterdam, a member of the City Council, and regularly, almost every year from 1655 to 1664, as a director in the WIC Amsterdam Chamber. His close identification with the True Freedom would lead to his dismissal from office after De Witt fell from power in 1672. Bontemantal then devoted himself to writing a study of the government of Amsterdam in the years he had served its government, 1653–1672.

Bontemantal was, like all senior office holders, a member of the public church. However, he publicly came out as a Remonstrant in 1682. His wife had always been a Remonstrant, and all of their children were baptized in the Remonstrant Church, even as Bontemantel attended the public church. Whether or not Bontemantel was a closet Remonstrant in the mid-1650s, his instincts certainly favored the Remonstrant way, as the policies he advocated for New Netherland indicate. A cornerstone of that policy was an aversion to dogmatic churchmen.[17]

Bontemantel expressed his attitudes toward uncompromising Calvinists in an outburst at the West India House in Amsterdam in January 1656. According to a report to the Amsterdam City Council, he was clearly upset about the assertiveness of doctrinaire ministers for a number of reasons. The "ecclesiastical hate is a damnable hate," he raged. Where lawyers could be flexible, churchmen simply condemned everything. He believed that "religion was often used as a cover for many evils." He blamed all the political troubles in the republic since the arrival of the Calvinist Duke of Leicester on the instigations of "men of the church." The man who complained about Bontemantel's outburst made it seem "as if he wanted to overthrow all ecclesiastical government." While Bontemantel denied this at the time, the history of Amsterdam's government he wrote after his fall from power made clear his view that preachers should be obedient to magistrates and not stir up trouble for whatever ostensibly religious cause they might advocate. According to Bontemantel, "Burgomasters have the authority to keep preachers within the bounds of respect and obedience regarding the State and the peace and quiet of the inhabitants," citing "numerous resolutions of Holland, such as the resolutions of 18 June and 16 December 1654, 7 November and 5 December 1655," all passed at the same time as New Netherland's ministers began agitating against religious diversity within the colony. If a minister went against those resolutions through ignorance or personal determination, then they could be cashiered, removed from their post, or otherwise punished. He then listed a few cases from the 1650s and 1660s and referenced the famous case of Adrianus Smoutius.[18]

Bontemantel was a colleague of the even more influential Coenraad van Beuningen, the leading Dutch diplomat in the 1650s and 1660s. From a wealthy regent family, Van Beuningen seems to have grown up with a friendly attitude toward Remonstrants, even if he had not actually been baptized as one himself. For a time he had served as Grotius's secretary in Paris. He did not serve as a director of the WIC, though he was a major investor in the VOC. Van Beuningen did serve in the Amsterdam city council between 1658 and 1660. Before that he had been ambassador for the republic to England, Sweden, and from 1655 to 1658, Denmark. After 1660, he would serve for years as the ambassador to France as well as returning to Amsterdam's city council and serving as burgomaster. A friend of Collegiants in the 1650s, toward the end of his life his penchant for mysticism and millenarianism secured his fame as a patron of religious dissent and speculation in Amsterdam.[19]

The exact connection between Van Beuningen, Bontemantel and the other directors in 1658–1660 is not clear, but it existed in some form. Amsterdam was very sensitive to the Baltic trade, which Johan de Witt named the "mother trade" of the republic. Bontemantel's January 1656 outburst had been prompted by concerns over the difficult political situation in the Baltic, where the Lutheran ministers in the Prussian territories were rumored to prefer an alliance with Roman Catholics over one with Calvinists. The directors' sensitivity to the conflict in the Baltic surely had something to do with their consideration for Lutheran sensibilities in the late 1650s. While the New Amsterdam Lutheran community was not particularly powerful or prestigious, the Amsterdam Lutheran community was. It included a number of wealthy and influential merchants, and it retained its ties to the German trading cities and Scandinavia.

The Dutch Republic's connection to Denmark was particularly tight in these years. From 1657 to 1660, Denmark was caught in a desperate war with Sweden for control of the Straights into the Baltic. Had the Dutch not intervened militarily on the side of the Danes in 1658, the Swedes might have gained more than they did, which was the Danish provinces on the northeastern side of the Straights. Swedish control of access to the Baltic would have severely disrupted Dutch trade to the region, on which it depended for many basic supplies, including wheat and timber. It should come as no surprise then, that Amsterdam's Lutherans now had the ear of the city's elite in a way they had not in 1653–1655.

Though the Lutheran petition campaign and subsequent effort to set up a "hidden" congregation under Gutwasser had failed, the efforts had expanded the contact between the colonial Lutherans and the Amsterdam church, and both with Amsterdam's city government and directors of the WIC. Concerned to maintain good relations with Denmark, and sensitive to the tribulations of trade and diplomacy in the Baltic, Amsterdam's burgomasters (some of whom also served at times as WIC directors) may not have wanted to allow Lutheran worship in America, but they certainly wanted to prevent the colonial Calvinists from causing too great an offence

to the Lutheran community in these dicey years. Somehow New Netherland's Lutherans had to be accommodated, if only superficially.

The directors did not portray themselves as urging a drastic change of
policy. They never formally objected to the colonial dominies' efforts to
incorporate Lutherans into the public church. On the contrary, they presented their proposed modification of the baptismal formulary as an opportunity to strengthen it. Their admonishment to Stuyvesant in May was to
"use the least offensive and most tolerant means, so that people of other
persuasions may not be deterred from the public Reformed Church, but in
time be induced to listen and finally gained over to it." Bontemantel ensured
that a postscript was added to a subsequent letter in June that the directors'
"opinions and intentions concerning the Lutherans, to attract them by moderate measures to the Reformed church," had led them to "the conclusion
to direct that hereby not only to use the old formula of baptism there in the
churches but also the phrase 'of here in church' ["alhier"] be entirely omitted, because we believe that thereby these and other dissenters will be satisfied and kept in the Reformed Church." It was a conflict over means rather
than ends. The Lutherans would not have to recite the baptismal formulary
with "alheir." However, they still would have no alternative but to baptize
their children in the public church. Their Lutheranism was not directly
threatened, but their religious future was constrained.[20]

Two weeks after Bontemantel announced the new policy of omitting
"alhier," two more of his colleagues reinforced the weight of the decision.
They remarked, "the legality concerning the formula was not apparent to
us then." Now, however, they were sure that it was "such that it may be
practiced there in such a manner without giving any offence to the Lutherans and other sects." They then sent along an "extract"—evidently a formal
opinion from several Dutch clergymen that has since been lost—to confirm
the propriety of their demand and ordered Stuyvesant and the colonial
clergymen to comply: "we want and desire that the same shall be observed
word for word in the church there, as we have found it to pertain to the
welfare and being of the state." That was the essence of the idea of the
public church, a servant of the state rather than the autonomous religious
institution many Counter-Remonstrants desired.[21]

The Amsterdam directors had authority over New Netherland, but they
could not easily compel the colonial establishment to do as they wished.
After Stuyvesant informed his dominies of the directors' comments, they
responded in August 1658 with an extended denial and a certain arrogant

defiance. In a formal written response to Stuyvesant, Megapolensis and Drisius dismissed the idea that the Lutherans had ever objected to the baptismal formulary or that they had coerced Lutheran parents to attend baptism and thus acknowledge the Reformed Church. They actually raised the problem of youths taking babies in for baptism that had been an issue in Holland years before. Some "young persons, who could hardly carry the child, and who had scarcely more knowledge of religion, baptism, and the vows, than the child itself, brought and presented other young children for baptism." The ministers then announced "from the pulpit, that no half grown youths should present other young children for baptism." Only "those who had arrived at years of discretion" and especially parents, who had a special duty to do so, should do it. Even then—in fact "only last Sabbath"—there continued to be "instances in which neither of the parents are present at the baptism of their child." The ministers felt they had "given sufficient proof that no undue strictness has been used toward the Lutherans in the baptism of their children, but that their own perverseness led them to make false representations to" the directors. In reality, the Lutherans "intend something else," namely to set up a church of their own (the ministers were right about this).[22]

The dominies belittled the problem by insulting the Lutherans. They admitted that "about two years ago one Peter Jansen a stupid northerner, who was neither a Lutheran nor of the Reformed Religion, and who had not intelligence enough to understand the difference between them, nibbled at these questions, but could not give any reasons against them, or receive and try to understand a reason in their favor." As "Paulus Schrick their leader in his wisdom once declared," the Lutherans were Lutherans and would remain so "because their parents and ancestors were Lutherans." The Dutch ministers called them "blind men" for they hardly knew "the teachings of Dr. Luther." They suggested the issue was not really the word "alhier" but the Lutherans' lack of spiritual worth. "We believe that, as the Pharisees were offended at the words of Christ, Matt[hew]. 15:12, 13, so also has it been in this case; that not only a few words in the Form of the administration of baptism, but also the preaching of the divine Word itself was objectionable to them."[23] In short, the Lutherans did not care or even understand enough about the actual baptismal ceremony for a legitimate controversy over it to exist.

The dominies had no intention of changing the baptismal formulary or accommodating Lutheran consciences in any way. Any concession was a step closer to a separate Lutheran congregation, not an expansion of the public church, the dominies believed. The dominies wanted to deny the Lutherans any chance to pretend they were not part of a Reformed community. Even if they left out the word "alhier," they would mean "the true Protestant and Reformed churches" and "not the Papal church," affirmed the dominies—leaving out the possibility of acknowledging the Lutheran church. Finally, "the Form now used has been so long employed," that to change it "in behalf of the Lutherans, may perhaps give offence to our own people."[24] The ministers were dodging the directors' question while asserting their determination to keep the colonial church as publicly Calvinist as possible.

Finally, New Amsterdam's clergymen invoked their own rights of conscience. In respect to the directors' statement that the older baptismal formula was still used in the republic, they agreed that when it came to "help on weaker brethren" it was customary in Scripture and according to several Dutch synods to be "moderate in all minor matters, and give indulgence." However, this was only for that which "does not affect truth and order," not with "reference to the obstinate and perverse," in this case the Lutherans. The dominies could only be as accommodating "as far as is consistent with truth and a good conscience." Since their conscience did not stretch nearly as far as the directors', they boldly opted for insubordination, much as the men of Flushing had a few months earlier. They concluded by deferring to their patrons in Amsterdam, the classis "to whom we are subordinate" and asking them for advice, once again appealing to a religious source of authority instead of the wisdom of the secular directors.[25]

The classis of Amsterdam also objected to the old, generic baptismal formula. However, there was not much they could do to stop the directors once the directors were set on a policy change. After receiving New Amsterdam's ministers' request for advice, the classis affirmed it was "of the opinion that the Brethren must be earnestly admonished not to depart from the customary formulae." The classis would "inform the Directors regarding several matters, as to which it is observed that their Honors are poorly informed," regarding the baptismal policy. It would also beg them "not to attempt to make any alterations in the customary Forms." However, the classis's deputies "noticed when they waited upon" the Amsterdam directors later that month, "that the broaching of this subject would be likely to awaken some displeasure in them." The reason apparently was "because of the small amount of correspondence of the Church there with the Directors." The classis agreed to "postpone addressing" the directors on the matter until it had corresponded more with New Amsterdam's ministers on the topic.[26]

The dominies' flagrant rejection of the directors' proposal provoked the Amsterdam directors into a decisive intervention. They wrote to Stuyvesant in February 1659, sending another copy of their orders "in regard to the Lutherans" of June 19, saying "our intentions are still the same." They saw "no reason, why the preachers there should raise difficulties about it; for it is an order practiced in most of the Reformed churches here." They sent an "open letter" to the ministers and told Stuyvesant to read it first before passing it on to them.[27] The Counter-Remonstrant autonomy of the colony's Dutch Reformed Church was about to end.

At first, it seemed the Lutheran matter might resolve itself to the ministers' satisfaction and their stubborn persistence would pay off. For the rest of 1659, neither Stuyvesant nor the dominies acknowledged the directors' order for a change in policy toward the Lutherans. Then in September the dominies reported on the arrest and deportation of the Lutheran minister Gutwasser, who had begun "to hold meetings and to preach" contrary "to his own solemn promises." There was "now again quietness among the people, and the Lutherans again go to church, as they were formerly accustomed to do." In fact, one of the leaders among the Lutherans who had helped bring Gutwasser over and held conventicles "is now one of the most punctual attendants, and has his pew near to the pulpit." They thanked "God that he has inclined the hearts of the Honorable Directors and those in authority, that the threatened split among the inhabitants, and the imminent injury to this infant church, have been averted by their vigilance and discretion." Stuyvesant, for his part, ordered a "Day of General Fasting and Prayer" in October to beseech God "that He may turn aside His wrath from us, and assist and bless us with His favor." No mention was made of the Lutherans, just a list of "sins of unbelief, dilatoriness in God's service, blaspheming His holy name, desecrating the Sabbath, drunkenness, lasciviousness, whoredom, hate, envy, lies, fraud, luxury, abuse of God's gifts, and many other iniquities," for which the colonists had justly suffered both a disease epidemic and a war with their indigenous neighbors.[28] It was a call to unity and conformity in the midst of many threats.

Not until the end of December 1659 did the directors announced their intention to treat New Amsterdam's church as they had been treating Amsterdam's church. They were going to send over "young preachers" to fill the colony's pulpits. They would not just be men who "lead a good

moral life." They also had to "be of a peaceable and moderate temperament," and they should "not be infected with scruples about unnecessary
forms, which cause more divisions, than edification." These were exactly
the same terms they had been using since the 1630s to describe the desirable
qualities in Amsterdam's ministers after the expulsion of Smoutius. They
were also not the qualities possessed by Megapolensis and Drisius. The
directors singled the two out as being "leaven" of fractiousness, for they
make difficulties in regard to the use of the old formula of baptism without
order from the Classis here." They accused the colonial ministers of innovation, claiming they had changed the baptismal formula "without the order
of the Church generally or of a Classis." In Holland, the "most moderate
preachers" affirmed that the formula was "an insignificant ceremony,
which may be performed or omitted according to circumstances and without hurting one's conscience." Why were the colonial ministers making
such difficulties over it? The Lutherans might "come to church now" and
matters continue "quietly and peaceably," but the directors worried that
things would not remain that way "as long as precise forms and offensive
expressions are not avoided." Megapolensis and Drisius had demonstrated
that they were not "of a peaceable and moderate temperament," and thus
precisely the sort of dominie that Bontemantel and other like-minded
Amsterdam magistrates despised.[29]

The infant nature of the colony justified the directors' intervention into
colonial religious affairs. Where the colonial Reformed establishment felt any
expansion of tolerance in the colony would be disastrous, the directors
argued that precisely because the colonial church was still "so weak and only
beginning to grow," precisionist scruples, what Megapolensis and Drisius
insisted was their conscience, must "be avoided." The directors suggested
that it was the hard line of the Calvinist clergy that threatened to push the
Lutherans to ask "permission to conduct a separate divine service there."
Now was a particularly delicate moment, "for the Lutherans would very
easily obtain the consent of the authorities here upon a complaint and we
[the directors] would have no means of preventing it." The WIC directors,
in other words, did not desire any special toleration of the Lutherans. They
did want to avoid confrontations that might provoke another Lutheran campaign to the magistrates of Amsterdam, the States of Holland, and the States
General. No doubt they feared that, in the midst of the current alliance with
Denmark, long a patron of Amsterdam's Lutheran church, they might be
compelled to recognize the Lutherans' right to worship. The directors

instructed Stuyvesant to "communicate all of this to the aforesaid preachers there and seriously admonish and recommend them to adopt our advice and use the old formula of baptism without waiting for further orders from here. That will allay dissensions in the state and of the church there."[30] As the directors presented it, the accommodation of the Lutherans in the matter of the baptismal formula was not a gesture at a more pluralistic society but rather an effort to prevent one from forming.

For the first time, the WIC directors were overriding Amsterdam's Reformed classis on questions of colonial religious policy. The classis had reached the limits of its influence. Reporting to New Amsterdam's ministers on March 1, 1660, the classis insisted that its deputies had "defended you" to the WIC directors "with all our might." Though the classis urged the ministers "not to depart from the usual Forms," they acknowledged the directors "would gladly see some moderation and laxity allowed on your part, in certain phrases, in the Formula of Baptism." As the directors told the classis deputies, they thought it "might be productive of much good in your locality." The deputies had repeated the claims of New Amsterdam's ministers about the "alleged false accusations of the Lutherans," but it proved counterproductive. The directors expressed "dissatisfaction at the infrequent correspondence of the church in New Netherland with their Honors." The directors were no longer willing to let the colonial church-men operate independently. They "strongly insisted on reading" the letters the ministers had sent the classis, which had no choice but to hand them over. It urged the ministers "to correspond more frequently with their Honors, as occasion may serve" so that "we will not be compelled, as pre-viously, to hand over to their Honors, your letters addressed to us."[31]

Stuyvesant, writing in April 1660, agreed to comply with the directors' orders, though he disagreed with their estimation of the colonial clergy. He was "sorry" to see the directors "so displeased, as your expressions make us presume, with the preachers here, whose zeal in teaching, admonishing and punishing, whose peaceable, and edifying life and conduct" was "agree-able not only to ourselves, but also to the whole community." He prayed, "that God may give them long life for the best of his infant church here," disagreeing with the directors' preference for new, younger ministers. He backed up the ministers as not having "any leaven of innovation or turbu-lence." To protect them, he "withheld" the directors' "expressions" about the dominies, saying he would "continue to do so, in order not to discour-age them in their good and faithful service." Though rejecting the directors' assessment of the clergy, Stuyvesant confirmed that they would observe and carry out the directors' orders with regard to the baptismal formula. To help, he requested "some psalmbooks or special liturgies of the Reformed church or formularies of baptism could be found somewhere and be sent over, in which the words 'here present' ["alhier"] are not used." Stuyvesant would comply, but not undermine the authority of his local church any more than necessary.[32]

The Amsterdam directors took further action even as Stuyvesant composed his response. They first sent "some books" to be used "for the public service," along with some "small psalters, prayers and catechisms, to be distributed and used as proper under the community in each respective place for teaching" for Stuyvesant to "hand to" the ministers. The directors repeated their commands to Stuyvesant, informing him also that they had secured the compliance of the two new ministers, Hermanus Blom and Henricus Selijns, with "the old formula of baptism." The two men affirmed what the directors wanted to hear, denying that "they would make difficulties about using it . . . considering it a matter of no importance and engaged themselves to make use of it in the exercise of their clerical duties." Along with Blom and Selijns went "notes, to be given to dominies Megapolensis and Drisius, that they too may use it at the proper occasions and carry out our good intentions and wishes, which they must not oppose." The Amsterdam directors did not trust the colonial ministers as Stuyvesant did. Continuing refusal "would displease us," they emphasized, "on account of the loss and injury to the province and the church there." A dent was made in the Counter-Remonstrant Dutch American church. It was still Reformed, but could not be as militantly Calvinist as before.[33]

The Lords Nineteen of the WIC, the superiors to the Amsterdam Chamber, shared its views on the supremacy of the Dutch Reformed Church in America. They had assured the Amsterdam classis in February 1660 that "from the beginning, they had established the rule, that only the Reformed Religion should be exercised" in New Netherland. They approved of Stuyvesant's "being very vigilant in that work" and claimed they "would not be backward in promoting the success of the same." When the classis checked with the directors again in 1661 after getting Schaets's complaint about Lutheran organizing at Fort Orange, the directors repeated that "they knew nothing" of promises made to the Lutherans that they "might institute public religious gatherings in the West Indies, or introduce a pastor or pastors," which the Lutheran consistory had recorded back in fall 1658, and had not "given their consent to such a thing." They reiterated their expectation that Stuyvesant "would not endure the existence of the Lutherans, if they should grow too bold." The classis told Schaets to "inform the good people concerning this, that they may dismiss their newly conceived hopes, since they may find abundant edification and comfort of soul, through the blessing of the Lord, in the Reformed worship, if they hearken diligently, an endeavor to walk before God and men with a good conscience." The message was clear. Colonial Dutch Lutherans would not be compelled to convert, but they would not be encouraged to remain Lutheran or allowed to worship as such. Instead of granting the Lutherans what they wanted, freedom of worship, the directors insisted only that the less explicitly Calvinist version of the baptismal formula be used so that Lutherans need not feel threatened with loss of their faith every time they baptized their children. It was a subtle distinction, but one that meant a good deal to both the directors and the Dutch Reformed churchmen who resisted it. Though done in the name of coping with the Lutherans, the baptismal modification was primarily a fight over theological tactics in the public church.[34]

The directors got their way. Samuel Drisius, Megapolensis's less polemical comrade, informed the classis of the colonial ministers' capitulation to the directors in October 1660. He expressed a sense of disappointment in the failure of the classis to change the directors' mind. "Our hope was that your Honorable body would have mediated with the Honorable Directors" in the matter of dropping "alhier" from the baptismal questions. However, "we cannot perceive this from your letter" of March 1, "much less from that of the Honorable Directors." The classis's insistence that the colonial ministers "adhere to the Formula" did not "change the opinion" of the directors "that we indulge in no unnecessary precision in matters of indifference; neither does it regain their approbation, or meet the intentions they have expressed." They had required Stuyvesant, "the Director-General to declare to us, in their name, that they simply demand that the old Formula should be used and observed by us, without any farther orders from Amsterdam, and without any farther opposition." The directors had outmaneuvered the dominies, gaining the approval of "several ministers in the Fatherland" who "judged it to be indifferent whether we use or omit the word 'alhier'" as well as the consent of dominies Blom and Selijns to use the "books which contain the old Formulas" that had been sent over.[35]

The directors' position was, to some extent, tolerant, for it removed a source of irritation to the Lutherans. Yet they did so precisely to deny the

Lutherans a motive for forming conventicles. As they insisted to the colonial administration, "greater evils may arise, and easily bring greater injuries to the church, by the formation of separate assemblies of other denominations." Deeming "it best" and embracing "the design of avoiding any division in the churches in this country" Drisius informed the classis that New Amsterdam's church would obey the directors and "use the old Formula," even though the classis objected. As if to smooth over the differences, Drisius went on to tell of a thirty-year-old Mennonite who was considering converting and becoming a member of the Reformed Church. His question was, did the man need to be rebaptized, or could they accept his Mennonite baptism? The classis responded that Dutch practice was to accept the baptism of "Papists" and Mennonites. As long as they made a "confession of their faith" they could become members. There was still hope for bringing other Christians into the public church.[36]

The controversy over the baptismal formula to be used in the colony's public church might seem a small matter. After all, it was just one word (in Dutch—three in English). Yet the controversy gets at some of the key issues at the heart of Dutch tolerance: the degree of magisterial influence in the functioning of the public church; the relationship between the public church and those who were not Reformed Protestants; the resulting variety of local religious arrangements. At stake was the religious future of New Netherland, which had preserved a strong Counter-Remonstrant flavor much longer than much of the rest of the Dutch world. If the Lutherans spoke the word "alhier," it implied they acknowledged the superiority of the colony's very Calvinist Reformed Church to their own and publicly began the process of abandoning Lutheranism. For the Reformed ministers of the public church this of course made sense. In the colonies as in Europe, baptism was the first step toward integrating the non-Reformed into the Reformed Church. Even if the parents did not fully embrace it, their children, in the absence of an alternative Lutheran Church, might very well do so as they grew up in the shelter of the public church. Ideally, within a generation or so, the Lutheran community would be absorbed into a unified Calvinist one.

The directors' solution of using a less obviously Calvinist formulary signaled that the New Amsterdam church was no longer to be overseen by Counter-Remonstrants alone. The directors insisted they did so explicitly to discourage the Lutherans of New Amsterdam from forming a separate congregation as they had been struggling to do for the previous ten years. In theory, then, the directors supported the Dutch Reformed ministers and classis in the ambition to convert as many Lutherans as possible. In practice, of course, the colonial Lutherans could now baptize their children as Protestant Christians in the public church without fear of being forced to abjure their faith and embrace Calvinism. The degree to which this let them continue to be Lutheran is ambiguous. Without a minister and congregation of their own there was only so much they could do. After the failed effort to let Gutwasser quietly get a Lutheran congregation going in the colony, the new policy helped quiet Lutheran resentment and activism, an important goal for the directors during the Baltic crisis of 1658–1660. Amsterdam needed to stay on good terms with the king of Denmark, a patron of Amsterdam's Lutherans. For the next few years, the policy seemed to work. There is no further mention of Lutheran challenges to hegemony in the remaining correspondence from either side.

Regarding the workings of Dutch tolerance more generally, it should be emphasized that this change in the baptismal formula, taken by many historians as a sign of the directors' tolerant inclinations, was made only in response to political pressures from within and without Amsterdam. Moreover, as so often in the Dutch world, it was a local and limited adjustment. The directors of the WIC did not make a general policy out of the shift in New Netherland. Elsewhere in the Americas, without an organized Lutheran community to challenge the baptismal formulary, the "customary Form" approved by the classis of Amsterdam with "alhier" continued to be used. New Netherland remained a distinct case.[37]

For the colonial Lutherans, the solution was less than fully satisfactory. New Netherland's Lutheran community benefited from its longstanding and increasing links with Amsterdam to retain a strong sense of what Lutherans could attain in the Dutch world. In 1663 a Lutheran colonist who had arrived only two years earlier sent an appeal to the Amsterdam consistory for help—the first such since Gutwasser had left in 1659. Hendrick Bosch, the writer, portrayed all the colonial Lutherans as intimately familiar with the "persecution and distress the Church of Christ, from the beginning until now, has had to endure and suffer." He noted with some irony that the suffering came "particularly from those who call themselves also members of Christ's" church, in other words, the Reformed ministers and magistrates of the public church. Bosch had lived in Leiden and knew how Amsterdam's Lutheran consistory had helped the Lutherans there. He implored them "to lend us the helping hand, in order that we may be provided with a pious, godly, and learned man." Though the Lutherans in America had not given up hope "that some day we may be rightly helped," many were beginning "to stray like sheep," that is, they were joining the Reformed Church. The rest "dare not come together here to offer any sign of devotion, much less trust themselves jointly to sign a petition to your honors, for fear of being betrayed." Sent in August the letter arrived at the Amsterdam consistory in October 1663. It was the last effort by Lutherans to form a congregation in Dutch North America. Before the consistory could act on Bosch's request—indeed, before anyone could really know what the impact of the new baptismal formula would have been on the Dutch religious community—the English conquered the colony and liberated the Lutherans from the public church.[38]

CHAPTER 8

BORDERS

He [the Jesuit Simon Le Moyne] has several times accompanied the Indians out of their own country, and visited Fort Orange. At length he came here to the Manhattans, doubtless at the invitation of Papists living here, especially for the sake of the French privateers, who are Papists, and have arrived here with a good prize.

The greatest challenge to the Calvinist hegemony in New Netherland came not from the Lutherans or Mennonites within the colony, nor from the directors in Amsterdam. Rather, it crossed the borders. Like much of the Dutch world, New Netherland was surrounded by neighbors of different religions. Jesuits entered from the north, via New France, and helped sustain the faith of the handful of Catholics in the colony. Quakers crossed in from the east, from Rhode Island, and made many converts among the English on Long Island. On the southwestern border, there had been the Swedish Lutheran colony of New Sweden and there still was the Catholic English colony of Maryland. Of course the harbor of New Amsterdam was open to ships from across the Atlantic world. This included ships that brought zealous Quaker missionaries, as well as French Catholic privateers. At the same time, borders offered the possibility of expelling religious dissidents from the colony, as had happened to the Lutheran minister Gutwasser, the Baptist Wickenden, and the first Quaker missionaries. The porous borders of the Dutch world ensured that Dutch religion did not develop in isolation. The story of religious diversity in New Netherland cannot be told without reference to its colonial neighbors.

As most places in the Dutch world were fairly close to an international border, borders arguably played a much more influential role for the Dutch than, say, the French, Spanish, or English. Until 1674, this was especially so because the frontiers of the entire Dutch world were extremely unstable: what was Dutch and where kept changing. Even in America, the borders of Dutch territory were in dispute. The southern frontier of New Netherland was challenged by New Sweden and then Maryland. The eastern frontier was contested by Connecticut and New Haven. New Netherland originally had encompassed the coast up to Narragansett Bay, but the intrusion of hundreds of English colonists made that untenable. Stuyvesant's government negotiated the Hartford Treaty with Connecticut in 1650 to create a clear eastern boundary between New Netherland and the English colonies. Though not recognized in Europe, the border proved fairly stable locally. After the English conquest it became, with small changes, the border between New York and Connecticut and, on Long Island, between today's Nassau and Suffolk counties.

The political and military uncertainty of what was and was not within the Dutch world meant that individuals were constantly moving in and out of those borders whether they willed it or not. Conquest brought various peoples into the Dutch world: Catholics in Europe and Brazil; Muslims, Buddhists, and Hindus in Asia. The result was a politically and culturally important phenomenon: individuals—often, but not always, men—who served as religious agents of other faiths and crossed into Dutch territory from neighboring foreign lands in order to proselytize or maintain the faith of non-Reformed peoples who had fallen under Dutch rule. In this way, priests, missionaries, and others who were not permitted by Dutch laws to live in Dutch territory or assemble a congregation, could prevent their co-religionists from completely dissolving into the public church by making forays to preach to, pray with, teach, and perform religious services for people, like Roman Catholics, who otherwise were denied those aspects of worship by the public church. They too formed a part of Dutch tolerance.

Borders were not just shifting lines or a frontier between Dutch and non-Dutch territory. There were various enclaves and exclaves, especially in Europe. Batavia, capital of the Dutch Asian empire, could be considered an enclave, surrounded by a sometimes hostile sultanate and linked by sea with other Dutch enclaves, the trading posts and islands scattered from Japan to Persia. Within the Dutch Republic, enclaves existed along the eastern and southern frontiers, small fiefdoms or portions of other territories that had never been acquired by the Hapsburgs and thus were not taken over by the Dutch rebels even when they controlled the land all about them.

Ravenstein, where Lutherans could get their Bible printed, was one of the most important. The enclaves remained part of the Holy Roman Empire until the French Revolution. In North America, "enclave" is one way to think of the Dutch position amid various Native American groups. The Dutch claimed from the Connecticut to the Delaware River valleys, but in reality they exercised direct control only over the few scattered European settlements within those borders. Native towns and villages surrounded the Dutch outposts. The indigenous settlements occasionally hosted religious dissidents from the Dutch Reformed order, like the Jesuits.

Finally, there were those who neither accepted Dutch conquest nor sneaked into Dutch territory to contest it but sought spiritual sustenance in neighboring lands. The Dutch Republic is famous as a country of immigrants and refugees from religious persecution. However the air of the republic did not hold the same sweetness for everyone. Roman Catholics, for example, had fled the advance of Dutch troops since the 1570s. They would do so in Brazil and Asia as well. Remonstrants fled abroad to Friedrichstadt in Schleswig-Holstein, after they lost their struggle for control of the Dutch Reformed Church in 1618. Indeed, during the dark days of the struggle for independence in the 1560s and 1570s, exile to neighboring lands had been crucial to the survival and formation of the Dutch Reformed Church, whose earliest synods were held in the German cities of Emden, East Friesland, and Wesel, Cleves. Protestant and Catholic dissidents who remained in the republic could always cross a border and find a friendly reception in neighboring territories. Along the southern border, Catholics developed traditions of pilgrimage to an enclave or Spanish held territory. In the east, Remonstrants in Nijmegen like Willemken van Wanray crossed the nearby border into the principality of Cleve to hear a Remonstrant minister preach during their time of persecution after 1618. Every faith in the Dutch world drew strength on connections and refuge across a nearby border somewhere.[1]

Catholics

Awareness of the possibilities offered by New Netherland's borders played a role in the Lutheran minister Johannes Gutwasser's struggle to form a congregation. When matters had become too hot for him in New Amsterdam in October 1657, the Lutherans sent him "quietly away to a farmer" in Middelburgh. Gutwasser explained to his consistory, "in order to save myself from violence, I have, with the consent of the congregation, been obliged to flee from the island of the Manhates to a colony, where I now reside." His congregants elaborated on the strategy. If Gutwasser were to "be further persecuted by the Director General and Council, we shall send him outside the jurisdiction, being about 6 or 8 miles away, under the jurisdiction of the English, to stay there until your honors send us a complete license from the fatherland to practice our religion here unmolested." In other words, if Dutch magistrates came looking for him, he could escape east into the English part of Long Island. Since he never did, one can only wonder how New England would have reacted to the sudden arrival of a German Lutheran minister.[2]

The Lutheran efforts to form a congregation provide much of the information we have about their community in New Netherland. Without the visits from Jesuits based out of New France, we would know virtually nothing about the existence of Roman Catholics in the colony, though there were some. Friendly relations between the French and Dutch made these visits possible in a way a visit from a Spanish Jesuit would not have been, for example. France was one of the oldest allies of the Republic, and remained so for almost a century after 1579. Thus, when the governors of New France agreed to open Quebec to trade with the Dutch in 1658, it was "as friends and allies of the Crown." Commerce did not lead to mutual religious liberty. New France was reserved for Roman Catholics much as New Netherland was for Protestants. Dutch Reformed visitors to New France were explicitly forbidden "the public exercise on land of their religion, which is contrary to the Romish." They would have to keep their worship on their ships.[3]

Isaac Jogues's 1643 visit was the first of a series by Jesuits to the Dutch colony. Had New Netherland not been conquered by the English, a situation resembling that of the republic could have evolved, where Jesuit and other missionary priests regularly crossed from its Catholic neighbors, infiltrating the republic to serve the needs of the Roman Catholics, who were not officially allowed a church of their own and could not create their own priests. As it was, the Jesuits who arrived came mostly by chance, as war captives and refugees from the Iroquois. A certain amount of pan-European solidarity in Native America created an affinity between Jesuits like Jogues and the Dutch colonists who helped them out of captivity. Freed by the Dutch commandant at Fort Orange, Jogues was smuggled to New Amsterdam, where he met a Polish Lutheran "lad." The youth "fell at his feet, taking his hand to kiss them, and exclaiming, 'Martyr, Martyr of Jesus Christ!'" Jogues "could not aid" his young admirer "for want of acquaintance with his language," though he considered it. They were "in a retired place." In the end, the only religious service he performed was to confess a Catholic Irishman. This was the first Roman Catholic priestly function performed in New Netherland. From such clandestine beginnings more could come.[4]

Iroquois warriors captured another Jesuit, Francesco Giuseppe Bressani, in 1644, the year after Jogues escaped. Ransomed to the Dutch, he too soon returned to New France and its missionary work. Bressani's account suggests how the religious conflict and competition of Europe permeated the American frontier. Though the Dutch had ransomed him, Bressani held them responsible for various "persecutions" the Jesuits faced in their missionary work. The "English, Dutch, and other heretical Europeans" who traded with the indigenous peoples had told them many things that rendered the Jesuit mission more difficult. The Protestants said the Jesuits were "wicked people, pernicious to the public weal, expelled from their countries, where, if they had us, they would put us to death; and that we had now fled to those lands in order to ruin them as soon as possible." The Dutch taught the Mohawks to "hate the sign of the holy Cross," calling it "a veritable superstition." They killed one French captive expressly because he had made the sign. Sympathy for captive Jesuits did not translate into an ecumenical spirit on the frontier.[5]

The third Jesuit to enter New Netherland came away with a more positive experience of the Dutch. Mohawks captured Joseph Poncet in August 1653. Soon thereafter, they made peace with the French, and conveyed Poncet to Fort Orange to begin his journey back to Canada. At Fort Orange, Poncet met two Catholics, a Brussels merchant and a young Frenchman acting as an interpreter for the Dutch. Several other colonists who were not Catholics, including "a good Walloon" and a "good Scotch lady," treated Poncet quite hospitably. He stayed in Fort Orange for a mere two weeks before heading back to Canada. Nevertheless, in that short stay he bolstered the Catholicism of the Catholics he met and laid the groundwork for friendly relations with the community—always a valuable asset for a missionary. He administered confession to the merchant from Brussels, whom he found to be "a good Catholic." The young French interpreter "set his conscience in order during the three nights that I spent with him under the roof" of one of his hosts. The Dutch officer in charge of the fort was clearly not happy to have a Jesuit around. He received Poncet "very coldly." None-theless, the kind treatment he received from the colonists left a strong impression. Poncet wrote, "I had to promise them to come back and see them the next Summer, so much affection and kindness did they manifest toward me." He did not return. Had he done so, he might have had a friendly place to stay and perhaps proselytize.[6]

Megapolensis, who had served at Rennselaerswyck and Fort Orange before settling at New Amsterdam, recognized the potential threat posed by the increasing contacts with New France and its Jesuits to the public church. In September 1658, he outlined the extent of Jesuit incursions into New Netherland, urging the classis to send "two more learned and godly ministers in this province" because "the Jesuits in Canada or Nova Francia are seeking to force an entrance among us, and introduce their idolatries and superstitions." First had been Jogues, about whom he had no com-plaints. Then Bressani, who had written a letter thanking Megapolensis for his help in which he said (according to Megapolensis) "that he had not argued, when with me, on the subject of religion, yet he had felt deeply interested in me on account of my favors to him; that he was anxious for the life of my soul, and admonished me to come again into the Papal Church from which I had separated myself." Megapolensis "returned such a reply that a second letter was never sent me." Megapolensis made no mention of Poncet.[7] He might have been unaware of his stay, since Poncet was in Fort Orange after Megapolensis had transferred to New Amsterdam. Had Megapolensis known of his activities, it is not difficult to imagine how he would have reacted.

The third Jesuit Megapolensis mentioned was Simon Le Moyne. Le Moyne was the first Jesuit to arrive in the colony in peace and dignity, not as a war captive. He came in fall 1657. Until then, the Mohawks' many wars with the French had kept Jesuits away from the Dutch frontier, providing a better shield against Catholic infiltration than any Dutch laws ever could. However, "when the French made peace with our Indians, the Mohawks, several Jesuits went among them, and have since continued there. One of them named Simon Le Moyne has been several times at Fort Orange, and last fall came here to Manhattan." Like most Calvinists, Megapolensis was suspicious of Jesuits. Le Moyne's journey to New Amsterdam was "doubt-less to encourage the papists, both Dutch and French, residing here, and to observe the condition of our affairs. He remained here eight days, and then returned to Fort Orange, and thence by land to Canada."[8] Megapolensis suspected Le Moyne was making first steps toward some sort of mission to the Dutch colony. After all, his Jesuit mission among the Mohawks was only "about four or five days journey from Fort Orange" and he "has several times accompanied the Indians out of their own country, and visited Fort Orange." A second letter claimed Le Moyne's visit to Manhattan was "doubtless at the invitation of Papists living here, especially for the sake of the French privateers, who are Papists, and have arrived here with a good prize," implying that Le Moyne had secret Catholic intelligence networks that spanned New Netherland. During his "eight days" in New Amsterdam, Megapolensis claimed Le Moyne "examined everything in our midst. He then liberally dispensed his indulgences, for he said to the Papists (in the hearing of one of our people who understood French) that they need not go to Rome; that he had as full power from the Pope to forgive their sins, as if they were to go to Rome."[9]

Megapolensis's personal encounter with Le Moyne gives a glimpse of the way religious issues could be discussed, and possibilities of conversion broached, when Jesuits were around. Raised a Catholic in the north of Holland and having studied with Jesuits before converting at the age of twenty-three, Megapolensis knew he was a likely target. When Le Moyne flattered him, telling him "he had heard the other Jesuits speak much of me, who had also highly praised me for the favors and benefits I had shown them" and saying he could not "neglect personally to pay his respects to me, and thank me for the kindness extended to their Society," Megapolensis responded with a disputatious disposition. After Le Moyne said "he had lived about twenty years among the Indians," Megapolensis "asked what fruit had resulted from his labors, and whether he had taught the Indians anything more than to make the sign of the cross, and such like superstitions." Le Moyne avoided an overt religious debate, saying he "wanted only to chat." However, on his way back to Mohawk Country, Le Moyne stopped at Fort Orange and sent Megapolensis three manuscripts he had composed, first "on the succession of the Popes; the second, on the Councils; and the third was about heresies, all written out by himself. He sent with them also, a letter to me, in which he exhorted me to peruse carefully these Catalogues, and meditate on them, and that Christ hanging on the Cross, was still ready to receive me, if penitent." The Dutch dominie answered with an extended point-by-point rebuttal in Latin, full of the polemical fire of a mature convert, accusing Roman Catholics of being idolaters and the true heretics, Jesuits of turning indigenous proselytes not into

Christians but only into papists, and many popes of having been "impious, atheist, epicurian, magicians," and otherwise less than respectable Christians men, including "sodomites."[10]

Megapolensis had personal reasons to be more sensitive to the Catholic threat than others. However, his reactions fit very well with Dutch policy toward Catholics in Europe and the colonies. Catholic individuals could and did live in Dutch territory, but were not allowed to practice their religion publicly. Catholics everywhere from Brabant to Batavia were deemed to be legitimate objects of proselytization by the Dutch Reformed Church. In fact, where the Dutch took over former Portuguese colonies, such as in Ceylon, Catholics often formed the majority of converts. Because the Dutch Reformed hoped to bring the Catholics to their camp, they looked on Jesuits and other Catholic priests with suspicion and discouraged them from performing their duties as much as possible. Even the Chinese in Batavia had more rights than Catholics. In the peace negotiations of 1648, as in the truce negotiations of 1609, the Dutch rejected Spanish proposals for toleration of Catholic worship. It was not an impossible arrangement. It existed in France after the 1598 Edict of Nantes and in some parts of the Holy Roman Empire. Instead, the States General imposed Calvinism by force on all its newly conquered territories. Only Maastricht had a German-style biconfessional simultaneum, because the bishop of Liège retained rights within the city. "Everywhere else . . . the Reformed church remained the only legally recognized confession, even if here and there Lutheranism managed, thanks to its support in commerce and the army, to obtain permission to maintain semi-public worship." However, the policy of imposing Calvinism on the Catholic borderlands of the republic largely failed. Counter-Reformation Catholicism had taken strong root in the localities that had still been in Spanish hands at the time of the 1609 truce. Even after the Dutch conquest, they could be fed spiritually from across the many nearby borders.[11]

One curiosity of the Dutch world is its comparative inability to convert Catholics after about 1620, even though much of it—in the republic as well as overseas—was built on Catholic terrain. The Dutch claimed the churches and church property, but to convert individuals took effort and skills that most Dutch dominies, like Megapolensis, who had their hands full just taking care of their own congregations, lacked. The best example of what the Dutch Reformed Church was capable of doing against the power of

Catholicism in the colonies comes in the story of a young Portuguese soldier in Asia named Joan Ferreira d'Almeida, who deserted to the VOC
troops—a reminder that many "Dutch" soldiers were neither Dutch nor
Dutch Reformed, yet another source of religious diversity in the Dutch
world. The soldiers in New Netherland, for example, were a mix of Catholics (a number came from the Catholic Southern Netherlands and at least
two from France), Lutherans (Scandinavians and Germans, some of whom
might have been Catholics as well), Anglicans from England, as well as
Reformed Protestants from the republic, Switzerland, and possibly elsewhere, like France. Such a mixture was typical of Dutch troops in the WIC
and VOC as well as Europe.[12]

Regardless of their original religious affiliations, soldiers in Dutch service were encompassed by the public church like everyone else in the Dutch
world. D'Almeida's experience indicates something of the Dutch Reformed
Church's ability to assimilate and convert at least some of those soldiers.
On a mission to Malacca in 1642, he read a Spanish-language anti-Catholic
book. He converted and decided to become a comforter of the sick for the
VOC. By 1650, he wrote a Portuguese anti-Catholic manuscript, *Differencia
da Christandade*, which would be published in Batavia in 1684 and in Dutch
translation in Amsterdam in 1673. His success in instructing slaves, mardijkers, and other Portuguese-speakers in Malacca in the Reformed religion
brought him to the attention of the Dutch authorities, who brought him to
Batavia in 1651. There he was such a success that the Dutch churchmen
encouraged him to become a minister, which he did in 1656. He then
became the leader of the Portuguese Reformed Church in Batavia. Elsewhere, he had less success. Sent to Ceylon after the Dutch conquest, he
failed to make much headway. There, local Catholic communities received
regular support from priests sent from the Portuguese base in Cochin. They
denounced Ferreira as an apostate rather than accept him as an evangelist.
After a few years he returned to Batavia, where he remained the minister
to the Portuguese community until his death in 1691. Shortly after his conversion he began a lifelong project to translate the Bible and other important Reformed texts, such as the Heidelberg Catechism, into Portuguese for
the first time. His translation of the New Testamen was published in the
Netherlands in 1681, but that of the Old Testament, finished by others after
his death, was not published until the mid-eighteenth century. In his life,
missionary work, and translations, Ferreira represented the greatest weapon

the Dutch had against Portuguese Catholicism. Though his was a singular accomplishment, his experience indicates some of the circumstances in which conversions from Catholicism might occur. A single man surrounded by Dutch Protestant culture, including its anti-Catholic propaganda, he could convert people of marginal status in places distant from the succor of Catholic territories like Malacca and Batavia, but not in the established communities of Ceylon that lay along a frontier with a free Catholic territory. For similar reasons, a Catholic community never managed to form in New Netherland, notwithstanding the presence of individual Catholics.[13]

Precisely because Roman Catholicism was such a powerful and pervasive force in Dutch Asia, the VOC never had more than the absolute minimal tolerance to offer it. The precepts of liberty of conscience did not prevent the Dutch from trying to stamp out Catholicism in their Asian colonies. On conquering Portuguese posts and colonies, they forbade the practice of Roman Catholicism and banned Catholic clergy, especially Jesuits, from their territory. Those caught would be fined, imprisoned, and banned from the colony. Their religious books and "ornaments" could be burned in public. Such was the fate of French Jesuit Alexandre de Rhodes, who arrived in Batavia with two others on a diplomatic mission regarding Malacca in 1646. When the council found Rhodes had taken part in secret worship services, he was fined 1,000 guilders, banned from the city, and had his religious books and other items burned publicly on the scaffold. If a priest was found celebrating a Catholic mass, as happened in Batavia in 1623, he was banned from the colony.[14]

No Catholic priest had a permanent post, however secret, in Batavia. A number of priests passed through, however, not unlike the Jesuits in New Netherland (albeit on a much larger scale). They stayed from a few days to a few months—around eight in 1652 alone. Ironically, the Dutch base of Batavia became the center of Catholic efforts to maintain the faith in Dutch Indonesia. Some 190 Catholic clergymen are believed to have visited Batavia between 1622 and 1783. Priests passing through Batavia on official business were kept under what seems to have been a closer watch than in New Netherland. Forced to lodge in the fort, they could move through the city only with a military escort. Those caught holding services were banned and sent as far away as possible, often all the way back to Europe. The oversight could be a bit loose at times, as in the case of Father Manuel Soares, in Batavia in 1661. Governor-General Maetsuycker let Soares stay in the city

under the watch of two not terribly strict soldiers. If Soares went in to visit
a house on a walk through town, they would wait patiently outside. Usually
a group of Catholics waited in the house to be baptized and have their
confessions heard. Soares later claimed to have performed 350 baptisms in
a few weeks. However that was all the time he had. Once Governor Maetsuycker learned how extensive his activities were, he put Soares under house
arrest and forced him to ship out.[15]

Batavia, with its variety of Catholics, Muslims, and more, was on the
opposite end of the spectrum from New Netherland. Nevertheless, the colonies existed in the same realm of possibilities and policies. The experience
of the greater number of Catholics in Batavia suggests something of what
might have been possible in New Netherland had the colony and its population survived longer than it did. It also captures the peculiar mix of Dutch
hostility to Catholicism and Jesuits priests in particular, along with their
ability to live in a world permeated by Catholic individuals and influences.
From Catholics to Chinese, Muslims, Lutherans, and Quakers, there was a
global effort by non-Reformed people to carve a space for worship in the
Dutch colonial world. In each case, the existence of nearby borders and
frontiers created possibilities that would not have existed otherwise.

Quakers

The New England frontier was one of the few the Dutch world shared
with a Protestant power. Instead of sheltering Jesuits, it enabled radical
Protestants like Baptists and Quakers to enter and reenter New Netherland.
Rhode Island, despised by Dutch Reformed ministers as the latrine of New
England, provided a valuable base and refuge for Protestant missionaries,
allowing them to stoke the fires of Quakerism even as Stuyvesant's government did what it could to extinguish them. After the dramatic events of
autumn 1657, the Quaker mission restricted itself to the English villages of
Long Island. Quakers no longer entered New Amsterdam to preach and
witness in the streets. Nominally under Dutch authority, the English towns
were proving increasingly difficult to manage and untrustworthy of allegiance. During the first Anglo-Dutch war there had been much grumbling
and organizing in favor of the English cause. During the second Anglo-
Dutch war, many colonists would come out in force to support the English
invasion and conquest of New Netherland.

Vlissingen, Rustdorp, and 's-Gravesende were the main sources of trouble for the Dutch. In the first two, there was a significant faction of English Reformed colonists willing to work with the Dutch public church against the Quakers. The Dutch authorities did not and could not police religious events in the English towns without their help. English informants and magistrates solicited Dutch interventions against conventicles in the English towns, pulling the Dutch into a religious struggle being fought across the English Atlantic community. While some took advantage of Dutch authority to help suppress conventicles of Quakers, others preferred to follow the Amsterdam path of connivance, or even joined the Quakers, permitting missions to circulate in their village and preach in their homes. The struggle on Long Island revived the typical Dutch dilemma over how far magisterial connivance would or could go. Stuyvesant found himself negotiating between the directors and his own local magistrates. Some allowed more connivance than he was willing to accept, while others, English and Dutch, supported his fight against conventicling.

The tensions within the English community between those willing and able to work with the Dutch Reformed and those who favored the Quakers came to a head in Rustdorp in January 1661. The village still had no minister of its own, so some inhabitants petitioned Stuyvesant's council to send a minister "to preach and baptize several children." Dutch minister Samuel Drisius, who spoke English and had lived in England for a time, went out on Saturday, January 8, arriving in the evening. The next day he "preached twice" and "baptized eight children and two aged women," returning to New Amsterdam in the evening. The Dutch Reformed Church could accommodate at least some of the needs and desires of the English Reformed.[16]

Drisius did not go to Rustdorp alone. Two officers of the Dutch court accompanied him: an Englishman, Resolved (Resolveert in the Dutch records) Waldron and a Dutchman, Nicolaes Bayard. Waldron and Bayard went along because "letters" from Rustdorp, Vlissingen, and Middelburg had informed Stuyvesant that "members of the sect, called Quakers" as well as "other Sects" were holding "private Conventickles" against "Order & Law." Two English residents of Rustdorp, Richard Everett and Nathaniel Denton, had provided the information. With their help, the officers were to find out in which houses conventicles had been held, which "men, or women there had beene present," and who else might have been involved in any way. Rustdorp's position near the border of New England and in the midst of the English towns of New Netherland made it an excellent base of operations for the Quaker mission to the English of New Netherland, and this seems to be exactly what was happening—much to the distress of at least some of the English.[17]

According to Henry Townsend's neighbors, Rustdorp remained a Quaker-friendly village thanks to his continuing efforts. Already convicted twice for hosting Quakers, Townsend continued to do so, giving them "uncommonly free access to" his house. Worse, Townsend had been caught going "from doore to doore" asking his neighbors if "they would nott come to his house for their was a learned man," Quaker George Wilson. Ten of Townsend's neighbors attended, seven men and three women, enough for a conventicle according to the anticonventicle ordinance. One of the other men, Samuel Spicer, was convicted of attending the conventicle in Rust-dorp and another in 's-Gravesende shortly thereafter, where he "lodged" the Quaker preacher and his followers "in his mother's house." In their defense, Townsend and Spicer "brought forward many frivolous excuses" (in the eyes of the court), such as "that they had only called on their friends, that no law forbade friends to meet each other." Both were fined. Town-send, a repeat offender, was banished.[18]

Rustdorp, on the eastern frontier with New England, was proving par-ticularly difficult to control. Stuyvesant complained of the excessive con-nivance in the town. The "Experiancy from tyme to tyme to our great displeasure and Contempt hath shewd us that our act & Orders, set forth against all the separate Conventicles were not kept and observed, according to the tenor of our good Intentions, Especially among you in the Towne of *Rustdorp*." He denounced the English colonists for abetting the Quakers' missionary activity, "giving Entertainment unto their Scatteringe preachers, leave and way unto their unlawful meetings and prohibited Conventicles." Worse was the problem of local magistrates' collaboration with the conven-ticlers. Some "in whom we had put trust & authority doth Connive with the Sect called quaeckers." Connivance was happening in New Netherland and Stuyvesant did not like it.[19]

Eleven days after convicting Townsend and Spicer, Stuyvesant deter-mined to take action. He resorted to perhaps his most desperate measure yet: what in Louis XIV's France would be called a dragonnade, namely billeting troops (dragoons in France) on religious dissidents. In France the goal was to compel Huguenots to convert to Catholicism by subjecting them to the outrageous behavior of raucous soldiers in the privacy of their own homes. In New Netherland the aim was to compel compliance with the anti-conventicle ordinance. No one was forced to convert, but just had to agree not gather for any sort of worship without approval of the public church. To add strength to his crackdown, Stuyvesant sent three new magistrates to replace those currently serving. They were all English: Richard Everett, Nathaniel Denton, and Andrew Messenger. With them went half a dozen soldiers, for whom the people of Rustdorp had "to furnish with Convenient Lodgeinge and diet until further order." Two and a half weeks later, the new magistrates of Rustdorp wrote to Stuyvesant with a list of signatures of those who promised to inform them "iff any meetings or Conventicles off quakers shall bee in the town of *Rustdorp*, that wee know" (they included Richard Everett and Nathaniel Denton). At the magistrates' urging, Stuyvesant released the nineteen men who signed the statement from having to quarter the soldiers. The soldiers were quartered on the six men who did not sign the statement "until further order." There is no evidence of what happened next. Jaap Jacobs concludes that they "probably decided to sign before long." However, it would take more than a mini-dragonnade to suppress the local Quakers.[20]

The crackdown in Rustdorp culminated just over a year and a half later, in October 1662, with a round of banishments from 's-Gravesande beginning with Samuel Spicer, who had been fined for the Rustdorp conventicle. Spicer's mother Michal, along with John Tilton and his wife Mary, were also condemned to leave the colony by the end of November on "payne of corporal punishment" for their support of the "abominable" and "heretical sect the Quackers." The court accused the Quakers of seeking to bring "God's Holy Word" and "worship" into contempt. The banishments were designed to prevent the "confusion and schism" the Quakers threatened to bring into "this barely developed province." The sentences also reflected the increasingly bilingual character of the province. The sentence against the Spicers was pronounced in Dutch, that against the Tiltons in English.[21]

Finally, perhaps the most famous case of persecution in New Netherland, that of John Bowne of Flushing in fall 1662, also involved the use and manipulation of the frontiers impinging on New Netherland. Bowne's arrest was prompted by magistrates from Rustdorp, who went to Stuyvesant's council at the end of August 1662 to complain that "the majority of the inhabitants of their village were adherents and followers of the abominible sect, called Quakers, and that a large meeting was held at the house of

John Bound in Vlissingen every Sunday." Bowne, who had lived in Vlissingen since 1651 but did not convert until around 1659, seems to have picked up the mantle of the now banished Townsend. Bowne certainly had the same enemies as Townsend, English magistrates Everett and Denton. The complaint against Bowne ended with a request that the meetings at his house "might be prevented one way or the other." Stuyvesant again turned to Resolved Waldron, providing him with a commission ordering "all Magistrates and Inhabitants of the English Townes, in the Jurisdiction of the New Netherlands" to assist him "to imprisson all such persons, which shall be found in a prohibited or in an unlawfull meeting." Waldron went in early September.[22]

Once again, Flushing's town charter rights of liberty of conscience would be summoned to defend the inhabitants' contravention of Stuyvesant's ordinances. John Bowne was a neighbor of the men who had signed the Flushing Remonstrance, but not a signer himself. However his case is arguably more important than the Remonstrance, because it forced the WIC directors in Amsterdam to confront Stuyvesant on his policy toward the Quakers. Given the limitations of the existing Dutch sources on Bowne's case, our primary source is Bowne himself, who kept a journal of his experience. Bowne went on to become a leading Quaker and correspondent of George Fox, his experience of persecution at the hands of Stuyvesant doing much to enhance his reputation and standing within the Quaker community. His story, along with that of Hodgson, provides rare details about enforcement of the laws against religious dissidents. At the same time, it needs to be treated with some caution.

Bowne begins his account with the arrival of the "scout" Resolved Waldron "with a company of meen with sords and guns" ordering him to report to "the generall" (Stuyvesant). Bowne pleaded that his wife and baby were sick in bed. When Waldron insisted, Bowne asked him to show the written order for his arrest. He constantly demanded written proof and the Dutch officials were always reluctant to grant it. When he finally got a glimpse of the order to arrest "such as be in unlawfull meetings" he noted that Waldron "found me in non." He was home alone with his family at the time. Here, the Englishmen were playing out a drama familiar to Dutch magistrates everywhere. They could not arrest someone for being of a different faith, only for holding illicit gatherings. The difficulty for magistrates was that to have proof of conventicling they had to catch people in the act, which Waldron had not done. Refusing to comply, Bowne was threatened to be bound "hand and fout" and, indeed, the "next day like a wicked hard-hearted man hee carried me in a bott to Monhatons" and the fort.[23]

Bowne found himself facing problems similar to Hodgson's. He did not speak Dutch, and the Dutch would not speak English to him. He would not take off his hat, and the Dutch insisted he do it. Seeing Stuyvesant about to get on a horse, he asked a Dutch sergeant to tell Stuyvesant he wanted to speak to him. The man returned "and tould mee in Duch and shewed mee by his actions that the generall sead if I would put of my hat and stand bare heded hee would speake with mee." Bowne could not, Stuyvesant would not, and so "the solgers did breke out in lafter at itt." The next day in court Bowne again refused to remove his hat. Stuyvesant had Waldron do it for him.

On trial, Bowne refused to acknowledge his guilt or Stuyvesant's portrayal of his actions. Stuyvesant showed him the law against conventicles (recently translated into English) "wherein he termed the sarvants of the lord to be heriticks dec[ei]vers seducers or such like" and asked Bowne "if I would deny that I had kept meetings." Bowne was holding to the legitimacy of his actions, using the Quaker term for their religious gatherings, meetings, and rejecting the word conventicle. He would not deny that he had hosted "meetings but that I had kept such meetings or entertained such persons as hee there read of I did deny for I could not owne them to bee such," that is, he denied Quakers were heretics and deceivers. Stuyvesant "would not reason it at all." He again asked Bowne if he would "deny meetings." Bowne would "neither deny nor afeirm." He virtually requested martyrdom of some sort, saying he was "in your hands redy to sufer what you shall bee suffered to inflict upon mee," once again using Quaker terminology ("sufferings" being their martyrological genre). He suggested that Stuyvesant would be to blame for any suffering of his sick wife and child while he was gone. Stuyvesant replied Bowne himself would be at fault and fined him 150 guilders.

Language continued to play a role in Bowne's story of persecution. The "scout" (Waldron presumably) returned to Bowne's cell the next day with a "writing in duch" that contained the court's sentence. If Bowne wanted it translated, he would have to pay three guilders. Bowne would not pay anything, nor would he accept the court's charge against him, though the "fyscall and scout in great rage" insisted on it. For his refusal, Bowne was carried "away to the dongon and there put." He was guarded day and night by soldiers who had "a stricket charge . . . to let no body com at mee or speke with mee," as had been the case with Hodgson. Eventually he was taken to a "cramped little space" in City Hall, where he was soon joined by Nicolas Davies and Hodgson, who had returned even after suffering what he had five years earlier.

Bowne was a colonist of some means and contacts. He solicited Dutch merchant friends in New Amsterdam to plead his case to Stuyvesant. Stuyvesant would not listen, saying Bowne must either pay the fine or be banished from the colony. William Leveridge (Leverich), an English Congregational minister who had recently arrived in the colony to serve Middelburgh, told Bowne that Stuyvesant would set him free if he would leave the colony in three months. When Bowne asked to get this confirmed from Stuyvesant himself, nothing happened except that Bowne soon found himself under close guard. Leverich later claimed he forgot to contact Stuyvesant. Bowne was left wondering "whether William Leveridge was the case of" his reduced freedom. The English Quaker had fallen afoul of an English Reformed minister as well as the Dutch.

Once again, matters were pushed to the extreme by the failure of the colonists to play by the rules of Dutch connivance. The sentence of banishment was carried out because Bowne offered himself up to it. Bowne was allowed to see his family before he left. When he returned to New Amsterdam, Heschout "torned himselfe about upon his heele and lafed and seemed to byte his tong and wonder." Bowne thought "its like hee thought I would not have come agene"; in other words, Waldron seemed surprised Bowne had not used his visit home to escape over the border to New England, which perhaps anticipated he might. Instead he was forcing Stuyvesant to carry out the banishment, which in Bowne's case was to Europe.

Stuyvesant was concerned with reducing religious diversity within his colony. Outside its borders was another matter. He said Bowne would be free if he left New Netherland willingly, but Bowne would not. He was intransigent, insisting on his innocence. At the same time, he was impressed that Stuyvesant "carried himselfe very moderate to mee all that time . . . and called me goodman bowne." Stuyvesant had clearly adopted a change of strategy, if not of heart, toward Quakers since he had sentenced Hodgson to hard labor and whipped him for refusing. Perhaps the fact that Bowne was a colonist and Hodgson an outside agitator colored his assessment. Nonetheless, the touching remark is reminiscent of earlier Quaker praise for Stuyvesant's moderation. In their eyes, his English lieutenants were the problem, not Stuyvesant. For Hodgson, the true persecutor had been Thomas Willet. For Bowne, it was English schout Resolved Waldron.

Bowne was sent back to Europe and ordered off the ship on arrival in Dublin after a spate of rough weather, where he took advantage of the occasion to visit local Quakers. Determined to press his case, he took another ship across the Irish Sea so that he could visit more Quakers—some of them in prison—in England before making his way to Holland. By 1663, when Bowne had arrived in England, a new series of religious penal laws, known as the "Clarendon Code," was being adopted by the Parliament of the restored English monarchy, intent on cracking down on all forms of religious dissent, especially Quakers. A number of Quakers in England would die in prison, suffer the loss of property seized to pay fines, and even be banished to the American colonies for insisting on gathering for worship. Compared to this treatment of religious dissidents, Stuyvesant was "moderate" indeed.

In Amsterdam, Bowne presented his case to the WIC directors in hopes of exoneration. Instead, he encountered a group of men unwilling to engage in any confrontation whatsoever. His case was helped by an English merchant who put him in touch with a Quaker minister in Amsterdam who knew Dutch and could translate for Bowne. The directors' first reaction was to ask Bowne to move to Amsterdam, saying "wee doe not give liberty there [New Netherland]," once again betraying the local specificity and variety of religious possibilities in the Dutch world. Bowne, like other men of Flushing, felt the town patent gave them the power to be more like Amsterdam than the rest of New Netherland. His plea for the rights of religious liberty granted in Flushing's patent met with the reply: "oh . . . that was before any or but few of your Judgement was harde of." The director who spoke most with Bowne was Jacob Pergens. Pergens displayed a Dutch capacity to qualify liberty of conscience with distinctions in time (before Quakers existed) and space (New Netherland versus Amsterdam) whose subtleties were lost on the determined Quaker.

The issue that evidently mattered most to the directors was obedience to the law. With Bowne, they encountered some of the same divinely inspired defiance that had animated the Flushing Remonstrance. Bowne insisted Quakers were a "peseable people." The directors then asked why they would not "be subject to the laws and placards which are published." His refusal to do so meant "wee cannot sufer you in our Jurisdiction." Bowne replied, "it is good first to consider whether that law or plackad that was published be according to Justis & righeousnesse or whether it be not quite contrarie to it." He produced a copy of the town charter, with its clause granting liberty of conscience. The directors read it and "did find it verie good and like it well," saying "some words about it." Bowne did not trust them, seeing "there wickednesse," and asked them to endorse his interpretation of the charter in writing. Pergens replied, they "will give you nothing under our hands" (not surprising, given the directors' earlier advice to Stuyvesant against agreements in writing). Instead, they offered to let Bowne return if he would sign an agreement to obey all future ordinances, which he eventually did, though he called it a "bad paper in duch which I gott translated." Recognizing him as a leader of the Quakers in the colony, they also insisted he "send all those that will not be subject to that plakad [Stuyvesant's anticonventicle ordinance] and all other [placards] that ether are all redy or shall be here after made shall not live in oure Jursidicion." The directors' insistence on obedience to the law was a demand not for religious conformity but simply for adherence to a law that prevented organizing by alternative religious groups. They were willing to accept Bowne as a Quaker, but not to have him organize a Quaker congregation.

Little as they wanted to persecute valuable merchant-colonists such as John Bowne, the Jews, or the Lutherans, the Amsterdam directors avoided ever actually defending the dissenters' legal right to worship. Stuyvesant's prosecutions remained an embarrassing challenge to their ideal of connivance, but they would do no more than chide him for it. On hearing of Bowne's deportation, the directors had told Stuyvesant they "heartily desire, that these and other sectarians remained away from there, yet as they do not, we doubt very much, whether we can proceed against them rigorously without diminishing the population and stopping immigration, which must be favored at a so tender stage of the country's existence," expressing an interpretation of the relationship between religious diversity and colonial development completely at odds with that of the colonial Dutch Reformed establishment. The directors asked Stuyvesant to "shut your eyes, at least not force people's consciences, but allow every one to have his own belief, as long as he behaves quietly and legally, gives no offense to his neighbors and does not oppose the government." After all, Amsterdam "has always practiced this maxim of moderation and consequently has often had a considerable influx of people, we do not doubt, that your Province too would be benefited by it." It is the most famous statement about Dutch tolerance in New Netherland and is frequently cited by those who see the activism of dissenting colonists finally prevailing on the directors to impose a more tolerant policy on Stuyvesant. However what they urged was nothing particularly new, and not an endorsement of the right to organize religions outside the purview of the public church.[24]

Some in the colony's Reformed religious elite who agreed with the Amsterdam directors' view and felt Stuyvesant's administration was being too harsh in its enforcement of the ordinance against conventicles. Dominie Polhemius, writing amid the turmoil on Long Island from his home in Midwout, sent a report to the Amsterdam classis in April 1664 that was critical of the way the public church was being run in the colony. He did not speak in favor of pluralism or toleration. In fact, he complained about the lack of a coordinated effort among New Netherland's churches to promote the Dutch Reformed faith by converting Native Americans, Englishmen, and others. "Those outside the church are hardly noticed," he complained. As a result, "they follow any opinions and whims of the community, from which we obtain our bread with troubles." For him, Stuyvesant's administration was weakening the public church, not strengthening it. "They who wield the scepter here, do so without let or hindrance," they were too severe. Quakers were "compelled to go before the court, and be put under oath; but such compulsion is displeasing to God." Polhemius wanted the Dutch Reformed Church to expand, but not through the coercive power of the state. Before the classis responded to his complaints, the colony was lost.[25]

The struggle over the tenor of religious policy in New Netherland was thus not simply a conflict between the directors in Amsterdam and the colonial Calvinists. Would the directors ever have pushed the colonists towards a new practice of tolerance? That is impossible to know, though doubtful. Bowne's case was the last of note for the history of tolerance in New Netherland: "no more arrests on religious grounds were made in New Netherland," as Jacobs puts it. However, the lack of prosecutions cannot be taken as a sign of a shift in the colony's practice of tolerance. It had barely a year of existence left, being conquered at the end of August 1664. Furthermore, by the time the directors' admonishment arrived (June 1663 at the earliest), Stuyvesant had lost control of the English towns on Long Island, which were rejecting Dutch authority and conspiring to put themselves under the government of Connecticut. He had much bigger fish to fry than conventicles. He had lost his English Calvinist allies in the seceding

towns and soon would lose the entire colony.[26] As for Bowne, his fate at
Stuyvesant's hands back in New Netherland will remain equally unanswer-
able. His ordeal in Amsterdam lasted well over a month. He took his time
getting back, stopping again in England to visit more Quakers, then went to
Barbados and Virginia before making his way back to New Amsterdam
returning in March 1664. By then, New Netherland had become New York.[27]

Religious diversity and the tolerance thereof in New Netherland echoed the
dynamics from elsewhere in the Dutch world, where borders increased the
range of religious options available to inhabitants of Dutch territory. From
Batavia to Fort Orange, Catholic missionaries could cross into Dutch territory from neighboring Catholic provinces to administer to local Catholics
who, legally, were not permitted to avail themselves of their services. In
North America, Quakers and Baptists did the same, crossing the Long
Island Sound from Rhode Island to proselytize to a receptive audience of
former Puritans. In Dutch America as elsewhere, borders with foreign powers provided access to alternative religious services the public church
denied. The proximate powers offered refuge to dissidents from the Dutch
system and produced a steady stream of missionaries. The combination of
these factors nourished the religious diversity in Dutch America that the
Dutch Reformed establishment worked so hard to reduce. It helped a small
group of Catholics cling to existence, forced the Dutch ministers to be on
their guard, and made possible the continual incursions of Quakers. Without their nearby bases in New France and Rhode Island, neither Jesuits
nor Quakers would have been able to make the impact they did on New
Netherland, which was otherwise sheltered by thousands of miles of sea
from the religious conflicts of Europe. In North America as everywhere
else, the Dutch could not get away from the constant competition for souls
out of which their republic had been born.

One factor that set New Netherland apart from many places in the
republic was the success with which Stuyvesant and much of the colony's
political and religious establishment—Dutch and English—had prevented
formal toleration of any sort from taking root. Defending the opinion that
a tender young colony as New Netherland could not support religious toleration, they effectively subverted any dreams WIC directors might have of
a cosmopolitan metropolis developing under the benevolent blindness of
connivance. New Amsterdam was not old Amsterdam. It was a small, heavily Calvinist outpost governed by a man determined to keep it that way,

supported by ministers of strict Calvinist zeal. Toleration and connivance attacked the orthodox ideal of uniformity in faith and, formally at least, uniformity prevailed in New Netherland to the end. The directors never replaced Stuyvesant or compelled him to permit the practice of any religion besides that of the Dutch Reformed Church.

New Netherland's Reformed hegemony was remarkably resilient. Within the constraints of liberty of conscience—constraints perfectly familiar to any Dutchman—Stuyvesant, his officers, and his ministers effectively reduced Dutch tolerance to its most basic level, the individual. With only a few occasional exceptions along the Long Island frontier, they held it there as long as the colony remained Dutch. All of this of course depended on how far their power and authority extended. The frontier with other colonies was one region where that power weakened. Another was when a separate Dutch colony was created. That is what happened after 1657 when the city of Amsterdam gained a colony on the South River.

CHAPTER 9

RADICALISM

... eschue the yoke of Temporal and Spiritual Pharaohs who have long enough domineered over our bodies and souls, and set up again (as in former times) Righteousness, love and Brotherly Sociableness, which are scarce any where to be found.

New Netherland was not the only Dutch society in North America. For almost a decade (1657–1664), the city of Amsterdam had a colony of its own on the South River. Technically a patroonship, a sort of fiefdom under the overall authority of the WIC, New Amstel inaugurated the most radical religious and social experiment the republic's colonies ever saw. While New Netherland clung to the legacy of the 1620s, New Amstel brought in the influences of the 1660s. The mix of radical religion, politics, and philosophy then available in the Dutch world could be called the Age of Spinoza, after the most famous and influential intellectual figure in the republic at the time. Baruch Spinoza never made it to America, nor did he include it much in his philosophizing. His influence was distant and indirect. Nevertheless, New Amstel's close connection to Amsterdam's city government opened up America to the republic's most progressive social visionaries, including men who knew Spinoza and his ideas.

The WIC never showed much interest in religious experimentation and held to a conservative version of the public church whenever possible. However, the financial troubles of the WIC after the loss of Brazil gave Amsterdam an opportunity to put into practice an alternate version of Dutch tolerance. Amsterdam had lent a warship for Stuyvesant's conquest of New Sweden. Unable to liquidate the debt, the cash-poor but now land-rich WIC granted the southern half of the South River as a patroonship to

Amsterdam. New Amstel, named after the river that flowed through the city, was the name of both the colony as well as its capital. Several years later, in December 1663, Amsterdam's patroonship was extended to cover the whole South River valley. Though the English soon seized the region for themselves, New Amstel's brief history contained the most radical approach to toleration and colonization the republic would ever see.[1]

Until the conquest of New Sweden, the Dutch had not had a strong enough presence to form a congregation on the South River or call a minister to serve it. After the 1655 conquest, the status of the Dutch Reformed Church was asserted, though there was still no significant group of Dutch colonists in the colony on the upper reaches of the river. From his base at Fort Altena, governor William Beeckman ruled over a mixed crowd of Dutch soldiers and traders surrounded by a largely Swedish and Finnish Lutheran population. Curiously, there was no mention of liberty of conscience in his instructions. He was sworn to "maintain and as much as is in my power promote the Reformed religion, as the same is taught and preached in the Fatherland and here conform to God's word and the Synod of Dordrecht."[2] The small Dutch community designated one of the Dutch freemen "to read to them on Sundays."[3] The Dutch community under WIC rule never reached a size justifying a Dutch Reformed minister. Religious services remained in the hands of devout laymen and approved religious texts. The only minister around was the Swedish Lutheran Lock, thanks to Stuyvesant's toleration of the Swedish Lutheran church.[4]

The first sign that change was in the air for Dutch America came with an act passed by the States General in conjunction with the WIC in February 1661. The Dutch were trying to take advantage of the religious uncertainty in England caused by the Restoration of the Stuart monarchy in 1660, which had led a number of English Protestants to rethink their position in the English world. Some fled as exiles and refugees to the Dutch Republic. In America, the strict Calvinists of New Haven began negotiations with Petrus Stuyvesant to settle what eventually became Newark, New Jersey. The WIC judged it a good time to offer discontented Englishmen a chance to establish new settlement in New Netherland. The act opened the colony to "all Christian people of tender conscience in England or elsewhere, oppressed," targeting the "English, good Christians" in particular. It gave no specifics on what the religious arrangements would be. It simply guaranteed the settlers "full liberty to live in the feare of the Lord." The majority of the text was concerned with the terms of land, taxes, and trade to be offered, which the Dutch considered quite favorable. There is no indication that any English other than the New Havenites considered the offer. Jews and Catholics clearly were not welcomed, nor did it lead to any change in the treatment of Quakers.[5]

As ever, local initiative modified the intent of acts proclaimed in Holland. When a genuine English religious refugee entered the WIC territory on the South River, nothing was done to encourage him to stay on as a colonist. Captain William Fuller, a Quaker, had participated in Maryland's revolutionary government. Fleeing the new Restoration regime to Fort Altena in 1661, he received the barest of indulgences from commandant Beeckman. When they first met, the Quaker excused his failure to doff his hat (unlike Bowne and Hodgson who never offered an explanation for their insistence on keeping them on). He "knew very well, it was proper to show some respect, but, said he, his conscience did not allow it." Beeckman replied, "our conscience could not tolerate such a persuasion or sect." He was willing to "tolerate" the Quaker, Beeckman wrote Stuyvesant, only if "he keeps still and no more followers of that sort shall arrive." In "case of increase," he explained, "I shall make him leave our jurisdiction pursuant to the praiseworthy orders made by your Honorable Worships," probably a reference to the anti-Quaker ordinance. Fuller moved on soon thereafter and there is no more mention of him in the Dutch documents. No Quaker congregation was established along the river until after the English conquest.[6]

New Amstel initially seemed a more promising land for the Dutch Reformed Church than the WIC's territory. Fewer Lutherans lived there, and Amsterdam's burgomasters did not begin their American colony with aspirations for pluralism. Instead they promoted the power of the Dutch Reformed Church, much to the satisfaction of the Amsterdam classis, which oversaw religious affairs in New Amstel as much as in New Netherland. After learning that Amsterdam's city government had gained control of the colony, the classis approached them to make sure that the public church would be supported and that there would not be "general license" which could permit the "divers sects, in that colony" to "lift their heads." Though maintaining that "they could not force the consciences of men, which indeed," the classis's deputies noted, "we had expressly stated we did not wish," the city councilmen affirmed that "should information arrive that the sects carried on their exercises of religion" in any public way, "they would look to it to prevent such a thing, after examination of the facts."[7]

New Amstel vice-director Jacob Alrichs expressed Amsterdam's desire for a strong Dutch Reformed community on the South River. Immediately on taking command, he urged that a clergyman be sent over, "so that all our work may begin in the fear of God, and obtain the blessing of the Almighty."[8] Within a year, some 150 colonists were settled in the outpost of New Amstel. Evert Pieterson, a comforter of the sick and schoolmaster, was employed to "publicly read God's Word, and sing the Psalms."[9] As soon as Amsterdam's burgomasters had assembled enough new colonists to start a congregation, they asked for and were granted a minister by the classis of Amsterdam. Dominie Everardus Welius arrived along with 300-odd colonists in the fall of 1657 and established the first Dutch Reformed consistory on the South River.[10] Alrichs was one of the elders, and schoolmaster Pietersen the deacon. The strength of local support for New Amstel's church was reflected in its membership, which grew from nineteen to sixty in two years.[11] When the city's commissioners in charge of the colony learned that the Swedish minister Lock had been so "bold" as "to preach in" New Amstel "without permission," they informed Alrichs that "as yet, no other religion but the Reformed can nor may be tolerated there, so you must, by proper means, put an end to or prevent such presumption on the part of other sectaries."[12] Stuyvesant's toleration of a Swedish Lutheran congregation was restricted to his colony of New Netherland.

The pluralism on the South River was unwelcome to local members of the Dutch Reformed Church. The presence of the Swedish Lutherans filled them with fears of apostasy and dissolution. Amsterdam's classis saw a common Lutheran problem on the North and South Rivers and had been disappointed to learn that New Sweden's treaty of surrender had allowed the Swedes to retain a Lutheran minister (Lock). When Dominie Welius went to New Amstel, the classis worried his "work of ministry will be very difficult," because there were "all manner of pernicious persuasions" and "in time more people will come" to add to the diversity. "Every one can therefore, easily perceive," they concluded, "how much diligence and labor are required to prevent false opinions and foul heresies from becoming prejudicial to the pure truth."[13] Nevertheless, the classis did not give up hopes of dominating the South River. Claiming "it is understood that the Swedes have mostly gone away," the classis argued that "further efforts should be made . . . to oppose the Lutherans and other sects." It encouraged the city of Amsterdam to follow the WIC's policy that "the Lutherans shall not be permitted any permission freely to exercise their forms of worship" (toleration of Lutheran worship in what had been New Sweden being the one great exception to this general WIC policy).[14]

Unfortunately for the Dutch Reformed, Welius's ministry marked the high point of their local hegemony, and his ministry proved brief. He died in December 1659, after just over two years of service. New Amstel's consistory immediately wrote and asked for a new minister "in order that the community may not run wild."[15] They were to be disappointed. Amsterdam's commissioners took three years before agreeing to support another minister in New Amstel, and a fourth year passed before the classis sent one over.[16] Then the appointed minister, Warnerus Hassinck, died en route. Dominie Selijns wrote from New Netherland to request yet another minister, claiming it was "very necessary" in no small part because "of the abominable sentiments of various persons there, who speak very disrespectfully of the Holy Scriptures." Selijns was referring to the Lutherans, who he felt had "done great damage among the sheep, who have so long wandered about without a shepherd."[17] Alas, New Amstel's flock obtained no relief. A few months after Selijns wrote, New Netherland fell to the English. Despite promising beginnings and official backing, the Reformed on the South River were in an inverse position from those on the North River, where the local minister was Reformed and it was the minister-less Lutherans who worried about their flock straying. Dutch Reformed religion on the South River would remain in lay hands for "nearly twenty three years" until New Amstel gained another Reformed minister.[18]

The enthusiasm of Amsterdam burgomasters for the Reformed Church in New Amstel proved short-lived. After Welius died, they began promoting pluralism instead of uniformity, taking some extraordinary steps. In the early 1660s, two separate Catholic priests were given permission to administer to Catholics in the region, provided they did so discreetly and privately (it is not clear if they actually went over).[19] New Amstel was thus the only colony outside Brazil where Dutch authorities gave some encouragement to Catholics. New Amstel abandoned its earlier opposition to the Lutheran church and extended support to it as well. When a young Lutheran student, Abelius Zetskorn, arrived in New Amstel in 1663, the Swedes there called him to be a pastor for their congregation. The authorities in New Amstel gave their approval to the call.[20]

Ironically, the greatest opposition to having a second Lutheran minister on the South River came from the one already there. Jealous of his authority, Lock objected "with all his influence," forcing the Swedes to "threaten him with a protest, before he could be persuaded to permit" Zetskorn to preach.[21] Thereafter, Zetskorn was invited to preach upriver, in the jurisdiction of WIC, which Stuyvesant apparently approved of on a one-time basis. The congregation there liked Zetskorn so much they offered him "as high a salary" as Lock received to entice him into being their schoolmaster, but the New Amstel congregation would not let him go.[22]

The exact outline of Zetskorn's career is rather hazy. However, his brief appearance stirred up speculations revealing the hopes and challenges New Amstel's increasingly liberal religious policy could raise for church life on the South River. In the early eighteenth century, Swedish Lutheran ministers asserted that at some point Lock received episcopal authority to ordain Zetskorn (a precedent for future ordinations), but there is no evidence Zetskorn ever was fully ordained or actually served as a minister in America.[23] He appears to have preferred teaching to ministering, for in 1664 one of the Dutch dominies noted that he had "exchanged the Lutheran pulpit for a schoolmaster's place."[24] In the eighteenth century, Zetskorn would be remembered as having ministered in New Amsterdam, where he had arrived in the fall of 1662.[25] However, no contemporary evidence supports this claim, or indicates that Stuyvesant ever allowed him to do more than preach once on the Delaware.[26] When a rumor reached New Amsterdam that Zetskorn had administered baptism, Beeckman denied it, saying he had preached only once to the Swedes.[27] To baptize would be to assume the function of a minister. Stuyvesant had reluctantly agreed to allow one Lutheran minister on the South River and his subordinate clearly did all in his power to ensure that matters stayed that way. Whether Zetskorn functioned as a minister in New Amstel is unknown, as is his ultimate fate. He disappears from the record after the English conquest.

Indulging Catholics and Lutherans still fit within the broader pattern of Dutch tolerance and was not without precedent elsewhere. However, Amsterdam's burgomasters would go one step farther and consider a set of radical tolerationist proposals made by two men influenced by new ideas from outside the major Christian churches. The primary sources were the Collegiants and, to a lesser extent, the philosophical circle around Spinoza that intersected with them. The Collegiants were a recent development, descended from Remonstrant dissidents. They had gained acceptance from Amsterdam's authorities in the 1650s because they knew the meaning of being "quiet" in a way none of the colonists in America ever grasped. As an officer who investigated their meetings on behalf of the burgomasters reported, their meetings were very calm. They read a chapter out of the Bible and then discussed it. As long as they remained peaceful and did not disturb the public peace or publish Socinian books, the Collegiants lived in security in Amsterdam, however much the Reformed consistory tried to thwart them. If anyone caused trouble through confrontational tactics, it was the consistory's spies. Collegiant gatherings were open to visitors and sympathizers: Mennonites, mystics, philosophers, and free-thinkers all found a welcome home in the Collegiant meetings, or colleges as they were called, whether they became Collegiants or not.[28] The experience of these quiet but intellectual meetings on religion inspired Franciscus van den Enden and Pieter Cornelisz Plockhoy to propose radical social and religious experiments for New Amstel.

The Collegiants offered a form and model for coexistence among people of very different ideas but common spiritual and intellectual passions. They did not offer a code of belief so much as a model for how religion could be something other than what a priest or minister told people it was. What mattered most to those involved in the planning and execution of the colony that brought these ideas to America was the radical decentralization of religious authority from what had once been the virtually supreme authority of the pope to the reasoned discussion of a thoughtful, informed, ecumenical Christian congregation. They went against the current trend in all the official churches—Dutch Reformed, Lutheran, Roman Catholic, Presbyterian, and so on—toward "confessionalization," in which members of the church were expected to adhere to a fixed set of dogmas to be accepted or rejected, a confession of faith. They spoke of the importance of tolerance, reason, and discussion in finding religious truth and relied on no higher source then the Bible and their relationship to it. They represented a radical extension of the democratization of religious authority that had begun with the Reformation.[29]

The most direct connection among Spinoza, the Collegiants, and America came in the person of the currently little known but at the time rather significant figure of Franciscus van den Enden. Van den Enden had ties to the Jesuits, having been one for a time in his native Spanish Netherlands. Born in Antwerp in 1602, he had distinguished himself as a teacher of Latin grammar, poetics, and rhetoric. However, when it came to teaching theology Van den Enden ran into trouble with his Jesuit superiors, and was expelled from the order in 1633. Thereafter he traveled, studied medicine, and married a woman from his native Antwerp before settling in Amsterdam around 1645. In Amsterdam, he practiced medicine and sold artistic prints until a bankruptcy in 1652 forced him to return to his original training and open a Latin school for those who did not wish to attend the official, but Reformed Protestant, Latin School of Amsterdam. Through this school, Van den Enden instructed several great figures of the Dutch Enlightenment. In addition to Spinoza, they included great Dutch artist Romeyn de Hooghe, noted doctor and chemist Theodoor Kerckrinck, and Nicolaes van Vlooswijck, scion of an important regent family. Van den Enden remained in Amsterdam until 1670, when he left for Paris to work as a personal physician of Louis XIV. He would be executed in 1674 for his part in organizing a pro-Dutch conspiracy in Normandy during the war with France (1672–1678).[30]

Van den Enden's philosophical influence among his contemporaries is difficult to gauge, though there is no doubt it existed. Contemporaries were not quite sure what to make of him. Through the 1650s, he was described as a Catholic. In spring 1662, a Danish doctor visiting Amsterdam described him as a Cartesian and an atheist. Around this time he met Adriaen Koerbagh, a free-thinker and friend of Spinoza, whose trial and imprisonment several years later remains a seminal case in the history of freedom of thought. Several scholars consider Van den Enden's house and school to have been one of the centers of Amsterdam's early "radical Enlightenment." He was friendly with poets like Johannes Antonides van der Goes and Pieter Rixtel, who may or may not have studied at his school. Through 1664, he, his family, and students put on several plays. Though Spinoza does not directly mention Van den Enden, several other contemporary sources associate the two. Whether or not Van den Enden helped Spinoza along his initial philosophical journey, by the 1660s they were moving in similar circles of Collegiants, humanists, and free-thinkers. Both earned reputations as Cartesians and atheists as a result.[31]

Van den Enden's impact on America, such as it was, would come through his possible connection with Pieter Cornelisz Plockhoy. Their acquaintance would have begun around 1661, at the peak of the True Freedom, when both were in Amsterdam proposing a colony founded on religious liberty in New Amstel. The years 1661–1664 were full of promise and hope in Amsterdam. They were the first years of peace since the end of a long series of conflicts: the first Anglo-Dutch War (1652–1654), the intervention in the Northern War as Danish allies against Sweden (1659–1660), and the long, global conflict with the Portuguese (1588–1661). A series of even larger wars gradually pulled the republic into a quagmire of debt and decline: another Anglo-Dutch War (1664–1667), the devastating war with France (1672–1678) to which belonged a third Anglo-Dutch war (1672–1674), the Nine Years War (1688–1697), and the War of the Spanish Succession (1701–1714). Between 1660 and 1672, in the eye of this hurricane of international conflict, the influence of radical philosophers and political theorists grew to such an extent that an open debate took place about the virtues of a republic over a monarchy. Implicitly, it was a debate over the virtues of a government with a prince of Orange. One central issue relevant to the story of Dutch tolerance in America was the value of restricting the power of the public church to its "proper" sphere. At the elite level, it was decided in favor of Republican rule and control over the church. While the debate raged, Amsterdam's regents endorsed the most radical religious settlement the Dutch colonies would ever see.[32]

The city of Amsterdam considered at least three, and more or less approved at least two, proposals for colonies that would offer a radical new, Collegiant-style form of religious coexistence.[33] In December 1661, the Amsterdam City Council first considered a proposal by Van den Enden for a colony at Hoornkill (named after the city of Hoorn in Holland). Though the negotiations eventually broke down, Van den Enden published an account of his efforts and his hopes for what the colony in America could mean for the Dutch Republic, *Brief Account of New Netherland's Situation, Virtues, Natural Advantages, and especial suitability for settlement*. His affinity for Collegiant-style piety is evident at the outset when he describes his target audience, readers "who are not concerned with the Preaching-Ministry and all the other mostly also idle scholarly delusive knowledge and are likewise not addicted to all worldly powers founded upon imposture and violence." In other words, it was not designed for those who belonged to or supported the public church and its ministry. Van den Enden was also one of the few thinkers on religious life in the colonies to be quite clear that what he was offering was a model for society in Europe as well as America: "all the main, appropriate and necessary foundations of a best and Free-People's-Government." He anticipated criticism, claiming he would take "no or little notice of the judgment of foolish, academically conceited Know-it-alls, cocky Grammarians, and such like envious Creatures of the Night." Van den Enden was a fighter with little respect for the Dutch intellectual establishment—an attitude that helps explain the failure of his proposal.[34]

Van den Enden's proposal is extraordinary in a number of ways. Drawing on existing accounts of New Netherland as well as reports by those recently returned from there, he painted a picture of Dutch America as a democratic, secular, equitable society just waiting to be realized. He praised indigenous Americans as living models of consultative democracy. He came out more strongly than virtually any of his contemporaries against slavery, seeing an "inconsistency implied by the keeping of slaves with regard to our free nature and government." Slavery was incompatible not just with the Dutch constitution but with Christianity itself, at least "in so far the Christian Religion is a reasonable Religion, that it consequently is also in conflict with it and with sure Reason, to hold humans as permanent slaves. It is likewise not allowed and against all human right and dignity to deal greedily in harmless people and to transport them into an irredeemable slavery." Van den Enden advocated for a society based on reason and equality. He called it "evened-equality" ("evengelijkheit"), a situation in which all men, rich and poor, stood a chance to improve their lives. Van den Enden spent considerable time demonstrating how society could be protected from tyranny, or "domination" as he also phrased it, and devoted to the common good. The possibilities of reasonable religion, rooted in the moderate climate of North America, made Dutch America the ideal place for a new and improved Dutch society. It is all quite extraordinary for what initially began as a proposal to settle a colony of six hundred families on the South River.[35]

Van den Enden's *Brief Account* contains the exchange of letters written with the burgomasters chronicling the fate of his radical proposal, revealing something of the mentality of the burgomasters in charge of colonizing New Amstel. Tellingly, they initially did not seem concerned by the radical tone of his vision. It was the question who would administer justice and whether the colonists really should receive the thirty-five-year tax break Van den Enden requested that gave them pause. There is some hint that as negotiations continued the burgomasters became a bit concerned by the radical implications of the proposal, and whether it would be wise to permit the establishment of such a society on its territory. However, Van den Enden's confrontational and uncompromising personality seems to have been the crucial factor in alienating their interest in his scheme. By April, the negotiations had broken off. His Dutch American utopia would never be.[36]

Van den Enden concluded his pamphlet, published in October 1662, with a renewed call for colonization that directly criticized Dutch foreign and colonial policy of the previous seventy years. He saw the nature of the republic as closely tied to its relationship with its colonies. The government of Holland had to be reformed, allowing more freedoms, including freedom of speech, before it could properly oversee colonization by "a freedom loving people." He then elaborated on his theory of how colonies could contribute to the common good. He saw the colonization of North America as an alternative to the "useless" wars that guzzled the "goods and blood of the common" people. Addressing "Holland," Van den Enden criticized the Orangist dreams of reconquering the southern Netherlands: "Towns and Places, who have nothing useful or valuable for you." The wars to capture them brought on a tremendous debt while the conquered cities, full of Catholics, were "a pressing burden to you, being mostly filled with inhabitants whom as suspected enemies you are necessitated to coerce with expensive garrisons, which garrisons mostly are composed of foreign, usually unfaithful and empty vagabonds and who . . . feed up their lusts at the cost of the dear sweat and labor of your frugal, industrious, and carefully living children." There was a strong nativist sentiment in the *Brief Account*. In addition to mistrusting Catholics and the mercenary soldiers needed to police them, Van den Enden feared WIC policy threatened to leave the colony too dependent on foreigners and render it vulnerable to a foreign takeover (correctly, it turned out). He saw his plan as an extension of proposals from the 1640s by Adriaen van der Donck to encourage migration from the Netherlands and thereby increase the Dutch population in the colony, making it stronger and more prosperous. A flourishing New Netherland would "deliver you in due time thousand fold fruits, without the least costs, and yet to your glory and relief." It was a radically different vision of Dutch expansion, one difficult to imagine before the era of True Freedom.[37]

Key to Van den Enden's proposal were democratic procedure, economic development, defense, and a new vision of Dutch tolerance. Turning completely against what had been Dutch policy in the colonies, Van den Enden argued for the establishment of "a Society of different people with conflicting sentiments." Here, for the first time, was an open advocacy of pluralism for Dutch America. However, it would not be pluralism of the sort emerging in Amsterdam through connivance, where individuals came together in separate congregations under their own religious leadership. Instead, it would be a society of free-thinkers, resembling nothing so much as a gathering of Collegiants. Clergy of all sorts must be kept out of the American settlement "without exception" as they "are feeders and stiffeners of every-one's particular opinion." The very presence of a minister would militate against pluralism, for "in case preachers from one sect were chosen, it would be impossible for so many people of different humors and inclination to agree with it." The alternative, "to appoint particular Preachers for each sect," would be both impractical for such a newfound society as well as "an unavoidable ruinous pest of all peace and concord" that would do anything but provide a firm basis for a new society. Curiously, Van den Enden's understanding of pluralism as a problem actually agreed with the Dutch Reformed ministers who judged a plurality of churches (and their attendant religious leaders) to be a threat to social stability. The difference was in their solutions. Where the dominies chose to preserve stability by suppressing pluralism, he chose to do the same by keeping out the ministers. After all, the settlers would be "as well supplied as they with the very best (which according to the judgment of most Preachers is the Holy Scripture)." What need had they of clerics to tell them what Scripture meant?[38]

The reliance on the Bible as the primary source of spiritual authority underscores just how Protestant Van den Enden's vision was. Without a minister to mislead them, the colonists would themselves be the judges of what was orthodox and not according to Scripture. If they followed Van den Enden's inclination, they would go farther than had all other radical Protestants, including the Collegiants. He held the sacred at a greater distance than they had by denying the two sacraments Protestants had retained after the Reformation: "Baptism and the Holy Supper" for him were but "ceremonies or memorials more becoming for weak children than for men in Christ." Nonetheless, his proposed Bible-based religion had much in common with Collegiant and even Mennonite worship. The best and cheapest way to provide for stability and "the common quiet, peace and concord" in matters of "the external or public service of God" would be to rely on the "very most peaceful and also cheapest Preacher, the Holy Scripture." Everyone would come together in a joint worship service at a set time in the morning on all Sundays and Holy days as in the Netherlands. They would then listen to an appropriate chapter of the Bible read by an adult or young, promising, qualified man.[39] The whole group would sing psalms before and after the reading for mutual edification. Then they would leave, as they had gathered, with all appropriate consideration and modesty—the "quietness" so crucial to Dutch connivance. The absence of a chance to discuss the day's reading is a notable difference from the Collegiants. It may have been part of Van den Enden's scheme to ban religious conflict by preventing religious confrontation or cathechizing.[40]

Van den Enden's religious pluralism was a reaction to the increasing institutional strength and influence of churches demanding and often enforcing adherence to specific confessions of belief, Lutheran, Reformed, or Catholic. Apart from banning religious leaders and relying on Scripture and Reason to order civil and religious life, his first rule was that "nobody, foreigner as well as simple inhabitant" was "in one way or another allowed to be molested on account of whatever assertion in matters of religion or opinion." At the same time, the religious inclinations of all the settlers were to be recorded. Despite the ecumenical (albeit clearly Protestant) tone of Van den Enden's pluralist Utopia, it was not a world in which confessional allegiances were irrelevant. On the contrary, it was constructed quite consciously against the threat of existing churches.[41]

Van den Enden's pluralism limited itself to a fairly select group of people with a shared Protestant vision of lay, scriptural religiosity without sacraments. It was not something for the majority of Europeans at the time, whether in Amsterdam or America. Nor did it in any way reflect the pluralism of a place like Batavia. Not many of his contemporary Europeans could meet his requirements for membership in a community founded to maintain "peace and unity" and avoid "all private quarrels and violent sectarianism concerning religious matters." Forbidding entry to priests and ministers was not enough. To prevent religious strife and preserve the "common peace," the following religious types had to be kept out of the colony: "all intractable people, such as obstinate Papists narrowly devoted to the Romish Chair, usurious Jews, obstinate English Quakers, Puritans and reckless, stupid believers in the millennium, together with all obstinate contemporaries claiming revelations, etc." There would also be a militia. Those, such as Mennonites, whose conscience would not permit them to serve in the militia would pay an extra tax in lieu of serving, just as Jews were being forced to do in New Amsterdam. For all its ambitious vision, it was a remarkably narrow and idiosyncratic scheme, a philosopher's paradise better suited for Van den Enden and his associates in Amsterdam than the Dutch overseas world.[42]

Van den Enden's vision for America was tied to his hopes for Europe. The failed effort to create society anew in North America inspired him to turn his energies toward reform at home. In 1665 he published one of the most radical political tracts of the era of True Freedom, *Free Political Propositions and Considerations of State, Grounded in the True Christian's Evenly Equal Freedom, striving for an honest and true Improvement of State, and Church*. Rather than list himself as author, Van den Enden called himself a "Lover of the evenly equal freedom of all well-educated Citizens." He ended the title page with two still revolutionary slogans: "The People's Prosperity is the Highest Law and The People's Voice is God's Voice." *Free Political Propositions* has drawn serious attention from scholars interested in radical Enlightenment philosophy and the origins of democracy.[43] It is a text of great interest, originality, and patriotism. Van den Enden wanted to make the Netherlands strong, and colonies were crucial to his plan. They would increase "free trade and shipping" and prevent overpopulation (especially by "foreigners and neighbours"). They would also provide an outlet for the Dutch economy "when in course of time the European Potentates might obstinately try to thwart us or also on account of the eventual death and ruin of trade in Europe." Colonies would ensure that "we would never be in a needy position but always have an abundance of countries and peoples for our subsistence." Written at the beginning of the war that would strip the Republic of New Netherland, this was an extraordinarily prescient judgment. Had the De Witts listened and not traded away New Netherland in the peace of Breda of 1667, things would have looked quite different for the Dutch, not to mention Dutch tolerance in America.[44]

Van den Enden was the first Dutchman since Willem Usselincx to articulate a scheme for free settler colonies in America tied to a religious and political vision for the Netherlands itself. Willem Usselincx is often credited as the intellectual inspiration for the West India Company, even though it paid little heed to his ideas. Associated with merchants doing business in Africa and the Caribbean, he was the most outspoken advocate for settler colonialism in his day. Born to a merchant family in Antwerp, he made his fortune trading with Iberia and the Azores in the late sixteenth century. A convinced Calvinist, he had fled to Middelburg by 1591. Like many fellow Flemish refugees, Usselincx took the side of Gomarus against Arminius. Before the 1609 truce was signed, he began agitating in person and in print for a company to create Protestant settlements in the West Indies. Rather than simply look for trade, they would extend Dutch power and True Religion, that is Calvinism, overseas. He proposed colonies of self-governing Dutch Protestant farmers overseen by a council of theologians and well

supplied with ministers to maintain their faith and missions to their indigenous neighbors. Toleration and religious pluralism were not part of Usselincx's vision. As with Van den Enden, his imperial vision was out of step
with his contemporaries' ambitions. North America produced nothing of
great value. It had no kingdoms or ports to trade with or significant Iberian
posts to conquer. Usselincx had some sympathizers, but no support. Failing
in Holland, he tried to convince the Protestant hero Gustavus Adolphus,
king of Sweden, to take up his vision. Adolphus was sympathetic, but the
Swedes did not have the money. When the WIC finally was launched in
1621, it made little provision for the sort of self-governing settler colonies
Usselincx wanted. He refused to partake in it and died a disappointed
man.[45]

Van den Enden's dream was quite the opposite of what Usselincx had
proposed. Usselincx wanted a Calvinist, Reformed body of citizens at home
and abroad; Van den Enden wanted a society founded on "Divine reason."
Free Political Propositions continued the struggle against "Sectarianisms and
Dissensions" begun in *Brief Account*.[46] In neither man's case did the proposals produce results. It is unclear just how many people stood behind
Van den Enden and his plan. He mentioned no specific individuals. It is
not even clear if Van den Enden himself intended to go over. However,
given who he was and knew, word of his schemes must have been in the
air in Amsterdam. Curiosity was piqued, providing an audience for Plockhoy and his plan for a similar sort of idealistic settlement in the same place.
Thanks to New Amstel, the religious possibilities, dreams, and conflicts in
Amsterdam in the era of True Freedom had an American colonial outlet.

The only successful effort to set up a colony grounded in religious liberty
came from Mennonites. Some of them may have been connected to Van
den Enden's efforts. In April 1662, the Amsterdam city council considered
the offer of twenty-five Mennonite families to settle in New Amstel if provided with a sufficient start-up loan. A month later, Plockhoy made his
proposal for a utopian colony in America. Plockhoy's is the only scheme
known to have resulted in an actual settlement in America. Whether he
learned any lessons or was inspired by Van den Enden's efforts is unclear.
Equally unknown is whether any of the Mennonite families who had
offered to go to America in April accompanied him. Plockhoy had been
out of the country for the previous five years or so on an international
quest to build an idealistic community of social, economic, and religious

equality. He thus had the experience and persistence that Van den Enden lacked to actually create a settlement. Plockhoy came from a very different background from Van den Enden and had few connections in Amsterdam, though both had connections to the city's Collegiants.[47]

Plockhoy is a relatively unknown but extraordinary figure in the history of Dutch tolerance and colonization. Unlike virtually everyone else who weighed in on both issues, he was not a well-educated child of privilege. An artisan's son, he spent his whole life working for a living, though his exact trade is unclear: probably carpenter, possibly cloth-worker, maybe tin-smith. Born about 1615 in Zierikzee, a once important town in Zeeland by then in decline, he moved to Zeeland's political, cultural, and economic capital of Middelburg as a young man. His parents were Mennonites, rather unusual for Zeeland, where most Protestants were strict Calvinists (a few Catholics lingered in scattered pockets). The bulk of Zeeland's Mennonite community lived in Middelburg, and most of them derived from the refugees who had fled the Spanish reconquest of the southern Netherlands. Consequently, they were known as the Flemish Mennonites, in contradistinction to Mennonite communities from Friesland (Frisian Mennonites) or North Holland (Waterlanders), each of which had distinctive cultural tendencies. The Flemish Mennonites were the largest community in Amsterdam, and Plockhoy may well have had some connections there through Galenus Abrahamsz, fellow scion of Zierikzee and head of Amsterdam's Flemish Mennonite community.[48]

Three factors proved decisive in pushing Plockhoy out of an otherwise humble existence and into the realm of colonial schemers and social and religious philosophers. First, though he was an artisan, a laboring man from a working family, he was of the middling sort. Second, his father died when he was young, exposing him to the struggles of poverty. Third, he seems to have had a certain charm and intelligence. Middelburg's Mennonites looked to him as one of their young talents for leading religious services. However, his charms extended to women other than his wife as well, and controversies over several incidents of dubious contact between Plockhoy and women prevented him from assuming a leading role in the Mennonite community, which eventually expelled him for his refusal to confess to wrongdoings with the women.[49]

Expelled from Middelburg's Mennonite congregation in 1654, Plockhoy's local prospects would not have looked good. The religious community was an economic community as well, ensuring and policing its members' creditworthiness and providing business contacts. Those who fell into disrepute lost both credit and business. Though still one of the larger cities in the Netherlands, Middelburg was losing its commercial dynamism. It did not draw the thousands of immigrants and offer the myriad opportunities Amsterdam did. Plockhoy may have stayed on for a while or tried his hand at life in Amsterdam or somewhere else in Holland. No evidence of his activities has been found until 1657, at which point he was in London.[50]

What is clear is that Plockhoy had embarked on a spiritual as well as physical journey after his expulsion. The first sign of his presence in England comes from the consistory records of the Dutch Reformed Church in London, Austin Friars. Something about what he did and said led them to conclude that he was a "Quaker." Indeed there are echoes of Quaker influence in his writings. Though he was not afterward seen as a Quaker and never called himself such, he was not unsympathetic to some of their ideas. A Quaker connection may have been what brought Plockhoy to England in the first place. Living in Zeeland, with its long history of connections to England, Plockhoy would have been aware of the tremendous religious and political changes there during the 1640s and 1650s. Shortly after his expulsion from the Mennonites, Quaker missionaries arrived in Middelburg: the first in 1655, several others in 1656, another in winter 1657. Quaker missionaries did not confine themselves to preaching to the local English congregation. They spoke up in the Dutch Reformed Church, provoking tremendous outcry and earning a stay in jail. Though most townsmen clamored against them, a few visited and showed an interest in their teachings. Plockhoy could not have missed the commotion. Perhaps he was one of the sympathetic visitors.[51]

Being sympathetic to the Quakers and their message did not make Plockhoy a Quaker. However, it could be additional evidence that he was becoming a Collegiant. Collegiants had given Quakers the only sympathetic hearing they received in Amsterdam. Until the 1670s, there was a steady dialogue between the two groups, who had much in common: not enough to unite, but some early Dutch Quakers had been Collegiants. There was no Collegiant College in Middelburg in the 1650s, but Plockhoy's brother Cornelis was one of the leaders of the Collegiant College in Utrecht, established by Mennonites in 1655. The brothers were still in touch, for that very year Cornelis appointed Pieter guardian of his daughter. Pieter's later writings make it clear he was drawn to various Protestant spiritualists of the radical Reformation. Utrecht's new Collegiant College, founded the year after his expulsion, offered him an alternative spiritual home. By 1661–1662, when he was in Amsterdam, he was attending its Collegiate College and contributing to its debates (most notoriously on the question of polygamy). As with Van den Enden, his vision of colonial religious pluralism and coexistence resembled a Collegiate meeting more than anything else. Whether or not he formally identified as a Collegiant, Pieter Plockhoy was certainly within their orbit.[52]

Plockhoy had gone to England with a vision for a harmonious religious and social order that he believed a man like Cromwell could implement. Soon after his arrival he seems to have developed a connection to Samuel Hartlib and his circle of internationally and ecumenically inclined Protestants. A 1657 draft of his first letter to Cromwell exists in the Hartlib papers, though he did not present his ideas to Cromwell until 1658. He laid out his scheme in two pamphlets published in London. In *The Way to the Peace and Settlement of These Nations*, Plockhoy reprinted three letters he had presented to Parliament outlining the way to universal religious toleration. In brief, his plan involved abolishing churches and ministers in England, Scotland, and Ireland, replaced them with "one general Christian assembling or meeting-place," in which "all people" could "orderly confer together concerning the Doctrine and Instruction of their Lord and Master Christ." His second work, *A Way Propounded to Make the Poor in These and Other Nations Happy*, proposed founding an egalitarian community to "eschue the yoke of Temporal and Spiritual *Pharaohs* who have long enough domineered over our bodies and souls, and set up again (as in former times) Righteousness, love and Brotherly Sociableness, which are scarce any where to be found." People from all walks of life would live together, mutually sharing in any mercantile profits and communally underwriting all capital investments. Medical care would be free and available to all, and widows and orphans would be cared for in a community centered on the life of the family.[53]

With the help of the Cromwellian government, Plockhoy came close to setting up a community based on his ecumenical ideals in Ireland. Unfortunately the Restoration of Stuart rule intervened and upset the plans. Even then, America was not his immediate choice for a fallback option. He first contemplated a move to a German city in the Calvinist County of Wied along the Rhine River just below Cologne. Wied had been devastated in the Thirty Years' War. Beginning in the 1650s, its count resorted to a policy of granting extensive religious freedom and civil rights to foreigners of any

faith who would come and settle in what he hoped would become a flourishing trading town on the Rhine: Neuwied. By 1661, a few Mennonites had
moved to the town along with some Jews. Soon thereafter it would, in fact,
become a thriving town famous for religious freedom, which persisted until
the collapse of the Holy Roman Empire. Neuwied thus fared somewhat
better than the earlier German havens of religious tolerance, Friedrichstadt
and Gluckstadt. However, Plockhoy ultimately chose not to settle in Neuwied, turning to America instead.[54]

In Amsterdam by 1661, Plockhoy petitioned for and received permission
to set up his utopian community on the South River. A second Dutch
pamphlet, *A Short and Clear Plan, Serving to a Mutual Accord to Lighten the
Burden of Work, Restlessness, and Difficulty of every sort of Artisan by Establishing a Mutual Company or Settlement . . . on the South River in New
Netherland*, confirmed that the egalitarian ideal he had proposed in
England could now be a reality in America. The pamphlet prints his agreements with the city of Amsterdam along with a commendatory poem by
Jacob Steendam. The ideas for the American settlement differed little from
what he had proposed in Britain, and the religious provisions were the
same.[55]

Never was a more idealistic community envisioned for New Netherland.
Alas for utopians, its existence was brief and tragic. Twenty-five families
totaling forty-one people landed at the Hoornkil in July 1663. Thirteen
months later, the budding settlement was thoroughly plundered by the conquering English. Plockhoy's family returned to Amsterdam, along with a
number of the other colonists. A mere handful of the rest, at most,
remained in America. Plockhoy's son would return in the 1670s and die a
blind pauper in Germantown, Pennsylvania. Plockhoy himself either died
in America by 1665 or in Amsterdam several years afterward, his dreams
and schemes devoured by the turbulent Atlantic world.[56]

The brief and disastrous history of radical Dutch tolerance in America is
an object lesson in the possibilities and limits of Dutch tolerance. The hopes
and ambitions for New Amstel in the 1660s were the most extraordinary
articulation of Dutch tolerance the Dutch colonial world would ever see.
Yet they were a unique product of peculiar conditions, the conjunction of
factors that put the city of Amsterdam in charge of a colony in the late
1650s, a highpoint of radical philosophizing, ecumenical gathering, and
millennial aspirations in the city, and made its rulers open to efforts by

Protestant groups beyond the public church to set up a community and protect it from the reach of the Dutch Reformed. Such schemes were unimaginable before 1651. The English conquest of 1664 destroyed Amsterdam's unique toehold in the Dutch empire before war and revolution in 1672 put a brake on the city's enthusiasm for liberal philosophizing.

It should be emphasized that the proposals for radical religious liberty in Dutch America were as restrictive as they were liberal. When the Dutch radicals imagined a colony of extraordinary tolerance, they could do so only by imagining most Dutch—most Europeans, in fact—out of it. There were certainly people who would have found the schemes of Van den Enden appealing, but they were mostly cosmopolitan urbanites like himself and preferred to stay in the republic, where the real struggle and hope for change lay, rather than chance a dangerous trip to a distant colony. A small group of people did find Plockhoy's plan congenial enough to risk the voyage. Whether many more would have come over time is difficult say. For in the end, as Plockhoy learned, all colonial idealism ultimately rested on one fact: imperial power. Unfortunately for Dutch America, that is what the Dutch did not have enough of in North America in 1664.

New Amstel's opportunities depended heavily on the political and diplomatic situation at home and abroad. When those changed, so did the possibilities in the colonies. War took New Amstel out of Dutch hands in 1664. Revolution and more war put a damper on the political and religious radicalism that had flourished during the True Freedom. After 1672, the climate in the Dutch Republic actively discouraged the sorts of schemes and philosophizing that lay behind the plans of Van den Enden and Plockhoy. The Dutch Reformed Church, with one or two brief exceptions, would continue to provide the primary framework for religious life in the Dutch colonies. For this reason, when the Dutch recaptured their North American territory in 1673, the religious system they put in place resembled not New Amstel but New Amsterdam instead.

CHAPTER 10

CONQUEST

The Dutch here shall enjoy the liberty of their consciences in Divine
Worship and church discipline.

The most decisive factor in bringing a change to tolerance in America was
military conquest. Conquest changed the terms of engagement and gave
groups new forms of negotiating power. Without it, the radical possibilities
of New Amstel would not have happened, nor would the one Lutheran
minister be tolerated on the South River, both legacies of the conquest of
New Sweden. In New Netherland, the struggles on the ground and in the
halls of power back in Holland had simply nudged matters back and forth
within a rather narrow framework. Quakers were converting ever more
colonists along New Netherland's eastern frontier, but were still subject to
harassment and banishment. The occasional Jesuit trickled into the province. The Lutherans had mobilized but were still compelled to remain part
of the public church. Indeed, the baptismal compromise imposed by the
WIC directors was intended to keep them there rather than tolerate them
as a separate entity. Thus there was religious diversity in New Netherland,
but it was largely under control. The majority of the population still
attended the public church, which was growing in strength and power as
new churches were built and more ministers recruited to serve the colony.
Left to its own devices, there was no indication that New Amsterdam would
emulate Amsterdam's religious climate. It was looking much more like
Middelburg, Kampen, or Cape Town. Then an English invasion fleet
appeared.

The Dutch knew all too well that wars and the treaties that concluded
them were powerful opportunities to effect radical change in a territory's

religious environment. The republic itself had only been made possible by eighty years of war. The recent losses of Brazil and Formosa, along with the gains of New Sweden and Ceylon, had all produced dramatic changes for the Dutch Reformed—driving them out or letting them in. In fall 1664, New Netherland joined the ranks of conquered colonies. However, its North American location once again put it in a slightly different category from the rest of the Dutch world, namely a Protestant one. A non-Christian Chinese army had driven the Dutch out of Formosa. A Roman Catholic insurgency had driven them out of Brazil. Catholic Spain, until 1648, and Catholic France, in 1672, threatened to conquer all or part of the republic and restore the Roman Catholic Church. The English conquest, on the other hand, as a Protestant conquest, did not entail such a dramatic adjustment to the religious climate of the colony. The conquerors were willing to extend formal recognition of toleration to the subjugated Protestant population, in ways neither the Dutch nor the English had been willing to do to Catholics anywhere else. Most colonists in New Netherland remained, leaving New York with essentially the same society Stuyvesant had presided over. The result was a remarkable degree of continuity into a new colonial life no longer dominated by the Dutch, but still very influenced by what they had created. However, the English conquerors made one major change: they actively fostered the pluralism the Dutch regime had done all within its constitutional power to restrain by replacing the public church with an Erastian system in which the English governor mediated between *all* religious groups in the colony equally. No single group had privileged support as the Reformed had had under West India Company rule.

Stuyvesant's godly colony came to an end on August 27, 1664, when he signed the Articles of Capitulation on the Reduction of New Netherland, surrendering the colony he had governed for a decade and a half to an English invasion force. The colony became New York, New Amsterdam became New York City, Beverwijck and Fort Orange became Albany and Fort Albany, and Fort New Amsterdam, where Stuyvesant's council had met and convicted Quakers, became Fort James. The new names were all references to the name and titles of New York's new ruler, James, duke of York and Albany, younger brother to King Charles II. Article Eight guaranteed that the "Dutch here shall enjoy the liberty of their consciences in Divine Worship and church discipline."[1] The Dutch Reformed had become a tolerated group.

Figure 7. New Amsterdam became New York as English warships sat in the harbor. This contemporary map dramatically conveys the transition in power from Dutch to English rule over the Mid-Atlantic. Copyright © The British Library Board.

The conquest was not the end of Dutch society in America. On the contrary, the attachment of the New Netherlanders to their American home led the vast majority of them, including Petrus Stuyvesant, all the resident ministers, Aaron Levy and his family, the Lutherans, and, of course, the English—Quakers, Baptists, Presbyterians, and Congregationalists—to stay on after the conquest. The ministers reported that they "could not separate ourselves from our congregation and hearers, but consider it our duty to remain with them for some time yet, that they may not scatter and run wild."[2] Within a few months their ability to leave was curtailed, as the Second Anglo-Dutch War began in earnest, cutting them off from the Dutch Republic.

The conquest of New Netherland in 1664 was one of a series of preemptive sneak attacks on Dutch posts in North America and Africa that began the Second Anglo-Dutch War (1665–1667). As with all the Anglo-Dutch wars, it was launched by the English. The Dutch Republic did not want to fight—it had little to gain and much to lose, particularly trade. Fortunately for the Dutch, France stood as their ally, ensuring that the Dutch came out of the war in much better shape than if they had been fighting on their own. Though the Dutch made no effort to recover New Netherland, in Africa and the Caribbean the story was different. The great Dutch admiral Michiel de Ruyter recaptured the African posts in 1665 and went on to plunder the English Caribbean. In retaliation, the English captured Saint Eustatius and Tobago in 1666. Later that year, the French allies of the Dutch took back both Tobago and Saint Eustatius. The final year of the war, 1667, was a year of triumphs for the Dutch. Their fleet invaded England, sailing up the Medway to capture and destroy much of the English fleet, which was too poorly funded to take to sea. They conquered Suriname and regained Tobago. The English looked weak. At the Peace of Breda, the Dutch retained Suriname, a potentially profitable sugar colony, in exchange for New Netherland. New Netherland was the only Dutch loss in what was otherwise a major triumph of Dutch arms.

Abandoned by its motherland, the Dutch Reformed Church lost its status as the public church. English policy in New York did not build on the precedent of New Netherland's religious policies. On the contrary, the English rulers encouraged the pluralism the Dutch had struggled to suppress. The new terms of religious life in New York were set in February 1665 when Colonel Richard Nicolls called an assembly of Englishmen at Hempstead. Under his direction the assembly came up with a new code of laws known as the Duke's Laws. Designed to accommodate the English inhabitants to the duke of York's government, the Duke's Laws would be extended to the Dutch only after restoration of English rule in 1674. The Dutch Reformed Church, once dominant, was now a merely tolerated church.

Though by the later standards of Pennsylvania the Duke's Laws were rather limited, compared to the Dutch arrangement it was a remarkable expansion of toleration. The Duke's Laws divided the English towns into parishes and allowed each to choose the sort of church it wanted by a majority vote of the householders. Choices were limited. Crucial conditions shut out Quakers, Baptists, and Catholics. For example, every church had to have a minister who could "produce testimonials to the governor that he hath received ordination either from some Protestant bishop or minister, within some part of his Majesty's dominions, or the dominions of any foreign prince of the Reformed religion." English ministers could not refuse "the sacrament of baptism to the children of Christian parents, when they shall be tendered, under penalty of loss of preferment." Nor could they exclude anyone from communion, unless demonstrably "of scandalous or vicious life," a matter determined by the administration, not the minister. In other words, they could not follow the restrictive practices of New England Congregationalists who opposed the Half-Way Covenant.[3] The beneficiaries of this toleration were the majority of the colony's population: Presbyterians, Lutherans, Dutch Reformed, and Congregationalists. Anglicans would also have been provided for, though there were virtually none. There is no record of an Anglican minister in New York before 1674 and no Church of England parish would be set up until the 1690s. Jews, who had only begun to return to the English world in London and the Caribbean, received special support of New York's governors. Initially little more than Asser Levy's family, the community grew steadily through immigration, and was able to form a congregation and build a small synagogue in the 1670s.

New York's religious tolerance was a byproduct of the conquest, not an inspired piece of colonial promotion. Because the expedition that conquered New Netherland had been launched in secret, there was no promotional material, as there was for Carolina and other colonies. One of the few efforts to promote New York was a short pamphlet by Daniel Denton, son of Richard Denton, the Presbyterian preacher of Hempstead. His brother had served as a magistrate enforcing Reformed hegemony under Dutch rule. The whole family were staunch allies of Stuyvesant and the Dutch Reformed Church. Though happy to live under English rule, they had not been unhappy with the Dutch public church. Denton published *A Brief Description of New-York: Formerly Called New-Netherlands* in London in 1670 to promote immigration. The subtitle accurately conveys the contents, which focused primarily on the geography and ethnography of the colony: the "Manner of its Scituation, Fertility of the Soyle, Healthfulness of the Climate, and the Commodities thence produced" together with a "Brief Relation of the Customs of the Indians there," as well as "Some Directions and Advice to such as shall go thither." It made absolutely no mention of religion, liberty of conscience, or church arrangement. The new tolerance was not billed as a draw for colonists.[4]

In some ways, more toleration in New York meant less autonomy for the religious groups in the colony. Church life became more influenced by the secular authorities since all were recognized yet none enjoyed a special status. Now the religious life of everyone in the province was supervised by the English governor, a far greater intrusion in the dissenters' religious lives than Stuyvesant had ever made. No longer the ally or protector of any particular church, the governor was now the mediator for *all* New York's religious groups equally, enforcing public order and religious limits. That the first two English governors (Richard Nicolls 1664–1668 and Francis Lovelace 1668–1673) were associated with the Church of England, a church virtually nonexistent in the colony, only reinforced their status as distinctly autonomous authorities who presided over, rather than participated in, the colony's religious life. Though essentially secular, their position had genuine religious consequences for the colony. Their support was needed for important aspects of church life, from recruiting new ministers to upholding the authority of ministers against dissenting congregants. Churches could thrive or fail depending on their support. Another result was that the governor could settle questions of doctrine within churches if he felt a dispute was producing too much conflict. Nicolls and Lovelace were not irreligious. They took their task seriously. However, what they saw fit to do to support "religion" in the colony was not always welcome to all the colonists. In theory, their enforcement of the Duke's Laws did not favor any denomination over another. But the new regime was a distinct loss for some and a gain for others.

Richard Nicolls, New York's first governor, was a royalist who had fought for the king during the civil war, then lived in exile with the Stuarts as a member of the household of James, duke of York. Though he fought for a while in the French army, he remained in York's service until he was killed in a naval battle against the Dutch in 1672. His religious affiliation is not entirely certain, though he was probably a conservative Church of England man for much of his life. A letter from Philip Calvert, a member of the Catholic family that owned and governed Maryland, indicates that by 1668, if Nicolls was not actually a Catholic, he was certainly friendly to them. Calvert wrote to thank Nicolls for sending a chalice and seven books, evidently related to Catholicism, hoping that "you may be as greate a practiser of the Religion, as you are a master of the honor of ancient Rome." He assured Nicolls that the chalice and books would "only be employd to the sacred use they were first consecrated for," and recognized the gift as

an "act of Adoration of the one ever living God which we both adore."[5]
There is very little record of what happened in the religious realm under
Nicolls's stewardship. He himself was remarkably tightlipped about religious issues, only noting in a report that "Liberty of Conscience is graunted
and assured."[6] Of course liberty of conscience under a Catholic or Catholic-
friendly Englishman was not the same thing as liberty of conscience under
a Calvinist like Stuyvesant.

The Dutch Reformed experienced their new condition as a tolerated
group as a distinct loss. In the gloomy years after the conquest, one would
write that it "appears as if God were punishing this land for its sins. Some
years (ago) there appeared a meteor in the air. Last year we saw a terrible
comet in the west, a little above the horizon, with the tail upward, and
hanging over this place. It showed itself for about eight days, and then
disappeared. So we fear God's judgments, but supplicate his favor."[7] At the
same time, the conquest revived the Counter-Remonstrant character of the
Dutch Reformed Church in North America. The Remonstrant-tinged public church foisted on them after 1658 evaporated with the newest and
youngest ministers: Dominie Selijns returned to Holland shortly before the
conquest and Dominie Blom returned as soon as the war was over in 1667.
The Calvinists persevered, though they were running out of energy. The
remaining four ministers were aging, and only Megapolensis aged well. Polhemius and Drisius lost coherence and stamina as they entered their sixties.
Schaets had his own problems, and lived long enough to have them derided
by a critical eyewitness in 1679: "He had a defect in the left eye, and used
such strange gestures and language that I think I never in all my life have
heard any thing more miserable." Schaets had probably suffered a stroke,
but his critic had his own theory. "As it is not strange in these countries to
have men as ministers who drink, we could imagine nothing else than that
he had been drinking a little this morning."[8] Though decrepit and addled,
the ministers preserved the memory and mission of Counter-Remonstrant
Calvinism well into the 1670s. Their parishioners would complain of their
feebleness, but never of their piety.

For other religious groups, the conquest was a boon. Few greeted the
conquest of New Netherland with more enthusiasm than the Lutherans. In
December 1664, the Dutch Lutherans petitioned Nicolls for the right to
form a congregation and call a minister—something they had been struggling for over a decade to achieve. Nicolls granted their wish the very next
day. The newly constituted Lutheran consistory of New York gleefully wrote

its fellow in Amsterdam to announce that "our faithful God, whose works are wonderful to behold, has, contrary to all human expectation, through this present governor placed us under his Royal Majesty of England's government, so that we have been spurred on by prominent persons of the English nation, yes, have even been furnished pens and hands, to carry on this Christian work." The war, and the unwillingness of several possible ministerial candidates to make the perilous crossing to America, forced the Lutherans to wait several years before getting their first official pastor in February 1669. It was a serendipitous find. Jacobus Fabritius was a refugee of Silesian origin, whose church in Hungary had been overrun by the Turks, and he needed a new post.[9]

On what now became the Delaware River, the radical experiment in New Amstel was eradicated, returning the religious situation to 1657. The Swedish colonists had come to peaceful terms with the English during the conquest. In return for standing back while the English captured the Dutch outposts, they secured the promise that "all people shall enjoy the liberty of Conscience in Church Discipline as formerly."[10] One thing that did change was the emergence of a small clique of Dutch Lutherans, who moved down from the Hudson Valley to take advantage of the new opportunities English rule opened up to them. The English conquest finally brought together the once separate Lutheran communities of New Netherland.[11]

For the Quakers as well, the English conquest created a more favorable climate, notwithstanding the limitations of the Duke's Laws, which discouraged proselytizing in the colony, a blow to the Quakers who were still spreading their faith. According to the laws, "no congregations shall be disturbed in their private meetings, in the time of prayer, preaching, or other divine service" and "every person affronting or disturbing any congregation on the Lord's day, and on such public days of fast and thanksgiving as are appointed to be observed . . . shall be punished by fine or imprisonment, according to the merit and nature of the offense." The laws were legislating against tactics that had been common in the Quaker campaign across the English world, but actually rare in New Netherland, where the Quakers had tended to gather in separate conventicles rather than confront a congregation at worship. Nonetheless, the Duke's Laws also protected Quakers in ways the Dutch government never had. The Dutch ordinances against conventicles and hosting Quakers were replaced by the provision that no "person shall be molested, fined, or imprisoned, for differing in judgment in matters or religion, who professes Christianity," all very Quaker-friendly terms.[12] Quakers no longer had to meet in secret or fear imprisonment for advocating their beliefs. Such evidence as exists suggests that they were emboldened by the possibilities unlocked by English rule. A 1677 petition from Huntington to New York's governor requests that "the Quakers may not be suffered to Come into our Meeting house in tyme of God's Worship to disturb us as they frequently doe," indicating the Quakers eventually became bold enough to take on existing congregations in a way they had not in the days of New Netherland.[13]

The one incident of possible religious conflict on Nicolls's watch can be read as a sign of Quaker activism. In summer 1667, a number of men in Flushing's militia company apparently refused to serve. We do not have their protest, but judging by Nicolls's reaction they were probably Quakers. The Quaker "Peace Testimony," which foreswore armed violence and military conflict, though articulated at the time of the Restoration in 1660, probably took a few years to be fully adopted by all Quakers in Britain.[14] How long it took to for New York's Quakers to accept it is unclear, but certainly by 1667 it would have been known and understood by them, if not their non-Quakers neighbors. Nicolls was shocked. He sent Flushing a letter, protesting, "you have given me just reason to suspect your fidelities & your courage." As punishment the militia company flags and "twelve Match Locks" had to be returned to Fort James. The men who offended him (presumably by refusing to serve) were also prohibited from entering New York City for three months. Another list of men was turned into Nicolls, this one preserved, containing the names of those in Flushing willing to serve. Flushing was as divided as ever. Nonetheless, the issue of Quaker pacifism was now added to the mix of claims to liberty of conscience in what had been New Netherland.[15]

One striking addition to the religious life of New York was the beginning of witchcraft trials. Under the Dutch, there had been no witchcraft trials, for witchcraft had not been treated as a prosecutable offense in the republic since the sixteenth century. The transition to English law, where witchcraft was still prosecutable, allowed colonists to take each other to court for witchcraft for the first time. The first accusation came scarcely a year after the conquest, in October 1665. Ralph Hall and his wife Mary were accused of having practiced sorcery on the person of George Wood and his infant son, beginning on Christmas Day 1664. They allegedly caused George and then his son to sicken and die. The grand jury of predominantly

Reformed colonists (Dutch and English) concluded that while there was reason for some suspicion about Mary, there was none against her husband Ralph. Exercising a discretion and caution that would be much missed in Salem twenty-seven years later, the court ordered Ralph to enter into a recognizance for his wife's good behavior. In August 1668, shortly before returning to England, Nicolls released the Halls from their recognizance, there "haueving beene no direct proofes nor further prosecuceon of them or either of them since" the 1665 trial.[16] In summer 1670 a witchcraft case came before Governor Lovelace. Katherine Harrison wanted to move from Wethersfield, Connecticut, to Westchester, New York, but the inhabitants of Westchester objected because she was "reputed to be a person lyeing under the supposicon of Witchcraft." Lovelace ordered her to move back to Connecticut to "end their Jealousyes & feares." However, he thought the "reasons" for their fears "do not so clearly appeare unto me." After Katherine gave "sufficient security for her Civill carriage & good behavior," Lovelace permitted her to "remaine in the Towne of Westchester" without "disturbance or molestation" until the next meeting of the Court of Assizes. After the court met in October 1670 and ruled there was "nothing appears against her deserving" prosecution or recognizance, she was allowed to remain in Westchester "or any where else in the Government during her pleasure."[17] With that, another potential incident was snuffed out. Witchcraft never again came before the courts of New York.

The English period fundamentally changed the religious dynamic of the region, most significantly by spurring English colonization of what is now New Jersey. At the time of the conquest the only settlement in the areas was the Dutch town of Bergen (now Jersey City), founded in 1661. Within months of the conquest, Governor Nicolls encouraged the group of puritans who had once negotiated with Stuyvesant to set up Newark (originally the "New Ark" of the Covenant). In the meantime, the duke of York granted the lands between the Hudson and Delaware Rivers to two of his supporters, Sir George Carteret and John, Baron Berkeley. In strictly legal terms, the duke's grant of New Jersey was no more than a grant of land ownership. Since he was not the king, he could not grant the powers of government the king had delegated to him in his proprietary of New York. New Jersey's proprietors overlooked this technicality and immediately began asserting their rule. The right of government over the territory became a bone of contention between New Jersey proprietors and governors of New York for the next several decades. Carteret's cousin and appointed governor, Philip Carteret, began the first expressly New Jersey settlement in 1665 with some thirty colonists from the Channel Islands (including Jersey, home of the Carterets and source of the new colony's name). Together with some English who had settled at the mouth of Newark Bay they began a town named Elizabeth, after Lady Carteret.

The New Jersey colony exceeded New York's policy of toleration. Unlike the Duke's Laws, no schema of semi-official establishment was provided for. On the contrary, the "Concessions and Agreements of the Lords Propriators of the Province of New Jersey" went out of their way to assure potential colonists that no sort of religious persecution would be possible. Settlers were authorized to "at all times truly and fully have and enjoy his and their Judgements and Conciences in matters of Religion throughout all the said Province." No one could be "any waies molested punished disquieted or called in Question for any difference in opinion or practice in matters of Religious concernments." As long as colonists behaved "themselves peaceably and quietly and" did not use "this liberty to Licentiousness, nor to the civill injury or outward disturbance of others," they were guaranteed a religious liberty unavailable in New York, England, or the Dutch Republic. Harassment, discrimination, and aggressive proselytizing were prohibited in New Jersey, "any Law Statute or clause conteyned or to be conteined usage or custome of this Realme of England to the contrary thereof in any wise notwithstanding," a direct affront to the Church of England, which would not gain a foothold in New Jersey for decades.[18]

Until 1675, most of the colonists in New Jersey moved there from another colony, many from New England. New Ark, begun by New Havenites, and Woodbridge (named after famous New England minister John Woodbridge), established by colonists from Massachusetts in 1667, were both Congregational settlements, as was Elizabeth. The following year, a group mostly of Baptists from New Hampshire settled Piscataway to the west, named after New Hampshire's major river. Finally, to the southeast, a number of Baptists and Quakers, mostly from Long Island, founded Middletown and Shrewsbury. New Ark, Elizabethtown, and Woodbridge were able to keep themselves supplied with Congregational ministers from New England.[19] Bergen depended on visits from New York's Dutch minister. In the other three towns, ministers were conspicuous by their absence—purposely so. Baptists and Quakers had more freedoms in New Jersey than in New York for they did not have to contend with the local establishment required by the Duke's Laws. New Jersey's radically decentralized religious system worked because every town was essentially segregated into a different faith. There were no divided communities, like Flushing, with conflicts that could draw the attention of higher authorities.

Governor Lovelace, who replaced Nicolls in 1668, was also a royalist who had spent some time abroad during England's revolutionary period. Like Nicolls he had fought for the king during the English Civil War, then spent time in exile, in Europe fighting for Louis XIV, in Virginia between 1650 and 1652, and finally back to Europe. His time in Virginia gave him more perspective on the colonial religious situation than Nicolls had had. On August 28, 1668, Lovelace explained to King Charles II that New York, situated between Maryland and New England, occupied "the middle position of the two distinct factions, the Papist and Puritan." On both a pan-colonial and local scale, Lovelace saw his role as balancing hostile religious factions while retaining their loyalty to the duke and king. Lovelace was a man of cosmopolitan experience and a firm supporter of "religion," albeit of an ecumenical Protestant bent. He expected New York's churches and ministers to carry out the basic functions of a parish minister to all inhabitants, whether their creed allowed it or not.

Lovelace confirmed Nicolls's religious policies, including the grant of freedom of worship to the Lutherans, who gained purchase with the arrival of their first openly tolerated minister. Lovelace licensed the minister, Fabritius, to preach after he swore the oath of loyalty to the king. Fabritius began the next day. With obvious pride, New York's Lutheran consistory reported the impact their new minister was making. As he preached, baptized, administered communion, and visited the sick, "many scattered Evangelical Lutheran members, of whom heretofore we had no knowledge, reveal themselves and come to us." Even a "50 year old Negro" came forward for baptism. The jealousy "among our adversaries" (the Dutch Reformed) was inflamed by Fabritius's success. "But it does us no harm," they reported, for Fabritius bore himself well, behaved modestly, and avoided confronting the Dutch Reformed. Moreover, the English officials respected him.

With his arrival, Fabritius became the most vigorous preacher in New York. Suddenly the shoe was on the other foot for the Dutch Reformed and their aging ministers. Whereas in the days of New Netherland they had boasted of the Lutherans who listened to their sermons, in New York the Lutherans could report that "Calvinists now come in large numbers to the preaching, and this because their three ministers have in these Easter holy

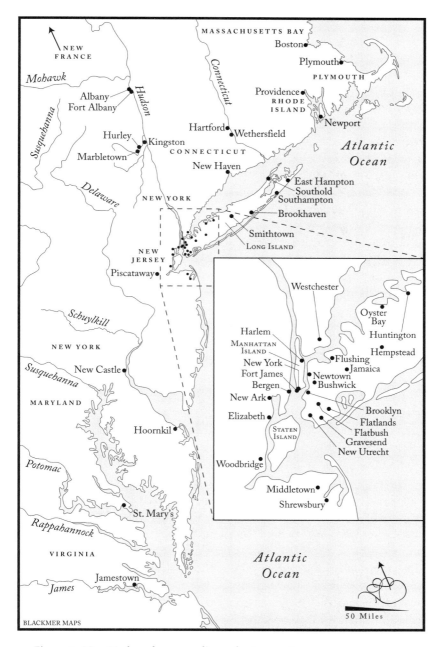

Figure 8. New York and surrounding colonies, c. 1672.

days held not more than one service, whereas our Rev. Magister held six, including Good Friday."[20] Meanwhile on October 13, 1669, Lovelace announced to those who were not Lutheran, most likely the Dutch Reformed, that the Lutherans enjoyed his special protection: "Gentlemen: I have lately received Letters from the Duke Wherein it is perticulerly signified unto me that his Royall Highness doth approve of the Tolleration given to the Lutheran Church in theise partes. I doe therefore expect that you live friendly & peaceably with those of that profession giving them no disturbance in the Exercise of their Religion, as they shall receive noe Countenance in, but on the Contrary strictly Answer any disturbance they shall presume to give unto any of you in your divine worship."[21] Neither Dutch Reformed nor Lutheran, Lovelace prioritized peaceful coexistence over the claims of a single church.

Alas for the Dutch Lutherans, their heyday was brief. Fabritius was a refugee in America, not a pilgrim. Driven out by the Turks from the eastern frontier of Christianity in Hungary, he had been desperate enough to accept a new position on its western frontier. However, he was not cut out for the humble work of building a new congregation. He proudly refused to present his preaching license to the court at Albany, which then banned him from preaching in its jurisdiction. His dismayed congregants discovered that he "is very fond of wine and brandy and knows how to curse and swear, too. In his apparel he is like a soldier, red from head to foot . . . he has had coats and a hat made like the pastors at Hamburg wear." Fabritius's behavior was making him the subject of scandalous gossip. The disillusionment was evidently mutual. After less than two years, he decided to move on to the Swedish Lutherans on the Delaware. His former Dutch Lutheran congregants called for another, hopefully more tractable, minister.[22]

Governor Lovelace continued to support the Lutheran Church, local scandal notwithstanding. He treated Fabritius with respect and recommended the minister to his commandant on the Delaware, Captain John Carr, whom he exhorted to show "all civill respect when he comes amongst you and take care he receives no affront there."[23] When the Amsterdam Lutheran consistory found a replacement for Fabritius, in the person of Bernhard Arnzius, Lovelace granted Fabritius permission "to give his Valedictory Sermon, and to Install the new Come-Minister according to the Custome used by those of their Religion." Lovelace's priority was to impart a certain dignity and authority to the office of minister, regardless how the man dressed or drank. Fabritius reciprocated, respecting Lovelace's authority by petitioning for the right to preach the sermon. Lovelace found the request "reasonable & (as I am Informed) according to the Custom of the Augustine Confession."[24] Arnzius proved a more tractable choice than Fabritius. A man of pietistic leanings, he quietly presided over New York's Lutherans for twenty years until his death in 1691. Under his guidance, the Lutherans garnered a small, stable corner of acceptance in New York society, building churches in both New York (1676) and Albany (1680).[25]

The Dutch Reformed dominies had little to be pleased with in the change of regimes. The tolerance of the English governors could not make up for the loss of the guaranteed salary and official support that had underwritten their authority under Dutch rule. As Megapolensis wrote the Amsterdam classis in 1669: "On Sundays we have many hearers. People crowd into the church, and apparently like the sermon; but most of the listeners are not inclined to contribute to the support and salary of the preacher. They seem to desire that we should live upon air and not upon produce." Governor Nicolls had deigned to tolerate the Dutch church, but he was not going to sustain it. When the ministers asked for help with their salaries, Nicolls's response was "that if the Dutch will have divine services their own way, then let them also take care of and support their own preachers, and thus, . . . nothing is done for our salary." Such was the experience of liberty of conscience for those who were tolerated rather than tolerating. Sixty-five-year-old Megapolensis stated his belief that God would take care of him for what little remained of his life. "But a thought often occurs to me, and troubles me," he concluded. "What will become of the congregation here, when I and Domine Drisius are dead? Since they care so little for a decent support of their preacher, I cannot see how they will procure another."[26] Lovelace did make more efforts to ensure the material welfare of the Dutch Reformed churches than Nicolls had. He relieved Dominie Polhemius from local taxes in January 1671, then in March, when there was resistance on the part of some to pay their share for the construction of a parish house for the Long Island congregations, ordered "those that are behinde in payment of their proportion" for the "Domine's House" in Brooklyn be compelled to pay.[27] But he could not sustain the Dutch ministry in the style to which they had been accustomed.

Without strong official support and funding, it became very difficult to find new ministers for the isolated colony. Blom left because his congregation could not afford to pay him. Megapolensis died in 1670, Drisius in

1673, and Polhemius in 1676. Schaets held on in Albany until 1694. After Megapolensis died, New York's Dutch Reformed Church asked that the classis send back Selijns, who had "left a deep impression among our membership by the faithfulness of his ministry, the piety of his life, his peculiar zeal in instructing and catechizing, and his kind and affectionate intercourse."[28] However, Selijns showed "but little inclination" to "consent to serve." As the classis pointed out, the lack of a fixed salary made it unlikely any able minister would willingly serve there.[29] Even Megapolensis's son Samuel, trained for the Reformed ministry at Harvard in hopes that he would return and serve the colony, was so discouraged by the lack of funds for the colonial church that he left New York and took a post in Holland.[30] The classis eventually found a replacement for Megapolensis in the person of William Nieuwenhuysen, who took over the New York City ministry in 1671.[31] The city's consistory gratefully acknowledged Nieuwenhuysen as "very agreeable to us, and his gifts fully satisfy the congregation. He labors daily and diligently in edifying our people, either by preaching God's Word, or by catechizing the young." Moreover, it reported it had finally settled on a means of paying the minister's salary through a mixture of beavers, silver coins, and wampum.[32] For the time being Nieuwenhuysen was the only young and vigorous minister the Dutch had in North America.

Among the English Reformed Churches, Governor Lovelace did as he did with the others, supporting the privileges of the ministers, regardless of their denominational affiliation. In March 1669 he ordered the town of Newtown (formerly Middelburgh) to pay 600 guilders back pay to Francis Doughty, a compromise settlement. It was less than Doughty demanded but more than Newtown claimed it could afford. Since Doughty was no longer Newtown's minister, the town was paying for past services and getting nothing for the future. It would be years before it had a minister of its own. Nonetheless Lovelace ordered the payment, adding, "all persons are hereby required to forbeare any further cavils or contests upon this account as they will answer the contrary at their perils."[33] This judgment suggests he worked to ensure that other ministers also got at least some of their financial due from their parishioners.

Remarkably, Lovelace extended his ecumenical support for organized religion to Quakers. George Fox, the great founder of Quakerism, passed through New York in spring 1672 on a journey to reinvigorate and organize Quaker congregations in the colonies. He had been in Jamaica, Maryland,

and New Jersey and would continue on to Rhode Island. In New York he stopped first at Gravesend, then Oyster Bay, where he participated in a general meeting that lasted "six days" and was "large." Afterward he went "through the woods to Flushing" and took part in a "large meeting at John Bowne's house." Fox remarked that Bowne "was banished by the Dutch into England," a somewhat garbled memory but a clear testimony to Bowne's status as a local sufferer for the faith. The Flushing meeting was a true public event, the greatest display of Quaker privilege the region had yet seen. There were "many hundreds of the world," that is non-Quakers, in attendance. This may have included the "governor" (Lovelace) who, Fox noted, "heard of me and was loving and said that he had been in my company."[34] Fox's journal, the sole source, is unclear on the exact nature of his contact with the governor, but Lovelace clearly made a positive impression on him.

New York under Lovelace also witnessed the first open disputation of religious doctrine the region had seen, when some local English Reformed Protestants confronted Fox. Fox returned to Flushing at the end of summer 1672 and held another meeting to which "many hundreds of the people of the world" traveled "about thirty miles" to attend. There was a justice of the peace "and his family, and many considerable persons." At the end of the meeting a "priest's son" (that is, the son of a minister—probably Daniel Denton) "stood up" and "laid down three things that he would dispute." These were three of the basic issues that Reformed Protestants held against Quakers, namely "the ordination of ministers," allowing women to speak in meetings, and "that we held a new way of worship."[35] Fox recounts the debate in some detail, demonstrating how he (of course?) emerged triumphant. How Reformed colonists perceived his performance is unknown. The occasion was highly significant for local history. Under the Dutch, Lutherans, Quakers, and Baptists had criticized the Reformed Churches, but never did the Reformed feel they had to respond in an open debate. Now, under English rule, it was possible for the leading English Quaker to travel peaceably across the colony, hold large meetings among his fellow Quakers, and even openly rebut Reformed Protestant criticisms. The contrast with the Dutch period is striking.

The budding pluralism of colonial New York was brought to a sudden halt by yet another conquest. On July 30, 1673, a Dutch fleet operating against the English in yet another (the third) Anglo-Dutch War (1672–1674) arrived in New York harbor and seized control of the colony. New Netherland was once again in Dutch hands. The experience was brief—a year later the Dutch negotiated peace in which they returned the colony to England—but significant. American historians like to think that there was a logic to religious toleration in colonial America: that it naturally grew and expanded over time. The Dutch did not share that logic. Rather than embrace the changes brought by the English to Dutch America, they turned back the clock as much as possible.

The contrast between how the Dutch and the English conquerors treated the religious diversity of the region underscores the contingency that shaped American pluralism. There was nothing inevitable or obvious about whom to tolerate or how. The Dutch approach is a reminder that there was more than one Dutch way of handling religious diversity, just as there was more than one way of being Dutch. The invading fleet came from Zeeland, the most fiercely Calvinist province in the Netherlands, a far cry from Amsterdam and its liberal connivance. Additionally, the fleet was sent out after a domestic revolution in Dutch politics, as the True Freedom under Johan de Witt collapsed under the pressure of a massive invasion by land and sea from France, England, and the bishopric of Munster. The young prince of Orange, Willem III, came to power to lead the war effort in a struggle for the very survival of the United Provinces. The Orangists once again had the upper hand in Dutch politics. Bontemantel and other liberal regents lost their positions. The environment that had made Plockhoy's experiment in New Amstel possible was replaced by a return to the ways of Petrus Stuyvesant, who died just as his beloved colony returned to Dutch rule.

The brief return of Dutch rule is also a reminder of how dependent colonial American developments were on European affairs. The Dutch had not bothered to recapture New Netherland during the Second Anglo-Dutch war, and they had not initially intended to do so in this third war either. The fleet that captured New York had embarked on a major trans-Atlantic raid to disrupt English shipping and trade in the Americas, from the sugar islands of the Caribbean to the tobacco fleet in the Chesapeake and the fisheries of Newfoundland. Only by chance did it discover that New York was an easy plum for picking. With the encouragement of some colonists, the fleet sailed into the harbor and, after a brief fight, overwhelmed the English defenses. Then most of the fleet sailed on to Newfoundland and back to Europe. Preserving Dutch America was not a consideration for the Dutch government, which offered to return New York in an effort to persuade the English to abandon the war. Placing its urgent European situation over the concerns of Dutch American colonists, the Dutch republic abandoned the opportunity to shape the religious and political future of North America. It might look as if English hegemony in North America was inevitable, but it did not seem that way in 1673.

Unfortunately for the English, New York's defenses could not withstand even a moderate military onslaught. The English garrison surrendered after a brief fight. New York became New Orange. Albany became Willemstadt. The new nomenclature reflected the Orangist inclinations of the new rulers. Zeeland, long a stronghold of Orangism and Calvinism, had been active in the conquest and government of Dutch Brazil as well as Suriname, Tobago, and parts of Guyana. It had long fostered a more expansionist vision of Dutch empire and religion than Amsterdam had. The restored colony stayed under Dutch control for just over a year, until it was returned to the English in November 1674 by the Treaty of Westminster. It was not long enough to effect lasting changes, but long enough to indicate how things would have gone had the Dutch retained New Netherland.

Naval Captain Anthony Colve headed the new Dutch government, receiving a temporary promotion to governor-general. Though he did not have much to work with, Colve strove energetically to restore New Netherland and the Reformed Church to their former glory. Only three ministers remained to uphold the church: Nieuwenhuysen in New Orange, the aging Schaets in Willemstadt, and Polhemius on Long Island. Drisius had died a few months earlier. Nonetheless, the new government made the Reformed Church once again the official religion of the colony. Dutch Reformed ministers were promised a secure income and could draw on the government to suppress dissent, as had been the case under Stuyvesant. The magistrates of New Orange affirmed the Reformed religion's public status by proclaiming days of humiliation and thanksgiving.[36]

Colve also resumed Stuyvesant's policy of cooperating with English Calvinists. When petitions from English Reformed communities on Long Island and New Jersey asked for freedom of religion, he granted it immediately. His preference for the Dutch Reformed emerged when he granted the Willemstadt Lutherans' petition for "free exercise of their religious worship, without let or hindrance." The goal, as with many such grants, was social and political stability: "to the end that they may live in peace with their fellow burghers." But there was one important condition. They must give no "offense to the congregation of the Reformed Religion, which is the official Church."[37] That had not been one of the English conditions for tolerating the Lutheran church. Dutch Reformed hegemony was restored, albeit somewhat weakened from its heyday a decade earlier. However, that could always change if New Netherland remained in Dutch hands. The Dutch Reformed Church had its champion back.

Colve's regime reinvigorated the previously struggling Dutch Reformed Church. In July 1674, Nieuwenhuysen happily reported to the Amsterdam classis that the "church in this place flourishes under God's blessing." There were now "between four and five hundred members; of whom, we can assure your Rev. Body, without boasting, more than one hundred have been received under our ministry." Nieuwenhuysen felt that "the present Dutch government" allowed the Lutherans "too much liberty," as "the late English" rulers had, but he was not intimidated by the competition. As he put it, "they do us no harm, while we occasionally gain a few from their small number," continuing the longstanding Dutch Reformed habit of trying to absorb the Lutherans. As far as Nieuwenhuysen was concerned, the Lutherans were the only group he had to worry about. Apart from them, there was "no other sect here."[38] The Dutch Reformed Church had weathered ten years of foreign occupation and stood ready to recuperate the ground it had lost under English rule.

Many colonists, Dutch and English alike, enthusiastically welcomed the restoration of the Dutch public church. The model of Anglo-Dutch Reformed cooperation that had prospered under Stuyvesant was resuscitated. The English Reformed churches petitioned for recognition and received it. In May 1674, Nathaniel Denton of Jamaica (son of Richard and younger brother of Daniel) asked that the local minister be maintained "as hitherto he hath bene maintained that is to say by the towne ingenerall every man paying according to proportion though they differed in judgement or would upon any other pretens deny payment." In other words, people could not object to paying for the local minister by claiming their conscience led them to dissent from the Presbyterian church. There were "two men in our towne which doth deny to pay theire proportion and giveth such threatening speeches that there is hardly any perswading of any one to goe with the marshall to assist him in the execution of his offis for they have a consaite that unless wee have an order from the governor to take it by distress of every one that wee cannot doe it of ourselves by the power wee have." The Dutch government approved. As had happened in New Netherland, the Dutch noted that the English Presbyterian minister was in "noe ways repugnant" to the Synod of Dort, and thus deserved government help in getting his salary collected.[39]

The religious tenor of Colve's government recalled that of New Netherland. Colve's foes were the same as Stuyvesant's—radical Protestants and Lutherans, both of whom found that the gains made under English rule could easily be restricted under the Dutch. Though the Dutch explicitly guaranteed "freedom of conscience" everywhere in the colony, it was limited (as it had been under New Netherland) by the prerogatives of the Reformed Church. Colve did not have the time or resources to go after the other religious groups as Stuyvesant had, but he kept them on a tight leash. He certainly did not encourage them as Lovelace had.[40]

The religious tolerance of New York was over. Colve did not harass Quaker congregations, but he did push Quakers out of the positions of power they had attained. Less than a year before the Dutch reconquest, George Fox had passed through Shrewsbury, New Jersey, and held "a very large meeting and a precious meeting" there, noting "the blessed presence of the Lord was with us." What impressed Fox even more than the spiritual power of the meeting was the fact that, in New Jersey, Quakers could be magistrates. In Shrewsbury he noted, "a Friend is made a justice."[41] By fall 1673 Shrewsbury had two Quaker magistrates. Both lost their positions under Dutch rule. Colve's justification for dismissing them was one generally used against Quakers. They were, he said, "Persons whoes religion Will Not Suffer them to take anij oath, or administer the Same to others wherefore they Can Nott be fit Persons for that office." In their place, he ordered the inhabitants to nominate "four Persons off the true Protestant Christian religion," from which he, in true Dutch fashion, would select two.[42] The ideological tone of the Dutch regime was unmistakable.

Though the Lutherans were allowed to continue to worship on their own, the Dutch Reformed began to harass them. At one point the Lutherans of Willemstadt protested to Colve that the Dutch Reformed "Sexton" was making them pay him "in cases of the burial of their dead . . . notwithstanding they employ their own Sexton." They complained that they paid their taxes and took care of their own poor, and "are therefore, as they consider, not in the least subject to such charges but on the contrary ought

to enjoy their (religious) exercises and Divine Service free and uncon-
strained, for which they have a written grant from the late Honorable Gov-
ernour Lovelace copy of which is hereunto annexed." Mr. Roosenboom,
the Dutch sexton, had seized and sold a Lutheran's goods to pay for his
burial. Under English rule, when the same Roosenboom had claimed jurisdiction over Lutheran burials, the response had been "Let the Dead bury
their Dead; for with what free conscience can" the Dutch "Precentor go and
act for the Lutherans, for they have more ceremonies than the Reformed.
Whereupon at that time he had no more to say, and it was well." Willemstadt's Lutherans pointed out that the Lutherans at New Orange had the
right to "bury their dead without notifying" the Dutch Reformed, yet their
local Reformed authorities threatened to deny them their newly gained
privilege.[43] There is no record of the response of Colve's government. However, the fact that Lutherans now had to struggle for a religious (and fiscal)
right that they had enjoyed freely under the English is significant. Dutch
Reformed colonists could take advantage of Colve's government to restore
the habits and prerogatives of the public church on their own initiative
(which could coincide with their own profit, as in Roosenboom's case).

The Dutch Reformed who remembered the days when the Lutherans
had to be part of their public church never seem to have accepted the
tolerated Lutheran congregations. Roosenboom's presumption is the only
incident for which there is evidence under Colve's government. Nevertheless, religious impatience bubbled along among the Reformed, occasionally
manifesting itself when a colonist was outraged enough to take someone to
court and the court was willing to hear the case. For example, in March
1680, after the English returned to power, Dominie Schaets took a Lutheran
couple to court for slander, claiming the man falsely accused him of trying
to convert the Lutherans' children (something Reformed ministers had
aspired to in the days of the public church). The Lutheran had told Schaets
"never to presume to speak to any of his Children on religious matters."
Upset, he accused the dominie of "sneaking through all the houses like the
Devill." Adding insult to injury, he claimed the Lutheran minister "does
not do so." The Lutheran's wife likewise "grievously abused & calumni-
ated" Schaets "behind his back," alledging he "abused her Religion as a
Devilish Religion." The Lutherans denied the accusations. Roosenboom
testified against them both. The court compelled the Lutherans to be formally reconciled with Schaets, acknowledge him to be an honest man, and
pay the court fees.[44] Given the long history of Lutheran subservience to the

Dutch Reformed in America, what seems most remarkable about this incident is not that the Lutherans lost the case, but that they felt they could express their grievances to Schaets's face. It is not hard to imagine that similar tensions and fears had existed all along but dared not be uttered.

On the Delaware, the Swedish Lutheran Lock managed to lay low during the restoration of Dutch rule. His colleague Fabritius, however, was dragged before the court in March 1674 for having "contrary to the laws of this government married Ralph Doxy and Mary van Harris on the 5th of February last past, without having any lawful authority thereto and without publication of bans." The prosecutor demanded he be publicly whipped "and then forever banished this government *cum expensis*." Fabritius humbly submitted, confessed his guilt, and promised "to behave properly in future." The court "would not proceed against him in the most rigorous manner, considering his age and position." Nonetheless, the offense, along with a report of Fabritius's "former bad behavior," was taken seriously. The Dutch court condemned him and declared him "incapable to perform the functions of a minister and what is connected with them within this province for the time of one year. After this time has elapsed," the sentence continued, Fabritius "shall be held to ask for a special consent, before he shall be re-admitted to the performance of the said functions." The sentence was harsher than anything Stuyvesant had mustered against the wayward Lock. And the court meant it. When Fabritius petitioned a month later for a mitigation of the sentence so that he "might at least be allowed to baptize, if he may not preach and act as a minister," his request was denied.[45]

The Dutch authorities did not share Governor Lovelace's respect for Fabritius's status as a minister. Had the Dutch stayed in power, his career, among other things, would probably have been over. In February, his estranged wife, Annetje Cornelis, petitioned the "Burgomaster & Schepens of" New Orange for permission to take possession of her house from her husband "a ci-devant Lutheran Preacher." They granted it to her. Unhappy about the decision, Fabritius tried to get into his wife's house despite the court's orders for him to stay away. When he physically resisted the efforts of the schout to stop him, the schout took him to court, where he was fined.[46]

The Dutch did not have much time back in power, but the few scraps of available evidence make clear how different their approach to religious diversity was from that of the English. Rather than encourage pluralism as the Duke of York's servants had, the Dutch restored the public church. Lutherans were permitted to retain their congregations—that was increasingly the case in the Netherlands at this time too—but there were clear restrictions and the steady pressure from Dutch Reformed colonists to erode their autonomy. The Dutch government also deposed one of the three Lutheran ministers in the colony, reducing the effectiveness of their church. It also dismissed Quakers from public office. As ever, liberty of conscience prevailed and no one was persecuted for their religion, at least not by Dutch Reformed standards. However, those who were not Reformed lost the support of the government while those who were—English as well as Dutch—once again had support for the financing and privileging of their church. The public church was not quite so strong and comprehensive as under Petrus Stuyvesant, but it could have regained its strength had the Dutch stayed in power.

Religious policy in the restored New Netherland reflected that of the republic, which took a reactionary turn after 1672. The expansion of debate and theorizing in the republic under the True Freedom came to an end with the "French War," as the Dutch called it, of 1672–1678. Begun with a surprise attack by French, English, and allied forces from the German ecclesiastical states of Cologne and Munster in the "Disaster Year" of 1672, the war saw the invaders quickly conquer virtually all the United Provinces save Friesland, Zeeland, and Holland—which only managed to save itself by breaking the dykes. The prince of Orange returned as stadholder of Holland and Zeeland, becoming again the key figure in the Dutch military and politics. Outraged at their government's failure to protect the country from invasion, Dutch mobs literally tore to pieces the De Witt brothers who had presided over the True Freedom. The Republican dream was over. Willem III led the fight against the French and their allies, who included, until 1674, the English. The Third Anglo-Dutch War (1672–1674), in which New York was recaptured, was just part of a desperate war for survival. The struggle against France's massive military machine compelled the Dutch to do what they could to deprive it of as many allies as possible. Hence they returned New York to the English in 1674, ending forever the ability of Dutch tolerance to determine religious life in the Mid-Atlantic.

The altered tenor of Dutch religious enterprise overseas after 1672 can be detected in the one new colony they founded in the Americas during the 1670s. Rejecting the True Freedom's propaganda and philosophizing in favor of toleration and trade, it was a colony for the Reformed church, not religious freedom. Curiously, like New Netherland, it had an element of Anglo-Dutch Calvinist cooperation. In 1675 John Price, English minister in The Hague, and son of William Price, a royalist Presbyterian who had been the minister in the English church in Amsterdam since 1648, submitted a proposal for a new colony in Guyana. The colony would be called Orange and situated on the Wiapoco River, along the border of the French colony of Cayenne. Given the loss of New Netherland, it would serve as a defensive outpost and a chance to open new trade outlets in a desperate war against the French. For Price at least, the primary goal was to create an orthodox and loyal Reformed Dutch Protestant settlement in America. Uninterested in pluralism, he wanted "to erect in that waste land a church of Jesus Christ, pure in word and deed to convert the poor blind Heathens from the darkness to the light and from the power of Satan to God." The result was a disaster. Poorly organized and supplied, the colony was quickly captured in a surprise attack by the French in 1677. Price was killed in the assault. The rest of the colonists were carried away as prisoners until the end of the war.[47]

The war was a hard one for the Dutch overseas and at home. Tobago, recently settled with another 500 Dutch colonists, was lost to the English in 1672 while the French captured Saint Eustatius. The following year, the same Dutch squadron that would retake New York recaptured Saint Eustatius, but the English captured it again. Tobago and Saint Eustatius were returned to the Dutch in the peace of 1674—reiterating the Dutch preference for territories in the greater Caribbean over North America. Reestablishing a fort on Tobago, the Dutch managed to fend off one French attack and almost successfully did so again when a lucky (for the French) cannon shot landed in the Dutch fort's ammunition dump, which exploded, destroying the fort and killing most of its defenders. The Dutch captured and then lost Cayenne to the French before the French captured Price's colony of Orange on the Wiapoco River. At the end of the war Dutch independence and territorial integrity were secured, as was tiny Saint Eustatius. But Cayenne and Tobago were lost to the French and New Netherland to the English.[48]

The Dutch Restoration of 1673–1674 is often overlooked in colonial American history, but it deserves attention for a number of reasons. At the very least, it serves as a reminder of how conquest made development of religious liberty in what became the middle colonies contingent, uncertain, and nonlinear. The dramatic transfers of authority from Dutch to English to Dutch and ultimately English played a decisive role in the Mid-Atlantic. With the English conquest of 1664, the tenor of tolerance in Dutch America changed dramatically. The budding radical experiment in New Amstel was cut short, and nothing quite like it would be seen until Quakers founded the colonies of West Jersey and Pennsylvania after 1674. New Netherland, on the other hand, was rendered openly pluralistic, with the English governors serving as patrons of *all* the faiths in the colony. The public church was gone. Whether one can say that the absolute result of the conquest was to increase toleration in the region is hard to say. New York was pluralistic in a way New Netherland was not, but it never encouraged the sort of anticlerical radicalism Amsterdam's burgomasters had permitted in New Amstel. Then the Dutch reconquest restored the public church and reduced the nascent pluralism of New York. It took a new European peace treaty to restore English rule in the Mid-Atlantic.

In the end, one could say that, thanks to the Dutch, America wound up with more religious freedom than it would have had without them. However, it should be remembered that the Dutch themselves had very little to do with it. Though they became a part of colonial American pluralism, it was the English authorities who took over from them who implemented the religious liberty that made the middle colonies America's hearth of religious pluralism. These English of the Restoration period (1660–1688) were a very particular bunch living in a peculiar moment of their nation's history, very different from the eras of Protestant and Church of England hegemony that preceded and followed it. Figures like William Penn could be friends with James, duke of York, and his brother, Charles II. After the return of New York in the Treaty of Westminster, the three supported the creation of three Quaker-dominated colonies by 1681: East Jersey, West Jersey, and Pennsylvania. It was an extraordinary conjuncture, one that could not have happened earlier and would not happen after the Glorious Revolution of 1688 drove James II from the throne. The great Dutch contribution to American religious diversity was to hold the Mid-Atlantic out of the English orbit long enough to surrender it at this singular period of English history.

CONCLUSION

What, then, is New Netherland's role in the story of American religious liberty? The 400th anniversary of Henry Hudson's arrival in what became New York prompted a new wave of reflections on the Dutch colony's contribution to American history. Joyce Goodfriend, a leading American historian of Dutch America, claims, "New Netherland was the site of America's first experiment in diversity." Notwithstanding its "shortcomings," the colony's history "offers the most candid version of American beginnings, one that highlights the pluralism and materialistic striving at the heart of the American experience." The colony's "version of pluralism, in which various groups of Europeans learned to coexist . . . still stands as a noteworthy precedent for the multicultural America in which we now live," however "flawed by modern standards" it was, including as it did the Dutch embrace of African slavery and wars against the indigenous inhabitants. Perhaps now, as the United States struggles "to become a pluralistic nation in practice as well as in rhetoric," Americans are "ready for decentering the opening acts of our national historical drama and casting the Dutch founders as leading players." Another leading scholar of Dutch America, David Voorhees, adds that "the concept of toleration" was a "key legacy of the Dutch influence" both in the region and on "the wider development of American political theory." They are correct that the Dutch brought a greater degree of religious diversity and a distinctive style of toleration to North America. However, the connections between what the Dutch did and what the United States became are not as direct as they imply.[1]

To gain a deeper understanding of just how Dutch tolerance fits into the broader scheme of early American history, this study has set the Dutch North American colonies within the broader context of the Dutch world both in Europe and overseas. Opening up the lens of analysis has suggested aspects that make the North American experience exceptional (a favorite topic of American historians), as well as others that make it less so, for both Dutch and American history. First off, compared to everywhere else in the

Dutch world, the New Netherland experience was distinctive because it was almost exclusively a Protestant one. The handful of Catholics in the colony figured only tangentially in the main controversies over religious diversity in the colony, which primarily pitted Dutch Reformed against Lutherans, Baptists, and Quakers. Unlike everywhere else in the Dutch world at the time, those being conquered by the Dutch (the Swedes) and those who conquered the Dutch (the English) were Protestants. The result was a very different set of confrontations from anywhere else, where Dutch Protestants conquered or were conquered by Chinese, or by Spanish, Portuguese, and French Catholics. Instead of the usual pivot of Protestant-Catholic relations, the story of toleration in New Netherland and New Amstel ran primarily along two Protestant axes, one across the North Sea to the English, the other into the Baltic and the Scandinavian and German powers. One would be hard pressed to find another such deeply Protestant-inflected colonial story anywhere in the European overseas world before the French Revolution. Suriname is a possibility, but there the important Jewish community played a central role quite unlike the marginal one of their fellows in New Amsterdam.

Putting the Dutch into the equation compels early American historians to think outside their usual North American frame of reference, much as the emerging field of Atlantic world history has urged us to do. For example, the Jewish connection to New Amsterdam is an excellent illustration of the parallels between North and South American history brought out by the Dutch experience. Most New Amsterdam Jews had been in Brazil first. Almost all eventually left for better possibilities elsewhere, like Suriname and Curaçao. Their opportunities varied with the fortunes of war on both sides of the Atlantic following in the wake of Dutch and, later, English conquests. Thinking about North America with the Dutch in it thus compels us to imagine a North American history decisively shaped by inter-imperial competition. Had postwar diplomacy turned out differently, North American history could have resembled that of the Greater Caribbean, with its many conquests and transfers of territory and subsequent failure to find a common national spirit of unity. Contingency laid the preconditions for American national unity. It could just as easily have taken them away.

The story I have presented here argues strongly against the habit of naturalizing the course of American history into a clear and simple narrative of progress. This is most importantly the case for the colonial Mid-Atlantic, where wars and treaties were the great drivers of change, not cultural habits or brilliant ideas. Only the English military conquest, the European treaties that confirmed it, and the peculiar religious and political conditions of Restoration England (1660–1688) made the middle colonies and the resultant pluralism so familiar to American historians possible. Pennsylvania, New York, New Jersey, and Delaware did not emerge as we have come to know them until after the Dutch had recaptured and relinquished the Mid-Atlantic one last time in the 1674 Treaty of Westminster. Had the Dutch held onto the region, we would write about those colonies as we do now of New Amstel—a fascinating flash in the pan of colonial American history. The Dutch experience is a reminder that wars and diplomacy that often figure marginally if at all in American history texts need to be incorporated more seriously into our thinking about what colonial America was.

The continuing role of Europe also needs to be taken more seriously in the study of religion in colonial America, another issue raised by some Atlantic world scholarship. The conquests of Dutch America are a stark reminder that colonial America was part of Europe and not separate from it, a relationship that could bring radical changes with virtually no input from colonists. Traditionally, the European contribution is noted at the beginning, at the moment colonists leave for America, but then it pretty much drops off, until some sudden controversy explicitly evokes colonial Americans' ties to Europe, most obviously with the American Revolution. Rather than seeing Europe as just the place whence colonists came and from which eventually declared their independence, we need to account for some two hundred years (Roanoke, 1585, to the Treaty of Paris, 1783, would be an apt Anglo-centric formula) of ongoing influence and relations between the colonies and Europe. This relationship affected the range of religious options open to the colonists, the composition of the clergy and the faithful, much of the content of religious instruction and controversy, and the very interpretation of colonial American religious life itself. After all, the comments by European observers of American religious life only make sense in comparison with what was possible and present in Europe at the time. The importance of evaluating the story of religious tolerance in the Dutch American colonies in the context of the Dutch world of the mid-seventeenth century rather than later manifestations of American society should be obvious. Tolerance is not a universal norm or category of analysis that can be applied equally to all cases. It must be understood in context, in the specifics of time, place, and the parties involved.

With the fate of religion in the Dutch world after 1664 in mind, it is clear that Dutch tolerance in the Mid-Atlantic would have created a degree of pluralism in colonial America, yet it would not have produced anything like the English middle colonies. Discerning readers will have noted that the struggles over toleration depicted in this book took place in certain places but not others. Vlissingen, Middelburgh, Rustdorp, 's-Gravesande, Heemsetede, and to a lesser extent Fort Orange witnessed agitation on the part of one group or another for rights to worship apart from the public church. However, these towns represented less than half the outposts established in New Netherland before the conquest of 1664. In others there was no challenge to the public church: Schenectady, Wiltwijck, Breukelen, Amersfoort, Midwout, Boswijck, Haarlem, Bergen, not to mention the scattered settlements at Kinderhook, Coxsackie, Claverack, and Staten Island. On the South River there was of course the Swedish Lutheran church and the emerging experiment in toleration at Hoornkill. However, there was a growing Dutch Reformed presence as well. Since the public church had been absent in the region in the days of New Sweden, one could argue that the South River was becoming a zone of expansion for the Dutch Reformed Church as well as a place of exceptional toleration—by New Netherland standards. In this it resembled the many frontiers of the Dutch world, from Maastricht to Brazil and Malacca, where the Dutch were able to expand thanks to the conquests of their armies. New Amsterdam, as the capital of New Netherland, experienced more than its fair share of the contests over diversity, from the arrival of the Jews to the Lutheran minister Gutwasser and the Quaker missionaries, but it was of course also the bastion of the Dutch Reformed establishment, reinforcing the hegemony of the public church across the colony. The geography of dissent in New Netherland must be balanced with the geography of assent, which points towards a very different future for the Mid-Atlantic from what actually happened after the English takeover.[2]

Religion in the American colonies was an extension of and variation on the European pattern. In the case of Dutch tolerance, the colonial American context was different than in the Netherlands, but it was not different enough to be excluded from the spectrum of Dutch possibilities. After all, regional variation was the Dutch norm. Apart from Native Americans and Africans (whose inclusion in Dutch colonial society was marginal at best), the mix of influences in the colonies—English Puritans, Lutherans, Jews, and Catholics—was the same as in Europe, albeit in different proportions.

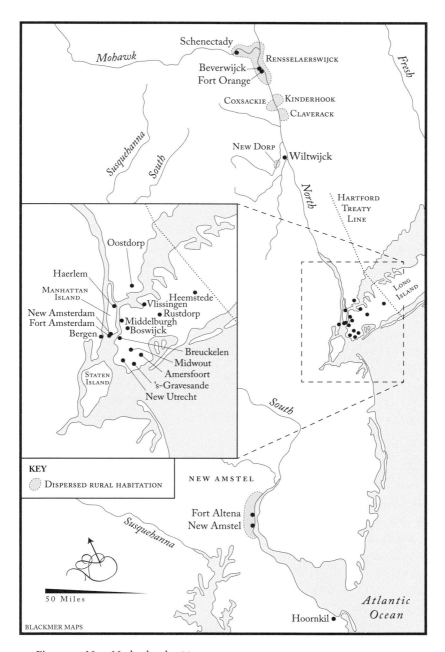

Figure 9. New Netherland, 1664.

European laws, habits, and cultural and historical referents set the terms by which those in power made decisions as well as how those Europeans with less power in America challenged those decisions. The American reality was different—the terrain, the climate, the history—but the Dutch (and more generally European) inclination was not to adapt to this alternate reality but rather to force it into their traditional frame of reference, as they did in Brazil, South Africa, and Asia. As long as they remained tied to Europe, the colonies were part of a European dynamic, not some autonomous American reality. Had the Dutch kept New Netherland in 1664 or 1674, there is little indication that it would have developed the liberal diversity of Amsterdam. A more likely comparison is the constrained pluralism of Zeeland.

This book deliberately ends in 1674 rather than 1664 to emphasize that there was more than one chance for a Dutch America. Dutch colonies were won and lost across the globe. It was an intrinsic part of the European expansionist experience. The Dutch could and occasionally did recapture colonies they lost. They only gave up on North America in the midst of a fight for the very survival of their nation, with a massive French army at the gates of Amsterdam and an English fleet off their coast. The importance of the Dutch restoration in New Netherland often gets lost in the great changes that came so soon afterward. Within two years of regaining control of the territory from the Dutch, the English rulers had divided the land into three separate colonies: New York, East Jersey, and West Jersey. In 1676 began the migration of thousands of Quakers to the Delaware River Valley and the Quaker-dominated colony of West Jersey. Within five years the west bank of the Delaware was turned over to the new colony of Pennsylvania. Quakers soon gained control of the East Jersey proprietorship as well, turning the whole region from the Hudson River south to Maryland into a Quaker empire of religious toleration. Thus began the religious pluralism that was the hallmark of the middle colonies and, later, the United States. It was a world very different from what most of the Dutch involved in colonizing America had envisioned. Throughout their tenure, the Dutch displayed a tenacious support for the supremacy of the Dutch Reformed Church and a deep disinclination to foster religious diversity. Both impulses were very Dutch—especially outside Amsterdam.

One of the most tangible Dutch contributions to American diversity and religious liberty was to import several players in the subsequent drama who would have been shut out had the Mid-Atlantic always been English.

A strong Dutch Reformed community comprised the majority of Dutch American colonists. The small Dutch and Swedish Lutheran community laid a foundation for the many German Lutherans who arrived in the eighteenth century. Likewise the seed of a Jewish North American community was planted. English radicals—Baptists and Quakers—gained a foothold outside Rhode Island they might not have otherwise been able to find. Without the Dutch, then, early America would have been less diverse both ethnically and religiously. Does this amount to a legacy of toleration and pluralism? Such generalizations need to be qualified and given more specificity. After all, the Dutch authorities expended much effort to reduce and constrain pluralism in the colony, just as they did most everywhere in the Dutch world. Thus, along with their toleration and pluralism the Dutch brought the impulse and ability to tame and assimilate both into a Reformed Protestant hegemony.

What really distinguished the Dutch was their strong sense of a significant difference between public and private worship and belief. Exactly where and how the line was drawn varied from place to place, but that it existed was crucial to the functioning of Dutch toleration. Its origins are uncertain, but it clearly grew out of the complicated history of the Dutch revolt and Reformation as well as the extraordinarily urban nature of Dutch society. The essence of Dutch tolerance was never to compel anyone to abandon their faith or convert, even though they frequently denied those of other faiths the capacity to practice their faith in any sort of organized, public fashion. For this reason it is easy to characterize the Dutch as both tolerant and intolerant. Depending on the criteria employed they could be either, or both. They both acknowledged and permitted a degree of religious diversity while facilitating the growth of the Dutch Reformed Church everywhere from Asia to the Americas, often in the teeth of Roman Catholic opposition. This powerful ambiguity was characteristic of the entire Dutch world in the seventeenth century.

Colonial America was not a place where new ideas about religious freedom emerged. Rather, it was a place where, occasionally, European dreams of religious toleration could find a home unavailable in Europe. None of the ideas or demands regarding tolerance in Dutch America grew out of the American experience. They all had origins and analogues in Europe. From Europe came the religious movements most closely associated with appeals to toleration (like Quakerism) and they all had to fight for a space in the American colonies. The combination of ingredients was of course distinct in Dutch America, but it was the structure in which the ideas operated, rather than the ideas themselves, that was new and different. Indeed, if anything, the tendency emerging from the American experience before 1675 was more often to shut down and limit religious diversity than expand it. Toleration spilled over to the colonies from Europe rather than emerging logically from the experience of colonizing America, in the case of Dutch America primarily through conquest, with New Amstel an exception of uncertain dimensions. Even Roger Williams and his charter for Rhode Island were products of England. The direction of influence was a decidedly one-way street.

What made the middle colonies so distinctive, then, was not the Dutch precedent or the frontier experience or the necessities of colonization. It was the *timing* of the settlement that mattered, the fact that they were granted and colonized in the Restoration period, under the patronage of Charles II and his brother James, duke of York. In the years 1664–1681, when the middle colonies were created, a unique combination of religious and political factors made it possible to establish not one but three Quaker-dominated colonies (East Jersey, West Jersey, and Pennsylvania), as well as to avoid the establishment of the Church of England. Nothing quite like it would ever be possible in the English world before or after. Yet, once in place, the religious diversity unleashed by the Restoration middle colonies would never be entirely reined in. American pluralism was the result. The Dutch who stayed on after the conquest became a part of it, but cannot be given much credit for it. They adapted to the English world, but not eagerly. Indeed, North America was one of the few places where the Dutch were in the unusual and unpleasant position of the conquered rather than the conquerors.

Though the English did the most to expand the frontier of religious liberty in the mid-Atlantic, the Dutch cannot simply be cast as intolerant or against pluralism. They extended their system, or more properly, systems, given the budding contrast between New Amstel and New Netherland, of religious liberty in America. Indeed, around the globe, wherever the Dutch gained control of territory, they installed their practice of religious liberty. On closer inspection, however, Dutch tolerance was not the same as what was promoted in the Restoration English colonies. Though it varied noticeably from place to place, it was a very Protestant system, and a Reformed Protestant one at that. Dutch tolerance was not a deliberately pluralistic vision. Rather it was a technique developed to foster the Dutch Reformed Church in a pluralistic world. From the beginnings of the Dutch revolt, the Dutch constantly operated in circumstances in which most people were not Dutch Reformed and, especially overseas, were not even Dutch. Underlying the enforcement of liberty of conscience was the hope, if not always the expectation, that ultimately all those subject to it would join and conform to the public Dutch Reformed Church. The conversions should be voluntary and not compelled, but they were no less desired. At times, it proved a powerful method for assimilation, at other times less so. Everywhere Dutch religious liberty proved an effective tool for articulating social stratification and inequality. The small, radical experiment in religious freedom that began in New Amstel was the great exception to the overall pattern during the Dutch Republic. It is yet another reminder of colonial America's dependence on the European context, for it could only have emerged from Amsterdam during the 1660s, not before or after.

If the Dutch can be granted a role in the development of American religious liberty, it is not as progenitors or models of its future but rather as participants, unwilling in the case of the Dutch Reformed, and very willing in the case of the Lutherans, Quakers, Baptists, and Jews, previously held in check by the public church. However, the greatest Dutch contribution toward the growth of American pluralism was less a positive than a negative impact on early English colonization. New Netherland succeeded in keeping the Mid-Atlantic out of English hands until 1664. Had that not happened, it most likely would have been a region divided between a greater Chesapeake and a greater New England. Even while the region was under Dutch control, both areas made efforts to expand into it. In the end, then, we can thank the Dutch for the possibility that there could be New York—as well as New Jersey and Pennsylvania. Without their tenure in North America, the United States would have been deprived of the unique hearth of religious and ethnic pluralism that the middle colonies became—even if it was the English of the Restoration era, not the Dutch, who created it. It is worth recalling the words of New Amsterdam's first minister, Michaelius, who reported to his colleague Smoutius back in Amsterdam soon after his arrival on Manhattan in summer 1628: "From the beginning we established the form of a church."[3] That is what the Dutch fought to maintain in New Netherland: a single kind of church, not many sorts of churches. Given the many constraints and challenges they faced, they were remarkably successful in doing so. Like it or not, it is an important part of the Dutch legacy that needs to be remembered alongside the emergence of pluralism in America.

ACA	Archief van de Classis Amsterdam van de Nederlandse Hervormde Kerk
AELG	Archief van de evangelisch-lutherse gemeente Amsterdam
Andros Papers	Peter R. Christoph and Florence A. Christoph with translations from the Dutch by Charles T. Gehring, *The Andros Papers, 1674–1676: Files of the Provincial Secretary of New York during the Administration of Governor Sir Edmund Andros, 1674–1680* (Syracuse, N.Y.: Syracuse University Press, 1989).
CM 1655–1656	Gehring, Charles T., trans. and ed., *Council Minutes, 1655–1656* (Syracuse, N.Y.: Syracuse University Press, 1995).
Corres. 1654–1658	Charles T. Gehring, trans. and ed., *Correspondence, 1654–1658* (Syracuse, N.Y.: Syracuse University Press, 2003).
DHM	*De Haelve Maen*
DHNY	Edmund B. O'Callaghan, ed., *Documentary History of the State of New York*, 4 vols. (Albany: Weed, Parsons, 1848–1853).
DRCHNY	Edmund B. O'Callaghan and Berthold Fernow, eds., *Documents Relative to the Colonial History of the State of New York*, 15 vols. (Albany: Weed, Parson 1853–1887).
ER	Edward T. Corwin, ed., *Ecclesiastical Records: State of New York*, 7 vols. (Albany, N.Y.: James B. Lyon, 1901–1916).
FOR 1654–1679	Charles T. Gehring and Janny Venema, trans. and eds., *Fort Orange Records, 1654–1679* (Syracuse, N.Y.: Syracuse University Press, 2009).
GAA	Gemeente Archief Amsterdam

JR   Reuben Gold Thwaites, *The Jesuit Relations and Allied Documents: Travels and Explorations of the Jesuit Missionaries in New France, 1610–1791* (Cleveland: Burrows Brothers, 1896–1901).

LChNY   Arnold J. H. van Laer, *The Lutheran Church in New York, 1649–1772: Records in the Lutheran Church Archives at Amsterdam, Holland* (New York: New York Public Library, 1946).

NJA   William A. Whitehead et al., eds., *Archives of the State of New Jersey*, 1st ser., 43 vols. (Newark, N.J., 1880–1949).

NNN   J. Franklin Jameson, ed., *Narratives of New Netherland, 1609–1664* (New York: Scribner's, 1909).

NOTES

Introduction

1. Nussbaum, *Liberty of Conscience*.

2. McLoughlin, *Soul Liberty*.

3. Hall, *Separating Church and State*; S. V. James, *John Clarke and His Legacies*; Pointer, *Protestant Pluralism*; Finkelman, "The Soul and the State," 78–105; Jacobsen, *An Unprov'd Experiment*; Frost, *A Perfect Freedom*; S. Schwartz, *"A Mixed Multitude"*; Buckley, *Church and State*; Underwood and Burke, *Dawn of Religious Freedom*.

4. Recently, popular attention has been drawn to New Netherland in part because of Shorto, *Island at the Center of the World*. For an overview of new work on Dutch North America see Goodfriend, *Revisiting New Netherland*.

5. Jacobs, *Colony of New Netherland*, 169, 171. See also Jacobs, "Between Repression and Approval."

6. Kaplan, *Divided by Faith*, 6–11.

7. Walsham, *Charitable Hatred*, 1–30. On negative attitudes toward toleration, and the difference between early modern ideas about it and more modern ones, see also Butterfield, "Toleration in Early Modern Times."

8. S. B. Schwartz, *All Can Be Saved*; Walsham, *Charitable Hatred*, 7, 29; Landsman, "Roots, Routes, and Rootedness," 273. For recent reviews and thoughts on the current state of writing about toleration, see Collins, "Redeeming the Enlightenment"; Haefeli, "Toleration."

9. Kaplan criticizes the Dutch nationalist argument that there's something inherently tolerant about the Dutch character, in his "'Dutch' Religious Tolerance."

10. *Amsterdam and her Other Hollander Sisters*, 3–4. The even more influential, and regularly republished, criticism of Dutch tolerance found in Andrew Marvell's poem, "The Character of Holland," was both part of the same war's anti-Dutch propaganda and a bid on the part of Marvell for patronage and employment, N. Smith, *Andrew Marvel*, 91–110. For more on English anti-Dutch propaganda, see Pincus, *Protestantism and Patriotism*.

11. Soll, "Accounting for Government," 228; Stoppa, *The Religion of the Dutch*, 46–47; Goslinga, *Dutch in the* Caribbean, 369. On the French, Stouppe, *La religion des Hollandois*, see Frijhoff, "Religious Toleration," 27–28, 43–45.

12. Frijhoff, "West India Company and the Reformed Church"; Frijhoff, *Fulfilling God's Mission*. Klein, "Shaping the American Tradition," 188–91, makes the teleological connections between New Netherland, New York, and America most explicit, but the interpretive habit runs back to the earliest American histories of the colony. The rubric of George Bancroft's *History of the United States of America* persists in studies of toleration in New Netherland from G. L. Smith, "Guilders and Godliness," to Rink, "Private Interest and Godly Gain" and Finkelman, "'A Land That Needs People'."

13. J. D. Bangs, "Dutch Contributions."

14. Prak, *Dutch Republic*, 219–20; Prak, "Politics of Intolerance"; Zwierlein, *Religion in New Netherland*. Citations refer to the Da Capo edition. Also, Zwierlein, "New Netherland Intolerance," and Williams, "'Abominable Religion'," and "Dutch Attitudes," which explore further the question of Dutch personal attitudes and judgments, as opposed to official policy.

15. Eekhof, *De Hervormde Kerk*; *Bastien Janszoon Krol*; *Jonas Michaëlius*. See also the review of Eekhof's work in Frijhoff, *Wegen van Evert Willemsz*, 823–38. Dutch scholarship on tolerance is becoming increasingly sophisticated, as in the excellent, and less ideologically freighted, essays by Pollman, "The Bond of Christian Piety" and Spaans, "Religious Policies."

16. For an excellent recent overview of Dutch religious politics at the time Eekhof and Zwierlein were writing, see van Eijnatten and van Lieburg, *Nederlandse Religiegeschiedenis*, 269–302.

17. Frijhoff, "From 'Case' to 'Model,'" 28, 35; Goodfriend, "Practicing Toleration," 100, 120–21.

Chapter 1. Dutch Tolerance

Epigraph: "Treaty of Union, eternal alliance and confederation made in the town of Utrecht by the countries and their towns and members, 29 January 1579," in Kossman and Mellink, *Texts Concerning the Revolt of the Netherlands*, 170.

1. "Treaty of Union . . . Utrecht," 170. Also see Van Gelderen, *Political Thought*, 51–52.

2. Frijhoff, "From 'Case' to 'Model,'" 37–39.

3. The following narrative of the Dutch Reformation and Revolt draws on several texts that should be consulted for further information, including Arnade, *Beggars, Iconoclasts, and Civic Patriots*; Van Deursen, *Bavianen & Slijkgeuzen*; Duke, *Reformation and Revolt*; Van Gelderen, *Political Thought*; Israel, *Dutch Republic*; Douglas Nobbs, *Theocracy and Toleration*; Pettegree, *Emden and the Dutch Revolt*; Prak, *Dutch Republic*; Price, *Holland and the Dutch Republic*.

4. For important Dutch studies of Dutch tolerance, see Van Erp, *Vrijheid in verdeeldheid*; Van Gelder, *Getemperde vrijheid*; Gisjwit-Hofstra, *Een schijn van verdraagzaamheid*; Van Rooden, *Religieuze Regimes*; Zilverberg, *Geloof en Geweten in de Zeventiende Eeuw*.

5. Israel, "Intellectual Debate About Toleration," 3, 5.

6. Parker, "To the Attentive, Nonpartisan Reader." L. J. Rogier advanced the forcible conversion theory in *Geschiedenis van het katholicisme in Noord-Nederland in de 16e en 17e eeuw*.

7. Van Rooden, "The Jews and Religious Toleration," 132, 140; Van Rooden, *Religieuze Regimes*, 169–99.

8. For an overview of the Inquisition and witch trials in the Netherlands along with the spread of the Reformed see Van Eijnatten and Van Lieburg, *Nederlandse Religie Geschiedenis*, 149–58.

9. For important studies, see Mack Crew, *Calvinist Preaching and Iconoclasm*; Arnade, *Beggars, Iconoclasts, and Civic Patriots*, 90–211.

10. [Philip Marnix of St. Aldegonde], *A True Narrative of what happened in the Netherlands in the matter of religion in the year 1566. By those who profess the reformed religion in that country, 1567*, in Kossman and Mellink, *Texts Concerning the Revolt of the Netherlands*, 78–81.

11. "A brief discourse sent to King Philip, our prince and sovereign lord, for the interest and profit of His Majesty and in particular of his Netherlands, in which are expounded the means that should be applied to obviate the troubles and commotion about religion and to extirpate the sects and heresies that abound in the Low Countries," in Kossman and Mellink, *Texts Concerning the Revolt of the Netherlands*, 56–59.

12. "Philip II to the Duchess of Parma, 17 October 1565 and Philip II to the Duchess of Parma, 31 July 1566," in Kossman and Mellink, *Texts Concerning the Revolt of the Netherlands*, 55, 72.

13. Israel, "The Intellectual Debate About Toleration," 6–8.

14. On William of Orange's efforts see Klink, *Opstand, politiek en religie bij Willem van Oranje*. For the Religious Peace in Haarlem (1577–1581) see Spaans, *Haarlem na de Reformatie*, 49–69. For the debate over religious peace in the 1570s, see Van Gelderen, *Political Thought*, 217–28. For Maastricht, see Ubachs, *Twee heren, twee confessies*. Ubachs points out that toleration did not extend past Catholics to Lutherans, Mennonites or others.

15. "Treaty of Union . . . Utrecht," 170.

16. *Verschooninghe van de Roomsche afgoderye* (Apology for Roman Idolatry, 1560).

17. Coornhert, *Synode over gewetensvrijheid*. See also Voogt, *Constraint on Trial*.

18. Van Deursen, *Bavianen & Slijkgeuzen* is the classic study of Holland; for Friesland see Wiebe Bergsma, *Tussen Gideonsbende en publieke kerk*.

19. Kaplan, *Calvinists and Libertines*; Kooi, *Liberty and Religion*; Spaans, *Haarlem na de Reformatie*.

20. Evenhuis, *Ook dat was Amsterdam*; Spaans, "Stad van vele geloven, 1578–1795."

21. Van Deursen, *Een Dorp in de Polder*; Trompeter, *Leven aan de rand van de Republiek*.

22. For an effective analysis of the differences between Calvinists and Libertines over Church membership and religious life, see Kaplan, *Calvinists and Libertines*, 28–110.

23. Frijhoff, "From 'Case' to 'Model,'" 39.

24. Israel, *Dutch Republic*, 276–67, 421–42, 446–47; Price, *Holland and the Dutch Republic*.

25. For an overview of the peculiar position and powers of the stadholders, see Rowen, *The Princes of Orange*.

26. Israel, "Intellectual Debate About Toleration," 11–13.

27. Israel, *Dutch Republic*, 393, 571–72. For a thorough study of Arminius and his theology, see C. Bangs, *Arminius*.

28. C. Bangs, *Arminius*, 302. One of his fellow diners, another minister, earned Plancius's enmity by "defending the Christian character of Rome."

29. On Woerden see Frijhoff, *Wegen van Evert Willemsz.*, 78–90.

30. See Israel, *Dutch Republic*, 433–49, for the fall of Oldenbarnevelt's regime.

31. Ibid., 450–65.

32. Ibid., 474–77.

33. On the Remonstrants, see Hoenderdaal and Luca, *Staat in de vrijheid*.

34. Israel, "Intellectual Debate About Toleration," 15–20.

35. Ibid. For Frederick Henry's religious moderation, see Rowen, *The Princes of Orange*, 61, 63–65.

36. Norton and Rous, *New-England's ensigne*, 19.

37. Norton and Rous, *New-England's ensigne*, 50–51; Harper and Gadd, "Norton, Humphrey (*fl.* 1655–1660)."

38. Israel, "Intellectual Debate About Toleration," 20–24.

39. The States of Holland, however, reissued in 1655 a 1624 prohibition against Lutheran services in the countryside, Frijhoff and Spies, *1650*, 400; Israel, *Dutch Republic*, 707–9; Van Gelder, *Getemperde vrijheid*, 95–96; Loosjes, *Geschiedenis der Luthersche Kerk in de Nederlanden*, 118–19; Frijhoff, "From 'Case' to 'Model,'" 40–43.

40. Frijhoff, "From 'Case' to 'Model,'" 40–43; Groenveld, *Huisgenoten des geloofs*.

41. Israel, "Intellectual Debate About Toleration," 24–31.

42. Van Limborch, *Korte wederlegginge*. See also "Limborch (Philippus van of á)," in Blok and Molhuysen, eds., *Nieuw Nederlandsch biografisch woordenboek*, 9: 609–10.

43. For Spinoza's biography and claims to his significance, see Israel, *Radical Enlightenment*, esp. 159–74.

44. For Plockhoy in Zierikzee and his probable birthdate of about 1615, see Looijesteijn, "'Born to the Common Welfare,'" 23–27.

45. Evenhuis, *Ook dat was Amsterdam*, 3:103–10; Abrahamsz and Spruit, *Bedenckingen over den toestant der Sichtbare Kercke Christi*. See also "Abrahamsz, Galenus," in Van der Aa et al., eds., *Biographisch woordenboek der Nederlanden*, 1:33–34. The Lamb's War was echoed by similar conflicts in England between Baptists and Quakers; see Underwood, *Primitivism, Radicalism, and the Lamb's War*.

46. Van der Wall, *De Mystieke Chiliast Petrus Serrarius*; Van der Wall, "The Amsterdam Millenarian Petrus Serrarius"; Rood, *Comenius and the Low Countries*.

47. Evenhuis, *Ook dat was Amsterdam*, 3:314.

48. Ibid., 313–17.

Chapter 2. Connivance

Epigraph: Lutheran Consistory to Lutherans at the Manhatans, May 4, 1655, in A. J. H. van Laer, *The Lutheran Church in New York*, 19.

1. Directors to Stuyvesant, April 16, 1663, DRCHNY 14:526.

2. See, for example, Kooi, "Paying Off the Sheriff," and Van Nierop, "Sewing the Bailiff in a Blanket."

3. Lutheran Consistory to Lutherans at the Manhatans, May 4, 1655, LChNY, 19.

4. Frijhoff, "From 'Case' to 'Model,'" 31–32; Spaans, "Religious Policies," 81, 85.

5. Spaans, "Religious Policies," 86.

6. Bradford, *Of Plymouth Plantation*, 10.

7. The following narrative draws from Happee, Meiners, and Mostert, *De Lutheranen in Amsterdam*, 1–26; Visser, *De Lutheranen in Nederland*, 39–61; Evenhuis, *Ook dat was Amsterdam*, 2:215–21; Kuijpers, *Migrantenstad*, 104–13; Spaans, "Stad van vele geloven," 414–16, 421–23.

8. GAA, AELG, inv. nrs. 19, 20, 21 cover the church books from 1647 (when they begin) until 1678. References are to GAA, AELG, inv. nr. 19 folios 43v, 65r, 268v and inv. nr. 20 folios 290, 684 and passim.

9. GAA, AELG, inv. nr. 19 folio 129 and inv. nr. 20 folio 462 and *passim*.

10. For The Hague see Wijsenbeek, "Geloof en Politiek."

11. For the Lutheran controversy in New Amsterdam, see Zwierlein, *Religion in New Netherland*, 187–212; Eekhof, *De Hervormde Kerk*, 2:1–36; G. L. Smith, *Religion and Trade*, 190–211; Jacobs, *Colony of New Netherland*, 161–67.

12. Frijhoff, *Fulfilling God's Mission*, 311, citing Hemmersam, "Reise nach Guinea und Brasilien, 1639–1645," 80–81.

13. GAA, AELG, inv. nr. 19 fo. 93v.

14. Frijhoff, "Seventeenth-Century Religion,"

15. Megapolensis and Drisius to Classis, October 6, 1653, ER 1:317–18; Petition, 1653, LChNY, 16. For the Mennonite, ER 1:513. He was admitted but in 1664 left for Curaçao with his wife, Drisius to Classis, August 5/14, 1664, ER 1:555.

16. Minutes of the Consistory at Amsterdam, October 12 and 19, 1649, LChNY, 13.

17. Israel, *Dutch Primacy*, 109–11; Rink, *Holland on the Hudson*, 24–49; Hart, *Prehistory of the New Netherland Company*.

18. LChNY, 14, 39.

19. Walraven to Classis, September 12, 1650, ER 1:281.

20. Petitions of 1653 and 1659, LChNY, 13–15, 39.

21. Minutes of the Consistory at Amsterdam, October 12 and 19, 1649, and Letter from Lutherans in New Netherland to the Consistory of Amsterdam, October 4, 1653, LChNY, 13, 15. Frijhoff and Spies, *1650*, 400.

22. Frijhoff and Spies, *1650*, 400; Israel, *Dutch Republic*, 707–9.

23. A point stressed by Jacobs, *Colony of New Netherland*, 162–63.

24. LChNY, 13–16.

25. LChNY, 17.

26. LChNY, 18.

27. For a discussion of free immigration to New Netherland, see Jacobs, *Colony of New Netherland*, 32–55.

28. LChNY, 19.

29. Megapolensis and Drisius to Classis, October 6, 1653, ER 1:317–18.

30. Schnoor, *Die rechtliche Organisation der religiösen Toleranz in Friedrichstadt*, 171. Carstensen, *Die Gründung und anfängliche Entiwicklung von Friedrichstadt*; Israel, "Central European Jewry during the Thirty Years' War," 13–15; Whaley, *Religious Toleration and Social Change in Hamburg*.

31. Classis of Amsterdam, Acts, January 1, 1654, ER 1:320–21.

32. Classis to Megapolensis and Drisius February 26, 1654, ER 1:322–23; Directors to Stuyvesant, March 12, 1654, in *Corres. 1654–1658*, 6.

33. Ibid.

34. Relevant works on Anglo-Dutch relations include Sprunger, *Dutch Puritanism*; Borman, "Untying the Knot?"; Grell, *Dutch Calvinists*; Grell, "Anglo-Dutch Communities in England"; Jones, *Anglo-Dutch Wars*.

35. Sprunger, *Dutch Puritanism*, 29–34.

36. Sprunger, *Dutch Puritanism*, 43–49; Bradford, "A Dialogue," 416.

37. Ibid., 49–59, 71–76.

38. Ibid., 60–70.

39. Ibid., 80–90; Bradford, "A Dialogue," 450–51.

40. The major scholarly study of religion in Leiden at this time notes that neither the Separatists nor the subsequently erected English Reformed Church in the city, both "small congregations . . . played any significant role in the city's collective religious life, and Leiden's political and religious elites paid scant attention to them," as does her book, see Kooi, *Liberty and Religion*, 165, and, for population and immigration figures, 21–22. For an effort to tell about all there is to tell about the Separatists in Leiden, see Kardux and van de Bilt, *Newcomers in an Old City*.

41. Kooi, *Liberty and Religion*, 2; Sprunger, *Dutch Puritanism*, 134–41.

42. Sprunger, *Dutch Puritanism*, 34–40, 262–84.

43. Ibid., 91–134, 142–45, 162–67, 187–89, 197–206, 262–84.

44. Ibid., 91–122; Carter, *English Reformed Church*.

45. Sprunger, *Dutch Puritanism*, 289–318.

Chapter 3. Toleration

Epigraph: Novum Belgium, by Father Isaac Jogues, 1646, in Jameson, ed., *Narratives of New Netherland*, 259–60.

1. Vaughn, *Creating the Creole Island*, 4.

2. Evenhuis, *Ook dat was Amsterdam*, 2:23.

3. Ibid., 2:322.

4. Frijhoff, *Fulfilling God's Mission*, 290–93.

5. Bontekoe, *Journaal*, 11; Evenhuis, *Ook dat was Amsterdam*, 2:324.

6. Ibid., 2:326.

7. Ibid., 2:338; Niemeijer, *Batavia*, 234–36.

8. Evenhuis, *Ook dat was Amsterdam*, 2:322.

9. Van Laer, *Documents Relating to New Netherland*, 2–5, 36.

10. Ibid., 2–5, 36.

11. For the Belgic Confession in the context of the early years of the revolt, see Van Gelderen, *Political Thought*, 62–109. Evenhuis, *Ook dat was Amsterdam*, 1:275–83, reflects on the issue in terms of Amsterdam's church politics.

12. Jogues, "Novum Belgium," 1646, in 259–60.

13. Jogues, NNN, 259–60.

14. "Antwoord van Trijn Quirijnendr. Op de eis van de Schout te Hoorn," August 24, 1609, in Van Deursen, *Bavianen & Slijkgeuzen*, 385.

15. Stoppa, *Religion of the Dutch*, 1, 30, 45–46. Frijhoff, "From 'Case' to 'Model'," 43–45, downplays the political purpose of the pamphlet and treats it more as a fairly accurate reflection of Dutch religious diversity.

16. Stoppa, *Religion of the Dutch*, 1, 30, 45–46; NNN, 262.

17. Jogues, NNN, 253.

18. NNN, 267–68, 272.

19. DRCHNY, 13:10; 14:26.

20. Van Laer, *Council Minutes*, 110, 305–6.

21. On the immigration and integration of New Englanders into New Netherland, see Zwierlein, *Religion in New Netherland*, 136–86; Jacobs, "Between Repression and Approval," 51–58.

22. Zwierlein, *Religion in New Netherland*, 161–62. On Kieft, see Frijhoff, "Neglected Networks."

23. Jacobs, *Petrus Stuyvesant*, 13–23; Van Baerle, *History of Brazil*, 128; Answer and Further Answer of the Director-General and Council to the proposals, November 28, 1661, March 11, 1662, DRCHNY 13: 210, 216; Concessions to be granted to the English-men, who desire to settle on the Kil van Kol, July 20, 1663, DRCHNY 13:281–82. On Stuyvesant's negotiations with English immigrants, see also Zwierlein, *Religion in New Netherland*, 175–86.

24. Stuyvesant to Endicott (no month or day) 1652, DRCHNY 14:179.

25. Report on the Surrender of New Netherland, by Peter Stuyvesant, 1665, NNN, 461.

26. Van Baerle, *History of Brazil*, 128; Israel and Schwartz, *Expansion of Tolerance*, 18–21. For something of a celebration of toleration in Dutch Brazil, which compares it to the convivencia of Medieval Spain, see Vainfas, "La Babel religiosa." Schwartz, *All can be Saved*, argues "Dutch Brazil and the period of Maurits of Nassau offer a limited opportunity to imagine what possibilities for tolerance might have existed in Portuguese society when the authority and power of the Church and especially the Inquisition had been diminished," 193. On Dutch Reformed propaganda regarding Brazil, see Van Groesen, "Herinneringen aan Holland, "A Week to Remember," and "Lessons Learned."

27. De Laet, *Historie ofte Iaerlijck verhael*, 336, 454–456. For the situation in Maastricht and the Overmass, see Ubachs, *Twee heren, twee confessies* and Ubachs, *Handboek*.

28. Schalkwijk, *Reformed Church in Dutch Brazil*, 272–88; Van Baerle, *History of Brazil*, 295.

29. Van Baerle, *History of Brazil*, 67, 128; Van der Dussen, *Relatório sobre as capitanias conquistadas*, 106; Soler, *Soler's Seventeen Letters*, 58–59.

30. Cited in Parker, *Faith on the Margins*, 57–58.

31. Calado, *O Valeroso Lucideno*, 261, 265, 267. Also translated as Divine Liberty, it was included in the declaration of revolt in October 1645. As a Dutch historian notes, the "declaration summarizes the limitations placed on the Catholic religion, expresses anti-Jewish and anti-Protestant feelings," and "reads much like a Declaration of Independence from the tyrannical WIC rule," Pijning "Idealism and Power," 229.

32. *A Rendição dos Holandeses*, 43–45; Israel and Schwartz, *Expansion of Tolerance*, 28, 30.

33. Schalkwijk, *Reformed Church*, 67–100. For the classis of Walcheren's enthusiastic involvement in recruiting ministers, sending Bibles, and proofing Church membership certificates, see Inv. nos. 73 & 74, Westindische kerk zakken, 1623–1641, Zeeuws Archief, Middelburg.

34. Van Goor, *De Nederlandse Koloniën*, 156–64.

35. On Dutch politics of toleration and proselytization in conquered territories see Israel, *The Dutch Republic*, 516, 598–601, 658–60. For all their privileges, matters did not always work out in favor of the Dutch Reformed. For a fascinating case study, in which the son of a Dutch Reformed minister in North Brabant converted to Catholicism in the 1650s and became a Jesuit missionary in Brazil, see Harline, "Religieoorlogen."

36. Starna, "Introduction," in *Indian Affairs in Colonial New York*.

37. ER 1:395–96; DRCHNY 12:105; Johnson, *Swedish Settlements on the Delaware*, 334, 373–74, 546–47, 668–69; Acrelius, *History of New Sweden*, 90.

38. DRCHNY 12:150–51, 307–8, 355, 357, 360, 366–68. Acrelius, *History of New Sweden*, 100–101, claims Lock was temporarily suspended from preaching, but restored by Stuyvesant after his marriage was approved.

39. Hartog, *Curaçao*, 159, 166–67, 199, 208.

40. Jews only arrived in South Africa after English takeover in 1795. Moorrees, *Die Nederduitse Gereformeerde Kerk in Suid-Afrika*, and Spoelstra, *Bouwstoffen voor de geschiedenis der Nederduitsch-Gereformeerde Kerken in Zuid-Afrika*; Evenhuis, *Ook dat was Amsterdam*, 3:62–65.

Chapter 4. Non-Christians

Epigraph: Petition of the Amsterdam Jews "To the Honorable Lords, Directors of the Chartered West India company, Chamber of the City of Amsterdam," January 1655, in Schappes, ed., *A Documentary History of the Jews in the United State*, 2.

1. By including Jews under the category non-Christians, I am following Jaap Jacobs, who argues that the Dutch relationship to Jews was distinct from that of other Christian groups. He does not include them in his chapter on "The Reformed Church and the Others," but puts them in "Burghers and Status," in which he also discusses Native Americans and enslaved Africans. According to him, "the Jews in New Netherland were second-class burghers . . . The decision to allow the Jews to stay in New Netherland . . . is not evidence of a desire for tolerance in the colony" (202).

2. For an overview of the Dutch Reformed efforts to expand their religion overseas up to the middle of the seventeenth century, see L. J. Joose, *"Scoone Dingen Sijn Swaere Dingen."* Toleration figures almost not at all in the text, with the small exception of Brazil.

3. Swetschinski, *Reluctant Cosmopolitans*, 11–25.

4. Ibid.

5. Ibid. For Jews in Hamburg, see Whaley, *Religious Toleration*, 70–110.

6. Swetschinski, *Reluctant Cosmopolitans*, 11–25; Evenhuis, *Ook dat was Amsterdam*; Spaans, "Stad van vele geloven, 1578–1795," 414–20; Bodian, *Hebrews of the Portuguese Nation.*

7. Schalkwijk, *Reformed Church*, 252; Hussen, "The Legal Position of the Jews"; Nusteling, "The Jews in the Republic of the United Provinces."

8. Megapolensis to Classis, March 18, 1655, ER 1:334–35. Polhemius's arrival can be tracked in ER 1:328, 330, 332–33, 36–39.

9. Van Baerle, *History of Brazil*, 128. See De Mello, *Gente da Naçao*, 208–32 for the emergence of Brazil's Jewish community.

10. Van Baerle, *History of Brazil*, 68, 128; Schalkwijk, *Reformed Church*, 255–56.

11. "Classicale acta van Brazilië," 329.

12. Soler, *Soler's Seventeen Letters*, 59, 74.

13. Remonstrance to the XIX by the Classis of Amsterdam, July 9, 1646, ER 1:203–4.

14. Israel and Schwartz, *Expansion of Tolerance*, 28.

15. Gelfand, "Jews in New Netherland," 42–46.

16. For the fascinating case of a Jewish man who was known and accepted as such by the Dutch yet worked in colonies where Jews were not officially allowed, see Meuwese, "Samuel Cohen (c. 1600–1642)."

17. Megapolensis to Classis, March 18, 1655, ER 1:335–36.

18. Ibid.

19. Petition of the Amsterdam Jews in Schappes, *Documentary History*, 2–4, 565n4.

20. Ibid.

21. Directors to Stuyvesant, April 26, 1655, in *Corres. 1654–1658*, 49.

22. Jacobs, *Colony of New Netherland*, 199–200.

23. Ibid. Finkelman, "'A Land That Needs People'," retains the older translation in his analysis.

24. Directors to Stuyvesant, March 13, 1656, in *Corres. 1654–1658*, 83.

25. Directors to Stuyvesant, June 14, 1656, in *Corres. 1654–1658*, 93.

26. Barlaeus, *History of Brazil*, 295–96; Schalkwijk, *Reformed Church*, 251–67; De Mello, *Gente da Naçao*, 257–366.

27. *CM, 1655–1656*, 68, 81, 128.

28. On the Jews in New Netherland, see most recently, Finkelman, "A Land That Needs People'"; Goodfriend, "Practicing Toleration"; Gelfand, "Jews in New Netherland," 39–49; Williams, "'Abominable Religion'." Earlier accounts can be found in G. L. Smith, *Religion and Trade*, 212–19; Eekhof, *Hervormde Kerk*, 2:69–76; Zwierlein, *Religion in New Netherland*, 247–65.

29. Ibid.

30. Ibid.

31. A small but dedicated circle of scholars have produced a significant amount of work on Jews and Protestant millenialists in the 1640s–1660s. For just a few of the relevant recent works see Cogley, "Ancestry of the American Indians"; Van den Berg and Van der Wall, *Jewish-Christian Relations*; Kaplan, Méchoulan, and Popkin, *Menasseh Ben Israel*; Van den Berg, *Religious Currents*; Wallenborn, *Bekehrungseifer, Judenangst und Handelsinteresse*.

32. Evenhuis, *Ook dat was Amsterdam*, 2:327. Indeed, for those accustomed to English Protestants' notorious reluctance (or inability) to translate their religion into a foreign idiom, the number of seventeenth-century Dutch religious texts in local Asian languages, especially Malaysian, is extraordinary. In the GAA, the ACA, toegangsnummer (aka archief nummer) 379 contains two: Nr. 195 "Dialang ca surga" catechetisch geschrift in het Maleis, by ds. Josias Spiljardus op het eiland Ay, 1657; Nr. 198 "Catechismus in het Maleis," by ds. Joannes Roman te Batavia.

33. Evenhuis, *Ook dat was Amsterdam*, 2:328, 341.

34. Ibid., 2:328–30. Two copies of the Formosan catechism, one translated into Dutch, can be found in GAA, ACA, toegangsnummer (aka archief nummer) 379; Gedeputeerden voor Buitenlandse Kerken, 1636–1804: Stukken betreffende de Werkzaamheden ten Aanzien van Afzonderlijke Gebieden (VOC-Gebied en WIC-Gebied), inv. nos 192 and 193.

35. ER 1:326–27. On the conversion of Native Americans in New Netherland, see Jacobs, *Colony of New Netherland*, 176–79. On Native American conversions in Brazil, see Meuwese, "Dutch Calvinism," 118–41.

36. "Classicale acta van Brazilië," 330. On Udemans and his justification of slavery see Nauta and Houtman, *Biografisch lexicon voor de geschiedenis van het Nederlandse protestantisme*; Boone, "'Om een woesten hoop te brengen tot de kerck'."

37. "Classicale acta van Brazilië," 329–30; Schalkwijk, *Reformed Church*, 151.

38. Walraven to Classis, September 12, 1650, ER 1:280–81.

39. Hartog, *Curaçao*, 1146. Acts of Deputies, Classis of Amsterdam, October 25, 1660, ER 1:493; Classis to Van Beaumont, July 8, 1661, ER 1:508; Van Deursen, *Bavianen & Slijkgeuzen*, 138–39.

40. November 1641, ER 1:142. Jacobs, *New Netherland*, 312–18.

41. Selyns to Classis, June 9, 1664, ER 1:548; Drisius to Classis, August 5/14, 1664, ER 1:554.

42. Evenhuis, *Ook dat was Amsterdam*, 2:339–40.

43. Niemeijer, *Batavia*, 65–81, population tables, 400.

44. Niemeijer, *Batavia*, 235–36.

45. Evenhuis, *Ook dat was Amsterdam*, 2: 335; Niemeijer, *Batavia*, 232, 235–37.

46. Niemeijer, *Batavia*, 233–34.

47. Ibid., 234–39.

48. Ibid., 239–41.

49. Ibid., 211–96.

Chapter 5. Babel

Epigraph: Petition of Reverends Megapolensis and Drisius to the Burgomasters and Schepens of the City of Amsterdam, New Netherland, July 6, 1657, ER 1:387.

1. Classis to Consistory in New Netherland, May 26, 1656, ER 1:348–49.

2. Acts of the Classis, May 7, 1657, ER 1:377.

3. Classis to Consistory in New Netherland, May 26, 1656, ER 1:349.

4. Megapolensis to Classis, March 18, 1655, ER 1:335–36.

5. Megapolensis and Drisius to Classis, August 5, 1657, ER 1:396–98 and DHNY 3:70–71; Pope, *Half-Way Covenant*, 3–74.

6. Megapolensis and Drisius to Classis, ER 1:396; *CM, 1652–1654*, 13; Jacobs, *New Netherland*, 311.

7. Moore returned from Barbados in 1657 only to die sometime between August and October "of a pestilential disease." On Moore and Middelburgh, see Megapolensis and Drisius to Classis, August 5, October 22, 1657, ER 1:397, 410–11. For conflict within the town, see The Petition and Order on a Petition, January 15, 1656, *CM 1655–1656*, 177–78; Petition of the Inhabitants of Middelburgh, January 22, 1657, *Corres. 1654–1658*, 119–20.

8. "Order on a Petition . . . concerning . . . Middelborch," January 15, 1656, *CM 1655–1656*, 177.

9. Consistory to the Manhatans, June 14, 1656, LChNY, 254; Megapolensis and Drisius to Stuyvesant, August 23, 1658, ER 1:429.

10. This and the next two paragraphs draw on "Ordinance Against Practicing any Religion other than the Reformed," February 1, 1656, in *CM 1655–1656*, 209–10, and Gehring, *Laws and Writs of Appeal,* 55–56.

11. Jacobs, *Colony of New Netherland*, 161. "Proposed Articles for the Colonization and Trade of New Netherland," August 30, 1638, DRCHNY 1:110–11. The WIC and the States General reviewed the proposal and neither objected at all to this statement on religion.

12. "Ordinance Against Practicing any Religion other than the Reformed," February 1, 1656, *CM 1655–1656*, 210; Jacobs, *Colony of New Netherland*, 160–61.

13. "Magistrates of Fort Orange/Beverwijck to Stuyvesant," March 10, 1656, *FOR 1654–1679*, 87–88; Jacobs, *Colony of New Netherland*, 160–61, 171.

14. Directors to Stuyvesant, March 13, 1656, *Corres. 1654–1658*, 84.

15. Consistory to Manhatans, June 14, 1656, LChNY, 254–55; Directors to Stuyvesant, June 14, 1656, *Corres. 1654–1658*, 93.

16. Directors to Stuyvesant, June 14, 1656, *Corres. 1654–1658*, 93.

17. Consistory to Manhatans, June 14, 1656, LChNY, 254.

18. Acts of the Classis, August 7, 8, October 3, November 3, 7, 1656, ER 1:354–55, 357, 360.

19. Consistory to Manhatans, June 14, 1656, LChNY, 254–55.

20. Directors to Stuyvesant, March 13, 1656; directors to Stuyvesant, June 14, 1656, *Corres. 1654–1658*, 83, 93.

21. Petition of the Lutherans, October 24, 1656, ER 1:358–59; Lutherans to Consistory, November 1, 1656, LChNY 20–21.

22. Megapolensis and Drisius to Classis, August 5, 1657, ER 1:397; Sentence of William Hallet . . . and of William Wickendam, November 8, 11, 1656, DRCHNY 14:369–70, 377. Eekhof, *De Hervormde Kerk* 2:56–57; Jacobs, *New Netherland*, 311. Jeremy Bangs claims Wickenden was a friend of Roger Williams and carried his ideas to the colonists in Flushing, "Dutch Contributions to Religious Toleration," 591.

23. Acts of the Classis, March 19, 1657, ER 1:372.

24. Acts of the Classis, April, 10, 23, May 25, June 5, 1657, ER 1:374, 376, 380–81, 382.

25. LChNY, 22–23.

26. Petition, July 6, 1657, ER 1:386–88. Ultimately, the issue of poor relief proved key to the gradual acceptance of separate congregations in the Netherlands, so long as each congregation took financial responsibility for its own poor, see Spaans, *Armenzord in Friesland* and "Religious Policies."

27. ER 1:388–89.

28. ER 1:389–90; Resolution, July 14, 1657, LChNY, 24. Goodfriend, "Practicing Toleration in Dutch New Netherland," argues that New Amsterdam's government cooperated with the anti-Lutheran initiative because, having only recently been granted the right to govern their city, they had "to be circumspect." She argues that their silence in other cases, especially the Quakers, their ability to deliver fairly impartial justice to the Jews, and the occasional act of kindness toward a religious dissident allow one to "postulate that Stuyvesant's opposition to religious toleration was not widely endorsed by New Netherlanders," 120.

29. Megapolensis and Drisius to Classis, August 5, 1657, ER 1:393–94.

30. Gutwasser to Consistory, August 14, 1657, LChNY, 24–26.

31. Goodfriend, "Practicing Toleration in Dutch New Netherland," 119–21.

32. Resolution, September 4 and Gutwasser to Consistory, September 8, 28, 1657, LChNY, 26–29.

33. Petition, October 10, Letter from Lutherans to Consistory, October 21, 1657, LChNY, 30–32; Petition, October 10, Gutwasser to Governor and Council, October 15, 1657, ER 1:405–9.

34. Megapolensis and Drisius to Classis, October 22, 25, 1657, ER 1:409–12.

35. Megapolensis and Drisius to Classis, September 24, 1658, ER 1:433.

36. Megapolensis and Drisius to Classis, September 10, 1659, ER 1:449.

37. Minutes of the Consistory, July 16, 1659, LChNY, 41.

38. Bosch to Consistory, August 19, 1663, LChNY, 47–48.

39. For examples, see Kooi, "Paying Off the Sheriff" and Trompeter, *Leven aan de rand van de Republiek*, 200–208, who presents the case of Mennonites on the republic's eastern frontier.

Chapter 6. Liberty of Conscience

Epigraph: Remonstrance of the Inhabitants of Flushing, 27 December 1657, DRCHNY 14:403.

1. Van der Pol, "Religious Diversity."

2. For other accounts of the Quakers in New Netherland, see G. L. Smith, *Religion and Trade*, 220–30; Eekhof, *De Hervormde Kerk*, 2:76–86; Zwierlein, *Religion in New Netherland*, 213–46.

3. Megapolensis and Drisius to Classis, August 14, 1657, ER 1:400.

4. Ibid., ER 1:399–400; Jacobs, *New Netherland*, 305–306.

5. Gandy, ed., *Sufferings of Early Quakers*, 182; Norton and Rous, *New-England's ensigne*, 15; Rous, Fox, and Cudworth, *Secret Works*, 12. For a good study of the genre of Quaker sufferings, see Gill, "Evans and Cheevers's *A Short Relation*."

6. On Quaker use of publicity to mobilize for their cause, see Moore, *Light in Their Consciences*, 155–63, Bitterman, "Early Quaker Literature of Defense," and especially K. Peters, *Print Culture*.

7. Megapolensis and Drisius to Classis, August 14, 1657, ER 1:400.

8. Gutwasser to Consistory, August 14, 1657, LChNY, 26; Megapolensis and Drisius to Classis, August 14, 1657, ER 1:400.

9. Worral, *Quakers in the Colonial Northeast*, 19.

10. Worral, *Quakers in the Colonial Northeast*, 7–23. See also Reay, "Popular Hostility Towards Quakers," and, for the appeal of early Quakerism, Moore, *Light in Their Consciences*.

11. DRCHNY 14:406; Norton and Rous, *New-England's ensigne*, 15.

12. Gandy, ed. *Sufferings of Early Quakers*, 182; Rous, Fox, and Cudworth, *Secret Works*, 1, 11.

13. Gandy, ed. *Sufferings of Early Quakers*, 182; Rous, Fox, and Cudworth, *Secret Works*, 1, 11. On Willet see E. Y. Smith, "Captain Thomas Willett," and Jacobs, *New Netherland*, 183, 332, 491. Willet does not appear at all in Jacobs's account of Hodgson's trial, which is based entirely on the original Dutch sources.

14. Jacobs, *Colony of New Netherland*, 168. Jacobs points out that nineteenth-century accounts that dramatized Hodgson's suffering as persecution were "largely based on hagiographic Quaker publications from the beginning of the eighteenth century, forty years after the event." However, one account dates from 1659, "being the substance taken out of his own true relation given under his hand, Robert Hodgshone" by Humphrey Norton, who claimed an "intire neerness betwixt the fore-mentioned sufferer & me, for whose innocency sake I cannot hold my peace, we having been partakers of the spirit of life and love together several dayes and years, and baptized we have been into many trials, which hath caused us for the comfort of each other to communicate what might administer strength to us," Norton and Rous, *New-England's ensigne*, 18. For additional accounts of Hodgson clearly based on the same source, see Rous, Fox, and Cudworth, *Secret Works*, 11–12; Gandy, *Sufferings of Early Quakers*, 182–83.

15. Ordinance, February 1, 1656, ER 1:344.

16. For Hodgson's story see Norton and Rous, *New-England's ensigne*, 15–18; Gandy, *Sufferings of Early Quakers*, 182–83; Jacobs, *Colony of New Netherland*, 167–68, and Worral, *Quakers in the Colonial Northeast*, 17, 19, 20, 65.

17. G. L. Smith, *Religion and Trade*, 222; Jacobs, *Colony of New Netherland*, 168; J. D. Bangs, "Dutch Contributions," 590. On the Swiss situation see J. D. Bangs, *Letters on Toleration*.

18. Braithwaite, *Beginnings of Quakerism to*, 402, 406–13. A recent study of the important role of women in seventeenth-century Quakerism, including their prominent role as missionaries, is Villani, "Donne quacchere nel xvii secolo."

19. See Pestana, "Quaker Executions as Myth and History," and "City upon a Hill Under Siege."

20. Megapolensis and Drisius to Classis, September 24, 1658, ER 1:433; Gandy, *Sufferings of Early Quakers*, 181–82; Worral, *Quakers in the Colonial Northeast*, 18–20. On Roger Williams's rebuttal of George Fox upon his visit to Rhode Island in 1672 and the ensuing political and doctrinal conflict in Rhode Island see Worral, *Quakers in the Colonial Northeast*, 31–41.

21. Megapolensis and Drisius to Classis, October 25, 1657, ER 1:410.

22. Norton and Rous, *New-England's ensigne*, 16–18; Gandy, *Sufferings of Early Quakers*, 182–83.

23. Megapolensis and Drisius to Classis, October 22, 1957, ER 1:410.

24. Megapolensis and Drisius to Classis, September 24, 1658, ER 1: 433. Jacobs, *Een zegenrijk gewest*, 457n170, confirms the lack of direct information on the ordinance.

25. Norton and Rous, *New-England's ensigne*, 19.

26. Rous, Fox, and Cudworth, *Secret Works*, 12.

27. The cases of Townsend and Tilton, 8, January 15, 1658, DRCHNY 14:405–8; Norton and Rous, *New-England's ensigne*, 20.

28. Remonstrance of the Inhabitants of Flushing, December 27, 1657, DRCHNY 14:402–4.

29. Gandy, ed. *Sufferings of Early Quakers*, 183; Rous, Fox, and Cudworth, *Secret Works*, 12; Norton and Rous, *New-England's ensigne*, 20.

30. Jacobs, *Colony of New Netherland*, 282n71. For recent accounts of the significance of the Flushing Remonstrance, see Garman, "Designed for the Good of All"; Maika, "Commemoration and Context; Voorhees, "The 1657 Flushing Remonstrance."

31. Garman, "Designed for the Good of All," 47–65, 81.

32. DRCHNY 14:404–5.

33. R. Ward Harrington traces the Biblical correspondences for many passages in the remonstrance, "Speaking Scripture."

34. DRCHNY 14:402.

35. DRCHNY 14:409.

36. DRCHNY 14:402–3.

37. DRCHNY 14:402.

38. DRCHNY 14:402–3.

39. DRCHNY 14:403.

40. R. Williams, *The Bloody Tenent*, cited in J. D. Bangs, "Dutch Contributions," 603.

41. J. D. Bangs, "Dutch Contributions," 596–97, citing Twisck, *Religions Vryheyt*.

42. DRCHNY 14:403.

43. J. D. Bangs, "Dutch Contributions," 599–600.

44. B. J. Kaplan, *Divided by Faith*, 321–22.

45. Ibid., 303–6.

46. Voorhees, "The 1657 Flushing Remonstrance," 13.

47. Quotes in Coffey, "Puritanism and Liberty Revisited."

48. Busher, *Religious peace*, 33, cited in Walsham, *Charitable Hatred*, 234. Not all Baptists agreed. See also Coffey, "Puritanism and Liberty Revisited," 961–85; Capp, *The Fifth Monarchy Men*, 181–84, on millenarian tolerance of Turks and Infidels.

49. Busher, *Religious peace*, cited in Walsham, *Charitable Hatred*, 234.

50. See Coffey, "Puritanism and Liberty Revisited"; Capp, *The Fifth Monarchy Men*, 181–84, on millenarian tolerance of Turks and Infidels.

51. R. Williams, *The Bloody Tenent*, A2 verso.

52. J. D. Bangs, "Dutch Contributions," 603–4.

53. On Roger Williams's rebuttal of George Fox on his visit to Rhode Island in 1672 and the ensuing political and doctrinal conflict in Rhode Island, see Worral, *Quakers in the Colonial Northeast*, 31–41.

54. Fox quotes in Walsham, *Charitable Hatred*, 235, and Moore, *The Light in Their Consciences*, 219. The later statement dates from 1661.

55. Here I am mostly in agreement with J. D. Bangs, "Dutch Contributions," 605, that the Flushing Remonstrance "has to be understood as an aspect of English interest in toleration, an interest that had arisen in the context of unofficial, dissenting discussions in the Netherlands, but not in New Netherland." See also Marshall, *John Locke*, 593–617.

56. DRCHNY 14:403.

57. DRCHNY 14:403. See DeRiggi, "Quakerism on Long Island," for the early history.

58. DRCHNY 14:403.

59. The argument figured in English debates in the 1660s, see De Krey, "Rethinking the Restoration Crisis."

60. DRCHNY 14:403.

61. DRCHNY 14:406–7.

62. DRCHNY 14:407, 409.

63. DRCHNY 14:407, 409.

64. Shattuck, "Heemstede," 31–33; Maika, "Commemoration and Context"; Jacobs, *New Netherland*, 308–09.

Chapter 7. Public Church

Epigraph: Directors to Stuyvesant, 20 May 1658, in Gehring, *Correspondence, 1654–1658*, 175.

1. For earlier studies of the baptismal controversy, see Eekhof, *Hervormde Kerk*, 24–35, G. L. Smith, *Religion and Trade*, 206–11.

2. Frijhoff and Spies, *1650*, 353–55. My sense of the long view of religious change in the Netherlands draws on Van Rooden, *Religieuze Regimes*.

3. Frijhoff, "Religion as Cultural Practice," 164; Goodfriend, "Practicing Toleration," 103–4; Jacobs, *Colony of New Netherland*, 163–64; G. L. Smith, *Religion and Trade*, 206–11.

4. Evenhuis, *Ook dat was Amsterdam*, 1:311–38.

5. For the Remonstrant approach to running the Public Church pre-1618, see, among others, Hoenderdaal and Luca, *Staat in de vrijheid*, 9–24; Kaplan, *Calvinists and Libertines*, 68–110; Spaans, *Haarlem na de Reformatie*, 113–38, 191–225.

6. DRCHNY 14:460–61. Berkin, "Moody, née Dunch, Deborah Lady Moody."

7. Acts of Classis, April 2, 15, May 6, 1658 ER 1:420–21, 422.

8. Directors to Stuyvesant, May 20, 1658, in *Corres. 1654–1658*, 174.

9. Directors to Stuyvesant, May 20, 1658, in *Corres. 1654–1658*, 174–75.

10. GAA, AELG, inv. nr. 20 [1656–1665, no. 2], f. 227–28.

11. Schaets to Classis, September 22, 1660, ER 1:483.

12. Ibid.

13. Evenhuis, *Ook dat was Amsterdam*, 1:234–37. Scholars sometimes have translated "alhier" as simply "here," which misses the emphasis on the locality where the phrase was spoken. I have preferred "of this place" to "here present" or other versions given in the translated documents.

14. For the controversies and policies regarding baptism in Holland before 1620, see Van Deursen, *Bavianen & Slijkgeuzen*, 135–44.

15. Megapolensis and Drisius to the Director-general, August 23, 1658, ER 1:428.

16. Directors to Stuyvesant, May 20, 1658, in *Corres. 1654–1658*, 174–75.

17. Bontemantel, *De regeeringe van Amsterdam*, 1: lxi–lxxxiv, makes the case of Bontemantel's affinity for Arminianism. O'Callaghan, *Register of New Netherland*, 1–5, provides a list of the known directors for the years 1648–1664. Bontemantel signed the crucial April 26, 1655, letter ordering admission of the Jews, and two important letters on policy toward the Lutherans of May 20 and June 7, 1658. He did not sign the important letter on Jewish and Lutheran policy of June 14, 1656, but Eduard Man, who did, also signed the April 26 letter and the 1658 letters Bontemantel did sign confirming the June 14, 1656 letter. See *Corres. 1654–1658*, 54, 97, 178, 182, 183.

18. Bontemantel, *De regeeringe van Amsterdam*, 1: lxii–lxiii, 140–41.

19. For Van Beuningnen's career and his close connection to events in the Baltic, see Postma, *Johan de Witt en Coenraad van Beuningen*.

20. Directors to Stuyvesant, May 20, June 7, 1658, in *Corres. 1654–1658*, 175, 182.

21. Directors to Stuyvesant, June 19, 1658, in *Corres. 1654–1658*, 185–86.

22. Megapolensis and Drisius to the Director-general, August 23, 1658, ER 1:430.

23. Ibid., 428–30. Their letter only discusses Matthew 15:12. Verse 13 reads "Every plant, which my heavenly Father hath not planted, shall be rooted up," scriptural backing for the dominies' opposition to tolerating a non-Reformed congregation.

24. Ibid., 429, 431.

25. Ibid.

26. Amsterdam Classis, February 3, February 24, 1659, ER 1:440–42.

27. Directors to Stuyvesant, February 13, 1659, DRCHNY 14:430.

28. Megapolensis and Drisius to Classis, September 10, 1659, and "Order Appointing a Day of General Fasting and Prayer," September 30, 1659, ER 1:449–53.

29. Directors to Stuyvesant, December 22, 1659, DRCHNY 14: 451.

30. Ibid.

31. Classis to New Netherland, March 1, 1660, ER 1:471.

32. Stuyvesant to Directors, April 21, 1660, DRCHNY 14:472.

33. Directors to Stuyvesant, March 29, April 16, 1660, DRCHNY 14:461.

34. Classis to New Netherland, March 1, 1660, ER 1:470; Classis to Schaets, December 15, 1661, ER 1:515–16.

35. Drisius to Classis, October 4, 1660, ER 1:485–86.

36. Ibid.; Classis to Drisius, December 15, 1661, ER 1:513–14.

37. On October 5, 1660, the classis told minister "Koningsvelt, about to go as minister to Kajana" [Guyana] "to abide by the customary Form" with "alhier" even though he had heard "that the Directors wish to have that word left out of the formulae," ER 1:492.

38. Bosch to Consistory, August 19, 1663, LChNY, 47–48, 256.

Chapter 8. Borders

Epigraphs: Megapolensis to Classis, September 28, 1658, ER 1:438.

1. For Catholic cross-border pilgrimages, see Wingens, *Over de grens*. The Remonstrant experience of persecution is well captured in Van Wanray, *Om den gelove*.

2. Lutherans to Consistory, October 21, 1657, and May 5, 1659; Gutwasser to Consistory, October 23, 1657, LChNY, 32, 34, 37.

3. DRCHNY 14:415.

4. NNN, 253.

5. JR 39: 77–79, 87, 141.

6. JR 40:141–45.

7. Megapolensis and Drisius to Classis, September 24, 28, 1658, ER 1: 434, 436.

8. Ibid., 434.

9. Ibid., 438–39.

10. Ibid. For the quote from the Latin letter see Eekhof, *De Hervormde Keerk*, 2:xxxi. My thanks to Adam Kosto for his translation help.

11. Frijhoff, "From 'Case' to 'Model,'" 40–43; Joose, *"Scoone Dingen Sijn Swaere Dingen"*.

12. Jacobs, "Soldiers of the Company," 19 identifies the national origins of the soldiers but not their religious affiliation, which is more difficult to determine.

13. Swellengrebel, "João Ferreira D'Almeida."

14. Niemeijer, *Batavia*, 245–46; Evenhuis, *Ook dat was Amsterdam*, 2:335.

15. For Catholics in Batavia, Niemeijer, *Batavia*, 242–56.

16. Court Minutes, January 1661, DRCHNY 14:489–92.

17. Ibid.

18. Ibid.; Jacobs, *New Netherland*, 308–10.

19. DRCHNY 14:491–92.

20. DRCHNY 14:492–93; Jacobs, *Colony of New Netherland*, 170.

21. New York State Archives, New York State Manuscripts 10–1:232–33 (my translation); Jacobs, *New Netherland*, 310. My thanks to Jaap Jacobs for sharing digital photos of the documents.

22. DRCHNY 14:515–16.

23. Quotations from this and the next ten paragraphs are from John Bowne, "Journal," f. 51–63 verso in John Bowne's Journal and Related Papers, 1649–1676, New York Historical Society. See also Bowne, *Journal of John Bowne*, 21–39.

24. Directors to Stuyvesant, April 16, 1663, DRCHNY 14:526.

25. Polhemius to classis, April 21, 1664, ER 1:544. For the classis's response, see ER 1:551, 554.

26. Jacobs, *Colony of New Netherland*, 171.

27. Bowne, "Journal," 1 ff., 64–69.

Chapter 9. Radicalism

Epigraph: Pieter Cornelis Plockhoy, *A Way Propounded to make the poor in these and other Nations happy*.

1. On patroonships in New Netherland, including New Amstel, see Jacobs, *New Netherland*, 112–132. Eekhof, *De Hervormde Kerk*, 1:246–67, provides a narrative of New Amstel's church.

2. DRCHNY 12:220.

3. ER 1:395; Zwierlein, *Religion in New Netherland*, 127.

4. Johnson, *Swedish Settlement*, 2:663–70.

5. DRCHNY 3:37–39.

6. DRCHNY 12:336. Quaker Captain William Fuller was in Barbados by 1671. See Papenfuse, *A Biographical Dictionary of the Maryland Legislature*, 1: 333–34, and R. M. Jones, *Quakers in the American Colonies*, 265–68, for the context of his 1657 conversion from puritanism to Quakerism.

7. Classis to Consistory of New Netherland, May 25, 1657, ER 1:379–80.

8. DRCHNY 2:7.

9. ER 1:378, 401–3.

10. DRCHNY 2:4; ER 1:373–74, 376, 378–79.

11. ER 1:457–8.

12. DRCHNY 2:61.

13. ER 1:379.

14. ER 1:377; DRCHNY 2:72.

15. ER 1:457–8.

16. ER 1:529–30, 543.

17. ER 1:549–50.

18. This was the reckoning of New Amstel's consistory in 1682, ER 2:823.

19. Grijpink, "Everard Stalpaert"; Looijesteijn, " 'Born to the Common Welfare'," 233.

20. DRCHNY 12:446.

21. DRCHNY 12:433.

22. DRCHNY 12:446.

23. Andrew Rudman to Justus Falckner, October 14, 1703, LChNY, 101–2.

24. Selijns to Classis, June 9, 1664, ER 1:550.

25. Acrelius, *History of New Sweden*, 101; Berkenmeyer, *Albany Protocol*, 191.

26. Kreider, *Lutheranism in Colonial New York*, 21.

27. DRCHNY 12:433, 446.

28. Evenhuis, *Ook dat was Amsterdam*, 3:313–17.

29. Fix, *Prophecy and Reason*.

30. Israel, *Radical Enlightenment*, 168–84; Klever, *Francisus van den Enden*, 7–83; Mertens, "Franciscus van den Enden."

31. Ibid.

32. Israel, *Dutch Republic*, 758–66.

33. G. L. Smith, *Religion and Trade*, 231–34, assumed the various initiatives were closely related if not the same. Looijesteijn, " 'Born to the Common Welfare,' " 234–39, argues that Van den Enden's and Plockhoy's efforts were separate endeavors, both separate from, though not necessarily unrelated to, the petition of twenty-five Mennonite families to move to the colonies. Looijesteijn examines the process of petitioning for a colony in "Petitioning, Colonial Policy."

34. Van den Enden, *Kort Verhael van Nieuw Nederlandts Gelegentheit*, ii.

35. Ibid., 21–22, 26, 29–30, 34–35.

36. Ibid., 43–67.

37. Ibid., 69–70.

38. Ibid., 28–29.

39. It was customary in Mennonite congregations to ask a young man to deliver a sermon, even if he did not want to; see Zijlstra, *Om de ware gemeente en de oude gronden*, 439; Looijesteijn, "'Born to the Common Welfare,'" 47–49.

40. Van den Enden, *Kort Verhael van Nieuw Nederlandts Gelegentheit*, 29, 44–45, 51.

41. Ibid., 38, 52.

42. Ibid., 36, 52.

43. For example, Israel, "The Intellectual Origins of Modern Democratic Republicanism."

44. Klever, *Van den Enden*, 130, 132, 188.

45. Jameson, "Willem Usselinx"; Ligtenberg, *Willem Usselincx.*

46. Klever, *Van den Enden*, 177.

47. Looijesteijn, "'Born to the Common Welfare,'" 221–22, discounts the assumption that these twenty-five Mennonites are connected to Plockhoy and his plan for a colony. His work supersedes G. L. Smith, *Religion and Trade*, 231–34 and all earlier work on Plockhoy.

48. Looijesteijn, "'Born to the Common Welfare,'" 23–46.

49. Ibid., 47–72.

50. Ibid.

51. Ibid., 89–97.

52. Looijesteijn, "'Born to the Common Welfare,'" 97–167. On the Collegiants' appeal to Mennonites, see Fix, *Prophecy and Reason*, esp. 42–48, 108–10.

53. Plockhoy, *A Way Propounded*, 3. Plockhoy's other English works are *The Way to Peace* and *An Invitation to the Aforementioned Society*; Looijesteijn, "'Born to the Common Welfare,'" 115–209.

54. Looijesteijn, "'Born to the Common Welfare,'" 210–15.

55. Both (Amsterdam, 1662) discussed in Eekhof, *De Hervormde Kerk*, 2:60–69.

56. Looijesteijn, "'Born to the Common Welfare,'" 241–62.

Chapter 10. Conquest

Epigraph: Articles of Capitulation on the Reduction of New Netherland, 27 August 1664, DRCHNY 2:251.

1. DRCHNY 2:251.

2. Drisius to Classis, September 15, 1664, ER 1:562.

3. The Duke's Laws, February 28, 1665, ER 1:570–72.

4. Denton, *A Brief Description of New York*.

5. Philip Calvert to Richard Nicolls, Head of Chesapeake Bay, March 22, 1668, Papers of William Blathwayt, 1657–1770, BL 59, Huntington Library. My thanks to Dan Richter for sharing this source with me. Nicolls's biography says nothing about his religion, though the fact that he received a doctorate in civil law from the University of Oxford in 1663 indicates that he conformed to the Church of England at least up to that point. Ritchie, "Nicolls, Richard (1624–1672)."

6. Governor Nicolls's Answers to the Several Queries, 1669, DHNY 1:59.

7. Samuel Megapolensis to a Friend, September 7, 1668, ER 1:597.

8. Danckaerts, *Journal of Jasper Danckaerts*, 45.

9. New York to Amsterdam Consistory, December 18, 1664; Consistory Minutes, November 21, Consistory to New York, November 28, 1668; Lovelace confirmation, February 20, 1669, LChNY, 50, 63, 64, 65–66.

10. Articles of Agreement, October 1, 1664, DRCHNY 3:71; Coll. Nicolls to Secretary of State, October 1664, DRCHNY 3:68–69.

11. See Christoph, "Delaware Under the New York Governors."

12. Duke's Laws, ER 1:572.

13. Petition from Huntingdon, ER 1:691.

14. Moore, *Light in Their Consciences*, 180–85.

15. DRCHNY 14:597–98.

16. DHNY 4:85–86.

17. DHNY 4:87–88.

18. NJA, 1:30.

19. The ministers were for New Ark: Abraham Pierson, 1667–1678, Abraham Pierson, Jr., 1678–1692, John Prudden, 1692–1699, Jabez Wakeman, 1699–1704; for Elizabethtown: Jeremiah Peck, 1668–1678, Seth Fletcher, 1680–1682, John Harriman, 1687–1705; for Woodbridge (which initially had trouble recruiting a minister at its low wage): John Allin, 1681–1686, Archibald Ridell (a Scot), 1686–1689, Samuel Shepherd, 1695–1702; Pomfret, *The Province of East New Jersey*, 371–79.

20. New York Consistory to Amsterdam, April 13, 23, 1669, LChNY, 68.

21. DRCHNY 14:626.

22. New York Consistory to Amsterdam, LChNY, 76.

23. Lovelace to Carr, April 13, 1670, DRCHNY 12:473.

24. August 11, 1671, DHNY 3:242.

25. Kreider, *Lutheranism in Colonial New York*, 23–29.

26. Megapolensis to Classis, April 17, 27, 1669, ER 1:602.

27. DRCHNY 14:650, 654.

28. Consistory of New York to Classis, January 29, 1669/70, ER 1:608.

29. Classis to Church of New York, September 10, 1670, ER 1:614.

30. Megapolensis to Classis, April 17/27, 1669, ER 1:602; Synod of North Holland, August 5, 1670, ER 1:613. Further discouragement came when Samuel's mother, even with the assistance of the Classis of Amsterdam, failed to persuade the West India Company to reimburse her for Megapolensis's unpaid back wages after his death, ER 1:683.

31. Acts of Classis, March 16, 1671, ER 1:617.

32. Church of New York to Classis, 1672, ER 1:624–25.

33. DRCHNY 14:619–20.

34. Fox, *Journal of George Fox*, 619–20.

35. Fox, *Journal of George Fox*, 629.

36. For ecclesiastical policy under Colve, see ER 1:628–52.

37. DRCHNY 2:617.

38. Nieuwenhuysen to Classis, July 26, 1674, ER 1:653–54.

39. Regarding the Maintenance of the Minister of Jamaica, L.I., May 9, 1674, DHNY 3:120–21, 194.

40. DRCHNY 12:508.

41. Fox, *Journal of George Fox*, 631.

42. Order, September 29, 1673, NJA 1:134.

43. DHNY 3:525.

44. DHNY 3:530–31.

45. DRCHNY 12:512.

46. DHNY 3:242, 243.

47. Blok and Molhuysen, *Nieuw Nederlandsch Biografisch Woordenboek*, 7:1024–26; Sprunger, *Dutch Puritanism*, 418–19; Goslinga, *Dutch in the Caribbean*, 429–30.

48. Goslinga, *Dutch in the Caribbean*, 467–82.

Conclusion

1. Goodfriend, "Why New Netherland Matters," 149, 158; Voorhees, "The Dutch Legacy in America," 411, 420.

2. A sense of how the texture of religious life in an unconquered New Netherland could have evolved can be garnished from existing studies of colonial Dutch Reformed communities, where the strength and persistence of the faith is a common theme. See, among others, Balmer, *A Perfect Babel of Confusion*; Corwin, *A Manual of the Reformed Church in America*; De Jong, *Dutch Reformed Church*; Fabend, *A Dutch Family*; Goodfriend, *Before the Melting Pot*; Hackett, *The Rude Hand of Innovation*; Haefeli, "A Scandalous Minister"; and Nooter, "Between Heaven and Earth."

3. Michaelius to Smoutius, August 11, 1628, ER 1:52.

BIBLIOGRAPHY

Manuscript Sources

British Library
  Egerton mss.
Gemeentearchief Amsterdam
  Archief van de evangelisch-lutherse gemeente Amsterdam
  Archief van de Amsterdam Classis
Huntington Library
  Papers of William Blathwayt, 1657–1770, BL 59,
Nationaal Archief, The Hague
  Oude WIC
New-York Historical Society.
  John Bowne's Journal and Related Papers, 1649–1676.
New York State Archives
  New York State Manuscripts.
Zeeuws Archief, Middelburg
  Westindische kerk zakken, 1623–1641.

Published Primary Sources

Abrahamsz de Haan, Galenus and David Spruit. *Bedenckingen over den toestant der Sichtbare Kercke Christi op aerden, kortelcyk in XIX artikelen voorgestelt.* Amsterdam, 1659.

Acrelius, Israel. *A History of New Sweden.* Trans. and ed. Willam M. Reynolds. Philadelphia: Historical Society of Pennsylvania, 1874.

Anonymous. *Amsterdam and her Other Hollander Sisters put out to Sea by Can Trump, Van Dunck, & Van Dumpe.* London, 1652.

Baerle, Caspar van. *The History of Brazil under the Governorship of Count Johan Maurits of Nassau, 1636–1644,* Trans. and ed. Blanche T. van Berckel-Ebeling Koning. Gainseville: University of Florida Press, 2011.

Bontekoe, Willem Ysbrantz. *Het Journaal van Bontekoe.* Trans. Thomas Rosenboom; ed. Vibeke Roeper. Amsterdam: Athenaeum-Polak & Van Gennep, 2007.

Bontemantel, Hans. *De regeeringe van Amsterdam soo in 't civiel als crimineel en militaire, 1653–1672.* Ed. G. W. Kernkamp. 2 vols. The Hague, 1897.

Bowne, John. *Journal of John Bowne, 1650–1694.* Ed. Herbert F. Ricard, preface Kenneth Scott. New Orleans: Polyanthos, 1975.

Bradford, William. "A Dialogue or a sum of a Conference between some young men born in New England and sundry ancient men that came out of Holland and old England, anno dom 1648." In *Chronicles of the Pilgrim Fathers of the Colony of Plymouth, from 1602 to 1625*, ed. Alexander Young. Boston: Little and Brown, 1841. 411–58.

———. *Of Plymouth Plantation, 1620–1647.* Ed. Samuel Eliot Morison. New York: Knopf, 1952.

Busher, Leonard. "Religious peace or a plea for liberty of conscience (London, 1646 edn)." In *Tracts on Liberty of Conscience and Persecution, 1614–1661*, ed. Edward Bean Underhill. London, 1846.

Calado, Frei Manuel. *O Valeroso Lucideno.* 5th ed. Ed. Leonardo Dantas Silva, preface José Antônia Gonsalves de Mello. 2 vols. Recife: Companhia de Pernambuco, 2004.

Christoph, Peter R. and Florence A. Christoph. *New York Historical Manuscripts, English: Books of General Entries of the Colony of New York, 1664–1673.* Baltimore: Genealogical Publishing, 1982.

Christoph, Peter R. and Florence A. Christoph with translations from the Dutch by Charles T. Gehring. *The Andros Papers, 1674–1676: Files of the Provincial Secretary of New York During the Administration of Governor Sir Edmund Andros, 1674–1680.* Syracuse, N.Y.: Syracuse University Press, 1989.

"Classicale acta van Brazilië." *Kroniek van het Historisch Genootschap* 6th ser. 4, 29 (1873): 298–317, 322–72, 375–419.

Coornhert, D. V. *Synode over gewetensvrijheid: Een nauwgezet onderzoek in de vergadering gehouden in het jaar 1582 te Vrijburgh.* Ed. J. Gruppelaar, J. C. Bedaux, and G. Verwey. Amsterdam: Amsterdam University Press, 2008.

Corwin, Edward T., ed. *Ecclesiastical Records: State of New York.* 7 vols. Albany: James B. Lyon, 1901–16.

Danckaerts, Jasper. *Journal of Jasper Danckaerts, 1679–1680.* Ed. Bartlett Burleigh James and J. Franklin Jameson. New York: Scribner's, 1913.

Denton, Daniel. *A Brief Description of New York, formerly called New Netherland.* Ed. Felix Neumann. Cleveland: Burrows Brothers, 1902.

Dussen, Adriaen van der. *Relatório sobre as capitanias conquistadas no Brasil pelos holandeses (1639).* Ed. and trans. José Antonio Gonsalves de Mello. Rio de Janeiro: Lucena, 1947.

Enden, Franciscus van den. *Kort Verhael van Nieuw Nederlants Gelegentheit, Deughden, Natuerlijke Voorrechten, en byzondere beqaeumheidt ter bevolkingh.* Amsterdam, 1662. In *Online documents regarding Franciscus van den Enden.* Ed. Frank Mertens. http://users.telenet.be/fvde/index.htm?Works1.

Fernow, Berthold. *Calendar of Council Minutes, 1668–1783.* Albany: State University of New York, 1902.

————, ed. *Records of New Amsterdam from 1653 to 1674*. 7 vols. New York: Knicker-bocker, 1897.

Fox, George. *The Journal of George Fox*. Ed. John L. Nickalls. Philadelphia: Religious Society of Friends, 1952. Rev. ed. 1997.

Gandy, Michael, ed. *Sufferings of Early Quakers: America (New England and Maryland), West Indies (Antigua, Barbadoes, Jamaica and Nevis), Bermuda, a facsimile of portions of Joseph Besse, A Collection of the Sufferings of the People called Quakers (1753)*. York: Ebor Press, 2001.

Gehring, Charles T., trans. and ed. *Correspondence, 1647–1653*. Syracuse, N.Y.: Syracuse University Press, 2000.

————. *Correspondence, 1654–1658*. Syracuse: Syracuse University Press, 2003.

————. *Council Minutes, 1652–1654*. Baltimore: Genealogical Publishing, 1983.

————. *Council Minutes, 1655–1656*. Syracuse, N.Y.: Syracuse University Press, 1995.

————. *Delaware Papers (Dutch Period): A Collection of Documents Pertaining to the Regulation of Affairs on the South River of New Netherland, 1648–1664*. Baltimore: Genealogical Publishing, 1981.

————. *Fort Orange Records, 1656–1678*. Syracuse, N.Y.: Syracuse University Press, 2000.

————. *Laws and Writs of Appeal, 1647–1663*. Syracuse, N.Y.: Syracuse University Press, 1991.

Gehring, Charles T. and Janny Venema, trans. and eds. *Fort Orange Records, 1654–1679*. Syracuse, N.Y.: Syracuse University Press, 2009.

Groenveld, Simon, ed. *Unie-Bestand-Vrede: Drie fundamentele wetten van de Republiek der Verenigde Nederlanden*. Hilversum: Verloren, 2009.

Grothe, J. A. *Archief voor de geschiedenis der Oude Hollandsche zending* 6 vols. Utrecht: C. van Bentum, 1884–1891.

Hart, Simon. *The Prehistory of the New Netherland Company: Amsterdam Notarial Records of the First Dutch voyages to the Hudson*. Amsterdam: City of Amsterdam Press, 1959.

Holm, Thomas Campanius. "A Short Description of the Province of New Sweden, now called, by the English, Pennsylvania, in America." Trans. Peter S. Du Ponceau. Historical Society of Pennsylvania Memoirs 3. Philadelphia: McCarty and Davis, 1834. 1–166.

Israel, Menassah Ben. *Indians or Jews: An Introduction by Lynn Glaser to a reprint of Manassah Ben Israel's "The Hope of Israel"*. Gilroy, Calif.: Boswell, 1973.

Jameson, J. Franklin, ed. *Narratives of New Netherland, 1609–1664*. New York: Scribner's, 1990.

Johnson, Amandus, ed. and trans. *The Instruction for Johan Printz, Governor of New Sweden*. Philadelphia: Swedish Colonial Society, 1930.

Klever, Wim, ed. and trans. *Francisus van den Enden: Free Political Propositions and Considerations of state (1665): Text in Translation, the Relevant Biographical Documents and a Selection from Kort Verhael*. "Vrijstad": n.p., 2007.

Kossman, E. H. and A. F. Mellink, eds. *Texts Concerning the Revolt of the Netherlands.* Cambridge: Cambridge University Press, 1974.

Laer, Arnold J. F. van, trans. *Council Minutes, 1638–1649.* New York Historical Manuscripts: Dutch, vol. 4. Baltimore: Genealogical Publishing, 1974.

Laer, A. J. F. van, ed. and trans. *Documents Relating to New Netherland, 1624–1626 in the Henry E. Huntingdon Library.* San Marino, Calif.: Henry E. Huntington Library and Art Gallery, 1924.

———. *The Lutheran Church in New York, 1649–1772: Records in the Lutheran Church Archives at Amsterdam, Holland.* New York: New-York Public Library, 1946.

———. *Van Rensselaer Bowier Manuscripts: Being the Letters of Kiliaen Van Rensselaer, 1630–1643, and Other Documents Relating to the Colony of Rensselaerswyck.* Albany: State University of New York, 1908.

Laer, Arnold J. F. van, trans., Kenneth Scott and Kenn Stryker-Rodda, eds. *Council Minutes, 1638–1649.* Baltimore: Genealogical Publishing, 1974.

Laet, Johannes de. *Historie ofte Iaerlijck verhael van de verrichtinghen der Geoctroyeerde West-Indische Compagnie, zedert haer begin, tot het eynde van 't jaer sesthienhondert ses-en-dertich.* Leiden, 1644.

Limborch, Philippus van. *Korte wederlegginge van 't boecxken onlangs (1653) uytgegeven by Jacobus Sceperus, genaemt Chrysopolerotus, waerin oder anderen gehandelt wert van de onderlinge verdraegsaemheyt.* Amsterdam: J. Rieuwertsz, 1661.

Myers, Albert Cook, ed. *Narratives of Early Pennsylvania, West New Jersey and Delaware, 1630–1707.* New York: Scribner's, 1912.

Nickalls, John L., ed. (See Fox).

Norton, Humphrey and John Rous. *New-England's ensigne: it being the account of cruelty, the professor's pride, and the articles of their faith . . . : This being an account of the sufferings sustained by us in New-England (with the Dutch) written by us whom the Wicked in scorn call Quakers.* London: Printed by T. L. for G. Calvert, 1659.

O'Callaghan, Edmund B., ed. *Calendar of Historical Manuscripts, in the Office of the Secretary of State.* Albany, N.Y.: Weed, Parson, 1866.

———. *Documentary History of the State of New York.* 4 vols. Albany, N.Y.: Weed, Parson, 1848–1853.

O'Callaghan, Edmund B. and Berthold Fernow, eds. *Documents Relative to the Colonial History of the State of New York.* 15 vols. Albany, N.Y.: Weed, Parson, 1853–1887.

Plockhoy, Pieter Cornelisz. *A Way Propounded to make the poor in these and other Nations happy, by bringing together a fit, suitable, and well-qualified People into one household-government, or little Common-wealth, wherein every one may keep his property, and be imployed in some work or other, as he shall be fit, without being oppressed. Being the way not only to rid these and other Nations from idle, evil, and disorderly persons but also from all such as have sought and found out many Inventions, to live upon the labour of others.* London, 1659.

———. *A Way to the Peace and Settlement of these Nations.* London, 1659.

————. *An Invitation to the Aforementioned Society or Little Common-Wealth, shewing the excellency of the true Christian love, and the folly of all those who consider not to what end the Lord of heaven and earth hath created them.* London, 1659.

A Rendição dos Holandeses no Recife (1654). Ed. José Antonio Gonsalves de Mello. Recife, 1979.

Rous, John, George Fox, and James Cudworth, *The Secret Works of a Cruel People made Manifest.* London, 1659.

Schappes, Morris U., ed. *A Documentary History of the Jews in the United States, 1654–1875.* New York: Citadel, 1950.

Soler, Vincent Joachim. *Seventeen Letters by Vincent Joachim Soler, Protestant Minister in the Service of the West Indies Company, written in Recife, Brazil, between 1636 and 1643.* Ed. B. N. Teensma, trans. Niels Erik Hyldgaard Nielsen. Rio de Janeiro: Editoria Index, 1999.

Spinoza, Benedict de. *Theological-Political Treatise.* Ed. Jonathan Israel, trans. Michael Silverthorn and Jonathan Israel. Cambridge: Cambridge University Press, 2007.

Stevin, Simon. *Het burgherlyck leven,* ed. Annie Romein-Verschoor and G. S. Overdiep. Amsterdam: Wereldbibliotheek, 1939.

————. *Vita Politica: Het burgherlyck leven: En nu alle menschen van hogen ende legen state in desen beroerlicken tijdt see nuttelick ghelesen.* Delft: Ian Andriesz, 1611.

Stoppa, Giovanni Battista. *The Religion of the Dutch represented in several letters from a Protestant officer in the French army to a pastor and professor of divinity at Berne in Switserland; out of the French.* London, 1680.

Stouppe, Jean-Baptiste. *La religion des Hollandois.* Cologne, 1673.

Temple, Sir William. *Observations upon the United Provinces of the Netherlands.* Ed. Sir George Clark. Oxford: Clarendon, 1972.

Thwaites, Reuben Gold. *The Jesuit Relations and Allied Documents: Travels and Explorations of the Jesuit Missionaries in New France, 1610–1791.* 73 vols. Cleveland: Burrows, 1896–1901.

Twisck, Pieter Jansz. *Religions Vryheyt. . . .* Hoorn: s.n., 1609.

Wanray, Willemken van. *Om den gelove: Wederwaardigheden van Willemken van Wanray als remonstrates weduwe in 1619 en 1622 te Nijmegen doorstaan en vervolgens eigenhandig opgetekend.* Ed. A. E. M. Janssen. Nijmegen: Valkhof Pers, 2003.

Whitehead, William A. et al., eds. *Archives of the State of New Jersey* 1st ser. 43 vols. Newark, N.J., 1880–1949.

Williams, Roger. *The Bloody Tenent, of Persecution, for Cause of Conscience.* London, 1644.

Wolley, Charles. *A Two Year's Journal in New York and Parts of Its territories in America,* ed. Edward Gaylord Bourne. Cleveland: Burrows Brothers, 1902.

Secondary Sources

Aa, A. J. van der, et al., eds. *Biographisch woordenboek der Nederlanden.* 21 vols. Haarlem: Van Brederode, 1852–1878.

Abicht, Ludo. *Geschiedenis van de Joden van de Lage Landen*. Antwerp: Meulenhoff/ Manteau, 2006.

Adriaenssen, Leo. *Staatsvormend Geweld: Overleven aan de frontlinies in de meierij van Den Bosch, 1572–1629*. Tilburg: Stichting Zuidelijke Historisch Contact, 2007.

Ahlstrom, Sydney E. *A Religious History of the American People*. New Haven, Conn.: Yale University Press, 1972.

Arbell, Mordechai. *The Jewish Nation of the Caribbean: The Spanish-Portuguese Jewish Settlements in the Caribbean and the Guianas*. Jerusalem: Gefen, 2005.

Arbell, Mordecai, comp., Dennis C. Landis and Ann P. Barry, eds. *Spanish and Portuguese Jews in the Caribbean and the Guianas: A Bibliography*. Providence, R.I.: John Carter Brown Library, 1999.

Arnade, Peter. *Beggars, Iconoclasts, and Civic Patriots: The Political Culture of the Dutch Revolt*. Ithaca, N.Y.: Cornell University Press, 2008.

Bachman, Van Cleaf. *Peltries or Plantations: The Economic Policies of the Dutch West India Company in New Netherland, 1623–1639*. Baltimore: Johns Hopkins University Press, 1969.

Balmer, Randall. *A Perfect Babel of Confusion: Dutch Religion and English Culture in the Middle Colonies*. New York: Oxford University Press, 1989.

Bancroft, George. *History of the United States of America from the Discovery of the Continent*. 6 vols., Vol. 2, *Colonial History, continued*. Boston: Little, Brown, 1876.

Bangs, Carl. *Arminius: A Study in the Dutch Reformation*. Nashville: Abingdon Press, 1971.

———. "Dutch Theology, Trade, and War: 1590–1610." *Church History* 39, 4 (1970): 470–82.

Bangs, Jeremy Dupertuis. "Dutch Contributions to Religious Toleration." *Church History* 79, 3 (2010): 585–613.

———. *Letters on Toleration: Dutch Aid to Persecuted Swiss and Palatine Mennonites, 1615–1699*. Rockport, Me.: Picton, 2004.

Barbour, Hugh. *The Quakers in Puritan England*. New Haven, Conn.: Yale University Press, 1964.

Berg, Johannes van den. *Religious Currents and Cross-Currents: Essays on Early Modern Protestantism and the Protestant Enlightenment*, ed. Jan de Bruin, Pieter Holtrop, and Ernestine van der Wall. Leiden: Brill, 1999.

Berg, J. van den and Ernestine G. E. van der Wall, eds. *Jewish-Christian Relations in the Seventeenth Century: Studies and Documents*. Dordrecht: Kluwer, 1988.

Bergsma, Wiebe. "Church, State and People." In *A Miracle Mirrored: The Dutch Republic in European Perspective*, ed. Karel Davids and Jan Lucassen. Cambridge: Cambridge University Press, 1995. 196–228.

———. "Reductie en Reformatie." In *Rondom de reductie: Vierhonderd jaar provincie Groningen, 1594–1994*, ed. P. Th. F. M. Boekholt et al. Assen: Van Gorcum, 1994. 236–54.

———. *Tussen Gideonsbende en publieke kerk: Een studie over het gereformeerd protestantisme in Friesland, 1580–1650*. Hilversum: Fryske Akademy, 1999.

Berkenmeyer, Wilhelm Christoph. *Albany Protocol: Wilhelm Christoph Berkenmeyer's Chronicle of Lutheran Affairs in New York Colony, 1731–1750.* Camden, Me.: Picton Press, 1971.

Berkin, Carol. "Moody, née Dunch, Deborah Lady Moody. c. 1585–1658/9." *Oxford Dictionary of National Biography,* online ed. January 2008. http://www.oxforddnb .com/view/article/71107.

Berknes-Stevelinck, C., Jonathan Israel, and G. H. M. Posthumus Meyes, eds. *The Emergence of Tolerance in the Dutch Republic.* Leiden: Brill, 1997.

Bitterman, M. G. F. "The Early Quaker Literature of Defense." *Church History* 42, 2 (1973): 203–28.

Blok, P. J. and P. C. Molhuysen, eds. *Nieuw Nederlandsch biografisch woordenboek.* 10 vols. Leiden: Sijthoff, 1911–1937.

Blom, J. C. H, R. G. Fuks-Mansfeld, and I. Schöffer, eds. *Geschiedenis van de Joden in Nederland.* Amsterdam: Balans, 1995.

Blomfelt, Frank. "The Lutheran Churches and Their Pastors in New Sweden, 1638–1655." In *New Sweden in America,* ed. Carol E. Hoffecker, Richard Waldron, Lorraine E. Williams, and Barbara E. Benson. Newark: University of Delaware Press, 1995.

Bodian, Miriam. *Hebrews of the Portuguese Nation: Conversos and Community in Early Modern Amsterdam.* Bloomington: Indiana University Press, 1997.

Bodle, Wayne. "The 'Myth of the Middle Colonies' Reconsidered: The Process of Regionalization in Early America." *PMHB* 113, 4 (1989): 527–48.

———. "Themes and Direction in Middle Colonies Historiography, 1980–1994." *WMQ* 51, 3 (1994): 355–88.

Bonomi, Patricia U. *A Factious People: Politics and Society in Colonial New York.* New York: Columbia University Press, 1971.

———. *Under the Cope of Heaven: Religion, Society, and Politics in Colonial America.* New York: Oxford University Press, 1986.

Boone, A. Th. "'Om een woesten hoop te brengen tot de kerck': Een onderzoek naar zendingsgedachten in piëtistische zeemansvademecums." In *Zending tussen woord en daad,* ed. A. Th. Boone and J. van Ekeris. Kampen: De Groot Goudriaan, 1991. 12–46.

Boone, A. Th. and van Ekeris, J. *Zending tussen woord en daad: Twee hoofdstukken uit de geschiedenis van gereformeerd piëtisme en zending.* Kampen: De Groot Goudriaan, 1991.

Boone, Marc and Maarten Prak. "Rulers, Patricians and Burghers: The Great and Little Traditions of Urban Revolt in the Low Countries." In *A Miracle Mirrored: The Dutch Republic in European Perspective,* ed. Karel Davids and Jan Lucassen. Cambridge: Cambridge University Press, 1995. 99–134.

Borman, Tracy. "Untying the Knot? The Survival of the Anglo-Dutch Alliance, 1587–1597." *European History Quarterly* 27, 3 (1997): 307–37.

Bouman, P. J. *Johan Maurits van Nassau: De Braziliaan.* Utrecht: Oosthoek, 1947.

Boxer, Charles R. *The Dutch in Brazil, 1624–1654.* Oxford: Clarendon, 1957.

———. *The Dutch Seaborne Empire, 1600–1800.* New York: Penguin, 1990.

———. *De Nederlanders in Brazilië, 1624–1654.* Trans. H. J. Nijk. Alphen aan den Rijn: Sijthoff, 1977.

Brathwaite, William C. *The Beginnings of Quakerism.* Cambridge: Cambridge University Press, 1955.

Bridenbaugh, Carl. *Fat Mutton and Liberty of Conscience: Society in Rhode Island, 1636–1690.* Providence, R.I.: Brown University Press, 1974.

Briels, J. *De Zuidnederlandse Immigratie, 1572–1630.* Haarlem: Fibula-Van Dishoeck, 1978.

Brodhead, John Romeyn. *History of the State of New York.* 2 vols. New York: Harper and Brothers, 1853.

Brunn, Gerhard and Cornelius Neutsch, eds. *Sein Feld war die Welt: Johann Moritz von Nassau-Siegen (1604–1679): Von Siegen über die Niederlande und Brasilien nach Brandenburg.* Münster: Waxman, 2008.

Buckley, Thomas E. *Church and State in Revolutionary Virginia, 1776–1787.* Charlottesville: University Press of Virginia, 1977.

Bumsted, John Michael. *The Pilgrim's Progress: The Ecclesiastical History of the Old Colony, 1620–1775.* New York: Garland, 1989.

Butler, Jon. *Awash in a Sea of Faith: Christianizing the American People.* Cambridge, Mass.: Harvard University Press, 1990.

Butterfield, Herbert. "Toleration in Early Modern Times." *Journal of the History of Ideas* 38, 4 (1977): 573–84.

Bye, John H de. *Geloof, hoop en liefde: Vesting van de Joden in de Surinaamse Jungle.* Schoorl: Conserve, 2002.

Capp, B. S. *The Fifth Monarchy Men: A Study in Seventeenth-Century English Millenarianism.* London: Faber and Faber, 1972.

Carstensen, Carl August. *Die Gründung und anfängliche Entiwicklung von Friedrichstadt an der Eider.* Plön: Kaven, 1913.

Carter, Alice Clare. *The English Reformed Church in Amsterdam in the Seventeenth Century.* Amsterdam: Scheltema and Holkema, 1964.

Cauwer, Peter de. *Tranen van bloed: Het beleg van 's-Hertogenbosch en de oorlog in de Nederlanden, 1629.* Amsterdam: Amsterdam University Press, 2008.

Christoph, Peter R. "Delaware Under the New York Governors, 1664–1681." *DHM* 65, 2 (1992): 26–31.

———. "The Freedmen of New Amsterdam." In *A Beautiful and Fruitful Place: Selected Rensselaerswijck Seminar Papers*, ed. Nancy Anne McClure Zeller. Albany, N.Y.: New Netherland Project, 1971. 157–70.

Clark, Henry B., ed. *Freedom of Religion in America: Historical Roots, Philosophical Concepts and Contemporary Problems.* Los Angeles: Center for Study of the American Experience, University of Southern California, 1982.

Cobb, Sanford Hoadley. *The Rise of Religious Liberty in America: A History.* Intro. Paul L. Murphy. 1902. New York: Johnson Reprints, 1970.

Coffey, John. "Puritanism and Liberty Revisited: The Case for Toleration in the English Revolution." *Historical Journal* 41, 4 (1998): 961–85.

Cogley, Richard W. "The Ancestry of the American Indians: Thomas Thorowgood's *Iewes in America* (1650) and *Jews in America* (1660)." *English Literary Renaissance* 35, 2 (2005): 304–30.

Cohen, Charles L. "The Post-Puritan Paradigm of Early American Religious History." *WMQ* 54, 4 (1997): 695–722.

Cohen, Robert. "The Egerton Manuscript." *American Jewish Quarterly* 52 (1973): 333–47.

Collins, Jeffrey R. "Redeeming the Enlightenment: New Histories of Religious Toleration." *Journal of Modern History* 81 (September 2009): 607–36.

Corbett, Theodore G. "The Cult of Lipsius: A Leading Source of Early Modern Spanish Statecraft." *Journal of the History of Ideas* 36, 1 (January–March 1975): 139–52.

Cornelissen, J. D. M. *De Eendracht van het Land: Cultuurhistorische studies over Nederland in de zestiende en seventiende eeuw.* Amsterdam: De Bataafsche Leeuw, 1987.

Corwin, Edward Tanjore. *A Manual of the Reformed Church in America. formerly Ref. Prot. Dutch Church, 1628–1902.* 4th ed. New York: Board of Publications, 1902.

———. "Recent Researches in Holland and the Ecclesiastical Records of the State of New York." *Papers of the American Society of Church History* 2nd ser. 1 (1909): 51–78.

Costigan, Lucía Helena, ed. *Diálogos da Conversão: Missionários, Índios, Negros e Judeus no contexto Ibero-Americano do Período Barroco.* Campinas: UNICAMP, 2005.

Curry, Thomas J. *The First Freedoms: Church and State in America to the Passage of the First Amendment.* New York: Oxford University Press, 1986.

Davis, J. C. *Fear, Myth and History: The Ranters and the Historians.* Cambridge: Cambridge University Press, 1986.

De Jong, Otto J. *De reformatie in Culemborg.* Assen, 1957.

De Krey, Gary S. "Rethinking the Restoration Crisis: Dissenting Cases for Conscience, 1667–1672." *Historical Journal* 38, 1 (1995): 53–83.

DeRiggi, Mildred Murphy. "Quakerism on Long Island: The First Fifty Years, 1657–1707." Ph.D. dissertation, SUNY Stony Brook, 1994.

Deursen, A. Th. van. *Bavianen en Slijkgeuzen: Kerk en kerkvolk ten tijde van Maurits en Oldenbarnevelt.* Assen: Van Gorcum, 1974.

———. *Een Dorp in de Polder: Graft in de 17de eeuw.* Amsterdam: Bert Bakker, 1998.

———. *Maurits van Nassau: De winnaar die faalde.* Amsterdam: Bert Bakker, 2000.

Dillen, J. G. van. "De West-Indische Compagnie, het Calvinisme en de Politiek." *Tijdschrift voor Geschiedenis* 74, 2 (1961): 145–71.

Dorren, Gabrielle. *Eenheid en verscheidenheid: De burgers van Haarlem in de Gouden Eeuw.* Amsterdam: Prometheus/Bert Bakker, 2001.

Duke, Alistair. "The Netherlands." In *The Early Reformation in Europe*, ed. Andrew Petegree. Cambridge: Cambridge University Press, 1992. 142–65.

———. *Reformation and Revolt in the Low Countries.* London: Hambledon, 1990.

Duke, A. C. and C. A. Tamse, eds. *Church and State Since the Reformation: Papers Delivered to the Seventh Anglo-Dutch Historical Conference*. Britain and the Netherlands 7. The Hague: Nijhoff, 1981.

Eekhof, Albert. *De Hervormde Kerk in Nord Amerika (1624–1664)*. 2 vols. The Hague: Nijhoff, 1913.

———. *Bastien Janszoon Krol: Krankenbezoeker, Kommies en Kommandeur van Nieuw-Nederland, 1595–1645*. The Hague, 1910.

———. *Jonas Michaëlius, Founder of the Church in New Netherland*. Leiden: Sijthoff, 1926.

Eijnatten, Joris van and Fred van Lieburg, *Nederlandse Religiegeschiedenis*. 2nd ed. Hilversum: Verloren, 2006.

Elton, G. R. "Persecution and Toleration in the English Reformation." In *Persecution and Toleration*, ed. J. J. Sheils. Studies in Church History 21. Oxford: Blackwell, 1984. 163–87.

Emmer, Peter C. "The First Global War: The Dutch Versus Iberia in Asia, Africa and the New World, 1590–1609." *e-Journal of Portuguese History* 1, 1 (Summer 2003): 1–14.

Enthoven, Victor. "Dutch Crossings: Migration Between the Netherlands and the New World, 1600–1800." *Atlantic Studies* 2, 2 (October 2005): 153–76.

———. "Nova Zeelandia and Cayenne: The Dutch on the Wild Coast, 1656–1666." In *D'un rivage á l'autre: ville et protestantisme aux xvie et xviie*, ed. G. Martinère, D. Poton, and F. Souty. Paris, 1999. 207–217.

———. "Suriname and Zeeland: Fifteen Years of Dutch Misery on the Wild Coast, 1667–1682." In *International Conference on Shipping, Factories, and Colonization*, ed. J. Everaert and J. Parmentier. Brussels, 1996. 249–260.

Erp, Stephan van. *Vrijheid in verdeeldheid: Geschiedenis en actualiteit van religieuze tolerantie*. Nijmegen: Valkhof Pers, 2008.

Evenhuis, R. B. *Ook dat was Amsterdam: De kerk der hervorming in de gouden eeuw*. 5 vols. Amsterdam: Uitgeverij W. Ten Have, 1965–1978.

Fabend, Firth Haring. *A Dutch Family in the Middle Colonies, 1660–1800*. New Brunswick, N.J.: Rutgers University Press, 1991.

Faber, Eli. *A Time for Planting: The First Migration, 1654–1820*. Baltimore: Johns Hopkins University Press, 1992.

Finkelman, Paul. "'A Land That Needs People for Its Increase': How the Jews Won the Right to Remain in New Netherland." In *New Essays in American Jewish History*, ed. Pamela S. Nadell, Jonathan D. Sarna, and Lance J. Sussman. Cincinnati: American Jewish Archives of Hebrew Union College-Jewish Institute of Religion, 2010. 19–50.

———. "The Soul and the State: Religious Freedom in New York and the Origin of the First Amendment." In *New York and the Union*, ed. Stephen L. Shechter and Richard B. Bernstein. Albany: New York State Commission on the Bicentennial of the U.S. Constitution, 1990. 78–105.

Fiske, John. *The Dutch and Quaker Colonies in America*. 2 vols. Boston: Houghton Mifflin, 1899.

Fix, Andrew C. *Prophecy and Reason: The Dutch Collegiants in the Early Enlightenment*. Princeton, N.J.: Princeton University Press, 1991.

Fletcher, Anthony. "The Enforcement of the Conventicle Acts, 1664–1679." In *Persecution and Toleration*, ed. J. J. Sheils. Studies in Church History 21. Oxford: Blackwell, 1984. 235–46.

Flint, Martha Bockée. *Early Long Island: A Colonial Study*. New York: Putnam's 1896.

Frijhoff, Willem. "Dimensions de la coexistence confessionelle." In *The Emergence of Tolerance in the Dutch Republic*, ed. C. Berknes-Stevelinck, Jonathan Israel, and G. H. M. Posthumus Meyes. Leiden: Brill, 1997. 213–38.

———. *Fulfilling God's Mission: The Two Worlds of Dominie Everardus Bogardus, 1607–1657*. Trans. Myra Heerspink Scholz. Leiden: Brill, 2007.

———. "A Misunderstood Calvinist: The Religious Choices of Bastiaen Jansz Krol, New Netherland's First Church Servant." *Journal of Early American History* 1, 1 (2011): 1–34.

———. "Neglected Networks: Director Willem Kieft (1602–1647) and His Dutch Relatives." In *Revisiting New Netherland: Perspectives on Early Dutch America*, ed. Joyce Goodfriend. Leiden: Brill, 2005. 147–204.

———. "New Views on the Dutch Period of New York." *DHM* 71, 2 (1998): 23–34.

———. "Religious Toleration in the United Provinces: From 'Case' to 'Model'." In *Calvinism and Religious Toleration in the Dutch Golden Age*, ed. R. Po-Chia Shia. Cambridge: Cambridge University Press, 2002. 27–52.

———. "Seventeenth-Century Religion as Cultural Practice: Reassessing New Netherland's Religious History." In *From De Haelve Maen to KLM: 400 Years of Dutch-American Exchange*, ed. Margriet Bruijn Lacy, Charles Gehring, and Jenneke Oosterhoff. Münster: Nodus, 2008. 159–74.

———. *Wegen van Evert Willemsz.: Een Hollands weeskind op zoek naar zichzelf, 1607–1647*. Nijmegen: SUN, 1995.

———. "The West India Company and the Reformed Church: Neglect or Concern?" *DHM* 70, 3 (1997): 59–68.

Frijhoff, Willem and Marijke Spies. *1650: Bevochten eendracht*. The Hague: Sdu Uitgevers, 1999.

Frijhoff, Willem et al. *Geschiedenis van Dordrecht*. 3 vols. Dordrecht: Gementearchief Dordrecht; Hilversum: Verloren, 1996–2000.

Frijhoff, Willem et al. *Geschiedenis van Zutphen*. Zutphen: De Walburg Pers, 1989.

Frost, J. William. *A Perfect Freedom: Religious Liberty in Pennsylvania*. University Park: Pennsylvania University Press, 1990.

Fuks-Mansfeld, R. G. *De Sefardim in Amsterdam tot 1795: Aspecten van een joodse minderheid in een Hollandse stad*. Hilversum: Verloren, 1989.

Gaastra, Femme S. *De geschiedenis van de VOC*. Zutphen: Walburg Pers, 1991.

Garman, Tabetha. "Designed for the Good of All: The Flushing Remonstrance and Religious Freedom in America." M.A. thesis, East Tennessee State University. 2006.

Gelder, H. A. Enno van. *Getemperde vrijheid: Een verhandeling over de verhouding van Kerk en Staat in de Republiek der Verenigde Nederlanden en de vrijheid van meningsuiting in zake godsdienst, drukpers en onderwijs, gedurende de 17e eeuw.* Groningen: Wolters-Noordhoff, 1972.

———. *De levensbeschouwing van Cornelis Pieterszoon Hooft: Burgermeester van Amsterdam, 1547–1626.* Utrecht: HES, 1982.

Gelderblom, Arie-Jan, Jan L. de Jong, and Marc van Vaeck, eds. *The Low Countries as a Crossroads of Religious Beliefs.* Leiden: Brill, 2004.

Gelderen, Martin van. *The Political Thought of the Dutch Revolt, 1555–1590.* Cambridge: Cambridge University Press, 1992.

Gelfand, Noah. "Jews in New Netherland: An Atlantic Perspective." In *Explorers, Fortunes and Love Letters: A Window on New Netherland,* ed. Martha Dickinson Shattuck. Albany, N.Y.: Mount Ida Press, 2009. 39–49.

———. "A People Within and Without: International Jewish Commerce and Community in the Seventeenth and Eighteenth Centuries Dutch Atlantic World." Ph.D. dissertation, New York University, 2008.

Geyl, Pieter. *Oranje en Stuart, 1641–1672.* Utrecht: Oosthoek's Uitgeverij, 1939.

———. *The Netherlands in the Seventeenth Century.* 2 vols. London: Ernest Benn, 1961.

———. *Pennestrijd over Staat en Historie.* Groningen: Wolters-Noordhoff, 1971.

Gill, Catie. "Evans and Cheevers's *A Short Relation* in Context: Flesh, Spirit, and Authority in Quaker Prison Writings, 1650–1662." *Huntington Library Quarterly* 72, 2 (2009): 257–72.

Gisjwit-Hofstra, Marijke, ed. *Een schijn van verdraagzaamheid: Afwijking en tolerantie in Nederland van de zestiende eeuw tot heden.* Hilversum: Verloren, 1989.

Glaser, Lynn, ed. *Indians or Jews? An Introduction to a reprint of Manasseh Ben Israel's* The Hope of Israel. Gilroy, Calif.: Roy V. Boswell, 1973.

Glezerman, Abraham. *Cleve, ein unerfülltes Shicksal: Aufstieg, Rückzug und Verfall eines Territorialstaates.* Berlin: Duncker and Humboldt, 1985.

Goodfriend, Joyce D. *Before the Melting Pot: Society and Culture in Colonial New York City, 1664–1730.* Princeton, N.J.: Princeton University Press, 1992.

———. "Black Families in New Netherland." In *A Beautiful and Fruitful Place: Selected Rennselaerswijck Seminar Papers,* ed. Nancy Anne McClure Zeller. Albany, N.Y.: New Netherland Project, 1971. 147–55.

———. "Burghers and Blacks: The Evolution of a Slave Society at New Amsterdam." *NYH* 59, 2 (1978): 125–44.

———. "Practicing Toleration in Dutch New Netherland." In *The First Prejudice: Religious Tolerance and Intolerance in Early America,* ed. Chris Beneke and Christopher S. Grenda. Philadelphia: University of Pennsylvania Press, 2011. 98–122.

———, ed. *Revisiting New Netherland: Perspectives on Early Dutch America.* Leiden: Brill, 2005.

————. "The Struggle over the Sabbath in Petrus Stuyvesant's New Amsterdam." In *Power and the City in the Netherlandic World*, ed. Wayne Te Brake and Wim Klooster. Leiden: Brill, 2008. 205–24.

————. "Why New Netherland Matters." In *Explorers, Fortunes and Love Letters: A Window on New Netherland*, ed. Martha Dickinson Shattuck. Albany, N.Y.: Mount Ida Press, 2009. 148–161.

Goor, J. van. *De Nederlandse Koloniën: Geschiedenis van de Nederlandse Expansie, 1600–1975*. The Hague: Uitgeverij Koninginnengracht, 1994.

Goslinga, Cornelis Ch. *The Dutch in the Caribbean and on the Wild Coast, 1580–1680*. Gainesville: University of Florida Press, 1971.

Gosses, I. H. and N. Japikse, *Handboek tot de Staatkundige Geschiedenis van Nederland*. The Hague: Nijhoff, 1947.

Graizbord, David L. *Souls in Dispute: Converso Identities in Iberia and the Jewish Diaspora, 1580–1700*. Philadelphia: University of Pennsylvania Press, 2004.

Grassmann, Antjekathrin. "Lübeck, Freie Reichsstadt und Hochstift, Wendische Hansestädte Hamburg, Wismar, Rostock, Stralsund." In *Die Territorien des Reichs im Zeitlater der Reformation und Konfessionalisierung: Land und Konfession, 1500–1650*, ed. Anton Schindling and Walter Ziegler. 7 vols. Münster: Aschendorffsche, 1992–1997. Vol. 6, *Nachträge*, 114–29.

Greenberg, Douglas. "The Middle Colonies in Recent American Historiography." *WMQ* 36, 3 (1979): 396–427.

Greer, Allan. "National, Transnational, and Hypernational Historiographies: New France meets Early American History." *Canadian Historical Review* 91, 4 (December 2010): 695–724.

Grell, Ole Peter. "The Anglo-Dutch Communities in England, 1648–1702." In *From Persecution to Toleration: The Glorious Revolution and Religion in England*. Oxford: Clarendon, 1991. 97–128.

————. *Dutch Calvinists in Early Stuart London: The Dutch Church in Austin Friars, 1603–1642*. Leiden: Brill/Leiden University Press, 1989.

————. "Merchants and ministers: the foundations of international Calvinism." In *Calvinism in Europe, 1540–1620*, ed. Andrew Pettegree, Alastair Duke, and Gillian Lewis. Cambridge: Cambridge University Press, 1994. 254–73.

————. "Scandinavia." In *The Early Reformation in Europe*, ed. Andrew Petegree. Cambridge: Cambridge University Press, 1992. 94–119.

————, ed. *The Scandinavian Reformation: From Evangelical Movement to Institutionalization of Reform*. Cambridge: Cambridge University Press, 1995.

Grijpink, P.M. "Everard Stalpaert van der Wiele ontvangt permissie om als missionaris naar Nieuw-Nederland te gaan. Anno 1662." *Bijdragen voor de Geschiedenis van het Bisdom van Haarlem*. 32 (1909): 180–81.

Groenveld, Simon. *Huisgenoten des geloofs: Was de samenleving in de Republiek der Verenigde Nederlanden verzuild?* Hilversum: Verloren, 1995.

Groenveld, S., M. E. H. N. Mout, and I. Schöffer, eds. *Bestuurders en Geleerden*. Amsterdam: De Bataafsche Leeuw, 1985.

Greyerz, Kaspar Von. *Religion and Society in Early Modern Europe, 1500–1800.* London: Allen and Unwin, 1984.

Groesen, Michiel van. "Herinneringen aan Holland: De verbeelding van de Opstand in Salvador de Bahia." *Holland* 41, 4 (2009): 291–303.

———. "Lessons Learned: The Second Dutch Conquest of Brazil and the Memory of the First." *Colonial Latin American Review* 20, 2 (2011): 167–93.

———. "A Week to Remember: Dutch Publishers and the Competition for News from Brazil, 26 August–2 September 1624." *Quaerendo* 40, 1 (2010): 26–49.

Güldner, Gerhard. *Das Toleranz-Problem in den Niederlanden im Ausgang des 16. Jahrhunderts.* Lübeck: Matthiesen, 1968.

Hackett, David G. *The Rude Hand of Innovation: Religion and Social Order in Albany, New York, 1652–1836.* New York: Oxford University Press, 1991.

Haefeli, Evan. "The Pennsylvania Difference: Religious Diversity on the Delaware Before 1683." *Early American Studies* 1, 1 (2003): 28–60.

———. "A Scandalous Minister in a Divided Community: Ulster County in Leisler's Rebellion, 1689–1691." *New York History* 88, 4 (Fall 2007): 357–89.

———. "Toleration." *Religion Compass* 4, 4 (2010): 253–62.

Hall, Timothy L. *Separating Church and State: Roger Williams and Religious Liberty.* Urbana: University of Illinois Press, 1998.

Hamilton, Alastair. *The Family of Love.* Cambridge: James Clark, 1981.

Hamming, I. *De kerk in Stad en Lande.* Zaltbommel: Europese Bibliotheek, 1975.

Happee, J., J. L. J. Meiners, and M. Mostert, eds. *De Lutheranen in Amsterdam (1588–1988).* Hilversum: Verloren, 1988.

Harline, Craig E. *Pamphlets, Printing, and Political Culture in the Early Dutch Republic.* Dordrecht: Nijhoff, 1987.

———. "Religie-oorlogen in eigen huis: De uitdaging van religious gemengde gezinnen na de Reformatie," *Trajecta* 16 (2007): 217–36.

Harper, Steven C. and I. Gadd, "Norton, Humphrey (fl 1655–1660)." In *Oxford Dictionary of National Biography.* Oxford: Oxford University Press, 2004–.

Harrington, R. Ward. "Speaking Scripture: The Flushing Remonstrance of 1657." *Quaker History* 82, 2 (1993): 104–9.

Hartog, Joh. *Curaçao van Kolonie tot Autonomie.* 2 vols. Aruba: D.J. de Wit, 1961.

Heijer, Henk den. *De geschiedenis van de WIC.* Zutphen: Walburg Pers, 1994.

Hemmersam, Michael. "Reise nach Guinea und Brasilien, 1639–1645." In *Reisebeschreibungen von deutschen beamten und kriegsleuten im dienst der Niederländischen west-und-ost-indischen kompagnien, 1602–1797,* ed. Samuel Pierre L'Honoré Naber. The Hague: Nijhoff, 1931. 80–81.

Heppe, Heinrich. *Geschichte des Pietismus und der Mystik in der Reformierten Kirche.* Leiden: Brill, 1879.

Hill, Christopher. *The World Turned Upside Down: Radical Ideas During the English Revolution.* 1972. London: Penguin, 1991.

Hoboken, W. J. van. "Een wederwoord inzake de Westindische Compagnie." *Tijdschrift voor Geschiedenis* 75, 1 (1962): 49–56.

———. "De West-Indische Compagnie en de Vrede van Munster." *Tijdschrift voor Geschiedenis* 70, 3 (1957): 359–68.

Hoenderdaal, G. J. and P. M. Luca. *Staat in de vrijheid: De geschiedenis van de remonstranten.* Zutphen: Walburg Pers, 1982.

Hoffecker, Carol E., Richard Waldron, Lorraine E. Williams, and Barbara E. Benson, eds. *New Sweden in America.* Newark: University of Delaware Press, 1995.

Hofman, T. M. *Eenich Achterdencken: Spanning tussen Kerk en Staat in het gewest Holland tussen 1570 en 1620.* Heerenveen: Groen en Zoon, 1997.

Horst, Irvin Buckwalter, ed. *The Dutch Dissenters: A Critical Companion to Their History and Ideas.* Leiden: Brill, 1986.

Hotchkins, S. F. *Early Clergy of Pennsylvania and Delaware.* Philadelphia: Ziegler, 1890.

Hsia, R. Po-chia and Henk van Nierop, eds. *Calvinism and Religious Toleration in the Dutch Golden Age.* Cambridge: Cambridge University Press, 2002.

Hühner, Leon. "Asser Levy: A Noted Jewish Burgher of New Amsterdam." In *The Jewish Experience in America*, ed. Abraham J. Karp. 3 vols. Waltham, Mass.: American Jewish Historical Society, 1969. 1: 51–65.

Hussen, Arend H. "The Legal Position of the Jews in the Dutch Republic, 1590–1796." In *Dutch Jewry: Its History and Secular Culture (1500–2000)*, ed. Jonathan Israel and Reinier Slaverda. Leiden: Brill, 2002. 25–41.

Ifrah, Lionel. *L'Aigle d'Amsterdam: Menasseh ben Israël (1604–1657).* Paris: Champion, 2001.

Israel, Jonathan I., ed. *The Anglo-Dutch Moment: Essays on the Glorious Revolution and Its World Impact.* Cambridge: Cambridge University Press, 1991.

———. "Central European Jewry During the Thirty Years' War." *Central European History* 16, 1 (March 1983): 3–30.

———. *Dutch Primacy in World Trade, 1585–1740.* Oxford: Clarendon, 1989.

———. *The Dutch Republic: Its Rise, Greatness, and Fall, 1477–1806.* Oxford: Clarendon, 1995.

———. "Dutch Sephardi Jewry, Millenarian Politics, and the Struggle for Brazil (1640–1654)." In *Sceptics, Millenarians, and Jews*, ed. David S. Katz and Jonathan I. Israel. Leiden: Brill, 1990.

———. "The Emerging Empire: The Continental Perspective, 1650–1713," In *Origins of Empire: British Overseas Enterprise to the Close of the Seventeenth Century*, ed. Nicholas Canny. Oxford: Oxford University Press, 1998. 423–44.

———. "The Intellectual Debate About Toleration in the Dutch Republic." In *The Emergence of Tolerance in the Dutch Republic*, ed. C. Berknes-Stevelinck, Jonathan Israel, and G. H. M. Posthumus Meyes. Leiden: Brill, 1997. 3–36.

———. "The Intellectual Origins of Modern Democratic Republicanism (1660–1720)," *European Journal of Political Theory* 3, 7 (2004): 7–36.

———. "Menassah Ben Israel and the Dutch Sephardic Colonization Movement of the Mid-Seventeenth Century (1645–1657)." In *Menasseh Ben Israel and His World*, ed. Yosef Kaplan, Henry Méchoulan and Richard H. Popkin. Leiden: Brill, 1989. 139–63.

———. *Radical Enlightenment: Philosophy and the Making of Modernity, 1650–1750*. Oxford: Oxford University Press, 2001.

———. "Religious Toleration and Radical Philosophy in the Later Dutch Golden Age (1668–1710)." In *Calvinism and Religious Toleration in the Dutch Golden Age*, ed. R. Po-chia Hsia and Henk van Nierop. Cambridge: Cambridge University Press, 2002. 148–59.

———. "De Republiek der Verenigde Nederlanden tot omstreeks 1750: Demografie en economische activiteit." In *Geschiedenis van de Joden in Nederland*, ed. J. C. H. Blom, R. G. Fuks-Mansfeld, and I. Schöffer Amsterdam: Balans, 1995. 97–126.

Israel, Jonathan and Reinier Salverda, eds. *Dutch Jewry: Its History and Secular Culture (1500–2000)*. Leiden: Brill, 2002.

Israel, Jonathan and Stuart B. Schwartz. *The Expansion of Tolerance: Religion in Dutch Brazil (1624–1654)*. Intro. Michiel van Groesen. Amsterdam: Amsterdam University Press, 2007.

Jacobs, Jaap. "Between Repression and Approval: Connivance and Tolerance in the Dutch Republic and in New Netherland." *DHM* 71, 3 (1998): 51–58.

———. *The Colony of New Netherland: A Dutch Settlement in Seventeenth-Century America*. Ithaca, N.Y.: Cornell University Press, 2009.

———. *New Netherland: A Dutch Colony in the Seventeenth Century*. Leiden: Brill, 2004.

———. *Petrus Stuyvesant: Een Levensschets*. Amsterdam: Bert Bakker, 2009.

———. "Soldiers of the Company: the Military Personnel of the West India Company in *Nieu Nederlandt*." In *Jacob Leisler's Atlantic World in the Later Seventeenth Century: Essays on Religion, Militia, Trade, and Networks*, ed. Hermand Wellenreuther. Berlin: LIT Verlag, 2009. 11–31.

———. *Een zegenrijk gewest: Niuew-Nederland in de zeventiende eeuw*. Amsterdam: Prometheus-Bert Bakker, 1999.

Jacobsen, Douglas. "American Puritanism Observed: New England and New Jersey." *NJH* 110, 1–2 (1992): 1–17.

———. *An Unprov'd Experiment: Religious Pluralism in Colonial New Jersey*. Brooklyn, N.Y.: Carlson, 1991.

James, Bartlett B. "The Labadist Colony in Maryland." *Johns Hopkins University Studies in Historical and Political Science* 17, 6 (1899): 1–45.

James, Sydney V. *John Clarke and His Legacies: Religion and Law in Colonial Rhode Island, 1638–1750*. University Park: Pennsylvania State University Press, 1999.

Jameson, J. Franklin. *Willem Usselinx: Founder of the Dutch and Swedish West India Companies*. New York: Putnam's, 1887.

Jamison, Wallace N. *Religion in New Jersey: A Brief History*. Princeton, N.J.: Van Nostrand, 1964.

Janssen, Antoon E. M. and Peter J. A. Nissen. "Niederlande, Lüttich." In *Die Territorien des Reichs im Zeitlater der Reformation und Konfessionalisierung: Land und Konfession, 1500–1650*, ed. Anton Schindling and Walter Ziegler. 7 vols. Münster:

Aschendorffsche Verlagsbuchhandlung, 1992–1997. Vol. 3, *Der Nordwesten*. 200–235.

Janssen, Hendrik Quirinus. *Catalogus van het oud synodaal archief*. The Hague: Hoogstraten en Zoon, 1878.

Janssen, J. A. M. M. "Zutphen in de maalstrom der kerkgeschidenis." In *Geschiedenis van Zutphen*, ed. W. Th. M. Frijhoff, B. Looper, J. van der Kluit, C. E. M. Reinders, R. C. C. de Savornia Lohman, F. W. J. Scholten, and R. Wartena. Zutphen: De Walburg Pers, 1989. 267–81.

Jernegan, Marcus W. "Slavery and Conversion in the American Colonies." *AHR* 21 (1916): 504–27.

Jessurun, J. Spinoza Catella. *Killiaen van Rensselaer van 1623 tot 1636*. The Hague: Nijhoff, 1917.

Johnson, Amandus. *The Swedish Settlements on the Delaware: Their History and Relation to the Indians, Dutch and English, 1636–1664*. 2 vols. New York: Appleton for University of Pennsylvania, 1911.

Jones, J. R. *The Anglo-Dutch Wars of the Seventeenth Century*. London: Longman, 1996.

Jones, Rufus M. *The Quakers in the American Colonies*. London: Macmillan, 1911.

Jong, Gerald F. de. "The Dutch Reformed Church and Negro Slavery in Colonial America." *CH* 40, 4 (1971): 423–36.

———. *The Dutch Reformed Church in the American Colonies*. Grand Rapids, Mich.: Eerdmans, 1978.

———. "Dominie Johannes Megapolensis: Minister to New Netherland." *NYHSQ* 52, 1 (1968): 7–47.

———. "The Formative Years of the Dutch Reformed Church on Long Island (Part I)." *Journal of Long Island History* 8, 2 (Summer–Fall 1968), 1–16.

———. "The *Ziekentroosters* or Comforters of the Sick in New Netherland." *NYHSQ* 54, 4 (1970): 339–59.

Jong, O. J. de. "Voetius en de tolerantie." In *De ongekende Voetius*, ed. J. van Oort, C. Graafland, A. de Groot, and O. J. de *Jong*. Kampen: Kok, 1989. 109–16.

Joose, L. J. *"Scoone Dingen sijn swaere dingen": Een onderzoek naar de motieven en activiteiten in de Nederlanden tot verbreiding van de gereformeerde religie gedurende de eerste helft van de zeventiende eeuw*. Leiden: Groen en Zoon, 1992.

Judd, Jacob and Irwin H. Pollock, eds. *Aspects of Early New York Society and Politics*. Tarrytown, N.Y.: Sleepy Hollow Restorations, 1974.

Kalff, S. "Joden op het eiland Curaçao." *Westindische Gids* 9 (1927): 69–84.

———. "Vreemdelingen in het Westindische Leger." *Westindische Gids* 10 (1928): 161–79.

Kammen, Michael. *Colonial New York: A History*. New York: Oxford University Press, 1975.

Kannegieter, J. Z. *Geschiedenis van de Vroegere Quakergemeenschap te Amsterdam, 1656 tot begin negentiende eeuw*. Amsterdam: Scheltema and Holkema, 1971.

Kaplan, Benjamin J. *Calvinists and Libertines: Confession and Community in Utrecht, 1578–1620*. Oxford: Clarendon, 1995.

————. *Divided by Faith: Religious Conflict and the Practice of Toleration in Early Modern Europe*. Cambridge, Mass.: Harvard University Press, 2007.

————. "'Dutch' Religious Tolerance: Celebration and Revision." In *Calvinism and Religious Toleration in the Dutch Golden Age*, ed. R. Po-Chia Shia and Henk van Nierop. Cambridge: Cambridge University Press, 2002. 8–26.

Kaplan, Yosef, Henry Mechouln, and Richard H. Popkins, eds. *Menasseh Ben Israel and His World*. Leiden: Brill, 1989.

Kardux, Joke and Eduard van de Bilt. *Newcomers in an Old City: The American Pilgrims in Leiden, 1609–1620*. 3rd ed. Leiden: Burgersdijk and Niermans, 2007.

Katz, David S. *Philo-Semitism and the Readmission of the Jews to England, 1603–1655*. Oxford: Clarendon, 1982.

Klein, Milton M. "Shaping the American Tradition: The Microcosm of New York." *NYH* 59, 2 (1978): 173–97.

Klink, Hubrecht. *Opstand, politiek en religie bij Willem van Oranje, 1559–1568: Een thematische Biografie*. Heerenveen: Groen en Zoon, 1998.

Klooster, Wim. *The Dutch in the Americas, 1600–1800*. Providence, R.I.: John Carter Brown Library, 1997.

Koedel, Craig. *God's Vine in This Wilderness: Religion in South Jersey to 1800*. Woodbury, N.J.: Gloucester County Historical Society, 1980.

Kooi, Christine. *Liberty and Religion: Church and State in Leiden's Reformation, 1572–1620*. Leiden: Brill, 2000.

————. "Paying Off the Sheriff: Strategies of Catholic Toleration in Golden Age Holland." In *Calvinism and Religious Toleration in the Dutch Golden Age*, ed. R. Po-Chia Shia and Henk van Nierop. Cambridge: Cambridge University Press, 2002. 87–101.

Kreider, Harry Julius. *Lutheranism in Colonial New York*. Ann Arbor, Mich.: Edwards Brothers, 1942.

Kroh, Deborah L. and Peter N. Miller, eds. with Marybeth De Filippis. *Dutch New York Between East and West: The World of Magrieta van Varick*. New Haven, Conn.: Yale University Press, 2009.

Krommen, Rita. "Mathias Beck und die Westindische Kompagnie: Zur Herrschaft der Niederländer im Kolonialen Ceará." Arbeitpapiere zur Lateinamerikaforschung II-01. Köln: Universität zu Köln, 2001. http://www.lateinamerika.uni-koeln.de/fileadmin/bilder/arbeitspap iere/krommen.pdf.

Kross, Jessica. *The Evolution of an American Town: Newtown, New York, 1642–1775*. Philadelphia: Temple University Press, 1983.

Kühler, W. J. *Het Socianisme in Nederland*. Leeuwarden: De Tille, 1980.

Kuijpers, Erika. *Migrantenstad: Immigratie en sociale Verhoudingen in 17e-eeuws Amsterdam*. Hilversum: Verloren, 2005.

Lacy, Margriet Bruijn, Charles Gehring, and Jenneke Oosterhoff, eds. *From De Haelve Maen to KLM: 400 Years of Dutch-American Exchange*. Münster: Nodus, 2008.

Lake, Peter. "Religious Identities in Shakespeare's England." In *A Companion to Shakespeare*, ed. David Scott Kastan. Oxford: Blackwell, 1999. 57–84.

Lambrechtsen van Ritthem, N. C. *Korte Beschrijving van de Ontdekking en der verdere Lotgevallen van Nieuw Nederland.* Middleburh: Van Benthem, 1818.

Lampe, Armando. "Christianity and Slavery in the Dutch Caribbean." In *Christianity in the Caribbean: Essays in Church History,* ed. Armando Lampe. Kingston: University of the West Indies Press, 2001. 126–53.

Landsman, Ned C. "The Middle Colonies: New Opportunities for Settlement, 1660–1700." In *Origins of Empire: British Overseas Enterprise to the Close of the Seventeeth Century,* ed. Nicholas Canny. Oxford: Oxford University Press, 1998. 351–74.

———. "Roots, Routes, and Rootedness: Diversity, Migration, and Toleration in Mid-Atlantic Pluralism." *Early American Studies* 2, 2 (2004): 267–309.

Landwehr, J. *VOC, a Bibliography of Publications Relating to the Dutch East India Company, 1602–1800.* Utrecht: HES, 1991.

Langdon, George D., Jr. *Pilgrim Colony: A History of New Plymouth, 1620–1691.* New Haven, Conn.: Yale University Press, 1966.

Leiby, Adrian C. *The Early Dutch and Swedish Settlers of New Jersey.* Princeton, N.J.: Van Nostrand, 1964.

Lewis, Dianne. *Jan Compagnie in the Straits of Malacca, 1641–1795.* Athens, Oh.: Center for International Studies, 1995.

Lieburg, Fred van. "The Dutch and Their Religion." In *Four Centuries of Dutch-American Relations, 1609–2009,* ed. Hans Krabbendam, Cornelis A. van Minnen, and Giles Scott-Smith. Amsterdam: Boom, 2009. 154–65.

———. "Geloven op vele manieren." In Willem Frijhoff et al., *Geschiedenis van Dordrecht.* 3 vols. Dordrecht: Gementearchief Dordrecht; Hilversum: Verloren, 1996–2000. Vol. 2, *Geschiedenis van Dordrecht van 1572 tot 1813,* 1998. 271–304.

Ligtenberg, Catharina. *Willem Usselincx.* Utrecht: Osterhoek Uitgeverij, 1914.

Linde, Jan Marinus van der. *Surinaamse suikerheren en hun kerk: Plantagekolonie en handelskerk ten tijde van Johannes Basseliers, predikant en planter in Suriname.* Wageningen: Veenman en Zonen, 1966.

Linde, W. van der. *Eindelijk Religieuze Tolerantie na 500 Jaar Religieuze Strijd in Geleen en in Zuid-Limburg.* Urmond: W. van der Linde, 2001.

Loker, Zvi. *Jews in the Caribbean: Evidence on the History of the Jews in the Caribbean Zone in Colonial Times.* Jerusalem: Misgav Jerusalem, 1991.

Looijesteijn, Henk. "'Born to the Common Welfare': Pieter Plockhoy's Quest for a Christian Life (c.1620–1664)." Ph.D. dissertation, European University Institute, 2009.

———. "Petitioning, Colonial Policy, Constitutional Experiment and the Development of Dutch Political Thought." Paper presented at Tenth International Conference on Urban History, Ghent, September 1–5, 2010.

Loosjes, J. *Geschiedenis der Luthersche Kerk in de Nederlanden.* The Hague: Nijhoff, 1921.

Macculloch, Diarmaid. *The Reformation: A History.* New York: Viking, 2003.

MacDonald, James M. *Two Centuries in the History of the Presbyterian Church, Jamaica, L.I.* New York: Carter and Brothers, 1862.

Mack Crew, Phyllis. *Calvinist Preaching and Iconoclasm in the Netherlands, 1544–1569.* Cambridge: Cambridge University Press, 1978.

Maika, Dennis J. "Commemoration and Context: The Flushing Remonstrance Then and Now." *Journal of American History* 89, 1 (2008): 29–42.

Marcus, Jacob R. *The Colonial American Jew, 1492–1776.* 3 vols. Detroit: Wayne State University Press, 1970.

Marshall, John. *John Locke, Toleration and Early Enlightenment Culture.* Cambridge: Cambridge University Press, 2006.

Mason, Peter, ed. *Indianen en Nederlanders, 1492–1992.* Leiden: Wampum, 1992.

McGregor, J. F. "The Baptists: Fount of All Heresy." In *Radical Religion in the English Revolution*, ed. J. F. McGregor and Barry Reay. Oxford: Oxford University Press, 1984. 23–64.

McLoughlin, William Gerald. *Soul Liberty: The Baptists' Struggle in New England, 1630–1833.* Hanover, N.H.: University Press of New England, 1991.

Méchoulan, Henry. *Amsterdam ten tijde van Spinoza: Geld and vrijheid.* Trans. Jelle Noorman. Amsterdam: De Arbeiderspers, 1992. From original *Amsterdam au temps de Spinoza.* Paris, 1990.

———. *Être juif à Amsterdam au temps de Spinoza.* Paris: Albin Michel, 1991.

Meiden, G. W. van der. *Betwist Bestuur: Een eeuw strijd om de macht in Suriname, 1651–1753.* Amsterdam: Bataafsche Leeuw, 1987.

Meilink-Roelofsz, M. A. P., ed. *Dutch Authors on West Indian History: A Historiographical Selection.* Trans. Maria J. L. van Yperen. The Hague: Nijhoff, 1982.

Mellink, Albert. *Amsterdam en de Wederdopers in de zestiende eeuw.* SUN: Nijmegen, 1978.

Mello, José Antônio Gonsalves de. *Gente da Nação: Cristãos-novos e judeus em Pernambuco, 1543–1654.* Recife: Fundacão Joaquim Nabuco, 1996.

Melnick, Ralph. *From Polemics to Apologetics: Jewish-Christian Rapprochement in 17th Century Amsterdam.* Assen: Van Gorcum, 1981.

Mertens, Frank. "Franciscus van den Enden: Former Jesuit, Neo-Latin Poet, Art Dealer, Philosopher, Teacher of Spinoza and Conspirator Against Louis XIV." Last modified March 31, 2010. http://users.telenet.be/fvde/index.htm?Home1, accessed November 13, 2010.

Merwick, Donna. "Becoming English: Anglo-Dutch Conflict in the 1670s in Albany, New York." *NYH* 62, 4 (1981): 389–414.

———. *Possessing Albany, 1630–1710: The Dutch and English Experiences.* New York: Cambridge University Press, 1990.

Meuwese, Mark. "Dutch Calvinism and Native Americans: A Comparative Study of the Motivations for Protestant Conversion Among the Tupis in Northeastern Brazil (1630–1654) and the Mohawks in Central New York (1690–1710)." In *The Spiritual Conversion of the Americas*, ed. James Muldoon. Gainesville: University Press of Florida, 2004. 118–41.

———. "Samuel Cohen. c.1600–1642: Jewish Translator in Brazil, Curaçao, and Angola." In *The Human Tradition in the Atlantic World, 1500–1850*, ed. Karen

Racine and Beatriz G. Mamigonian. Lanham, Md.: Rowman and Littlefield, 2010. 27–41.

Molhuysen, P. C. and P. J. Blok, eds. *Nieuw Nederlandsch biografisch woordenboek*. 10 vols. Leiden: Sijthoff, 1911–1937.

Molitor, Hansgeorg. "Politik zwischen den Konfessionen." In *Der Niederrhein im Zeitalter des Humanismus: Konrad Heresbach und sein Kreis*, ed. Meinhard Pohl. Bielefeld: Verlag für Regionalgeschichte, 1997. 37–55.

Moore, Rosemary. *The Light in Their Consciences: The Early Quakers in Britain, 1646–1666*. University Park: Pennsylvania State University Press, 2000.

Moorrees, A. *Die Nederduitse Gereformeerde Kerk in Suid-Afrika, 1652–1873*. Kaapstad: Bybelvereniging, 1937.

Mörke, Olaf. "The Political Culture of Germany and the Dutch Republic: Similar Roots, Different Results." In *A Miracle Mirrored: The Dutch Republic in European Perspective*, ed. Karel Davids and Jan Lucassen. Cambridge: Cambridge University Press, 1995. 135–72.

Mowrer, Lilian T. *The Indomitable John Scott: Citizen of Long Island, 1632–1704*. New York: Farrar, Straus, 1960.

Mulder, W. Z. *Hollanders in Hirado, 1597–1641*. Haarlem: Fibula-Van Dishoeck, n.d.

Münch, Paul. "Nassau, Ottonische Linien." In *Die Territorien des Reichs im Zeitlater der Reformation und Konfessionalisierung: Land und Konfession, 1500–1650*, ed. Anton Schindling and Walter Ziegler. Münster: Aschendorffsche Verlagsbuchhandlung, 1992–1997. Vol. 4, *Mittleres Deutschland*. 234–53.

Munroe, John A. *Colonial Delaware: A History*. Millwood, N.Y.: KTO Press, 1978.

Murrin, John M. "Religion and Politics in America from the First Settlements to the Civil War." In *Religion and American Politics from the Colonial Period to the 1980s*, ed. Mark A. Noll. New York: Oxford University Press, 1990. 19–43.

Nauta, Doede and C. Houtman. *Biografisch lexicon voor de geschiedenis van het Nederlandse protestantisme*. Kampen: Kok, 1978–2006. 6 vols. 1: 385–86.

Niemeijer, Hendrik E. *Batavia: Een koloniale samenleving in de 17de eeuw*. Amersfoort: Balans, 2005.

Nierop, Henk van. "Sewing the Bailiff in a Blanket: Catholics and the Law in Holland." In *Calvinism and Religious Toleration in the Dutch Golden Age*, ed. R. Po-Chia Shia and Henk van Nierop. Cambridge University Press, 2002. 102–11.

Nissenson, S. G. *The Patroon's Domain*. New York: Columbia University Press, 1937.

Nobbs, Douglas. *Theocracy and Toleration: A Study of the Disputes in Dutch Calvinism from 1600 to 1650*. Cambridge: Cambridge University Press, 1938.

Nooter, Eric. "Between Heaven and Earth: Church and Society in Pre-Revolutionary Flatbush, Long Island." Ph.D. dissertation, New York University, 1994.

———. "Between Heaven and Earth: The Dutch Reformed Church in Flatbush Society, 1654–1664." *DHM* 66, 4 (1993): 66–74.

Nussbaum, Martha. *Liberty of Conscience: In Defense of America's Tradition of Religious Equality*. New York: Basic Books, 2008.

Nusteling, Hurbert P. H. "The Jews in the Republic of the United Provinces: Origin, Numbers, and Dispersion." In *Dutch Jewry: Its History and Secular Culture (1500–2000)*, ed. Jonathan Israel and Reinier Slaverda. Leiden: Brill, 2002. 43–62.

Nuttall, Geoffrey F. *The Holy Spirit in Puritan Faith and Experience*. Intro, Peter Lake. 1946. Chicago: University of Chicago Press, 1992.

O'Callaghan, Edmund B. *History of New Netherland; or New York Under the Dutch*, 2 vols. New York: D. Appleton, 1846.

———. *The Register of New Netherland, 1624 to 1674*. Albany, N.Y.: J. Munsell, 1865.

O'Connor, Thomas F. "Religious Toleration in New York, 1664–1700." *NYH* 17 (1936): 391–410.

Onderdonk, Henry. *Antiquities of the Parish Church, Jamaica*. Jamaica, N.Y.: Charles Welling, 1880.

Oostindie, Gert. *Paradise Overseas: The Dutch Caribbean: Colonialism and Its Transatlantic Legacies*. Oxford: Macmillan, 2005.

Panetta, Roger, ed. *Dutch New York: The Roots of Hudson Valley Culture*. New York: Fordham University Press, 2009.

Papenfuse, Edward C., Alan F. Day, David W. Jordan, and Gregory A. Stiverson, eds. *A Biographical Dictionary of the Maryland Legislature, 1635–1789*. 2 vols. Baltimore: Johns Hopkins University Press, 1979.

Parker, Charles H. *Faith on the Margins: Catholics and Catholicism in the Dutch Golden Age*. Cambridge, Mass.: Harvard University Press, 2008.

———. "The Moral Agency and Moral Autonomy of Church Folk in the Dutch Reformed Church of Delft, 1580–1620." *JEH* 48, 1 (1997): 44–70.

———. "To the Attentive, Nonpartisan Reader: The Appeal to History and National Identity in the Religious Disputes of the Seventeenth Century Netherlands." *Sixteenth Century Journal* 28, 1 (Spring 1997): 57–78.

Parker, Geoffrey. "Success and Failure During the First Century of the Reformation." *Past and Present* 136 (1992): 43–82.

———. ed. *The Thirty Years' War*. London: Routledge, 1987.

Pestana, Carla Gardina. "The City upon a Hill Under Siege: The Puritan Perception of the Quaker Threat to Massachusetts Bay, 1656–1661." *New England Quarterly* 56, 3 (1983): 323–52.

———. *Liberty of Conscience and the Growth of Religious Diversity in Early America, 1636–1786*. Providence, R.I.: John Carter Brown Library, 1986.

———. "The Quaker Executions as Myth and History." *Journal of American History* 80, 2 (1993): 441–69.

Peters, H. "Geloof, onderwijs en cultuur, circa 1600–1807." In *Geschiedenis van Assen*, ed. H. Gras et al. Assen: Van Gorcum, 2000.

Peters, Kate. *Print Culture and the Early Quakers*. New York: Cambridge University Press, 2005.

Pettegree, Andrew. "Coming to Terms with Victory: The Upbuilding of a Calvinist Church in Holland, 1572–1590." In *Calvinism in Europe, 1540–1620*, ed. Andrew

Pettegree, Alastair Duke, and Gillian Lewis. Cambridge: Cambridge University Press, 1994. 160–80.

———. *Emden and the Dutch Revolt: Exile and the Development of Reformed Protestantism*. Oxford: Clarendon, 1992.

———. "The Netherlands." In *The Early Reformation in Europe*, ed. Andrew Pettegree. Cambridge: Cambridge University Press, 1992. 142–65.

———. "The Politics of Toleration in the Free Netherlands, 1572–1620." In *Tolerance and Intolerance in the European Reformation*, ed. Ole Peter Grell and Bob Scribner. Cambridge: Cambridge University Press, 1996.

Pijning, Ernst "Idealism and Power: The Dutch West India Company in the Brazil Trade (1630–1654)." In *Shaping the Stuart World, 1603–1714: The Atlantic Connection*, ed. Allan I. Macinnes and Arthur H. Williamson. Leiden: Brill, 2006. 207–32.

Pincus, Steven C. A. *Protestantism and Patriotism: Ideologies and the Making of English Foreign Policy, 1650–1668*. Cambridge: Cambridge University Press, 1998.

Plooij, Daniel. *The Pilgrim Fathers from a Dutch Point of View*. New York: New York University Press, 1932.

Pointer, Richard W. *Protestant Pluralism and the New York Experience: A Study of Eighteenth-Century Religious Diversity*. Bloomington: Indiana University Press, 1988.

Pollman, Judith. "The Bond of Christian Piety: The Individual Practice of Tolerance and Intolerance in the Dutch Republic." In *Calvinism and Religious Toleration in the Dutch Golden Age*, ed. R. Po-Chia Shia and Henk van Nierop. Cambridge: Cambridge University Press, 2002. 53–71.

Pol, Frank van der. "Religious Diversity and Everyday Ethics in the Seventeenth-Century Dutch City Kampen." *Church History* 71, 1 (March 2002): 16–62.

Pomfret, John E. *Colonial New Jersey: A History*. New York: Scribner's, 1973.

———. *The Province of East New Jersey, 1609–1702: The Rebellious Proprietary*. Princeton, N.J.: Princeton University Press, 1962.

———. *The Province of West New Jersey, 1609–1702: A History of the Origins of an American Colony*. Princeton, N.J.: Princeton University Press, 1956.

Pope, Robert G. *The Half-Way Covenant: Church Membership in Puritan New England*. Princeton, N.J.: Princeton University Press, 1969.

Post, R. R. *Kerkelijke verhoudingen in Nederland voor de Reformatie, van c. 1500–c 1580*. Utrecht: Uitgeverij Het Spectrum, 1954.

Postma, Mirte. *Johan de Witt en Coenraad van Beuningen: Correspondentie tijdens de Noordse Oorlog (1655–1660)*. Deventer: Scriptio, 2007.

Powicke, F. J. *John Robinson (1575?–1625)*. London: Hodder and Stoughton, 1920.

Prak, Maarten. *The Dutch Republic in the Seventeenth Century*. Trans. Diane Webb. Cambridge: Cambridge University Press, 2005.

———. "The Politics of Intolerance: Citizenship and Religion in the Dutch Republic, Seventeenth to Eighteenth Centuries." In *Calvinism and Religious Toleration in the Dutch Golden Age*, ed. R. Po-Chia Shia and Henk van Nierop. Cambridge: Cambridge University Press, 2002. 159–75.

Price, J. L. *Culture and Society in the Dutch Republic During the Seventeenth Century.*
    London: Batsford, 1974.

————. *Holland and the Dutch Republic in the Seventeenth Century: The Politics of
    Particularism.* Oxford: Clarendon, 1994.

Reay, Barry. "Popular Hostility Towards Quakers in Mid-Seventeenth-Century
    England." *Social History* 5, 3 (1980): 387–407.

————. "Quakerism and Society." In *Radical Religion in the English Revolution,* ed.
    J. F. McGregor and Barry Reay. Oxford: Oxford University Press, 1984. 141–64.

Riker, James. *The Annals of Newtown in Queens County, New York.* New York: Fans-
    haw, 1852.

————. *Revised History of Harlem.* New York: New Harlem Publishing, 1904.

Rindler, Edward P. "The Migration from the New Haven Colony to Newark, East
    Jersey: A Study of Puritan Values and Behavior, 1630–1720." Ph.D. dissertation,
    University of Pennsylvania, 1977.

Rink, Oliver A. *Holland on the Hudson: An Economic and Social History of Dutch New
    York.* Ithaca, N.Y.: Cornell University Press, 1986.

————. "Private Interest and Godly Gain: The West India Company and the Dutch
    Reformed Church in New Netherland, 1624–1664." *NYH* 75, 3 (1994): 245–64.

Ritchie, Robert C. *The Duke's Province: A Study of New York Politics and Society, 1664–
    1691.* Chapel Hill: University of North Carolina Press, 1977.

————. "Nicolls, Richard (1624–1672)." *Oxford Dictionary of National Biography,*
    online ed. January 2008. http://www.oxforddnb.com/view/article/20182.

Roberts, Michael. "The Swedish Church." In *Sweden's Age of Greatness, 1632–1718,* ed.
    Michael Roberts. London: Macmillan, 1973. 132–73.

————. *The Swedish Imperial Experience, 1560–1718.* Cambridge: Cambridge University
    Press, 1979.

Roeber, A. G. "'The Origin of Whatever Is Not English Among Us': The Dutch-
    Speaking and German-Speaking Peoples of Colonial British America." In *Strangers
    Within the Realm: Cultural Margins of the First British Empire,* ed. Bernard Bailyn
    and Philip D. Morgan. Chapel Hill: University of North Carolina Press, 1991.
    220–83.

Rogier, L. J. *Geschiedenis van het katholicisme in Noord-Nederland in de 16e en 17e eeuw.*
    3 vols. Amsterdam, 1945–47.

Rohm, Thomas and Anton Schindling, "Tecklenburg, Bentheim, Steinfurt, Lingen."
    In *Die Territorien des Reichs im Zeitlater der Reformation und Konfessionalisierung:
    Land und Konfession, 1500–1650,* ed. Anton Schindling and Walter Ziegler. 7 vols.
    Münster: Aschendorffsche Verlagsbuchhandlung, 1992–1997. Vol. 3, *Der Nordwes-
    ten,* 182–99.

Romijn, H. M. *Kroniek van de Doopsgezinden in Zaandam.* Zaandijk: J. Heijnis Tsz.,
    1971.

Rood, Wilhelmus. *Comenius and the Low Countries: Some Aspects of Life and Work of
    a Czech Exile in the Seventeenth Century.* New York: Abner Scram, 1970.

Rooden, Peter van. "Conceptions of Judaism as a Religion in the Seventeenth-Century Dutch Republic." In *Christianity and Judaism: Papers Read at the 1991 Summer Meeting and the 1992 Winter Meeting of the Ecclesiastical History Society*, ed. Diana Wood. Studies in Church History 29. London: Blackwell, 1992. 299–308.

———. "Dutch Concepts to Express Religious Difference, 1572–2002." In *Baupläne der sichtbaren Kirche: Sprachliche Konzepte religiöser Vergemeinschaftung in Europe*, ed. Lucian Hölscher. Göttingen: Wallstein, 2007. 136–50.

———. "The Jews and Religious Toleration in the Dutch Republic." In *Calvinism and Religious Toleration in the Dutch Golden Age*, ed. R. Po-chia Hsia, and Henk van Nierop. Cambridge: Cambridge University Press, 2002. 132–47.

———. *Religieuze Regimes: Over godsdienst en maatschappij in Nederland, 1570–1990*. Amsterdam: Bert Bakker, 1996.

Roodenburg, Herman. *Onder censuur: De kerklijke tucht in de gereformeerde gemente van Amsterdam, 1578–1700*. Hilversum: Verloren, 1990.

Roorda, D. J. *Partij en factie: De oproeren van 1672 in de steden van Holland en Zeeland, een krachtmeting tussen partijen en facties*. Groningen: Noordhoff, 1978.

Rooze-Stouthamer, Clasina Martina. *Hervorming in Zeeland (ca. 1520–1572)*. Goes: Koperen Tuin, 1996.

Rowen, Herbert H. *The Princes of Orange: The Stadholders in the Dutch Republic*. New York: Cambridge University Press, 1988.

Saxby, T. J. *The Quest for the New Jerusalem: Jean de Labadie and the Labadists, 1610–1744*. Dordrecht: Nijhoff, 1987.

Schalkwijk, F. L. *The Reformed Church in Dutch Brazil (1630–1654)*. Zoetermeer: Boekencentrum, 1998.

Schilling, Heinz. *Religion, Political Culture and the Emergence of Early Modern Society: Essays in German and Dutch History*. Leiden: Brill, 1992.

Schindling, Anton and Walter Ziegler, eds. *Die Territorien des Reichs im Zeitalter der Reformation und Konfessionalisierung: Land und Konfession, 1500–1650*. 7 vols. Münster: Aschendorffsche Verlagsbuchhandlung, 1989–1997.

Schoor, Arie van der. *Stad in aanwas: Geschiedenis van Rotterdam tot 1813*. Zwolle: Waanders Uitgevers, 1999.

Schnoor, Willi Friedrich. *Die rechtliche Organisation der religiösen Toleranz in Friedrichstadt in der Zeit von 1621 bis 1727*. Husum: n.p., 1976.

Schwartz, Sally. *"A Mixed Multitude": The Struggle for Toleration in Colonial Pennsylvania*. New York: New York University Press, 1987.

Schwartz, Stuart B. *All Can Be Saved: Religious Tolerance and Salvation in the Iberian Atlantic World*. New Haven, Conn.: Yale University Press, 2008.

Shattuck, Martha Dickinson, ed. *Explorers, Fortunes and Love Letters: A Window on New Netherland*. Albany, N.Y.: Mount Ida Press, 2009.

———. "Heemstede: An English Town Under Dutch Rule." In *The Roots and Heritage of Hempstead Town*, ed. Natalie A. Naylor. Interlaken, N.Y.: Heart of the Lakes, 1994.

Shomette, Donald G. and Robert D. Haslach. *Raid on America: The Dutch Naval Campaign of 1672–1674*. Columbia: University of South Carolina Press, 1988.

Shorto, Russell. *The Island at the Center of the World: The Epic Story of Dutch Manhattan and the Forgotten Colony That Shaped America*. New York: Doubleday, 2004.

Siminoff, Faren R. *Crossing the Sound: The Rise of Atlantic American Communities in Seventeenth-Century Eastern Long Island*. New York: New York University Press, 2004.

Smid, Menno. "Ostfriesland." In *Die Territorien des Reichs im Zeitlater der Reformation und Konfessionalisierung: Land und Konfession, 1500–1650*, ed. Anton Schindler and Walter Ziegler. 7 vols. Münster: Aschendorffsche Verlagsbuchhandlung, 1992–1997. Vol. 3, *Der Nordwesten*, 130–47.

Smit, J. G. and Eelco Beukers, eds. *Den Haag: Geschiedenis van de stad*. 3 vols. Zwolle: Waanders Uitgevers, 2004.

Smith, Elizur Yale. "Captain Thomas Willett." *NYH* 21 (1940): 404–17.

Smith, George L. "Guilders and Godliness: The Dutch Colonial Contribution to American Religious Pluralism." *Journal of Presbyterian History* 47 (March 1969):

———. *Religion and Trade in New Netherland: Dutch Origins and American Development*. Ithaca, N.Y.: Cornell University Press, 1973.

Smith, Nigel. *Andrew Marvel: The Chameleon*. New Haven, Conn.: Yale University Press, 2010.

Smolinsky, Heribert. "Humanistische Kirchenordnungen des 16. Jahrhunderts als kirchenpolitische 'via media' in Jülich-Kleve-Berg." In *Der Niederrhein im Zeitalter des Hunamismus: Konrad Heresbach und sein Kreis*, ed. Meinhard Pohl. Bielefeld: Regionalgeschichte, 1997. 75–90.

———. "Jülich-Kleve-Berg." In *Die Territorien des Reichs im Zeitlater der Reformation und Konfessionalisierung: Land und Konfession, 1500–1650*, ed. Anton Schindling and Walter Ziegler. 7 vols. Münster: Aschendorffsche Verlagsbuchhandlung, 1992–1997. Vol. 3, *Der Nordwesten*, 86–107.

Soll, Jacob. "Accounting for Government: Holland and the Rise of Political Economy in Seventeenth-Century Europe." *Journal of Interdisciplinary History* 40, 2 (2009): 215–38.

Spaans, Joke. *Armenzorg in Friesland, 1500–1800: Publieke zorg en particuliere liefdadigheid in zes Friese steden, Leeuwarden, Bolsward, Franeker, Sneek, Dokkum en Harlingen*. Hilversum: Verloren, 1998.

———. *Haarlem na de Reformatie: Stedelijke cultuur en kerkelijk leven, 1577–1620*. The Hague: Stichting Hollandse Historische Reeks, 1989.

———. "Religious Policies in the Seventeenth-Century Dutch Republic." In *Calvinism and Religious Toleration in the Dutch Golden Age*, ed. R. Po-Chia Shia and Henk van Nierop. Cambridge: Cambridge University Press, 2002. 72–86.

———. "Stad van vele geloven, 1578–1795." In *Geschiedenis van Amsterdam: Centrum van de wereld, 1578–1650*, ed. Willem Frijhoff and Maarten Prak. Amsterdam: Sun, 2004. 384–467.

———. "Unity and Diversity as a Theme in Early Modern Dutch Religious History: An Interpretation." In *Unity and Diversity in the Church*, ed. Robert Norman Swanson. Oxford: Oxford University Press, 1996. 221–34.

Spoelstra, Cornelis. *Bouwstoffen voor de geschiedenis der Nederduitsch-Gereformeerde Kerken in Zuid-Afrika*. Amsterdam-Kaapstad: Hollandsch-Africaansche Uitgevers-Maatschappij, 1906.

Sprunger, Keith L. *Dutch Puritanism: A History of English and Scottish Churches of the Netherlands in the Sixteenth and Seventeenth Centuries*. Leiden: Brill, 1982.

Spufford, Margaret. "Literacy, Trade and Religion in the Commercial Centres of Europe." In *A Miracle Mirrored: The Dutch Republic in European Perspective*, ed. Karel Davids and Jan Lucassens. Cambridge: Cambridge University Press, 1995. 229–83.

Starna, William A. Introduction to *Indian Affairs in Colonial New York: The Seventeenth Century*, rev. ed., ed. Allen W. Trelease. Lincoln: University of Nebraska Press, 1997. 138–48.

Stols, Eddy " 'Brazil Versuymd' andersom gezien: De Brazilianen over hun Hollands verleden." In *De Nieuwe Wereld en de Lage Landen: Onbekende aspecten van Vijfhonderd Jaar ontmoetingen tussen Latijns-Amerikca en Nederland*, ed. J. Lechner, H. Ph. Vogel, et al. Amsterdam: Meulenhoff, 1992. 115–36.

Streng, J. C. *"Stemme in staat": De bestuurlijke elite in de stadsrepubliek Zwolle, 1579–1795*. Hilversum: Verloren, 1997.

Sullivan, Winnifred Fallers. *The Impossibility of Religious Freedom*. Princeton, N.J.: Princeton University Press, 2005.

Sutherland, N. M. "Persecution and Toleration in Reformation Europe." In *Persecution and Toleration*, ed. W. J. Sheils. Studies in Church History 21. Oxford: Blackwell, 1984. 153–61.

Swellengrebel, J. L. "João Ferreira D'Almeda: de eerste vertaler van de Bijbel in het Portugees." *De Heerbaan* 13 (1960): 179–218, 240–73.

Swetschinski, Daniel M. *Reluctant Cosmopolitans: The Portuguese Jews of Seventeenth-Century Amsterdam*. London: Littman Library of Jewish Civilization, 2000.

Te Brake, Wayne. "Emblems of Coexistence in a Confessional World." In *Living with Religious Diversity in Early-Modern Europe*, ed. C. Scott Dixon, Dagmar Freist, and Mark Greengras. Burlington, Vt.: Ashgate, 2009. 53–79.

Teensma, B. N. "Resentment in Recife: Jews and Public Opinion in 17th-Century Dutch Brazil." In *Essays on Cultural Identity in Colonial Latin America: Problems and Repercussions*, ed. Jan Lechner. Leiden: Talen en Culturen van Latijns Amerika, 1988. 63–78.

Templin, J. Alton. *Pre-Reformation Religious Dissent in the Netherlands, 1518–1530*. Lanham, Md.: University Press of America, 2006.

Terrell, Michelle M. *The Jewish Community of Early Colonial Nevis: A Historical Archaeological Study*. Gainesville: University Press of Florida, 2005.

Thomas, Werner. *In de Klauwen van de Inquisitie: Protestanten in Spanje, 1517–1648*. Amsterdam: Amsterdam University Press, 2003.

Trelease, Allen W. *Indian Affairs in Colonial New York: The Seventeenth Century*. Intro. William A. Starna. Lincoln: University of Nebraska Press, 1997.

Trompeter, Cor. *Leven aan de rand van de Republiek: Stad en gericht Almelo, 1580–1700*. Amsterdam: Bert Bakker, 2006.

Ubachs, P. J. H. *Handboek voor de geschiedenis van Limburg*. Hilversum: Verloren, 2000.

———. *Twee heren, twee confessies: De verhouding van staat en kerk te Maastricht, 1632–1673*. Assen: Van Gorcum, 1975.

Underhill, Edward Bean, ed. *Tracts on Liberty of Conscience and Persecution, 1614–1661*. London: for the Society, 1846.

Underwood, James L. and William L. Burke, eds. *The Dawn of Religious Freedom in South Carolina*. Columbia: University of South Carolina Press, 2006.

Underwood, T. L. *Primitivism, Radicalism, and the Lamb's War: The Baptist-Quaker Conflict in Seventeenth Century England*. Oxford: Oxford University Press, 1997.

Vainfas, Ronaldo. "La Babel Religiosa: Católicos, calvinistas, conversos y judíos en Brasil bajo la dominación holandesa (1630–1654)." In *Familia, religión y negocio: El sefardismo en las relaciones entre el mundo ibérico y los Países Bajos en la Edad Moderna*, ed. Jaime Contreras, Bernardo J. García García, and Ignacio Pulido. Madrid: Fundación Carlos de Amberes, 2002. 321–42.

Van Rensselaer, Marianna Schuyler. *History of the City of New York in the Seventeenth Century*. 2 vols. New York: Macmillan, 1909.

Van Zandt, Cynthia J. "The Dutch Connection: Isaac Allerton and the Dynamics of English Cultural Anxiety in the *Gouden Eeuw*." In *Connecting Cultures: The Netherlands in Five Centuries of Transatlantic Exchange*, ed. Rosemarijn Hoefte and Johanna C. Kardak. Amsterdam: University of Amsterdam Press, 1994. 51–76.

Vaughn, Megan. *Creating the Creole Island: Slavery in Eighteenth-Century Mauritius*. Durham, N.C.: Duke University Press, 2005.

Venema, Janny. *Beverwyck: A Dutch Village on the American Frontier, 1652–1664*. Albany: State University of New York Press, 2003.

———. *Kinderen van weelde en armoede: Armoede en liefdadigheid in Beverwijck/ Albany. c. 1650–c. 1700*. Hilversum: Uitgeverij Verloren, 1993.

Villani, Stefano. "Donne quacchere nel xvii secolo." *Studi Storici* 42, 2 (1999): 585–611.

Visser, C. Ch. G. *De Lutheranen in Nederland: Tussen Katholicisme en Calvinisme, 1566 tot heden*. Dieren: De Bataafsche Leeuw, 1983.

Voogt, Gerrit. *Constraint on Trial: Dirck Vockertsz Coornhert and Religious Freedom*. Kirksville, Mo.: Truman State University Press, 2000.

———. "Primacy of Individual Conscience or Primacy of the State? The Clash Between Dirck Volckertsz Coornhert and Justus Lipsius." *Sixteenth Century Journal* 28, 4 (Winter 1997): 1231–49.

Voorhees, David William. "The 1657 Flushing Remonstrance in Historical Perspective." *DHM* 81, 1 (2008): 11–14.

————. "The Dutch Legacy in America." In *Dutch New York: The Roots of Hudson Valley Culture*, ed. Roger Panetta. New York: Fordham University Press, 2009. 411–29.

Wagman, Morton. "Corporate Slavery in New Netherland." *Journal of Negro History* 65, 1 (1980): 34–42.

Wall, Ernestine van der. "The Amsterdam Millenarian Petrus Serrarius (1600–1669) and the Anglo-Dutch Circle of Philo-Judaists." In *Jewish-Christian Relations in the Seventeenth Century: Studies and Documents*, ed. J. van den Berg and Ernestine G. E. van der Wall. Dordrecht: Kluwer, 1988. 73–94.

————. *De Mystieke Chiliast Petrus Serrarius (1600–1669) en zijn wereld*. Leiden, Ph.D. dissertation, 1987.

Wallenborn, Hiltrud. *Bekehrungseifer, Judenangst und Handelsinteresse: Amsterdam, Hamburg und London als Ziele sefardischer Migration im 17. Jahrhundert*. Hildesheim: Georg Olms, 2003.

Walsham, Alexandra. *Charitable Hatred: Tolerance and Intolerance in England, 1500– 1700*. Manchester: Manchester University Press, 2006.

Ward, Christopher. *New Sweden on the Delaware*. Philadelphia: University of Pennsylvania Press, 1938.

Warnsink, J. C. M. *Abraham Crijnssen: De Verovering van Suriname en zijn aanslag op Virginië in 1667*. Amsterdam: N.V. Noord-Hollandsche Uitgeversmaatschappij, 1936.

Watts, Michael R. *The Dissenters: From the Reformation to the French Revolution*. Oxford: Clarendon, 1978.

Weis, Frederick Lewis. *The Colonial Clergy of Maryland, Delaware and Georgia*. Lancaster, Mass.: Society of the Descendants of the Colonial Clergy, 1950.

————. *The Colonial Clergy of the Middle Colonies: New York, New Jersey, and Pennsylvania, 1628–1776*. Worcester, Mass.: American Antiquarian Society, 1957.

Weslager, C. A. "The City of Amsterdam's Colony on the Delaware, 1656–1664; With Unpublished Dutch Notarial Abstracts." *DH* 20 (1982): 1–26; 72–97.

————. *Dutch Explorers, Traders, and Settlers in the Delaware Valley, 1609–1664*. Philadelphia: University of Pennsylvania Press, 1961.

————. *The English on the Delaware, 1610–1682*. New Brunswick, N.J.: Rutgers University Press, 1967.

————. *New Sweden on the Delaware, 1638–1655*. Wilmington, Del.: Middle Atlantic Press, 1988.

Whaley, Joachim. *Religious Toleration and Social Change in Hamburg, 1529–1819*. Cambridge: Cambridge University Press, 1985.

White, B. R. *The English Separatist Tradition: From the Marian Martyrs to the Pilgrim Fathers*. Oxford: Oxford University Press, 1971.

White, Philip L. *The Beekmans of New York in Politics and Commerce, 1647–1877*. New York, 1956.

Wijsenbeek, Thera. "Geloof en Politiek." In *Den Haag: Geschiedenis van de stad*, ed. J. G. Smit and Eelco Beukers. 3 vols. Zwolle: Waanders Uitgevers, 2004. 2:207–27.

Wilbur, Earl Morse. *A History of Unitarianism: Socianism and its Antecedents*. Cambridge, Mass.: Harvard University Press, 1945.

Williams, James Homer. "'Abominable Religion' and Dutch (In)tolerance: The Jews and Petrus Stuyvesant." *DHM* 71, 4 (1998): 85–91.

———. "Dutch Attitudes Toward Indians, Africans, and Other Europeans in New Netherland, 1624–1664." In *Connecting Cultures: The Netherlands in Five Centuries of Transatlantic Exchange*, ed. Rosemarijn Hoefte and Johanna C. Kardak. Amsterdam: University of Amsterdam Press, 1994. 23–50.

Wingens, Marc. *Over de grens: De bedevaart van katholieke Nederlanders in de zestiende en achttiende eeuw*. Nijmegen: SUN, 1994.

Worden, Blair. "Toleration and the Cromwellian Protectorate." In *Persecution and Toleration*, ed. W. J. Sheils. Studies in Church History 21. Oxford: Blackwell, 1984. 199–233.

Worral, Arthur. *Quakers in the Colonial Northeast*. Hanover, N.H.: University Press of New England, 1980.

Zijlstra, S. *Om de ware gemeente en de oude gronden: geschiedenis van de dopersen in de Nederlanden, 1531–1675*. Hilversum: Verloren, 2000.

Zilverberg, S. B. J. *Geloof en Geweten in de Zeventiende Eeuw*. Bussum: Fibula van Dishoeck, 1971.

———. "Van gedulde tot erkende geloofsgemeenschap." In *Staat in de vrijheid: De geschiedenis van de remonstranten*, ed. G. J. Hoenderdaal and P. M. Luca. Zutphen: De Walburg Pers, 1982. 57–88.

Zwarts, Jac. "Een episode uit de Joodsche kolonisatie van Guyana (1660)." *Westindische Gids* 10 (1928): 519–30.

Zwierlein, Frederick J. "New Netherland Intolerance." *Catholic Historical Review* 4, 2 (1918): 186–216.

———. *Religion in New Netherland, 1623–1664*. 1910. New York: Da Capo, 1971.

INDEX

ACKNOWLEDGMENTS
———————

To recast this piece of colonial American history I have had to adopt a larger scope than I initially had imagined. First drawn to the topic during the late 1990s, I found myself embarking on a long trans-Atlantic endeavor, drawing on scholarship, archives, and people in both Europe and America, whose assistance it is my pleasure here to acknowledge. Most of all I must thank John Murrin, who invited me to come to Princeton University and encouraged me to follow my instincts on what was important in American history, even if they led me over the Atlantic to Europe and back in time to the Middle Ages. John first alerted me to the wonders of the seventeenth-century middle colonies, imparting a scholarly fascination for a time and place that I have yet to shake. His kindness, humor, knowledge, dedication, and enthusiasm for history remain a constant inspiration. Peter Lake's engaging seminars on Tudor-Stuart ecclesiastical politics provided me with the key to the mysteries of the middle colonies and emboldened me to go where I had not dreamed. Scholars with whom I worked in one capacity or another—Theodore K. Rabb, Kenneth Mills, Natalie Zemon Davis—and other colleagues made early modern history fascinating. For someone trying to understand and explain colonial America it was a godsend.

If one is going to seriously study New Netherland, a crucial requirement is a familiarity with Dutch language, culture, and history, something rather difficult to acquire in the United States these days, even at leading research universities. Fortunately, there was at least one Dutch person in Princeton, Helene van Rossum, willing to teach me Dutch and, through her friends and family, introduce me to Dutch society, for which I am forever grateful. After that, I was able gradually to build up my knowledge of all things Dutch, even as I began teaching at Tufts University, where my colleagues supported my wide-ranging interests with gracious generosity. My growing involvement in colonial Dutch studies would have been impossible without the New Netherland Project (now the New Netherland Institute) based at the New York State Library and Archives in Albany. Its importance for Americans interested in not just New Netherland but the seventeenth-century Dutch world cannot be underestimated. Charles Gehring has been on a longstanding quest to make Dutch history and sources accessible to non-Dutch-speaking Americans through a steady flow of published translations that are an invaluable source of information and analysis. Janny Venema has ably joined Charlie in his efforts, and added her own scholarship to what is now a dynamic and diverse field of study. Joyce Goodfriend pioneered research on Dutch colonial New York and has been a consistent supporter of all work in the field ever since, including my own. David Voorhees has been an invaluable guide and fellow researcher, raising questions and illuminating sources. Through the friendly but scholarly series of Rensselaerswyck seminars on early Dutch American history begun years ago by Charlie, a real community of scholars and nonscholars has emerged, all of whom are in no small way indebted to the work of the Project (now the Institute). I am grateful for all the interest they have shown in my work. I do not think I would have been able to write this book without the foundation they have laid for Dutch American studies.

In 2005 I had the good fortune of finding a post at Columbia University, one of the few places in America where I could expand my approach to the early modern Dutch world with ready institutional and collegial backing. The libraries and staff at Columbia University are outstanding. If they did not have something I needed on Dutch history (and they have a surprising amount), they quickly obtained it for me. The Nederlandse Taalunie (Dutch language union) in connection with the Queen Wilhelmina Visiting Professorship at Columbia University has proven a tremendous resource. With the able guidance of Martha Howell heading a committee of colleagues, and the enthusiastic participation of a growing body of interested graduate students, I have enjoyed invaluable opportunities to organize and participate in conferences, workshops, and talks on Dutch language, culture, and history that enhanced my appreciation of all three. Wijnie de Groot, Columbia's exemplary teacher of Dutch language and culture, has been an invaluable guide to seventeenth-century Dutch language and paleography. The university supported me for a year of leave in 2008–2009 that made it possible for me to mature as a historian of the Dutch. Without that opportunity I would not have dared write this book.

My colleagues in the Columbia history department have proven a vital source of support and intellectual exchange. Special thanks must go to my chair, Mark Mazower, who held his hand over my head in the crucial final stage of the writing process. Adam Kosto readily assisted with a last-minute Latin translation. Christopher Brown and Matthew Jones deserve outstanding recognition for their sharp reading of a monstrous manuscript at a difficult time in the semester. Peter Walker gave the subsequent version the appreciative reading of a sharp graduate student, which gave me hope that it had something worthwhile after all. Over the past two years Leslie Ribovich has been an outstanding research assistant, an irreplaceable editor, and my ideal undergraduate reader. No one else has worked as hard on this manuscript as she.

In the Netherlands, a range of people over the years have assisted my efforts in the study of things Dutch. On the historical side I must begin with Jaap Jacobs, the doyen of New Netherland history. He has been critically supportive of my work for years and an endless source of knowledge and research about the colony. Victor Enthoven has long been my guide to the Dutch national archives and seventeenth-century Dutch Atlantic history, introducing me to obscure corners of the Dutch world and, as a scholar interested in trade rather than religion, helping me keep my research in perspective. Ben Kaplan kindly allowed me to visit him at an archive in Zwolle and has been an encouraging and stimulating interlocutor on the history of toleration ever since. Henk Looijestein graciously shared his work on Plockhoy, on which I have relied greatly. His delightful walking tours made me feel as at home in seventeenth-century Amsterdam as I now do in its twenty-first-century manifestation. Frank Mertens likewise generously shared with me his important research on Franciscus van den Enden, without which I would have been at a loss about this fascinating figure. Michiel van Groesen at the University of Amsterdam has offered friendship and encouragement to my interest in Dutch history. Hospitable and stimulating conversations about Dutch religious history in Leiden with that outstanding scholarly pair, Joke Spaans and Peter van Rooden, made me feel like I had something to contribute after all. The staffs of the University of Amsterdam libraries, the Dutch National Archives, and the Royal Library in The Hague, and particularly the Municipal Archive in Amsterdam, were models of the sort of kindness and efficiency that make historical research a real pleasure—and success. I look forward to the chance to work with them more in the future.

The English language has a series of unfriendly expressions regarding the Dutch, all belied by my personal experience with Dutch individuals.

Ingeborg Seeleman has helped me feel at home in Amsterdam and the Dutch language since my first stay in the city back in 1996. My urbane and creative Dutch language teacher, Simone Klink, has made fluency seem both an attainable and a desirable goal. Joanne van der Woude graced me with her knowledge of Dutch culture and society, giving me a deeper perspective on the Dutch trans-Atlantic experience in the seventeenth and twenty-first centuries. Most especial thanks go to Ieneke and Andries Suidman, without whose friendship and hospitality this book would lack the vitality it has accrued over my last few research trips to Holland.

Additional friends have expanded my horizons to the South Atlantic. Mark Meuwese kindly shared his research on Dutch Brazil, and has been my principal guide to the wonderland of its history. Andie Davis deserves special thanks for getting me to visit Brazil much sooner than I had imagined, spurring me to learn Portuguese and incorporate the Dutch experience there into my thinking about North American history.

Next I must thank those responsible for turning my ramblings into a published book. Bob Lockhart, the editor for University of Pennsylvania Press, has overseen the process from the beginning with great competence and energy. Dan Richter, editor of the series on early American history for the press, has provided a critical but helpful eye. The two readers for the Press, Willem Frijhoff and Frank Bremer, accepted the manuscript on the first go but provided enough penetrating comments that I was driven to radically revise it. Zara Anishanslin gave the entire manuscript a final, crucial, and effective reading that has made this a better book than before. Alison Anderson ably saw me through the final editorial process.

Additional research for this book was undertaken at the New York State Archives, the New-York Historical Society, and the British Library, whose staff and collections were of great assistance. The interest and support of the Bowne House Historical Society in Flushing is also much appreciated. The assistance of all these and more such institutions and individuals has been crucial to the completion of this project. We historians get to put our names on the covers of our books, but we really could not do it without the resources and networks they make available to us. Of course in all cases, any faults with the book or quirks of interpretation must be ascribed to me alone.

Finally, thanks are due to my family and nonacademic friends for indulging my drawn-out quest to be a scholar and a gentleman. Since I am the first Ph.D. in the family, I do not think they knew what I was getting into when I went off to graduate school. I certainly did not. That I have made it this far in reasonably good shape says much about their love, consideration, and patience, even when they did not fully understand what I was up to, in no small part because too often I could not adequately explain it to them. Hopefully this book will clarify things a bit.

Portions of this work have been presented in various forums over the years. In reverse chronological order, they are the University of Amsterdam; the European History Workshop at Columbia University; the University Seminar on the City at Columbia University; the Colonial Americas Workshop in the History Department of Princeton University; the Scherer Center for the Study of American Culture at the University of Chicago; the Herbert H. Lehman Center for American History at Columbia University; the Center for Ethical Culture in New York City; the American Antiquarian Society; the American Historical Association. I thank the participants at all these events for the shared knowledge, challenging questions, and perceptive comments, without which I probably would have published this book a lot sooner.